Civil Rights in My Bones

To: Ellen Creane

Great to meet you at the Fairhope Unitarian Fellowship.

May God bless + protect you in all things.

John T. McWhatMy Jr.

3-11-2018

ALSO BY JULIAN L. McPHILLIPS JR.

From Vacillation to Resolve: The French Communist Party
in the Resistance Movement against the Nazis, 1939–1944 (1968)

The People's Lawyer (2005, WITH CARROLL DALE SHORT)

The History of Christ the Redeemer Episcopal Church (2006)

CIVIL RIGHTS IN MY BONES

*More Colorful Stories from
a Lawyer's Life and Work*

2005–2015

JULIAN L. MCPHILLIPS JR.

FOREWORD BY CONGRESSWOMAN TERRI SEWELL

NewSouth Books

Montgomery

NewSouth Books
105 S. Court Street
Montgomery, AL 36104

Publisher's Cataloging-in-Publication data

McPhillips, Julian L., Jr.
Civil rights in my bones : more colorful stories from a lawyer's life and work,
2005–2015 / Julian L. McPhillips Jr. ;
with a foreword by Congresswoman Terri Sewell.
p. cm.

ISBN 978-1-60306-417-0 (paperback)
ISBN 978-1-60306-418-7 (ebook)

1. McPhillips, Julian L., Jr. 2. Lawyers—Alabama—Biography. I. Title.

2016934358

Design by Randall Williams

Printed in the United States of America
by Thomson-Shore, Inc.

This book is dedicated first to the "Love of My Life," Leslie McPhillips. It is also dedicated to my three children, Rachel, Grace, and David, each of whom, equally, are my heart, and my grandchildren, Laurel, Jude, and Nanette.

This book is dedicated secondarily to my clients, but especially to Emerson Crayton Jr., an innocent, unarmed 21-year-old African American shot and killed by an Alexander City police officer on March 8, 2014.

This book is also written in honor of my incredibly wonderful parents, who gave their best, and did their best, to raise five children, including me.

Finally, but most significantly, this book is written in honor of the God the Father, who created me; God the Redeemer, who has saved me; and God the Sustainer, who has enabled me. That is God, the Father, Son, and Holy Spirit.

CONTENTS

FOREWORD

U.S. Representative Terri Sewell

One of the interesting things about Alabama is that while the state has many problems, it also has had over the years many people willing to put themselves on the firing line to change things, to right wrongs, to bring progress. These admirable people haven't always triumphed, of course—or the state wouldn't still be in the shape that it is—but they have put forth the effort. In Alabama's history over the past six decades, much of this effort has revolved around civil rights. And ironically, much of it still does, because discrimination, injustice, and inequality were not magically resolved just by getting rid of Jim Crow laws.

So civil rights work is still necessary, and thankfully there are still people willing to do that work. One of those people is my long-time friend and supporter, Julian McPhillips. I have known Julian for many years. In fact, he recruited me out of high school in 1981 to attend Princeton University, his alma mater.

Julian is a lawyer, and he's a good one. The same dogged determination that made him a champion heavyweight amateur wrestler makes him a formidable advocate in the courtroom. Over the past thirty-five years, I've gotten to know Julian pretty well. He has remained a loyal Democrat—a rarity these days among white males in the Deep South—and I have seen him at many political events. I also see him at some Princeton events. We have visited in Washington. He and Leslie, his wife, have hosted fundraisers for me in their home. And so forth.

We have talked enough about issues and politics that I was already familiar with the general nature of his law practice. Yet I didn't fully grasp the extent to which his passion for the law, for fairness, for equal rights and treatment, extended into his law practice. *Civil Rights in My Bones,* I discovered, is a very fitting title for this book.

He has handled case after case after case that are modern-day examples of the same sort of issues that motivated the warriors for civil rights in the 1950s and 1960s. Like those earlier advocates, he demonstrates a principled belief in democracy and fair play. He believes that the state should not be able to convict a person unjustly. He believes in law enforcement, but he also believes that police should not be able to shoot unarmed people and get away with it just because the victim was poor and/or minority. He believes that big business should not be able to get away with cheating consumers and hiding behind arbitration agreements. He believes that the courts should not automatically side with business. He believes that the more powerful our institutions, the more they should err on the side of protecting human dignity and looking out for the poor and powerless.

In the chapters of this book—which he wrote over the course of two years, in bits of time grabbed here and there—one also learns a lot about Julian's beliefs outside the courtroom.

He comes from a family whose roots go deep in Alabama, chiefly in Mobile and Cullman. It is a family with tradition in both religion and politics, though outside the Baptist, Methodist, and Pentecostal denominations held to by most white Alabamians. Instead, the McPhillips forebears were Catholic, Presbyterian, and Episcopalian. Julian's own father left a prominent family business in midlife to become an Episcopal priest, one who in the turbulent 1960s was racially liberal and politically active. Julian Sr. became director of the Peace Corps in India; Julian's mother worked in Calcutta with Mother Teresa. Later, they ran George McGovern's presidential campaign in Alabama.

Julian himself was away at college and law school, and then working in Wall Street law firms, during most of those years, but his parents' political and religious instincts obviously sank in.

They motivated him to come back to Alabama at a most interesting time—1975, during the years right after the civil rights movement, when Bill Baxley was recruiting bright young lawyers from top law schools to work for him in the Alabama attorney general's office.

Julian became one of those young assistant attorney generals who set about helping Baxley shake things up in the state by prosecuting polluters,

---

Congresswoman Terri Sewell has represented Alabama's 7th District since 2010. She sits on the House Committee on Financial Services, among others. She was the first black valedictorian of Selma High School, is a graduate of Princeton University and Harvard Law School, and practiced law in Birmingham before winning election to Congress.

corrupt politicians, white supremacists, and fraudulent businesses. Julian made a few headlines himself, and then he got the political bug for the first time, running for AG himself when Baxley moved on to higher office.

Julian lost that first campaign, but then he went into private practice and began taking on the typical cases handled by plaintiff's lawyers: accidents, business disputes, and so on. But he was also fearless in taking on cases of race discrimination, police brutality, judicial misconduct, political malfeasance—cases most private lawyers didn't handle.

Julian's early legal practice, including many of his civil rights cases, were described in another book about him published 15 years ago, and updated and republished 10 years ago. This book picks up where that one left off and focuses on the past decade. Significantly, the civil rights work continues right up to the present day. He and his firm have won a lot of cases that have made good money. But there have been many cases taken on a pro bono basis just because Julian believed the client's case needed to be heard.

I admire that about him.

I also admire how he and Leslie have supported churches, schools, and museums, sponsored immigrants, worked for children, and assisted other candidates for public office (including me). I admire how Julian put himself in the political arena again in 2002 when he ran for the U.S. Senate, and how, after he lost that race, he has stayed active helping others.

All this and more are in this book. It's an enjoyable and educational read.

Julian is a fascinating, complex character. Some of what he has done over the years has been controversial. But you can't read his memoir without coming away with an appreciation for his deep sincerity, compassion, and commitment to fundamental human values.

And he fights for the underdog. I like that.

PREFACE

It's been more than 40 years since I returned to Alabama in April 1975 with my gorgeous newlywed, Leslie. We met in Manhattan in 1973 and were married a year later. She bolstered my confidence and spirits. All these years later, she is still the apple of my eye, an engaging life partner, and a wonderful mother to our children.

It's been 45 years since my May 1971 graduation from Columbia Law School. My father was right to encourage my brother Frank and me to go into the legal profession. It has worked well for us.

The first four years on Wall Street, two with a big international law firm (Davis Polk & Wardwell), and two more with American Express, seasoned me. New York was an exciting start for our marriage and a base for great international travel. The Big Apple also allowed me to continue my passion for amateur wrestling, via participation on the New York Athletic Club team. But those four years also showed me what I *did not* want to do with the rest of my life.

We arrived back in Montgomery on April 28, 1975, and spent our first days at "the Pea Level," the Wetumpka-area cottage of Clifford and Virginia Durr. What an honor and a privilege it was to be inspired by those two greats. They motivated me to pursue civil rights cases and other challenging legal work. Cliff was in the last two weeks of his life, though no one could have guessed it. He regaled Leslie and me with Alabama stories. Not to be outdone, Virginia spiced the mix and stirred the pot.

Fast forward 40 years to my own senior vantage point—I turned 69 in November 2015—and I have updated my story with this third book. Writing it turned out to be even more a joy than I had expected. I had my first taste of the autobiographical craft in 2005, when I wrote a 90-page update to my biography, *The People's Lawyer, the Colorful Life and Times of Julian L. McPhillips, Jr.* (NewSouth Books, 2000). That first edition was written by Carroll Dale Short, an Alabama journalist, poet, essayist, novelist, and—in the style he employed on my story—writer of creative nonfiction.

Dale's first edition covered not only the 1946–2000 years of my life, but parental and ancestral roots as well. The second edition included my supplement covering the next five years, 2000–2005, with a special chapter dedicated solely to my wonderful parents, who went to heaven in 2001 (Dad) and 2002 (Mom).

Both editions subsequently sold out, and with so much more happening in my life and career over the past 10 years, I felt it worthwhile to update the saga with this new book, which makes ample reference to the earlier books but does not incorporate them. While concentrating on the next ten years (2005–2015), this new book stands alone, with different adventures, candid observations, and a myriad of experiences.

The present volume has been sparked by a combination of historical appreciation, creative literary instincts, theological inspiration, and civil rights idealism—a common denominator of much of my legal work has been civil rights, hence the title of this new volume.

What do I have to share that is worth a reader's time? The answer arrives in the form of candid and adventurous legal stories and history worth preserving. There are also some humorous tales and some humbling experiences. These should help readers connect. The chapter on the depression I experienced in 2006 may speak to someone. I hope it does. Although I fully and openly share that experience now, the four dreary months from April through July 2006 were the worst period of my life, worse even than breaking my leg twice, ten weeks apart, in 1965–66, as a sophomore Princeton athlete.

For me, the writing has been catharsis and therapy. Maybe it's a family trait. My parents wrote a four-volume autobiography, "The Drummer's Beat." Although their work remains unpublished, I am only following in their footsteps.

Leslie and I are extraordinarily grateful to God for many blessings. We do not take them for granted. That includes life itself, good health, peace, prosperity, and a wonderful marriage and family. As we move along in the aging process—the "cycle of life" as daughter Rachel calls it—we realize increasingly that this life is the beginning of a greater life beyond the grave.

We've also come to realize, to quote theologian Paul Tillich, that "God is the ground of our being." We wouldn't be here in the first place but for his creating us, redeeming us, and sustaining us. That is the Triune God, also known as the Trinity. This is God the Father, God the Son, and God the Holy Spirit. I am committed to all three, but I know they are One God.

Leslie and I take seriously the words of our Lord in Luke 12:48 that "to whom much is given, much will be required," and this has motivated much of our life and story.

This third edition also has an update on our grown children, son David, 25, and daughters, Rachel, 38, and Grace, 35, and their respective husbands, Jay and Corbett. All have been an enormous joy to Leslie and me, as have our precious grandchildren, Jay and Rachel's children Laurel, 7, and Jude, 4, and Corbett and Grace's first child, Nanette Lillabelle, who was born in February 2016 just as this book was going to press.

In sharing the above, I intend no slight to my friends who have no children. Nor in discussing my long and happy union with Leslie am I diminishing my many friends who have been divorced. I've often joked that had I married any of the first seven to eight girlfriends before meeting Leslie, I, too, would be a divorce statistic. I concede that I am not the easiest person to live with. Leslie was strong and secure enough to put up with me, and she brings out the best in me. She has loads of common sense, patience, and family values, and she could put up with my foibles. We both thank God that he has entrusted us with three wonderful children and a growing brood of grands.

Along the way, the major lessons learned include (a) the enormous Creativity, Grace and Love of God the Father, Son and Holy Spirit, (b) the dignity and worth of every human life, (c) the importance of humility, humor, and hard work, and (d) the significance of forgiveness and reconciliation, foundational to healing. Get these principles right and there is meaning and purpose aplenty in life, and a joy and peace worth more than silver and gold.

While there have been many serious experiences in my life, there have been many lighthearted moments. Some escapades started off solemnly, yet ended up with good laughs (see Appendix 1).

I hope you, the reader, find something intriguing or worthwhile in this book. It is far from a literary masterpiece, and it might be my final autobiographical account. I challenge you, however, to write, preserve and share your own story, whether through a written, audio, or visual medium. As I have experienced with my two previous books, your history may enlighten and uplift others more than you expect. To me, real life stories are often more interesting than fiction. My story is real life, and so is yours.

As to the future of this book, I can only cite the French phrase, *on vera*— we'll see. Indeed, we'll have to wait and see and hope that this book "has legs." I hope it does, and I hope readers, even if they skip around among the stand-on-their-own chapters, will find it enjoyable and uplifting.

ACKNOWLEDGMENTS

First and foremost, I thank God for giving me life itself and the skills, life experience, prosperity, and desire to craft this work.

At the top of my list of humans to thank is my dear, devoted wife and life partner, Jeanne Leslie Burton McPhillips. She has been such a huge encourager and supporter, not only of me, but of our children and grandchildren. God truly polished a jewel when he sent Leslie to Earth. She has supported me from the beginning of the writing of this book to the end, roughly a two-year period.

Indeed, it was in early 2014 that *Pride of Montgomery* magazine did a cover feature story on Leslie and me and referred to the two earlier editions of *The People's Lawyer*. In that magazine, I first stated that "a third update beckons in 2015." That sort of committed me to doing this book.

The writing was done in bits and pieces between carrying the average load of 100 to 130 legal cases, ministering to and administering Christ the Redeemer church, being chief executive of a museum, and enjoying my three children, their families, and Leslie.

Given the candid nature of this book, I acknowledge that any critical comments about others are to be considered as my opinion only, written in good faith, and based on truth as I perceive it. I do not exclude myself from a self-effacing admission of my own faults, such as the need for more patience and humility. Of course, there is ample room for differences of opinion on almost any subject. Therefore, anyone offended is welcome to write his or her own book, or a letter to an editor, in reply.

There are others I must thank. Of course, Randall Williams has not only been the co-publisher of this book and a great encourager, but also a friend and client.

While my office manager Amy Strickland and former paralegals Vicki Morrison and Denise Bertaut all significantly helped in the typing of this book, the real hero of its typing, editing, and continuous revisions has been my new friend and associate attorney Chase Estes, 27 at the time this book went to press in December 2015. Thus, as I sometimes say, he is young enough to be my grandson.

Where did time go so quickly? My place in the "cycle of life" keeps accelerating, as does everyone else's.

I use three affectionate nicknames for Chase interchangeably, depending

XVI   CIVIL RIGHTS IN MY BONES

on the mood of the moment: "Chase Manhattan," "Cut to the Chase," and "Chase, Rattle and Roll." Chase is gracious and savvy enough to know that the nicknames are "terms of endearment."

Anyway, to Chase . . . who is probably somewhat awkwardly typing this line . . . thank you, thank you, thank you, for the excellent job you have done.

I also must thank the several people who have read all or parts of the several drafts of this book. That includes my long-time friend and attorney, Bobby Segall. It also includes attorney and educator Dr. Jim Vickrey. It includes the great encourager and Episcopal priest friend, Doug Carpenter, who, along with his father the Bishop, encouraged me to go to Princeton for college, a most beneficial step.

I also thank Sandra Long for being a reader of an earlier draft. I thank Tyna Davis for her input on the "Civil Rights in My Bones" chapter, Tommy Gallion for input on the Don Siegelman chapter, Shawn Sudia-Skehan for input on the Fitzgerald Museum chapter, and my daughter Grace for suggested revisions on the family chapter.

Part I

Background and Inspiration

1

CIVIL RIGHTS IN MY BONES

That's right—civil rights in my bones or DNA. How did it get so deeply embedded?

This is not meant to sound sanctimonious. A high percentage of people would say that at some level they are pro-civil rights, in the broad sense of the term. After all, that's what the early colonists exercised against the British, who even earlier had used civil rights against King John to get his signature on the Magna Carta. Accordingly, civil rights is synonymous with freedom, or a desire for it. It's something deep in the human psyche, deep in the soul. Deep in my soul.

In America, the words *civil rights*, at least since the 1950s when the modern-day movement ignited, have taken on a more specialized meaning: that is, where do you stand on treating African Americans? In the southern United States, where slavery was rooted for more than two centuries, this was and is no small question.

Yet civil rights has never been an exclusively Southern concern. Due in part to the Great Migration of the early 20th century when millions of blacks moved to the North, West, and Midwest to escape Jim Crow segregation in the South, civil rights became a national issue. California, with its Watts riots of 1968, was a manifestation. So was Newark, New Jersey. In many respects, civil rights, or the denial thereof, has been the most compelling issue in America during the last hundred years. Civil rights underlies so many related issues, from welfare to unemployment, to health care, to education, to the identity of the current American president. It also includes our justice system, both criminal and civil.

Of course, Martin Luther King Jr., Fred Shuttlesworth, Rosa Parks, Ralph Abernathy, E. D. Nixon, Fred Gray and other giants of the civil rights movement deserve all the honors they have received for their courageous and effective moving of mountains during the bloody 1950s and 1960s in Alabama and elsewhere. All inspired and influenced me, as they did countless others.

Joe Reed, through the Alabama Democratic Conference and the Alabama

Education Association, helped many blacks gain public office in Alabama from the 1970s to the present, thus enhancing civil rights. State Representative Alvin Holmes has vigorously raised civil rights consciousness in Montgomery and the Alabama legislature over the past 40 years. Meanwhile, State Representative John Knight, with a quiet dignity, helped the historically black Alabama State University achieve parity in funding with major white state universities.

There are many other lights in the civil rights world, some very bright, some less so, but all have contributed to making Montgomery and America a better place.

On the Caucasian side, Clifford and Virginia Durr will always be great heroes in civil rights to me, not only for coming to Rosa Parks's rescue when she was arrested on December 1, 1955. The Durrs also stood tall against McCarthyism and encouraged progressivism from the 1930s until their deaths. They will long be remembered. Likewise, Bob and Jeannie Graetz, the white Lutheran pastor and his wife who survived multiple bombings of their parsonage during the Montgomery Bus Boycott, are walking-talking civil rights monuments, still active at ages 87 and 85. They encourage modern-day Montgomerians to be a part of the "beloved community" espoused by Martin Luther King Jr.

I CAME FROM A different background. Given my father's first career in the vegetable canning business, I grew up from 1946 to 1959 in Cullman, Alabama, a town with essentially no blacks. The only black community in Cullman County was Colony, a small town that dated to the Reconstruction era. The rest of the county's residents were white, many of German heritage. Our family's business, King Pharr Canning Company, was Cullman's largest employer, but the employees were all white. Perhaps because of the absence of blacks in Cullman, I really never heard racial slurs being used while I was growing up. When black maids came from Colony, their sons sometimes played ball with us and other neighborhood kids in our big backyard. This was in the 1950s. There were no incidents. We all had fun together and gave no thought to racial differences.

Only later did I learn of Cullman's bad reputation on the race issue. I never saw it personally, but photographs apparently exist of an infamous sign posted on the edges of town that threatened, "N-----, don't let the sun set on you here." Ironically, many Cullman friends of about my age ended up, as I did, doing things that helped black people. Even politicians from Cullman, including father and son former governors Big Jim Folsom and

Jim Folsom Jr., were progressive on the race issue. And ironically a black native of Colony, James Fields, was elected to represent Cullman County, which is still predominantly white, in the Alabama Legislature.

It was at the young age of nine, in December 1955, that I first started learning what civil rights, as a modern-day issue, was really about. When I was about six, my father responded to my normal kid's interest in baseball by teaching me how to follow the major league teams' box scores in the *Birmingham News*. As I gradually learned to read better, I started glancing at other news stories. Thus, when the Montgomery Bus Boycott started making headlines in late 1955, I followed the story with interest. I was fascinated to read about Rosa Parks, Martin Luther King Jr., Ralph Abernathy, and others and their cause. My parents were also interested and talked about the developments. At an early age, I found myself cheering for the civil rights leaders and their cause.

When my hero, Reverend Fred Shuttlesworth, emerged on the scene in the 1950s and '60s in nearby Birmingham, my fascination grew and my curiosity soared. The *Birmingham News* prominently covered most of these developments, and I read the articles.

Meanwhile, I was being raised on a fairly heavy dose of the Christian gospel at home. The famous Sermon on the Mount words of Jesus ". . . inasmuch as you have done it unto the least of them my brethren, you have done it unto me . . ." were meaningful to me at an early age. Words like that were not to be ignored. But in what context? Jesus didn't say "except for civil rights" or "except for black people."

When Dad left Cullman and the family business in 1959, and took the entire family of seven with him to seminary in Sewanee, Tennessee, to study to become an Episcopal priest, the meaning of the civil rights movement took on a deeper context. I could hear Mom and Dad discussing or debating it with other seminarians. I was in my precocious teen years then, as a cadet at Tennessee's Sewanee Military Academy from 1959–1964.

Mom and Dad were avant-garde on the race issue. It was in their bones and roots as well. While their parents were more traditionally conservative, Mom's great-grandfather, the Reverend Dr. David Sanderson, was minister at Eutaw's First Presbyterian Church (in Greene County in the Alabama Black Belt) from 1860–91. His congregation before, during, and after the Civil War was half-white and half-black. In 1871, Dr. Sanderson co-founded, along with his best friend and colleague, Dr. Charles Alan Stillman, the Tuscaloosa College for Black Preachers, now Stillman College.

Dad came from the Jesuit tradition of the Catholic Church but also had served four years in the U.S. Navy, mostly in the Pacific. He was not as radical as the Berrigan brothers, but his strong faith compelled him to be pro-civil rights and anti-the Vietnam War, at early stages of both movements. Dad's famous words about why he left the family business and went to seminary were: "Son, I've decided to bet my life on the fact that everything Jesus Christ said in the Gospels is true." Those words became a foundation of my own faith.

Dad finished seminary in 1962. As fate would have it, where would he be called to minister but to Montgomery, Alabama, at the Church of the Ascension, in the Garden district. Our home was immediately adjacent to the church. Of the seven siblings who moved to Montgomery, I was the only one not at home full-time. Older sister Sandy studied at Huntingdon College, and my younger siblings attended the Montgomery public schools. After an agonizing bout of indecisiveness in the summer of 1962, I decided to return to Sewanee Military Academy to finish up my last two years of high school. Yet I ended up as the only one of my siblings to return permanently to Montgomery.

The early 1960s were key years in civil rights across the South and in Montgomery. The bus boycott was over, but sit-ins came in 1960 and the Freedom Riders in 1961, and Fred Gray and his colleagues were bringing a steady stream of lawsuits to desegregate schools, parks, housing, public accommodations, and more. Segregation was also challenged in churches and clubs.

Dad had made it clear, as a condition to his coming to the Church of the Ascension, and based on his understanding of the Christian faith, that the church doors must be open to all people, black and white. Despite having lost an earlier rector, Tom Thrasher, on this issue—or perhaps because they had—the Ascension's vestrymen agreed.

During Dad's two years in Montgomery, 1962–64, he also pastored regularly at the Church of the Good Shepherd, an all-black Episcopal church at Grove and Jackson streets, near Alabama State University. Some worried that this might be a dangerous ministry for a white priest, but Dad's gentle reply was the Holy Spirit had him covered. Dad's statement inspired me to think similarly in future times when I became engaged in my own civil rights work.

The warnings were not unfounded. We had arrived in Montgomery less than a year after the Freedom Rides and the ugly incident at the black First Baptist Church on Ripley Street, where a white mob was barely stopped by U.S. marshals and federalized National Guardsmen from storming the church. Inside the church the beaten Freedom Riders, Reverends King, Abernathy, and Shuttlesworth, and 1,500 concerned black men, women, and children had gathered to pray and organize.

In the spring of 1963, the year after we moved to Montgomery, Fred Shuttlesworth led an escalation of the movement in Birmingham, bravely resisting Public Safety Commissioner Bull Connor's dogs, firehoses, and billy clubs. Then in September 1963 came the infamous church bombing which killed four black girls.

So IT WAS IN those dangerous days that my dear parents became a part of the circle of Virginia and Clifford Durr. The Durrs' home in Montgomery before they moved to rural Elmore County was at 2 Felder Avenue, near Sidney Lanier High School. Their large two-story house was a central meeting place in the early 1960s for white Southern liberals, their black brethren, and visiting journalists, lawyers, and Northern liberals. (In 2005, I was privileged to lead the effort to erect a historic marker there, honoring the Durrs, with a well-attended dedication ceremony.)

The Kings had left Montgomery by the time Mom and Dad arrived, but the Durrs took my parents over to Atlanta to meet them. The inspiration they gained was passed on to me. I remember mother saying how impressed she was with both Coretta and MLK. I didn't fully grasp the significance of their meeting at the time. Now I do. Dr. King is an enormous hero to everyone who takes civil rights seriously, and he is a double hero to me for his early opposition to American's misguided Vietnam war. I've been humbled to win several MLK awards from civil rights organizations.

I will always consider President John Kennedy and his brother Attorney General Robert Kennedy heroes of the civil rights movement as well. The November 22, 1963, assassination of President Kennedy was a tragic historical moment for all of America. It also figured into my family's Montgomery civil rights experience in a uniquely personal way. On that date, I was a senior at Sewanee Military Academy. About an hour after the assassination was reported on the national news broadcasts, I wrote a letter (see appendix) home to my parents, expressing profound grief but also hope for America. Three days later, I received a call from Dad saying how touched he and Mom were with my letter. Dad explained that my expression was very different from the reactions of many Montgomery high school students at Sidney Lanier and Robert E. Lee high schools, where cheering took place. Dad asked permission to submit my letter to the local newspaper, as an expression of a different viewpoint. I was honored by the suggestion and readily agreed. On November 29, a week after JFK's death, the letter was printed in the

Alabama Journal, the afternoon newspaper, under the headline "A Letter from a Teenager Who Didn't Cheer" (see Appendix 4).

That letter, 53 years ago, was my first contact with the Montgomery media about an issue of public concern. It was not to be my last.

Dad moved the family to Birmingham in the summer of 1964, as I prepared to enter my freshman year at Princeton. During the next two years at his new pastorate, St. Luke's Episcopal Church in Mountain Brook, Dad preached a number of bold sermons on civil rights-related topics. One of Dad's sermons in 1965 expressed anguish over the acquittal of the murderer of Jonathan Daniels, the Episcopal seminarian shotgunned to death in Lowndes County, Alabama. A framed copy of that sermon now hangs prominently in the Rosa Parks Library and Museum in Montgomery.

I am proud of Dad. He pulled no punches. The index to J. Barry Vaughn's *Bishops, Bourbons, and Big Mules: A History of the Episcopal Church in Alabama* (University of Alabama Press, 2013), has nine page references to the Rev. Julian L. McPhillips. Virtually all are related to Dad's confronting racism in the church. One reference is to the Church of the Ascension in Montgomery in 1962, and the remainder are to St. Luke's Episcopal Church in Birmingham, 1964–1966.

Truth be told, my civil rights sensibilities and those of my siblings came equally from our mother. Eleanor Dixon McPhillips was so deeply committed spiritually and emotionally to the movement that she had prepared to go to Selma in the spring of 1965 to be a part of the famous march to Montgomery. Dad was okay with her going, though a little nervous. But Alabama's Episcopal Diocesan Bishop George Murray got wind of her plan and wrote Dad a kind but firm letter stating that, if Mom did march, it would mean the end of his ministry at St. Luke's Episcopal in Birmingham and quite possibly in all of Alabama.

It wasn't that Murray could have prevented Dad or Mom from acting, but he speculated that no Alabama church would want Dad after that. Sadly, that was the climate of the times among white Alabamians. In the end, Dad still supported Mom's marching, but she pulled back because she didn't want to be the cause of ending his ministry.

I was away at Princeton at the time, but my brother Frank was still living at home with our parents and heard more of the ins and outs about it, and still knows more. People who are inclined to scoff at recollections of such incidents weren't living in Alabama then and were unaware of how many people, whites and blacks, were being killed or seriously injured in those days. The common denominator is that all the victims were pro-civil rights.

I was coming to the conclusion that I didn't want to return after college to such a deeply racist state as I felt Alabama was at that time.

THEN, IN 1966, DAD and Mom left Birmingham so Dad could become America's Peace Corps director in India. Mother worked during that period on the streets of Calcutta with an amazing Catholic nun who would later be known to the world as Mother Teresa.

Meanwhile at Princeton, my own commitment to civil rights grew exponentially. When I first arrived, I had been bombarded by other students about the church bombing. An article in the 1965 *Princeton Wrestling News* about me being elected captain of the wrestling team contained the statement that "Julian McPhillips comes from Birmingham, where people use clubs, rather than wrestling holds." Unlike some fellow Princeton freshmen from Alabama (there were only five of us), I didn't try to defend Alabama. Instead, I agreed with the criticism.

In my junior and senior years, I was also involved in the Princeton-in-Harlem Project. That brought me to New York City, to work with African American teenagers there. In turn, I hosted Harlem students coming to Princeton for reciprocal visits intended to educate, motivate, and inspire the black teens.

I finished Princeton in June 1968. That summer and the preceding summer of 1967, I traveled first to Europe, and then to India, where Mom and Dad were engaged in Peace Corps work. Despite all the controversies of the Vietnam War era, somehow Columbia Law School accepted me as a student.

The next seven years in New York City exposed me to a strong social justice agenda. Hence my commitment to civil rights kept growing and growing. That is why I turned down a free membership at the New York Athletic Club in 1973, as a reward for my winning two individual Eastern AAU Wrestling championships for the club and helping the NYAC team win two national championships—I didn't want to be an official part of a club that excluded black members. I politely shared this with head coach Bill Farrell, who solicited me; he seemed to understand. That is also why, after I had moved back to Montgomery with my new bride, Leslie, we resisted as diplomatically as possible invitations to join the Montgomery Country Club.

WHEN LESLIE AND I returned to Montgomery on April 28, 1975, we were invited by Virginia and Clifford Durr to stay at their Pea Level home in Wetumpka until we found a place to live.

The Durrs were a remarkable couple. Virginia was the sister-in-law of U.S. Supreme Court Justice Hugo Black. While still in the U.S. Senate, Black had brought Cliff Durr to Washington to work in FDR's New Deal; Durr was general counsel to the Reconstruction Finance Corp. and director of the War Defense Plant, and thus helped America through two of its most difficult times. Later he served on the Federal Communications Commission and deserves much of the credit for creating public broadcasting. Virginia was an ally of progressive politician Henry Wallace and was close to Eleanor Roosevelt. There are several good books about both Durrs and a documentary film. As editorialist Ray Jenkins stated, the true role model for Atticus Finch in *To Kill a Mockingbird* could have been Cliff Durr. He has certainly been a role model for me.

It was inevitable that we would become a part of the local "civil rights circle." And soon we did. That was a wonderful circle to be a part of, as Virginia introduced me in the mid-1970s personally to Rosa Parks, E. D. Nixon, Johnnie Carr, and other local civil rights activists or sympathizers, black and white. One might say the "die was cast." However, this was precisely where my heart was, and it is where my heart has remained for more than 40 years.

Unfortunately, about two weeks after we returned to Montgomery, Clifford Durr died. While it was nice to meet the rest of the family at his funeral, I profoundly regretted that I didn't have more time to visit with Cliff about the amazing historical events he was involved in.

I had already been blessed, however, to get to know the Durrs' daughter, Lucy Hackney, at Princeton. I took three Princeton history courses under the Durrs' distinguished son-in-law, professor Sheldon Hackney.

The Hackneys fanned the flames of my civil rights enthusiasm, as they did for many other Princeton students of our 1960s era, including Ray Arsenault, a year behind me, who has since written major works of history, including on the Freedom Rides. Montgomery native Mills Thornton, Class of 1966, was another Hackney student who has also written extensively and excellently on civil rights history. Mills, Ray, and I, along with so many other Princeton students, were much influenced by Sheldon Hackney.

Virginia Durr remained close personally to Leslie and me for our first 20 years back in Montgomery. I will always appreciate Virginia encouraging me to prepare a resolution for the Young Lawyer's section of the Alabama State Bar Convention that summer of 1975, honoring her dear Cliff. Leslie helped me install the words on a homemade plaque. I remember Mike House (Senator Howell Heflin's future chief of staff) and other young law students at the meeting in Mobile whispering behind my back, as I presented the resolution, "Oh, he must be a liberal."

Liberal I was, and proudly so, especially by Southern standards in a region that reveres "conservatism." Yet, like most people, I am not a doctrinaire anything, and I cannot be placed easily in a box. On faith and family issues, like many of my black friends, I tend to be more traditional, or conservative.

MY FIRST TWO YEARS and three months back in Montgomery, I worked as an assistant attorney general under the progressive Bill Baxley, who had been a district attorney at age 25 and then became Alabama's attorney general when he was only 28. At the time, he was the youngest state attorney general in U.S. history. Many called Bill "liberal," especially on the race issue, because he so vigorously prosecuted the church bombers in Birmingham. Bill was also a populist generally, and I found his approach philosophically quite compatible with my own. I admired Bill greatly at the time and still do.

I was successfully pursuing white-collar crime and other public-interest cases. Meanwhile, Bill—and Virginia Durr—kept me involved in civil rights matters. That provided a great connection in the black community, and when Bill decided in 1978 to run for governor, several other assistant attorneys general encouraged me to run to succeed him. I did, and before it was over, every black political group in the state was supporting me. That included the powerful black wing of the Alabama Democrats, the Alabama Democratic Conference (ADC), whose endorsement was a valuable political asset.

The ADC endorsement was considered adequate to propel me into the run-off. Thus, after I alone received the endorsement, out of the 9 candidates in the attorney general's race, it suddenly elevated me into front-runner status. I was then promptly attacked by three of my opponents, Ray Acton, Bob "Hawkeye" Morrow, and Bill Stephens. Acton's and Morrow's attacks were harmless, but Stephens got a straw man to challenge my residency qualifications as a candidate. I was served with a lawsuit in Huntsville shortly before the first-round primary election. The intent was to harm me with negative news, even if the suit itself were unsuccessful. In the end, it probably helped a little more than it hurt.

Fortunately, with the expert help of my long-time friend and personal attorney, Bobby Segall, the Alabama Supreme Court denied Stephens's efforts to keep me off the ballot. When the results were tallied, I was in second, 5,000 votes ahead of the third-place candidate, Joe Fine, president of the Alabama Senate, and securely in the run-off. I know the ADC endorsement was highly instrumental.

I campaigned hard for the next week, but was shocked to discover at the end of the first week, that my run-off place had been stolen from me. During the week after the election, Fine's totals went up about 5,000 votes in six counties, and mine went down about 5,000 votes, a swing of 10,000 votes.

I contested the obvious theft for a week but had to abandon the challenge, due to its futility and exorbitant costs. Fine, as president of the Alabama Senate, held a lot of IOUs, but I primarily blame the probate judges. I later learned how easy it was to change totals, like "stealing candy from a baby."

THE NEXT CHAPTER OF my life was about to begin, in which I increasingly became known as both a civil rights attorney and trial lawyer.

Returning to law practice in 1978, I started building up a law firm from ground zero. This was very different from my two years in a big Wall Street law firm (1971–73), two years with American Express Company in New York (1973–75), and two years and three months as an Alabama assistant attorney general (1975–77).

It helped to have name recognition and a good rapport with the public, left over from the 1978 campaign, to help build the practice. This included a number of relationships with African American leaders, especially ministers in Montgomery. Many saw that my spiritual orientation as the son of a priest was real. It was not just a charade to win votes. The ministers and other leaders referred plenty of prospective cases and clients to me. They also invited me to preach at their churches.

It wasn't hard to do civil rights work, with Virginia Durr grooming me and recommending me to so many people. Two of my most famous cases came from her in the mid-1980s. One was the class-action Johnny Reynolds race discrimination suit. The Reynolds suit, filed in 1985, opened up jobs to minorities in the infamous Alabama Highway Department, which had become a cesspool of unceasing racism. A great effect of the Reynolds case was that it spilled over into other departments and agencies of Alabama state government. Fearing a similar suit, these agencies and employers started hiring more blacks.

The other landmark civil rights suit I filed in 1986 was the famous Michael Timmons case that struck down Montgomery's vagrancy law. I argued that it violated both the 4th and 14th amendments to the U.S. Constitution. I called it Montgomery's South Africa law, because it was used to harass and arrest poor people, mostly black, who could not identify themselves to police officers with a written form of identification. Again, I credit my hero U.S. District Judge Myron Thompson for his astute rulings on both cases.

One of my most significant civil rights cases in the early 1980s was one I call the "Shades of the Scottsboro Boys Case." That is because I had to travel to Scottsboro in north Alabama to represent a white real estate broker, Charlotte Payne, whose office burned down after she showed a home in a white neighborhood to a black couple. The KKK element was still strong in the Scottsboro area at that time, and Charlotte's insurance broker, a former chief of police, allegedly had ties to that element. So I sued the insurance company, Nationwide Insurance, when it denied her claim on the basis that she had committed the arson herself, even though there had not been enough evidence to charge her criminally. Charlotte and I were heartened when an all-white jury returned a substantial verdict for us against Nationwide—a white lady's civil rights were vindicated.

My civil rights legal work has involved many cases challenging unlawful employment discrimination based on race, sex, age, national origin, religion and/or disability. Some of these cases are discussed in the two editions of *The People's Lawyer* and others will be discussed in more detail in this present volume. I don't just represent only blacks and women in race and sex discrimination cases, but anyone who has been wrongfully discriminated against.

Some white males have also been wrongfully discriminated against, due to their race and/or sex, and sometimes both. I've seen it and defended against it. Also, persons of one race or gender can and do discriminate against other persons of the same race or gender. Indeed, jealousies within groups can contribute to such cases. It all depends on the facts and circumstances of each case. Legal proof requires much more than "a feeling." The federal courts have set high, concrete standards.

I also have a great interest in helping immigrants, especially from African countries such as Kenya, Nigeria, Benin, Senegal, and Uganda. Our law firm has also helped Hispanic immigrants. We too easily forget that our country was founded by immigrants.

One area of my civil rights work has roiled my liberal friends, including some very close to me. This is my pro-life work. Numerous sophisticated and intellectual people, many very secular and independent-minded, see this issue quite differently. They are also mostly ethical and moral, and many are religious. They consider a women's right to an abortion to be a paramount, absolute U.S. Constitutional right, which it is, thanks to *Roe v. Wade*.

Unfortunately, I feel there is a blindness operating here. These people don't realize that there is a great life in the womb after only five weeks. There is a brain wave so strong that if it was in was an adult on life support, the law would not allow you to remove the life support. There is an equally strong heartbeat. There is also great physical pain on the part of the unborn child ripped from his or her mother's womb.

The problem with pro-choice is that it is absolutely "no choice" for the one and only life really at stake, namely the unborn child. So I make no apologies about having a "heart for the unborn," something my opponent Susan Parker strongly and successfully used against me in my 2002 campaign for the U.S. Senate.

As a civil rights attorney, I unequivocally assert that the greatest civil right is life itself. I am encouraged that the famous ACLU lawyer, New Yorker Nat Hentoff, who is both Jewish and atheist, now says he is very pro-life due to the overwhelming scientific evidence about "real life inside the womb."

My heart for civil rights carries over into a sideline of ministerial work. I was ordained in 2003 by a black denomination, the Global Evangelical Christian Church. It was my civil rights work, not going to seminary or passing a canonical exam, which led Global Evangelical Christian to ordain me. Since April 2013, I also have served as a lay minister and administrator at Christ the Redeemer Episcopal Church in Montgomery. Our congregation is about "half and half" racially. That includes not only four African Americans in our church jazz band, but immigrants from Kenya, Nigeria, and Benin. Our congregation has been served by both African and Korean priests. Thus, we've had three races worshiping together. We celebrate first our Lord Jesus, but we also celebrate our diversity. We emphasize the healing ministry and enjoy Spirit-filled praise and worship music. We begin every service with the words "Let the Glory of the Lord fill this House."

THE CIVIL RIGHTS BATTLE, on many fronts, is far from over, as I will discuss in more detail in the next to last chapter. Meanwhile, I will continue to do my part to try to help society's problems. I thank God that he has given me and many others a heart for civil rights. A fertile field of opportunity, with many serious challenges, still remains for those of us in Alabama to pursue this interest well into the 21st century.

2

CIVIL RIGHTS INSPIRATIONS AND ALLIES

Montgomery's place in civil rights history is so great that hundreds if not thousands of books, movies, museums, art exhibits, plays, songs, and historical markers now tell its stories. Having moved back to Montgomery in 1975, and coming immediately into the embrace of Virginia and Clifford Durr, it was inevitable that I would be caught up in the civil rights history and that the key figures of the movement would influence me both personally and professionally. As already mentioned, I met many of the heroes of the movement and even came to know some of them quite well. Of course, thousands of local citizens, anonymous today, participated in their own collectively heroic ways. Many of these unsung persons have become friends, clients, and acquaintances over the years.

I would be extraordinarily remiss not to acknowledge that in the greater Montgomery area, there are living people with much bigger civil rights names than my own. Fred Gray, with his pioneering legal work in the Montgomery Bus Boycott and many other cases, is a national hero. Likewise, Bryan Stevenson, who created the Equal Justice Initiative, is in a class by himself. Federal judge Myron Thompson is also a big-time civil rights hero (as was his predecessor, the legendary Frank M. Johnson Jr.), and so is Judge U. W. Clemon in Birmingham. Morris Dees and his colleagues at the Southern Poverty Law Center have handled many significant civil rights cases.

I credit Charles Steele, the national president of the Southern Christian Leadership Conference, and Alabama NAACP President Benard Simelton with many great civil rights initiatives.

My latest hero in the civil rights arena is like a daughter or niece, namely Terri Sewell, the first African American congresswoman from Alabama. She gives me more credit than I deserve for pulling her out of what she calls "the cotton-patch of Selma" by recruiting her for Princeton. I prophesied in my 1981 recommendation letter that she would one day be a member of Congress. Her incredible combination of intellect, wit and humor, and habits of hard work have made her a great leader at a young age. I compare her to Barbara Jordan of Watergate fame. Meanwhile, Terri holds the safest seat in the U.S. House and is the highest-ranking Democrat in Alabama. She comes by her gifts honestly: Nancy Sewell, Terri's dynamic mother, was the first black elected to the Selma City Council.

Credit for their political action also goes to black Montgomery political leaders Joe Reed, Alvin Holmes, John Knight, and Thad McClammy, and their judicial counterparts Charles Price and Johnny Hardwick. Ditto for former U.S. Magistrate Judges Delores Boyd and Vanzetta McPherson, talented lawyers dedicated to justice, and courageous in dispensing it.

Robert James, president of the seminal Montgomery Improvement Association and long-time head of the Cleveland Avenue YMCA, has contributed greatly to the civil rights movement in Montgomery. I first met gracious Robert in the late 1970s, when I became a director for 10 years of what was once known as the "black YMCA," and I have supported it financially every year since. The Montgomery Improvement Association is the organization that coordinated the bus boycott; Dr. Martin Luther King Jr. was its first president.

Nelson Malden, Martin Luther King Jr.'s barber, deserves his place in Montgomery's civil rights lore. Nelson, at age 21, first met Rev. King—he wasn't a "Doctor" yet—in 1954 when the newly arrived young preacher settled into Nelson's chair at the College Hill Barber Shop for a trim. Nelson was also a member of King's congregation at Dexter Avenue Baptist Church. King became a loyal customer and followed Nelson in 1958 to the new Malden Brothers Barber Shop on south Jackson Street near ASU. Nelson continued to cut Dr. King's hair until he left Montgomery in 1960 and occasionally afterwards when the increasingly prominent civil rights leader would be back in town on civil rights or legal business. Nelson, now 82, is a frequent participant in civil rights commemorations. I see him and his wife, Dean, every year at a home reception my wife and I host for the Clifford and Virginia Durr lecture series. Malden Brothers Barber Shop is still in business, and Nelson is still cutting hair. His shop is a treasure trove of civil rights photographs, signs, and memorabilia.

Filling a special niche in Montgomery's and Alabama's civil rights lore has been actress Tommie "Tonea" Stewart, a star in *Mississippi Burning* and other movies and television shows. She has especially inspired students as dean of the College of Visual and Performing Arts at Alabama State University. Civil rights is always a theme in her work.

No list of civil rights personalities would be complete without mentioning Sheyann Webb-Christburg, one of the subjects of the book and movie,

Selma, Lord, Selma. Sheyann, at nine years of age, was the youngest person on the Edmund Pettus Bridge when state troopers and sheriff's possemen attacked marchers in 1965.

Civil rights enthusiasts abound in Montgomery's historically black churches. The Dexter Avenue King Memorial Baptist Church may be the best-known because of its location a block from the capitol and because Dr. King famously pastured it from 1954–1960. The church is led today by the Reverend Cromwell A. Handy and lay leaders such as Vanzetta and Thomas McPherson and Ed and Alma Collier.

First Baptist Church on Ripley Street (Montgomery also has a white First Baptist Church on Perry Street), led by the Reverend E. Baxter Morris and lay stalwarts like Warren and Tyna Davis, frequently brings in leading civil rights figures, especially during Bus Boycott and Freedom Rides commemorations, since this church was a key site in both momentous civil rights episodes.

A great number of African American ministers have provided spiritual and moral leadership to the civil rights movement in the Montgomery area over the years. The ones with whom I have had the most contact are the Reverends John Alford of Mt. Gaillard Missionary Baptist Church (now retired), Jiles Williams of New Providence Missionary Baptist, Calvin McTier of Bethel Missionary Baptist Church, Edward J. Nettles of "Enough is Enough" fame, Kyle Searcy of Fresh Anointing Church, Father Manuel Williams of Resurrection Catholic Church, and Thomas Jordan of Lilly Baptist Church.

I also include the esteemed pastor and civil rights activist Reverend George Washington Carver Richardson of Hutchinson Missionary Baptist Church. Not to be left out is the Reverend Leon Henderson of Montgomery, who pastors in Alexander City; he has helped in my police brutality case over the wrongful death of Emerson Crayton Jr.

There are many others, churches and individuals, too numerous to mention, and I apologize to anyone omitted. Collectively, however, they have helped move Montgomery more forward in civil rights and race relations.

Educator Tyna Davis deserves comment. Sharing my birthday, November 13, but born seven years earlier in 1939, she was a Montgomery teacher when the black Alabama State Teachers Association (ASTA) merged with the white Alabama Education Association (AEA) in 1969. The two groups of respective officials alternated in leadership until 1973, when elections were thrown open for the first time with candidates from both organizations eligible.

The first five AEA presidents elected by the combined body were white. Tyna became the first black elected AEA president in 1978. She later served as the highest-level official under Paul Hubbert and Joe Reed, the co-executive secretaries of AEA. Now 76, Tyna remains energetic and articulate as the chairwoman of the Montgomery County Democratic Party.

Though most of the leaders from the bus boycott era have passed on—Fred Gray, Bob Graetz, and Uriah Fields are the only living MIA principals from 1955–56—the Montgomery area is home to a long list of living men and women who have made significant contributions to civil and human rights. A few have already been named, but among the still active "civil-righters" are Gwen Patton, Janet May, Dorothy Autry, Connie Harper, Ella Bell, Doris Crenshaw, and Georgette Norman.

Hank and Rose Sanders of Selma are also fierce civil rights advocates, even if they can't quite leaven their activism with the humor and wit of their former law partner, the late J. L. Chestnut. He was another who inspired my legal career. People sometimes called Chestnut the "conscience of the civil rights movement." He once gave me the high accolade of calling me the "white J. L. Chestnut." I was honored to be one of the three eulogists at his funeral in 2007.

Tuskegee's Johnny Ford was first elected mayor of his historic town in 1970 and has intermittently been reelected over the years. Johnny also founded the World Conference of Black Mayors. He is diplomatic and kind but has long stood up to civil rights abusers in Tuskegee and Montgomery. Johnny led the fight to restore the Victoryland dog track and casino business that has employed 2,000 people in Macon, Montgomery, and nearby counties. That's civil rights work at its best.

Donald Watkins, native of Montgomery and one time city-councilman, but now of Birmingham, has been an exceedingly articulate civil rights advocate and has courageously stood up to power.

I would be remiss not to mention Alabama State University's new president, Gwendolyn Boyd, who had some rocky moments in her first year but nonetheless has brought badly needed new leadership to the venerable institution. She is a dynamic public speaker, whom I've enjoyed getting to know personally.

Likewise, the National Center for Civil Rights and African American Culture on Carter Hill Road, under the leadership of Janice Franklin, Dorothy Autry, Howard Robinson, and Gwendolyn Boyd, keeps the civil rights flame burning strong. I also include the dynamic couple of Jackie and Joe Trimble. Jackie chairs ASU's English Department. Joe is a great author, among other talents.

Whites have also made significant contributions to civil rights and inspired me in my life and work, including some who are still alive. I have already mentioned Bob and Jeannie Graetz, Bill Baxley, Morris Dees, and Paul Hubbert. I also add Ray Jenkins, fearless editor of the *Alabama Journal*, who lived and worked in Montgomery from 1954 to 1979. He and my father were good friends.

I thank Dees and Joe Levin for creating the Southern Poverty Law Center and Richard Cohen for running it today. The Center has done much good civil rights work, especially in defying agents of hate and in helping immigrants. I have disagreed with some of their initiatives, but I appreciate the SPLC's stands for tolerance and justice.

Former SPLC staffer Randall Williams, editor of NewSouth Books, is also an important part of the civil rights fabric in Alabama. A longtime board member of the Montgomery Improvement Association, Randall was also an original member of the Friendly Supper Club, a diverse group that has met monthly in Montgomery since the Todd Road racial crisis in 1983. At the SPLC, he was the first director of the Klanwatch Project, but his greatest contribution to civil rights may be the many books he has edited and written to preserve civil rights history. Randall is very independent-minded, but decent to the core.

Randall, Bob & Jeannie Graetz, and I were the only four Caucasian members of an original group of about 35 civil rights foot-soldiers honored by the Rosa Parks Museum in 2004 with bronze imprints of our hands, permanently installed on black marble at the Museum.

Of course, there are many other civil rights heroes, sung and unsung, as well as other anonymous folk, all over America and in other parts of Alabama, who have fought for civil rights. I therefore apologize to anyone whose name I have wrongfully left out. This list is far from exhaustive and was never meant to be a Who's Who. My references in this chapter are primarily limited to those whose paths have come through Montgomery, the birthplace of the civil rights movement, and to those who are still living.

However, over the months while I was writing this book, several people I included in early drafts have died, and I do want to mention them even if they do not still walk among us.

Montgomery lost a great civil rights leader with the September 2015 passing of Solomon Seay Jr. at age 81. The son of civil rights pioneer Reverend Solomon Seay Sr., the younger Seay became a lawyer, joined Fred Gray's law firm, and was a part of many landmark civil rights cases from the 1960s through the 1990s. Tough on the outside against injustice, Solomon had a kind and tender inside. I got to know him and his wife Ettra soon after my return to Montgomery. Solomon was a member of the Episcopal Church of the Good Shepherd when my father ministered there. Solomon left us a great autobiography, *Jim Crow and Me.*

Amelia Boynton Robinson of Selma, who was over 100 years old when she recently died, was an enormous spark plug for the civil rights movement. An early proponent of voting rights, she was severely beaten on the Edmund Pettus Bridge on Bloody Sunday in March 1965. Her son, Bruce, by the way, is now the Dallas County attorney, but as a student at Howard Law School, he was arrested in Virginia in 1958 for trying to eat in a whites-only interstate bus terminal cafe. His became a landmark U.S. Supreme Court case and precipitated the 1961 Freedom Rides.

Other recent losses in central Alabama in 2015 were Beverly Ross of Montgomery and Barbara Howard of Tuskegee, both long-time civil rights soldiers. I must also include the late Richard Boone, a humble but sacrificial civil rights warrior, and his energetic wife, Mary. Both were clients and friends of mine. I spoke at Richard's memorial service in 2013.

FOREMOST AMONG AFRICAN AMERICAN ministers encouraging my civil rights work has been Rev. John Alford, long-time president of the Montgomery chapter of the Southern Christian Leadership Conference (SCLC). Over the years, I have been blessed to receive five different awards from the Southern Christian Leadership Conference and several more from the Alabama NAACP and other local civil rights organizations.

My close friendship with John began in 1977–78 in my attorney general's campaign, was strengthened while we both helped Bill Bradley in his 2000 presidential campaign, and grew much more in my own 2002 U.S. Senate campaign. John, too, has been my pastor. On September 11, 2001, when I was uncertain about whether to continue in the U.S. Senate race, John invited me to his home swimming pool and shared a "word of knowledge" from Proverbs 3:6 that lifted my spirits.

John was the most valuable player in my Senate campaign. The group he brought into leadership roles included Martin Luther King III, Fred Shuttlesworth, and Andrew Young. John also introduced me to State Senators Sundra Escott of Birmingham and Charles Steele of Tuscaloosa. I developed solid friendships with all of them. Each was enormously helpful in the campaign, not only in their own hometowns, but statewide. Steele is now the national SCLC president and remains a close friend with whom I frequently communicate, as I do with Sundra Escott.

John also introduced me to Rev. T. L. Lewis, and the Birmingham minister brothers, Revs. Abraham and Calvin Woods. Both committed to me early in the U.S. Senate race of 2002, as did former Birmingham Mayor Richard Arrington and Senator Escott, both great civil rights champions. They supported me even though U.S. Attorney Doug Jones of Birmingham was in the race. Doug had recently successfully prosecuted a church bombing, leading to a full-page picture of himself in *Newsweek*, but had stepped on some local toes.

The Rev. Fred Shuttlesworth deserves special mention. This hero of the Birmingham civil rights campaign has enormously inspired me. At first, it was his work in the early 1960s fighting the dogs, hoses, and policemen in Birmingham, and standing up to great racial injustice, which I read about in the *Birmingham News* and saw on television. Secondly, Fred personally encouraged me in my work fighting police brutality. I was in awe of Shuttlesworth. His undaunting commitment to civil rights, despite having been bombed three times, elevated and set an example for my own commitment. Thirdly, when I ran for U.S. Senate in 2002 he campaigned for me in Birmingham and the Black Belt. Finally, when I was ill in 2006, Dr. Shuttlesworth's two personal visits to my home in Montgomery greatly contributed to my recovery, and set an enormous pastoral example, one that I want to follow.

MANY CIVIL RIGHTS CASES and employment discrimination plaintiffs have come to me from a prominent east Alabama civil rights leader, Bishop Arthur Dowdell of Auburn. "Bishop," as I respectfully call him, has long been a city councilman there. He has also been much involved in the healing ministry and deliverance. Dowdell heads up the black denomination known as the New Testament Potter's House Full Gospel Church.

Nurses need help, too. I've been especially disappointed by the way the Baptist hospitals, especially Baptist South, treat their nursing staff. I know Baptist Hospital often renders good medical services, but it has caused a lot of its employees to come running to me for help. It has also very badly treated a medical doctor client of mine, Dr. Rochelle Janush. The Baptist Foundation that owns the hospitals would be dismayed if it knew how much Baptist spent in legal fees to fight an employee's case that could have initially settled for $5,000. I am especially aware of numerous age discrimination cases by older nurses against Baptist, having handled 3–4 in 2014–2015 alone.

The same could be said for Rheem Manufacturing Company. Unfortunately, settlement agreements with confidentiality and non-disparagement clauses prevent us from commenting on any individual cases with that business.

One of the greatest deprivations of civil rights for average ordinary consumers, black and white, has been the growth of arbitration. Arbitration is involuntarily imposed on a consumer, as a precondition to buying a car, or attending a college. One of the worst offenders has been Virginia College, which I have fought in the courts, trying to defeat the involuntary shackles of arbitration that Virginia College has deceitfully and fraudulently, in my opinion, tried to impose on students the college has abused. (See Chapter 24).

Battling police brutality is a huge form of civil rights work. This is covered at length in Chapters 4 and 5 of this book. Interestingly, however, my civil rights work has spawned two different reactions from a prominent and progressive family of white judges in Montgomery, namely Truman Hobbs Sr. and Truman Hobbs Jr. In 1987, the senior Hobbs, a federal judge, observed wryly "How would you like it, Mr. McPhillips, if someone said you were white on the outside, but black on the inside." I laughed, and replied "Your Honor, they've been saying that about me for a long time. It's true, and I'm proud of it."

Fast forward to 2015, and I'm before his son, Montgomery County Circuit Judge Truman Hobbs Jr. (10 years younger than me) on a summary judgment motion, where a white police officer, with a bad history at the MPD, used his police car to run over my client Myreico Broaden, breaking his leg. Broaden had committed no crime. Just like the famous Bernard Whitehurst, Broaden was simply running from the police, in fear of being shot. Anyway, the Montgomery police officer jumped out of his car, and told my client "you're a fast nigger," while Broaden was anguishing in pain under the police car's wheels. To my great surprise, the younger Hobbs ruled in favor of the officer. The case is on appeal to the Alabama Supreme Court.

A law partner of both Hobbses was Bobby Segall. He is, in my opinion the best lawyer in Alabama. Bobby has helped me obtain great results on several civil rights-related cases. He is currently assisting me in representing Kolea Burns, the administratrix of the estate of Emerson Crayton Jr. Crayton was an unarmed 21-year-old black male, shot and killed by police on March 8, 2014, as he backed his car out of the Huddle House parking lot in Alexander City.

Another emerging civil rights attorney, Eric Hutchins, an African American in his late 30s from Alexander City, got me involved in the Emerson Crayton Jr. case (see Chapter 4). Although from a modest background, Eric was well-educated at Brown University and Northern Ohio Law School. He has been a tenacious and highly motivated co-counsel in pursuing justice in the outrageous police killing of Mr. Crayton. I see Eric as a great civil rights warrior, present and future.

I especially appreciate Montgomery County Circuit Judge Johnny Hardwick for standing up firmly against police brutality. Likewise, former presiding judge Charles Price was strong enough to stand up to the establishment. Notwithstanding, both judges are pro-law enforcement, with a heart for victims of crime.

I HAVE TO CONCEDE that Montgomery's thrice-elected Mayor Todd Strange, though originally a Republican, has shown a heart for civil rights, which helped reelect him, as it did city councilman Tracy Larkin and the other African American councilmen. Ditto the trio of our great African American county commissioners, Dan Harris, Elton Dean, and Jiles Williams, all men of integrity. I supported Dan in his unsuccessful candidacy in the most recent August 2015 mayor's race, and helped him defend a vigorous challenge in the March 2016 county commissioner's race. He is a good friend.

State Senator Quinton Ross of Montgomery is also a strong civil rights advocate. It is also in his DNA. Quinton also knows what it's like to be wrongfully indicted and bullied. I contributed financially to his defense. He was charged by federal prosecutors in 2013 with alleged wrongdoings connected with gambling legislation related to Milton McGregor. Quinton was acquitted on all counts in a first trial, whereas the alleged co-conspirators, including McGregor, due to a mistrial the first time around, had to endure a second trial before acquittal. Joe Espy and Bobby Segall led an excellent defense.

Lewis Gillis and Tyrone Means, law partners and both African Americans, have also been real civil rights advocates, as has been a former law partner of theirs, Troy Massey.

I also acknowledge that such well-known and successful private practice attorneys as Jere Beasley (especially in the products liability field) and Joe Espy (defending against unjust criminal prosecutions) have also promoted the civil rights of minorities, and others, in special ways.

I am the first to acknowledge that I have had other good in-house legal help in pursuing many of my cases. Earlier on, and still, my law partner Kenneth Shinbaum has been most helpful. Partner Joe Guillot has also assisted me greatly. More recently, my two associate attorneys, Chris Worshek and Chase Estes, have been very helpful, as has office manager-paralegal Amy Strickland. A new African American paralegal, Carlton Avery, is also assisting me on the Crayton case and another wrongful death case inside the Montgomery City Jail, involving the loss of life of Tony Lewis Jr.

Of course, the theme story of *The People's Lawyer* involved a Montgomery police officer wrongfully running over and badly injuring my client, Reggie "Pee Wee" Jones in 1998. The city was held accountable in a substantial way in that case.

REPRESENTING PEOPLE WRONGFULLY CHARGED with a crime is true civil rights work and addressed in more detail later. It is wrong, and reckless, the way some prosecutors get caught up in the competition of getting a conviction, no matter what the truth, or what the cost. It is also very wrong the way some district attorneys fail to investigate and/or prosecute police misconduct cases. These are both clear violations of civil rights, either way, in my opinion.

On the other hand, I commend Montgomery's current district attorney, Daryl Bailey, for the professional and careful way he handles his cases. Former Montgomery district attorney, Ellen Brooks, also did a good job. Both are sensitive to minority issues, although blacks are no longer the minority in the city of Montgomery, but the majority.

ONE DOESN'T HAVE TO be a lawyer, minister, teacher, or political figure to be active in civil rights and one doesn't have to be black to promote the cause, even at an historically black institution like Alabama State University. I cite two examples, both much younger than me and both Caucasian. Ken Mullinax, 56, is the public relations officer at Alabama State University. He drove me around Alabama in my attorney general's campaign in 1977. Ken energetically promotes civil rights history for both ASU and otherwise. David Campbell, 48, my third cousin, has been Alabama State University's photographer for 15 years. He is beloved on that campus. We're both directly descended from David Davidson Sanderson, 1821–1890, co-founder of Stillman College in Tuscaloosa.

Another Caucasian with a heart for civil rights is educator-lawyer Dr. Jim Vickrey. A native Montgomerian who grew up in segregated Montgomery in the 1940s and 1950s, Jim was the youngest college president in America when he took over at Montevallo University in 1977 at age 35. His enlightened view on race relations and gender fairness contributed to his leaving in 1988. In later years as a Troy University professor, Jim's progressive views have remained steadfast.

No list of Caucasian leaders helpful to the civil rights movement in Alabama would be complete without mentioning the late Paul Hubbert and the imprisoned Don Siegelman. Hubbert's enlightened leadership in merging AEA with ASTA helped cause higher quality public education to be available for African Americans. Siegelman also did much to help his black brethren, including a lottery initiative that was so wrongfully used to imprison him.

There are also many physicians who do important civil rights work of a different sort. That includes repairing bodies, souls, and minds injured by exercising civil rights, or battered by the absence of civil rights. Especially worth mentioning are three doctors I know personally, John Winston, Jefferson Underwood, and Warner Pinchback, all African Americans. I am continually inspired by the 85-year-old Dr. Winston, whom I see at Lions Club meetings on Fridays. This usually smiling doctor still treats students at Alabama State University. There are many more physicians, white and black, who have certainly contributed to the cause, including Dr. Duncan McRae, a Caucasian.

UNFORTUNATELY, ONE OF THE things holding back the progress of civil rights is not just white opposition but rivalries, jealousies, and egos within the so-called "black community." Books can be written about this. Perhaps it's simply a maturing of the black community, as the same social phenomena also exist in the so-called "white community." Increasingly, thankfully, we are becoming one community of mixed colors and races, but rivalries and jealousies persist in human nature generally.

Montgomery and its nearby sister cities of Selma and Tuskegee are good at celebrating civil rights. Annually, the Montgomery Bus Boycott, the Edmund Pettus Bridge crossing, and the Selma-to-Montgomery March are re-enacted and celebrated. We just celebrated the 50th Anniversary of the March, and the 60th Anniversary of the Montgomery Bus Boycott was vigorously celebrated in Montgomery from December 1–7, 2015.

Additionally, the Rosa Parks Museum, the Civil Rights Museum, the more recent Freedom Riders' Museum (thanks to Myron Thompson and Ellen Mertins), the Dexter Avenue King Memorial Baptist Church, the First Baptist Church Ripley, and many other local Montgomery churches in the African American community celebrate important historical moments.

Appropriately, the modest homes inhabited by Martin Luther King Jr., Ralph Abernathy, and Nat King Cole have historical markers in front, and are regularly opened up as house museums.

Selma, Birmingham, Tuskegee, and Mobile, and other Alabama cities also have great civil rights memorials and museums. My dear, younger brother Frank has long served on the board of directors of the Birmingham Civil

Rights Institute, and has contributed to it generously. Frank gets his heart for civil rights from the same set of parents that I have.

There will be people who criticize me for not mentioning them in this book. One who kidded me for not mentioning him in *The People's Lawyer* was fellow attorney Jimmy Poole, now a Montgomery County District Court judge. I respect Jimmy. He is well connected with Montgomery's black community. Jimmy has been also a strong advocate for trial lawyers, Democrats, and for law and order, including "not driving under the influence of alcohol or drugs." Jimmy, please be advised I have now corrected the problem, and I appreciate your leadership.

Part II

My Professional Life

3

THE LEGAL PROFESSION, ITS CHANGES, AND ITS PERSONALITIES

So much has changed in the legal profession since my 1971 graduation from Columbia Law School. Indeed, so much has changed in America and the world, which certainly includes Montgomery in the more than 40 years since I returned here in 1975.

My first job was on Wall Street from 1971–73, on the 44th floor of the Chase Manhattan Bank Building. The work polished my skills and opened my eyes to what I didn't want to do the rest of my life—helping the rich get richer. The second job, as in-house counsel for American Express Company, gave me enough insight into the mega-corporate world to learn that it was not my cup of tea, either. My heart was really back in the South and on the side of seeking justice for ordinary people.

Returning to Alabama, I found much more exciting work on the staff of dynamic Attorney General Bill Baxley. I enjoyed fighting while collar crime, doing environmental law, and involving myself in the ongoing civil rights movement. That led to my running for Alabama attorney general in 1978, a story in itself. In the years after that election, I reentered private law practice, but one way or another I've been a lawyer for 45 years. Over those four-plus decades, I have gradually developed an understanding of the legal profession and its myriad changes, some for the better, many for the worse.

In 1978, Alabama was a one-party state, Democratic. That being the case, many populist candidates were successful in statewide races, including judicial races—in Alabama, almost all judges are elected rather than appointed. That meant the little guys had a better chance of being treated fairly in the Alabama Supreme Court. That also meant that justice was usually better served in the trial court. Summary judgment against a plaintiff (the side I usually represented in civil cases) was denied if there was a "scintilla" (a trace) of evidence in the plaintiff's favor.

Then along came the infusion of much bigger money into judicial races. More pro-business candidates were elected in statewide judicial, legislative, and executive races. Suddenly, the standard for denying summary judgment changed. Soon it became "substantial evidence," a much higher and more challenging burden. Less chance for the little guy. Also, some judges have made themselves "triers of fact," eliminating the right to a jury.

My law partners Jim Debardelaben, Kenneth Shinbaum, and I got a big judgment against Auburn University in a 1986 jury trial in federal court under federal age discrimination laws. Auburn's defense was that it relied upon a market-rate theory in paying newly arrived Chinese assistant professors as much as older, full professors who had written textbooks. We convinced a jury in Opelika that this defense by Auburn University was inherently age-discriminatory.

Today, unfortunately, an age discrimination case against Auburn University would be "dead in the water" for two reasons. First, the 11th U.S. Circuit Court of Appeals has upheld the market-rate theory as a valid defense. Second, the 11th Circuit and the U.S. Supreme Court, in *Garrett v. University of Alabama in Birmingham*, ruled that the Age Discrimination in Employment Act, when passed by the U.S. Congress, was somehow not properly vetted on the issue of states' sovereign immunity. Therefore, the court ruled that while the law did apply to the private sector, it did not apply to state institutions.

The same highly questionable rationale was used to strike down the applicability of the Americans with Disabilities Act against state actors. Fortunately, the federal Vocational Rehabilitation Act still applies to state actors, so long as the state entities receive federal money for their budgets, as Auburn does. Thus, I can still pursue disability discrimination cases against Auburn University and have done so successfully in more recent cases.

All of my anti-discrimination cases based on race, sex, age, national origin, religion and/or disability are civil rights cases, one way or the other. When we represent plaintiffs under the Family Medical Leave Act, our cases also protect a civil right given to employees by the federal government. The employee must have worked for more than a year and must leave to take care of close family health needs or one's own health, which leave cannot exceed 90 days in any one-year period. The FMLA has opened up a whole new area of the law, sadly for some employers, happily for conscientious employees hit by legitimate health issues that might otherwise cost them their jobs.

ANOTHER HORRENDOUS DEVELOPMENT IN the 1980s and 1990s was the emergence of arbitration. Arbitration is extremely unfair, and it has been intentionally designed to be disastrous for consumers and other claimants wronged by corporate wrongdoers. *The People's Lawyer* detailed the story of my client Ron Mays and the "Arbitration Albatross." Arbitration essentially imposes excessive costs on a grievant, win, lose, or draw. Worse, arbitrators hearing the cases often lean toward corporate defendants, for the self-interested reason that the arbitrator, at $250–$350 per hour, wants to be hired again. A corporate defendant is much more likely to be a repeat user of arbitration than an individual with a one-time claim, and the arbitrator's reputation for deciding cases quickly reverberates around corporate arbitration selection circles.

Arbitration has proven to be a deceitful trick employed by corporations to stop complaints in their tracks. Many plaintiff's attorneys refuse to handle mandatory arbitration cases, leaving many wronged consumers dangling without legal representation. Those attorneys who do take plantiff's arbitration cases face an uphill, often losing proposition. Arbitration thus undeniably equals the loss of a valuable civil right for members of the consuming public, especially poorer individuals. I will say more about arbitration later in the book.

Mediation, on the other hand, has been a more positive development for aggrieved parties. Mediation is not mandatory. Both sides must agree to mediation, and the procedure has helped some plaintiffs achieve decent settlements without the great cost of litigation. My law firm has frequently benefited from it. Mediators are generally much fairer than arbitrators. Some of the best mediators in central Alabama include Phil Adams of Auburn and Jim Rives, Randy James, and former circuit judge Randy Thomas, all of Montgomery.

For litigation-oriented attorneys, such as our firm, the courts, especially on the federal side, have become very clogged. In the Middle District of Alabama, headquartered in Montgomery, my hat of admiration is off for Judges Keith Watkins, Myron Thompson, and Harold Albritton, especially after Judge Mark Fuller was removed from his cases in August 2014. Worse, Judge Fuller tied up the process for appointment of two badly needed judges, causing a major logjam in our federal court.

Apparently, U.S. Rep. Terri Sewell, a Democrat, and U.S. Senators Richard Shelby and Jeff Sessions, Republicans, are deadlocked over the choice of a new judge from Alabama for the 11th Circuit and the two vacant seats in the Middle District of Alabama. President Obama defers to the recommendations of all three. Terri won't budge, neither will the senators. President Obama has the power to nominate, and I wish he would go ahead, but the Senate must approve. Hopefully, something soon will be worked out.

Thus, we are left with only one full-time, non-senior federal judge for the Middle District of Alabama, namely Keith Watkins. Although pleasant and reasoned in his opinions, he is very conservative on employment discrimination cases, especially those involving race. Myron Thompson works full-time as a federal judge, but is my age, 69, and thus several years past entitlement to become senior judge with half a case load. The overcrowded court schedule has forced full-time service on him. Judge Harold Albritton, 79, does carry a half load but is conservative on civil rights cases. Judge Thompson is the federal judge good for plaintiffs wrongfully losing their job. Without him, it's an uphill struggle.

I am very pleased with most of the six judges we have in the Montgomery County Circuit Court, namely Johnny Hardwick, Truman Hobbs Jr., Gene Reese, Greg Griffin, J. R. Gaines, and Bill Shashy. Being subject to reelection in an overwhelmingly Democratic county makes these judges more accountable to the people. I am also pleased that seasoned attorney James Anderson, who is reasonable, friendly, and bright, was the favorite at this writing to succeed Shashy in the March 2016 Democratic primary.

The majority Democratic electorate in Montgomery County has led the election of more African American judges (Hardwick, Griffin, and Gaines, as well as their predecessor, Charles Price, now retired). Moreover, at the domestic relations level, Calvin Williams and Anita Kelly are black and Bob Bailey is white. Likewise, at the Montgomery County District Court level, Troy Massey and Pamela Higgins are black while Jimmy Poole is white. These are all outstanding jurists.

Thus, the "almighty vote," and the increasing number of African American voters in the urban centers of Montgomery and Jefferson counties has made it possible to elect African American judges in those circuits. As a result, the judiciary—even the white judges—has become more sympathetic to legitimate civil rights issues. Of course, some are more sympathetic than others.

In the private practice of law in Montgomery, several other excellent attorneys have impacted positively for civil rights. I refer especially to Bobby Segall (educational issues); Jere Beasley (products liability issues), and Joe Espy (defending against unjust prosecution). I love to quote Jere Beasley that "Everyone is looking for the million dollar case. Guess what? It's already in your office. It is just a matter of working it up properly." That statement certainly refers to civil rights cases as much as any others. Indeed, the civil rights of victims have been greatly enhanced by financial recoveries from wrongdoers in jury trials but greatly damaged by heinous arbitration.

Speaking of Beasley, I admire and respect the giant plaintiff's law firm that Jere and his partners have put together here in Montgomery at Beasley Allen. Perhaps Jere's greatest talent in law is that he is an organizational genius. He is also very savvy in talking to juries, and he knows how to work politics in his favor. Jere's younger partners, Tom Methvin and Cole Portis, have both been state bar presidents. Another partner, Gibson Vance, who got his start working for me, is a past president of the American Association of Justice (the national trial lawyers' organization). Greg Allen is a whiz at product liability cases, and partners Michael Crow and Dee Miles are also talented, as are partners Graham Esdale, Ben Baker, LaBarron Boone, and Frank Woodson. Frank Wilson and Kenneth Mendelson are two sharp former Beasley Allen partners who now have their own firms.

I still insist that the best lawyer in Alabama, pound for pound, is Bobby Segall, one month younger than me. Bobby's hairstyle looks like Albert Einstein's and his brain is also in that arena. He's represented me and my firm successfully on several occasions. Further, I've teamed up with Bobby on a number of great results. He is currently working with me in the Alexander City case, seeking compensation for the wrongful police shooting death of Emerson Crayton Jr. (See Chapter 4). Bobby is humble, has a wonderful sense of humor, and has always been generous for worthy community causes.

There are numerous other excellent lawyers in Montgomery. The defense bar has its share of colorful and effective lawyers. Foremost on the civil side are Tommy Gallion, Spud Seale, David Boyd, Bill Brittain, Winston Sheehan, Richard Broughton, Liz Carter, Kelly Pate, Alex Holtsford, Chuck Stewart, Ham Wilson, Henry Barnett, Bruce Downey, Mark Bain, Chip Nix, and Dorman Walker. I throw in Randall Morgan and Randy McNeill for being very scrappy. Leading criminal defense attorneys include the aforementioned Joe Espy, Susan James, Bill Blanchard, David Vickers, and Richard White. I've worked with all of these lawyers and know personally how skilled they are.

A number of very sound plaintiff's lawyers have worked in my office but since gone out on their own in private practice. That includes Jim Debardelaben, Frank Hawthorne Jr., and William Gill. My present partners, Kenneth Shinbaum, Aaron Luck, Jim Bodin, and Joe Guillot, are excellent and have sharpened their tools over years of practice. Kenneth reaches his 30th year with me in April 2016, Jim and Aaron have been with the firm for more than 20 years, and Joe is in his 18th year. Two younger associates, Chris Worshek, 30, and Chase Estes, 27, bring new energy from their generation, including superior electronic skills.

The Copelands are a talented family of Montgomery lawyers. Patriarch Albert was one of the lions of the bar when I returned to Montgomery in

1975. He was then practicing with the distinguished Truman Hobbs Sr., later a federal judge. Son Lee has followed in his father's footsteps in becoming president of the Alabama Bar Association. Lee's brother, Paul, and Paul's wife, Susan Copeland, are also astute attorneys.

Another good Montgomery father-son combination of lawyers is Doyle and Jacob Fuller. The younger Jacob is developing a tort remedy for mold cases. Doyle is the younger brother of the late Millard Fuller, Morris Dees's original law and business partner and later the founder of the worldwide housing ministry of Habitat for Humanity, often working over the last few decades with former President Jimmy Carter.

I mentioned James Anderson, twice a statewide candidate for public office who now has a very good chance of being elected to the circuit judge vacancy. His brother, Charles Anderson, has developed a fine law firm.

Corkie Hawthorne and Tom Edwards are fine lawyers and good friends of mine who practice together out of a Scott Street office. About ten years younger than me, both helped considerably when I ran for the U.S. Senate in 2002. Corkie comes from a family of lawyers. His father, Frank Hawthorne Sr., was a distinguished Balch and Bingham partner. Corkie's brother, Frank Jr., was my law partner 1983–1993. Corkie's sons, Raymond and Charlie, are also eager attorneys. The youngest, Charlie, worked for me in 2013–2014.

Experienced attorneys Larry Menefee and Marvin Campbell have a strong social conscience, obvious in their legal work. Likewise, the father-son team of Wayne (now retired) and Mark Sabel have handled groundbreaking civil rights cases, including one that brought greater rights to women on the Montgomery police force. Attorney Mark Wilkerson has developed special expertise in administrative law matters, and frequently sits as a hearing officer for the Alabama Board of Nursing.

Montgomery also has many excellent attorneys in the domestic relations field, including Ron Wise, Judy Barganier, John Henig, and Floyd Minor. Richard Shinbaum, my law partner's brother, has expert knowledge of the bankruptcy field, and others specialize in taxation and corporate housekeeping. Hank Hutchinson of Capell Howard and Joe Warren are especially talented in trusts and estates; I have used both on wills. Inge Hill Jr. and Shawn Cole are two other lawyers skilled in legal fields that I do not handle.

Bradley Arant attorneys Chuck Stewart, Stan Gregory, and Bill Mc-Gowin—my fourth cousin once removed—have a multitude of talents. Gregory is very astute in estate litigation. Stewart helped mediate an employment litigation settlement worth $400,000 for a client of mine in 2015. Phillip Butler, my age, is another seasoned attorney with that firm.

Landis Sexton is a general practitioner whose multiple legal skills I greatly appreciated and occasionally used when he was on the third floor of my office building in 2010–2012. Charlie Edmondson is great at handling real estate-related legal problems and property closings. Richard Dean is in a league by himself as a collection lawyer, although Mark Chambless is also very good. These are all areas I do not touch.

I MUST TIP MY hat to a strong contingent of younger lawyers who have positively impacted the greater Montgomery legal scene. Three were high-school age when I recruited them to Princeton in the late 1970s (Susan Price, deputy chancellor of Post-Secondary Education), the 1980s (Shannon Holliday, partner at Copeland, Franco, Screws, and Gill), and 1990s (Rick McBride Jr., partner at Rushton, Stakely, Johnston and Garrett).

Speaking of the Princeton connection, two fine local lawyers, Mark Davis of Ball, Ball, Duke and Matthews and William Haynes of Ruston Stakely Johnston and Garrett, have sent sons to Princeton in recent years: Will Davis is training to be a doctor, and William Haynes Jr. is only in his sophomore year at Old Nassau.

Many other young lawyers make a difference in Montgomery. Chuck James is influential and smart. His law partner, Joe Hubbard, is a former state representative and a Democratic nominee for attorney general. Joe's father, Lister Hubbard, about eight years younger than me, has long been a distinguished member of the Capell Howard law firm. Lister's grandfather was U.S. Senator Lister Hill; Joe would love to follow in his footsteps someday.

The Teague brothers, Matt and Clay, are also impacting the Montgomery legal scene, as did their distinguished father, Barry Teague, a former state senator and U.S. Attorney. Matt is one of Jere Beasley's talented young lawyers. Clay, a solo practitioner, is married to one of my daughter Grace's good friends growing up, the former Jamie Tatum. Clay is fortunate to have his mother Diane Teague's sparkle.

Two younger female lawyers making a difference for their law firms are Barbara Wells of Capell Howard and Emily Marks of Ball Ball. I have worked with both and know how talented they are.

Austin Huffaker of Rushton Stakely is an exceptionally sharp attorney. A former neighbor, Austin is widely admired in Montgomery for displaying incredible grace and endurance in surviving the premature deaths of his father, brother, and wife in close proximity.

Joe Reed Jr., James Wilson IV, and Terry Davis are seasoned and talented lawyers who are well-connected with the African American community. Joe

Jr. is the son of legendary ADC leader Joe Reed Sr., and Terry is Joe Sr.'s nephew. James is the nephew of the late Solomon Seay Jr., the great civil rights lawyer.

Other talented local lawyers include Jimmy McLemore of the Capell Howard firm, Joe McCorkle of Balch and Bingham, Montgomery city attorney Mickey McInnish, and Micky McDermott, who used to be a city policeman and is now an all-purpose lawyer. You might call them and me the "McBrigade" of Montgomery attorneys. All the other Macs are also active in projects outside their law practices that benefit the greater Montgomery community.

One young lawyer with a good future is one I affectionately refer to as "the Poet Virgil"—Virgil Ford. He made a lot of friends in the county courthouse working under Judge Tracey McCooey. He is competent, confident, and has a good sense of humor. Ditto young attorney Tim Gallagher.

It's also interesting that there are four Faulk attorneys practicing in Montgomery: Win and Peyton in Montgomery, Robert in Prattville, and Joe in Troy. I have practiced with all these competent lawyers. Interestingly, to my knowledge, they are not related to one another.

Of course, there are a large number of attorneys working for state, county, and federal governments as assistant attorneys general, assistant district attorneys, and as assistant U.S. attorneys. Many are brilliant and dedicated public servants. I won't attempt to list their names, but I've had a special friendship with two: Rosa Hamlett Davis, who retired in 2015 after more than forty years but then went to work for the Alabama Judicial Inquiry Commission; and John J. Davis, who worked for me as a law clerk in the early to mid-1980s and afterward made a solid career as an Alabama assistant attorney general. John and Rosa both have great senses of humor, which has surely contributed to their longevity.

There are two Alabama assistant attorneys general, Stephanie Billingslea and Ternisha Miles, both mentioned in subsequent chapters, with whose professional skills I have been quite impressed.

Also worthy of mention in the Montgomery legal scene are municipal court judges Les Hayes and Milton Westry, and city prosecutors Ed Parish and Buster Russell. Ed's motto is "to turn negatives into positives," as he often acts as peacemaker resolving disputes between city residents.

The above list is far from exhaustive, as there are many other fine lawyers whose names I did not call. A flood of young attorneys is coming into the bar without experience or seasoning. It is incumbent upon the more senior attorneys to make the effort to help mentor these young men and women.

GREAT RESPECT GOES TO Montgomery's senior-most attorney, George Azar, who at age 84 was still slugging it out but has finally retired. The "force of nature" known as Jere Beasley turned 80 in December 2015.

Another senior attorney I admire immensely is 74-year-old U.S. Attorney George Beck. I came to know George when he was the top deputy attorney general under Bill Baxley from 1975 to 1977. We were co-counsel on several big cases. George is related to Clifford Judkins Durr, through the Judkins branch.

Other senior lawyers, now retired, whom I greatly appreciate include brothers John Scott, 85, and Jim Scott, 79, formerly of Capell Howard, and Leon Capuano, 83. The distinguished Scott brothers are directly descended from John Scott, an original founder of Montgomery, as well as from U.S. President John Tyler. (The Scotts' father, incidentally, was the Montgomery municipal judge who convicted Rosa Parks in 1955 of violating the city's bus seating segregation law, precipitating the Montgomery Bus Boycott.) Capuano, a man of great conscience, supported me in both my statewide political races, in 1978 and 2002.

Other lawyers in their mid-70s include the semi-retired Billy Hill, whose sense of humor has lightened many a moment; Samuel Masdon, a retired Winston County district judge taking criminal defense appointments; and Barry Leavell and Richard Gill, who are still working hard.

Since I am "only" 69 and still in God-blessed good health, I can see remaining in the legal arena for a while, but 75 looks like a good outer limit on retirement age. That would be in 2021, and would hopefully allow enough time, and decent physical and mental health, to concentrate more fully on other interests, of which I have many. That includes traveling, writing, hiking, enjoying family, encouraging amateur wrestling, the healing ministry, and ministry in general, and doing my part to help make the world a better place to live in. I still might come in to the law office occasionally to handle a special case or two. Or I might be wise enough to learn how to fully retire.

I must confess that I miss certain senior lawyers who've moved on to greater life beyond the grave. Red Bell died at 87 in 2013, and projected energy and humor to the end. Others include Alvin Prestwood, Paul Lowery, Euel Screws, Robert Huffaker, Tommy Thagard, Rick Williams, Maury Smith, and Bobby Black. Bobby's mantle of effective but humorous advocacy has been picked up by his son, Robert Black, who left his father's Hill Hill Carter law firm to create a new firm, also doing insurance defense work. Charles Crook is another whose witty personality is missed; his spirit and flag have been picked up by his son, McDowell Crook, an attorney who has long worked with Tommy Gallion. Attorneys Tom DeBray and Mays Jemison are also missed.

A helpful development pushed by former presiding Circuit Judge Charles Price was the creation of the Public Defender's Office. Led by the determined Aylia McGhee, an African American female, the office employs 14 attorneys to defend indigent defendants in criminal cases before the six Montgomery County circuit judges and three district judges. These lawyers are trained to better represent poorer defendants, who previously had inexperienced and sometimes inadequate contract lawyers.

I salute with appreciation the Legal Services Corporation of Alabama. In Montgomery, their lawyers represent indigent parties in civil cases, including landlord-tenant disputes and other civil matters many private-practice attorneys avoid. I commend all these attorneys, and hope that state and/ or private sources will continue to provide the necessary financial support.

I'm not just a civil rights attorney but also very much a trial lawyer. Our professional organization changed its name several years ago from the Alabama Trial Lawyers Association to the more neutral Alabama Association of Justice (AAJ); the earlier name had developed negative connotations, especially with the business community. The AAJ has moved to a beautiful Victorian style mansion two doors immediately south of the McPhillips Shinbaum office. The energetic Ginger Avery, Cathy Givhan, Amy Herring, and Johnnie Smith run the day-to-day operations. Those four, plus the officers, are all that prevent the plaintiff's practice from being wiped out by the Republican so-called tort-reformers of the Alabama legislature.

The nine Republicans on the Alabama Supreme Court have developed a reputation for knocking down big judgments for plaintiffs or reversing them all together. Alabama citizens as a whole have no understanding of the negative consequences of this trend. Strong judgments for deserving plaintiffs serve the dual purpose of compensating injured parties for their suffering and losses *and* giving a warning to other potential offenders.

My worst experience involved the reversal of a multi-million-dollar verdict in a wrongful death case on behalf of LAMP Magnet High School senior Brittany Timmons's estate. In a 5–4 vote in 2006, the Supreme Court, on its own initiative on an issue not raised by either side, overturned a just verdict. Buddy Brown of Cunningham Bounds of Mobile was the lead attorney, but our firm assisted.

Current Supreme Court Chief Justice Roy Moore, who was not on the Court when the Timmons verdict was overturned, has sparked both sides of moral issues such as the Ten Commandments and same-sex marriage. What caused him to be removed earlier from office was not his initial stand on the Ten Commandments, which had broad support, including mine, but his failure to remove the tablets when ordered to do so by the federal court. Under the doctrine of federalism and the U.S. Constitution, Moore should have removed the monument and put it somewhere else.

Roy Moore actually attracts his share of liberal political support in Alabama, because he is the most pro-plaintiff of the nine Supreme Court justices and seems to have a heart in court cases for the common man, or little guy. That is why Moore historically has retained strong support both from the African American community and the Alabama trial lawyers.

Moore has also been a strong advocate towards urging the governor and Alabama legislature to restore funding to the Alabama court system. The legislature's "no tax, no brains" stinginess has badly hurt the state court system, and that negatively impacts justice in Alabama. The ones most hurt by injustice in Alabama are the poor, which disproportionately includes African Americans and Hispanics.

As a conscientious civil rights attorney trying to obtain, or maintain, a judgment for his client, I must also be political savvy. To be a successful plaintiff's attorney, one must be a good architect, painter, electrician, plumber, and carpenter all at one time, or the jury will not "buy the house" you are building in its courtroom. To be a successful defense attorney, one must simply be a good demolition man. If the defense lawyer can make any room look unattractive, the jury will not buy the house.

These are pressures and tensions aplenty for trial lawyers and civil rights attorneys. They are part of the professional life. Even deciding which cases to take in the first place requires great care and discretion. I remember Morris Dees years ago saying that "the success of a law practice often depends more on the cases an attorney turns down than on the ones he takes." And while Dees's Southern Poverty Law Center has famously pursued many groundbreaking cases, it is also known for turning down many important cases.

The requirements of law practice also include keeping up with elaborate federal scheduling orders and their many deadlines, as well as preparing for and taking depositions. Likewise, preparing and filing motions for summary judgment and/or responding to such motions can be pressure-oriented, and "discovery disputes" (the information exchange process between opposing counsel) can be time-consuming and protracted.

Speaking of federal practice, two 11th Circuit legal giants, Ed Carnes and Joel Dubina, must be recognized. Their territory includes not only all of

Alabama, but Georgia and Florida as well. It is Montgomery's honor to have two such high-level judges one step below the U.S. Supreme Court. Dubina, by the way, is the father of able young U.S. Congresswoman Martha Roby.

In recent years, I have represented many attorneys and other professionals experiencing disciplinary problems. That includes two judges out of Birmingham and one from Selma. I consider it a high honor to be a "lawyer's lawyer." It is an even higher honor to be a "judge's lawyer."

I was raised by my parents to view every profession and any job as a ministry. This makes me want to help, one way or another, virtually everyone who comes to see us. That is sometimes a problem. If the ingredients for winning are not there, then it is not worth the cost of money or time for either the client or the firm to take on the case.

It matters not to me what a person's political party, philosophical outlook, religious view, or sexual orientation is when it comes to representing someone unjustly treated. We are all God's children, and all of us deserve decent and competent representation.

4

BATTLING POLICE BRUTALITY

I respect good law enforcement as much as anyone. Indeed, without ready and well-trained policeman, the peaceful pursuit of democracy would turn to chaos and anarchy. Without justice and competent officers to enforce it, the noble principles of freedom, democracy, and liberty quickly melt away.

Over the years, I've also represented many police officers in trouble, mostly out of sorts with their bosses. As an assistant attorney general in 1975–77, I prosecuted white collar crime and helped start Montgomery's Crime Prevention Program. So how did I end up taking on so many cases of police brutality? In part, it goes back to the mid-1980s clashes I had with former Montgomery Mayor Emory Folmar's administration, mostly over police issues. One case involved a challenge to the promotional practices of the police department in 1986. Another case involved my representing police officer Steve Eiland who wrote an unflattering poem about Emory, posting it inside the elevator doors of the MPD.

I also represented police officers as defendants in back-to-back federal trials as recently as 2005–2006. In 2007 I successfully defended a Lowndes County police officer charged with vehicular homicide. We obtained an acquittal before a Lowndes County jury.

The early and strong support I received in 1978 from black political groups while running for Alabama attorney general, and again in 2002, while running for the U.S. Senate, greatly sensitized me to the issue of police misconduct. This included not only brutality and racial profiling by police but also the risks of "driving while black" or even "riding while black." My hero, Fred Shuttlesworth, himself a champion against police brutality, also motivated me.

So it was natural that people with complaints about local police started gravitating towards me and my law office in the 1980s and 1990s. One was Michael Timmons, in his late 20s, sent to me by Virginia Durr and by his sister, Rosa Timmons. Michael was rough-cut and mumbled his words; he was beaten badly when Montgomery police stopped him one night and he lacked identification papers. I filed a suit challenging Montgomery's vagrancy law as overly broad and vague in violation of the 14th Amendment's due process clause. I also threw in a 4th Amendment claim of unreasonable seizure. How fortunate we were to draw federal jurist Myron Thompson, who ruled in our favor on both grounds. Thus Montgomery's version of South Africa's paddy wagon pick-up law was struck down.

Most of my police brutality cases originated with wrongful acts by a younger, Rambo-esque set of bullies in uniform. Standing up strongly to such rogues is an instinct developed from my father's Christian gospel teachings but encouraged by my success as an amateur wrestler.

Undoubtedly, police brutality cases are not a good way to make a living as a lawyer. The better living comes more from personal injury, employment litigation, and criminal defense. Yet, in terms of an impact on society, or on the public generally, I know we've made a positive difference. I've been told so by several police officers. Hopefully police locally think twice before they beat someone up, or shoot to kill. If so, we've saved some lives or prevented more serious injuries. That's meaning and purpose aplenty in life for any lawyer.

Although I've never been arrested, I have been stopped for traffic violations, primarily speeding, over the years. I always try to be gracious and thank the officer. This diffuses tension. In early 1991, running late to church while traveling down Vaughn Road, I was stopped for going too fast. After giving the officer my driver's license, and then hearing some chuckling going on in the police car behind me, I thought "Oh boy, I'm in for it now."

The officer then came up to me with my driver's license in hand and said, "Are you really Julian McPhillips?" I answered, "Yes." The officer then replied, "You don't know how much your name is cussed and discussed at the police department. The top brass, they hate you, but the rest of us, we love you." And I received only a warning about the speeding.

The list of people I've represented against police brutality over the years could easily exceed 100. I had many actual or prospective cases before Emory Folmar went out of office in 1999 and was succeeded by Bobby Bright. Dissatisfied with progress against racial profiling and police brutality in the Bright administration, local and state civil rights leaders, including the Revs. John Alford and Richard Boone, and State Senator Charles Steele, staged a sit-in at the mayor's office, demanding a civilian police review board. Mayor Bright resisted. All three SCLC officials were arrested when they laid down on his floor, and they were carried out of Bright's office by local police. I visited all three in jail and prayed with them. They were released.

Unfortunately, I have continued to receive numerous brutality complaints, not only involving local Montgomery police, but also from surrounding localities, especially the Elmore County Sheriff's office.

Most of my police brutality cases involve unjustified excessive force that wounds both bodies and souls of human beings. These strong-arm tactics are also counterproductive to law enforcement, creating enormous resentment and hostility, especially in the African American community.

The cases of Kamesha Williams, Miguel Johnson, Dashad Berry, Devonna Chapman, and Chiquita Brooks are worth peeking at to understand the culture of how these cases so easily occur.

Kamesha Williams, Miguel Johnson, and Dashad Berry, all brutalized and injured in 2009, were originally three separate cases. They were consolidated into one lawsuit in the Circuit Court of Montgomery County based on my argument that they reflected a pattern and practice of misconduct within the Montgomery Police Department. The common denominator was that all three involved disabled African Americans who were unjustifiably subjected to excessive force by police. Fortunately, we drew Circuit judge Johnny Hardwick on these cases. In his trial lawyer years, Hardwick had handled a few police brutality cases himself.

Dashad Berry is a T-4 paraplegic, paralyzed from the chest down. On March 18, 2009, two friends literally picked Dashad up at his house to go purchase cigarettes—they took him out of his wheelchair and placed him in the backseat of their car. On the way, they were stopped by the police at a driver's license checkpoint. The officers demanded that all three get out of the car. When Dashad objected that he was paraplegic, the police responded mockingly, "What's paraplegia?" The officers threatened to use a Taser on him if he didn't get out of the car. Dashad asked if he could telephone his mother to bring his wheelchair, but he was told, "No, we don't want any mama drama here." The officers pulled Dashad out of the car and later dropped him on the ground, hurting his back. Dashad's mother subsequently did come and took him to an emergency room for medical treatment.

Kamesha Williams was 38 as of July 30, 2009, when she was badly roughed up by the Montgomery police. She suffered from avascular necrosis, modecular necrosis, arthritis, and had had two hip replacement surgeries. She also had serious psychological issues. Due to her disabilities, Kamesha was unable to "hit the ground" immediately when ordered by an MPD officer to do so. Instead, she squatted down. According to multiple eyewitnesses, an officer reacted by kicking Kamesha in the back and stomping on her, leaving his boot-print clearly on her T-shirt.

The bullying officer ignored Kamesha's pleas and those of two daughters that she was disabled. They forced her to lie on the ground, over an ant pile, for thirty minutes. She suffered numerous bites and subsequently required much medical treatment.

Miguel Johnson was also 38 when he was bullied by the MPD on September 30, 2009. Weighing 360 pounds, Miguel had screws in his knee and his hip from previous surgeries. He also suffered from spinal stenosis, causing great back pain. He had recently received treatment for a shoulder injury just before his bad day with the MPD occurred.

On that day, an MPD officer, with a history of theft of drug money, stopped while Miguel was lying on side of the street, next to a curb, trying to jack up his vehicle to change a flat tire.

The officer demanded to see Miguel's driver's license, and Miguel, still lying on the ground, handed up his wallet. Also in the wallet were eight $100 bills. When the police officer flipped Miguel his wallet back, it contained only one $100 bill. This caused Miguel to scream at the officer for "stealing my money." As the officer's cover-up ensued, other officers were dispatched and subjected Miguel to much profanity and roughhouse treatment. Included was a football-style tackle of Miguel into the police car. Afterwards Miguel was treated for back, leg, neck, and shoulder pain. See *Ex parte City of Montgomery*, 99 So.2d 282, 288–89, 290–291 (2012).

The three consolidated cases came before the Alabama Supreme Court on a petition for Writ of Mandamus filed by the City of Montgomery in 2011, after Judge Hardwick had denied summary judgment. The City of Montgomery was relying upon its discretionary immunity defense, to which we asserted a "bad faith exception." In a substantial victory for the plaintiffs, the Alabama Supreme Court, in a long opinion by Judge Michael Bolin, denied the City's petition in Williams's and Johnson's cases, but surprisingly granted mandamus in Berry's case.

Accordingly, the Williams and Johnson cases returned to the Circuit Court of Montgomery for February 2013 trial dates. Judge Hardwick astutely turned the trial into a mediation. With help from Judge Hardwick, a successful settlement was worked out for both Kamesha Williams and Miguel Johnson. Unfortunately, it took almost four years to get there (2009–2013). By holding the bullying police's feet to the fire, however, and through dogged persistence, we established the principle that "law enforcement must also obey the law." Hopefully, a message was sent to the MPD, and to other police and sheriffs, to treat local citizens, including disabled African Americans, with respect and dignity.

Other successful outcomes on police brutality cases were obtained in 2012 for Devonna Chapman and her daughter Quinnettria Chapman, both of whom were roughed up and thrown down by the MPD, causing significant injuries to both.

Sometimes these brutality cases come at the most inconvenient times. A Thanksgiving vacation had long been set with my wife Leslie's "Burton family" for Chicago in 2012. That is also where our daughter Grace and her husband Corbett live. Unfortunately, I had to fly back early Sunday morning to Birmingham, to drive down to Montgomery to prepare witnesses for a Monday morning trial before Judge Truman Hobbs Jr. This involved my client, Chaquita Brooks, another disabled African American roughed up by the Montgomery police.

The trial started Monday morning with picking the jury. We were fortunate to have a venire of about 60 percent blacks for a case that was innately racial. Brooks had her head repeatedly slammed against the window of her car by a heavy-set white officer. Her children were witnesses, and four testified at trial. For the jury we had nine blacks and three whites. We were faked at jury selection into keeping an older white woman who said her nephew was badly beaten by the police. All nine of the blacks and one other white lady on the jury were strongly for us. However, the older white lady dug in against us, and persuaded one young white man to side with her, in a 10–2 jury vote, in our favor.

In my opinion, Judge Hobbs declared a "hung jury" mistrial much too early, after only three hours of deliberation. If the jury had been allowed to deliberate longer, as in most criminal cases, I believe the two against us would have folded. Overall, I felt Judge Hobbs was fair, and the City's defense attorney, Jason Paulk, was a gentleman and very professional.

Two to three months later, and with a second trial date approaching, the City made an offer which my client, Ms. Brooks, found satisfactory. The case was settled on confidential terms.

The City of Montgomery is not the only repository of abusive, bullisome cops. In fact, under former police chief Kevin Murphy and public safety director Chris Murphy (they are not related) an effort was made to reign in roughhouse tactics and become more user-friendly with African Americans. I appreciated that, even though as of mid-2014 I still had two cases pending for trial, those of Myreico Broaden, deliberately run over by the MPD, and Ester Cannon, beaten up by police officers until they realized he was not the person they were looking for. No apologies.

I have also found the Elmore County sheriff's office to be especially rough with citizens, both before and after taken to jail. I couldn't believe my ears when I heard Sheriff Bill Franklin tell a Montgomery Lions Club audience in 2010 that he frequently warned young people that the penalty for drug abuse might well include being beaten up or raped in jail. It was as if he felt this was an expected part of justifiable punishment.

AND THEN THERE IS the Alexander City police force! There it has been open season for some time by white cops—despite the occasional presence of a black police chief—on black citizens, Especially infamous was the planned murder of Vincent Bias, encouraged by a white officer and caught on audiotape in 2013 but stopped at the last moment. That case has been settled, for only $30,000, but Bias was not killed. A more recent big case has involved a white police officer who shot and killed Emerson "Junior" Crayton Jr., a 21-year-old black man, outside the Alexander City Huddle House restaurant on March 8, 2014. At this writing, the Crayton case was ongoing, and the Bias case was a foundation to Crayton's claim against Alexander City of wrongful death and negligent failure to train its officers (see Appendix 2).

Crayton's wrongful death lawsuit was filed not just against the City of Alexander City and police officer Donald "Tommy" Maness, who did the actual shooting. Additional defendants were a group I call "the Huddle House Defendants." That included the owners of the Huddle House in whose parking lot the shooting occurred, namely Daniel Yates and Lynn Paterson, but also the business name of their restaurant, D&L Foods, Inc. It also included their manager Legina Watson and the Georgia franchisor corporation, known as Huddle House, Inc.

What precisely did they do wrong? Paterson is the one who, according to witnesses, falsely attributed to Emerson Crayton Jr. the words, "I'll blow your place up." A male cook, Danny Radford, did not hear Crayton say those words, but he heard Paterson say them. This caused Radford to follow Emerson outside into the parking lot and signal to Maness to come down from the immediately adjacent hill to constrain Crayton.

The Huddle House defendants correctly state that they never told Officer Maness to shoot and kill young Crayton. However, they were a "but for" link, without which the shooting would never have occurred. Our theory was that Huddle House, through Watson and Radford, had "wrongfully incited" the killing. We also argued that this wrongful behavior sprang out of a highly racial and hostile environment towards their black customers, in violation of federal law.

The main part of the wrongful death suit, which is in federal court because of our U.S. Constitutional 4th Amendment "wrongful seizure claim," was against Alex City and Officer Maness. Five eyewitnesses exist, all black—none of whom were consulted by the ABI in its investigation—who say Officer Maness didn't have to shoot. They say Maness had adequate space in the Huddle House parking lot to avoid being hit by Emerson's car, without shooting Emerson, as Emerson was about to exit towards Highway 280.

The central question of the case, and the central defense of Alex City and Maness, is that Maness shot Crayton in self-defense to keep Crayton from running over him. However, Crayton was unarmed, had committed no crime, was only in the process of backing up, and had yet to move his car forward. Multiple eyewitnesses also say Maness was sufficiently to the side of the front of the car that he wouldn't have been hit. In fact, instantaneously *after* Maness fired his initial shots, the car lunged straight forward and did not hit Maness. We say the shooting of Crayton was unnecessary and unjustified by law.

After the killing on March 8, 2014, it took us two months to get Kolea Burns qualified as administratrix of Crayton's estate. Kolea is the mother of two-year-old Germani, the only child of Emerson Jr., and thus, under Alabama law, his sole heir. In May 2014, we filed suit in Montgomery. Emerson's parents, Kolea, and the baby, and several other supporters were present at the news conference in which I and co-counsel Eric Hutchins called for justice.

About eight attorneys soon filed motions to dismiss for the multiple defendants. The case was assigned to Judge Mark Fuller, but by August 2014, before he would rule, Fuller had been arrested in Atlanta on charges of beating up on his wife. As a result, the federal court administration took away all of Fuller's cases, including ours.

Meanwhile, Eric, co-counsel Bobby Segall, Chase Estes, and I were working hard to prepare and file responsive pleadings on all the motions to dismiss. We were also securing witnesses and procuring tapes and well over a thousand pages of documents from Alex City. We were ably assisted in August 2014, by two young law students from Northern Ohio University, Renee Drollette and Shawna Maurice.

To our delight, we discovered that our case was reassigned to Judge Myron Thompson, who by then had gone on senior status. However, because the U.S. District Court for the Middle District of Alabama was two judges short, Thompson was unable to devote the necessary time to focus on the serious issues raised. Accordingly, the case rocked on through the fall and winter months of 2014–2015, with no ruling on the motions to dismiss. Without rulings, no formal discovery could begin.

I filed motions that got Birmingham U.S. Magistrate Judge Paul Greene—on loan to the Middle District to help with the case load—assigned to us. He heard our arguments in March and by late April 2015 had issued an opinion and order in our favor on most salient points. Discovery slowly began.

Finally, in mid-August 2015, we had four days of depositions in Alexander City at the old City Hall. Twelve depositions were taken. One skillful day-long deposition of Officer Maness was taken by Bobby Segall. Eric Hutchins took one more the next day, and I took the other ten over several days.

Interestingly, all four of the primary attorneys at the depositions were 68 years old and born within months of one another. I was the oldest, born November 13, 1946; Bobby Segall, December 5, 1946; Bill Brittain, counsel for the Huddle House defendants, and George Royer, counsel for Alexander City defendants, were born in 1947. What does that tell us about age, or trial lawyers particularly, and the legal profession in general?

In any case, the depositions were helpful. It was early September before Jeanna Boggs had the key depositions ready. Based on the same, I dictated a letter, with attorney Chase Estes typing, for Bobby's signature on Copeland Franco letterhead. The letter was addressed to Bill Brittain.

On October 2, 2015, the case was resolved with the Huddle House defendants for $100,000, with no confidentiality clause. A formal settlement agreement has been signed and the case is now dismissed against the Huddle House defendants. Suffice it to say that plaintiff Kolea Burns and Emerson Crayton Jr.'s parents were satisfied, especially since Huddle House's degree of culpability was less than that of Maness and Alexander City.

A pro-tanto release allows us to continue our suit against Alex City and Maness. That case is not, and will not be, easy, given Maness's defense that he shot Crayton to keep himself from being run over. We have hired experts on proper police procedures and accident reconstruction. Both experts cost substantial money, but the settlement with Huddle House helps cover those expenses. It's unfortunate but true that justice in a wrongful death case is measured in financial terms.

I have the highest respect for George Royer, counsel for Alexander City and Maness. He is very astute. I first knew George in 1975–1977 when we worked together as young assistant attorneys general under Bill Baxley in Montgomery.

At this writing, mediation was scheduled with the Alexander City defendants for February 5, 2016. The seasoned mediator from Opelika, attorney Phil Adams, will try to help us resolve the case. Notwithstanding the usual risks of litigation, we are aiming for a very substantial settlement.

5

BERNARD WHITEHURST JR.

No police misdeed has shaken Montgomery harder than the Montgomery Police Department's wrongful killing of Bernard Whitehurst Jr. in December 1975. The subsequent cover-up and related events toppled Montgomery Mayor Jim Robinson, Chief of Police Ed Wright, and Donnie Foster, the policeman who fatally shot Whitehurst.

In April 1977, the *Washington Post* devoted a full newspaper page to a lengthy story by Myra McPherson entitled, "Alabama's Watergate." The sordid story of the great police cover-up was and is spellbinding.

When I was running for attorney general in 1977–78, I kept hearing the phrase "Whitehurst affair" or "Whitehurst investigation." It was the apparent clue to whether Montgomery's district attorney Jimmy Evans might get into the race himself. The word was that he was too caught up in the Whitehurst investigation to even think about running for higher office. Additionally, the controversy was making Evans unpopular in the law enforcement community.

The "Whitehurst affair" was also having an effect on the 1978 governor's race in Alabama, since Attorney General Bill Baxley was running for governor. Many were saying that Baxley, as the state's top law enforcement official, was shirking his duty by not personally heading up the Whitehurst investigation.

I remembered that in 1976 young Montgomery attorney Donald Watkins pursued a case in federal court against the City of Montgomery and its police department. Unfortunately he ran into a disastrous gutting of his case by the difficult U.S. District Judge Robert Varner, who was widely viewed as racist in effect if not philosophy. Varner wrongfully concluded that Whitehurst's civil rights had died with him, therefore, any conspiracy to violate Whitehurst's civil rights had also ended with his death. So instructed, the jury returned a verdict in favor of former police chief Wright, former deputy chief Charles Swindall, and Foster, the trigger man. The 11th Circuit Court of Appeals later denied the Whitehurst family's appeal.

Fast forward three and a half decades from the December 1975 death and the October 1976 denial of justice to April 2012 when Whitehurst's oldest son, Stacy, called me. He said, "You are the only one who stands up to police brutality in Montgomery." My handwritten note of April 24, 2012, reflected that Stacy was calling about a situation that occurred 37 years ago, when he had just turned three. *His father was killed. He was shot in the back by a police officer,* said my note.

I immediately felt an electric current course through my body, because I knew who and what Stacy was talking about. Younger attorneys who grew up in Montgomery law practice in the 1980s, 1990s, and 2000s couldn't have known as much.

Three days later, on April 27, 2012, Stacy brought in his mother, Florence, and two sisters, Tracy and Sheila. They signed an attorney-client agreement for me to represent them in seeking belated justice for the murder of Bernard Whitehurst. The agreement read:

> Represent Bernard Whitehurst Jr., via his widow Florence Whitehurst, son Stacy Whitehurst and daughter Tracy Whitehurst to explore and pursue creative options for recovery, due to murder of Bernard Whitehurst and cover-up by the Montgomery police in 1975. Among the options to explore would be a (financial) return from the Montgomery City Council and/ or some other governmental entity (such as State of Alabama or federal government, although it is recognized that either will be difficult); another option is to explore obtaining whatever copyright or intellectual property protection (may exist) and then seek to find a writer and/or ultimately a moviemaker interested in pursuing the story. Attorney does not agree to file lawsuit because statute of limitations has run and other defenses exist; also the alleged murderer has recently died. (Would also like apology from Mayor of Montgomery on behalf of City.)

My attorney's fee would be a contingency of one-third of anything recovered. Later, in preliminary negotiations, I reduced my fee to zero in hope of being more persuasive to present Montgomery Mayor Todd Strange, who thought the City owed nothing due to the long-since running of the statute of limitations. Legally yes, I conceded, but morally no.

From that point onward, knowing it would be difficult to recover anything, yet possessing a strong-sense of meaning and purpose, I began a two-fold effort. The first was to see if it were possible to get this still-aggrieved family anything, especially financially, for their loss. The second was to find a book writer for their story.

Addressing the second issue first, it was actually fun to contact potential writers. I started with friend Randall Williams, the book editor extraordinaire. He gave me the names of seven prospects. I also called Dr. Jackie Trimble, chairwoman of the English Department of Alabama State University. She suggested one good possibility.

I personally contacted Kendal Weaver, the Associated Press's retired Alabama bureau chief, and Howell Raines, former executive editor of the *New York Times*. Both thought a book was a great idea, but they were caught up in other projects. Ditto for Frank Sikora, retired from the *Birmingham News* and author of several books on civil rights subjects. I had a long-running set of conversations with Dr. Tennant McWilliams, recently retired UAB historian. I spoke with freelance writer Tom Gordon, formerly of the *Birmingham News*; He considered the project a good idea but was too busy. I even reached Myra McPherson, the original writer of the lengthy 1977 *Washington Post* story. She was 78 in 2012 and was working on another project.

I also spoke with my Princeton friend, Mills Thornton, who graduated from Ole Nassau only two years ahead of me. A civil rights historian, Mills also declined.

I was even referred to Foster Dickson, a teacher at Booker T. Washington Magnet High School. He was interested but said "the real thing's he's struggling with is that so many of the key players have passed away." I finally had to put the book project on the back burner, given the negative responses I received. More recently, in 2015, I learned that Mr. Dickson had decided to work on the project after all.

Meanwhile, in May 2012, I went to see Mayor Strange and the Montgomery City Council. In my initial letter dated May 17, 2012, I wrote:

> Dear Todd,
>
> This is not a legal letter of my usual sort. There is not a threat, actual or implied, of litigation, so I don't think you need to turn this over to one of your attorneys.
>
> . . . [I represent the] widow and children of Bernard Whitehurst, deceased . . . shot and killed by the Montgomery police back on December 2, 1975, at the age of 32

I added that Whitehurst was not a fleeing felon. I also said Whitehurst did not meet the physical description, including the color of clothes, of a burglar the police were searching for in his neighborhood, at the time he was shot and killed. I enclosed the *Washington Post* full-page article and discussed how bad the cover-up made Montgomery look. I referred to how the MPD had planted a gun by the hand of Mr. Whitehurst, making it look like Whitehurst was shooting at them first and that the police simply shot back at him in self-defense. I also pointed out that the MPD was now using the Whitehurst case at the Police Academy to teach what police should not do. I conceded to the mayor that the statute of limitations had long since run on any civil claims or criminal prosecution. I also recognized that the one who pulled the trigger, Donnie Foster, was dead, as were Robinson and Wright and others implicated in the cover-up.

But I suggested that an apology from the City of Montgomery was due the Whitehursts, as well as some compensation. I further asked that the matter be put on the agenda of the next City Council meeting.

Along with Stacy Whitehurst, I met personally with Mayor Strange and City Councilman Tracy Larkin on May 26, 2012. Both were conciliatory and acknowledged the City's wrongdoing. While no commitments were made, Larkin shared his view that an amount in the neighborhood of $25,000 for each of the five Whitehurst family members— the widow and four now adult children—was reasonable. I gathered from a nod and wink by the mayor that he might be able to go along with that. Yet Mayor Strange was worried about "opening the floodgates," especially when there was no existing legal obligation on the part of the City.

On Tuesday, June 5, 2012 I escorted widow Florence Whitehurst, Stacy Whitehurst, and other family members to a City Council meeting. I told the council members that "the Whitehurst case is unprecedented, and undisputed, with an odor so strong there is no other case comparable." I distinguished it from the "famous Todd Road case" of 1983, where no lives were lost.

On June 7, 2012, I sent a carefully worded letter to Mayor Strange and all nine of the Montgomery City Councilman. I cited "the tears in her eyes, the anguished struggle to say something by Florence Whitehurst." I referred to "the deep pain wallowing up so intensely in Stacy Whitehurst." I asked again for an apology, downplayed the risk of opening any floodgates of City liability, and said *I appeal to you on a moral basis."* (Emphasis added).

I concluded by saying:

> As to the issue of financial compensation, I have previously recommended $25,000, or a total of $125,000, for the family. Some family members, after the meeting, expressed a feeling that $25,000 was not really adequate to compensate them for their pain and injury and loss. Of course, no amount of money really is, as the senior Mr. Whitehurst's life was worth far more than any amount of money to his family. However,

if the City does $25,000 each, or wanted to do more than $25,000 each, the family members would be grateful.

I added that:

> Whatever the City of Montgomery does financially, the Whitehurst family, for the sake of their privacy and dignity, would like it kept confidential. I trust this would better serve the City's interests also. I hope it can be done. I could work with you or your counsel on a statement with appropriate and sensitive language.

Meanwhile, my well-meaning friend and *Montgomery Advertiser* columnist Vanzetta McPherson picked up on the local news coverage and wrote a June 7, 2012, column, stating that the family should not get any compensation. The *Advertiser* allowed me to submit a reply column on June 11, 2012 (see Appendix 6).

My battle, unfortunately, wasn't with the City of Montgomery and its mayor alone. A fourth Whitehurst sibling emerged, namely Bernard Whitehurst III. He claimed to be the only biological son of Bernard Whitehurst Jr., saying the other three children were adopted. Somehow, someway, someone had filled his head with the notion that the case was worth millions and the family members were being shortchanged. Bernard III eventually convinced his mother of the same. Young Bernard used some harsh words towards me.

I was off the case, then back on, then off again.

Meanwhile Mayor Strange, trying to protect the City's pocketbook, not only from the Whitehursts' claims but potentially from others, got Alabama Attorney General Luther Strange to issue an opinion that the Whitehursts couldn't be legally compensated financially. I could have challenged that legally, but when widow Florence sided with her son Bernard III, I withdrew at the end of June 2012.

Before withdrawing, however, on June 17, 2012, I succeeded in getting the Montgomery City Council to issue an apology on behalf of the City. After nearly forty years of silence, Montgomery city leaders finally issued a public apology to the Whitehurst family members. Hooray.

"I was very emotional and more than a little shaken," said oldest son Stacy Whitehurst.

"We've taken a gigantic step, and it was all unanimous," said Mayor Strange. He also announced the City had created a historic marker for

Whitehurst. That fall a large historic marker was erected in the park across from City Hall. It stated on the front side:

Bernard Whitehurst and the Whitehurst Case

On December 2, 1975, Bernard Whitehurst was shot to death by a police officer in Montgomery, Alabama. He died behind a house on Holcombe Street, running from police officers who mistakenly believed he was the suspect in a robbery of a neighborhood grocery store.

The facts were slow to emerge in this shooting of a black man by a white police officer. But investigations urged by the Whitehurst family, the city's daily newspaper, and the local district attorney revealed the following of that tragic event: that Whitehurst, 32, did not match the robbery suspect's description; that he was unarmed, despite police claims that they returned fire after being fired upon; that the gun found by his body had been confiscated by police in a drug investigation a year earlier, and was placed at the scene as part of a police cover-up.

The shooting that cost Bernard Whitehurst his life ultimately led to the resignation of the city's mayor and public safety director, the resignation or termination of eight police officers, and the perjury indictment of three police officers. These events, known collectively as the Whitehurst Case, are considered pivotal in the history of the City of Montgomery.

On the back side, the marker read:

Montgomery: Learning from the Past

The Whitehurst Case has proven transformative in Montgomery and is part of the body of events and individuals that have shaped both the struggle for civil rights and the relationship between the Montgomery community and the Montgomery Police Department.

Decades after Bernard Whitehurst was shot and killed by a Montgomery police officer, the Montgomery Police Department employs a case study of this fatal shooting and subsequent events to help officers learn about policing in a capital city that is both the "Cradle of the Confederacy" and the "Birthplace of Civil Rights."

The Whitehurst Case forms a significant part of the police curriculum, *"Policing in a Historic City: Civil Rights and Wrongs in Montgomery."* This case, which embodies both private grief and public tragedy, continues to teach powerful lessons to police officers seeking to understand the line between right and wrong.

I was not present at the ceremony installing the marker, because no one ever told me the ceremony was taking place. I was gratified anyway; I hadn't taken on the case for personal recognition.

Months later, at Stacy Whitehurst's request, I contacted State Senator Dick Brewbaker to see if the Alabama legislature could do anything. Dick was sympathetic and interested but he said that with all the state's financial problems and obligations, it couldn't afford to help. Again, no luck.

There's an old saying in legal negotiations that "pigs get fat, and hogs get slaughtered." $25,000 is not pocket change. $125,000 is not peanuts either. I don't want to call it a bad name, but the $125,000, split equally five ways, could have helped each of the surviving Whitehursts in a significant way. Yet, as of late 2015, they haven't received a penny.

On January 7, 2015, the *Montgomery Advertiser* announced that Bernard Whitehurst III was seeking to have a portion of Holcombe Street, where the killing took place, named after his father. As of this writing, that had not happened.

Nonetheless, on December 2, 2015, some 20 people, including myself and paralegal Carlton Avery, gathered for the dedication of another historic marker installed at the spot where Bernard Whitehurst Jr. was shot and killed. The Whitehurst family members were present, as were Public Safety Commissioner Chris Murphy, Mayor Todd Strange, author Foster Dickson, the press, and some friends. The mayor spoke a few words, as did Bernard III. The mayor insisted that I say something, and I did.

The next day, the two brothers, Stacy and Bernard Whitehurst III (who is now quite friendly towards me), came to my office to discuss the issue of financial restitution and how to achieve it. We're exploring some ideas.

Meanwhile author Dickson is working on a book about the Whitehurst case and changes in Montgomery since the 1970s, for which the Whitehurst case has been a catalyst.

As the French say, *on vera* —we'll see.

6

Nick Autrey and the Case from Hell

Nick Autrey is quite a character. About six years younger than me, he is plenty smart, has good integrity, and works hard—a good combination. But he could be better organized, and that weakness gets him trouble sometimes. A first cousin of former Lieutenant Governor George McMillan Jr., the politically savvy Autrey remained a good Democrat, even after white Alabamians left the party in droves in the 1980s and 1990s.

After energetically helping me in my 2002 U.S. Senate campaign, Nick came to me a year later for legal help. He and his business, First National On-Line Processing (FNOP), which installed and distributed automatic teller machines (ATMs), had gotten into disputes with too many people on too many fronts. In November, 2003, at a tailgate party in Auburn before the annual football game with Alabama, I showed Nick a lawsuit I had drafted for him.

The suit was filed in December 2003 in the Macon County Circuit Court. The defendants were Coastal ATM, Inc., and numerous other individuals and corporate entities. By the time it got to trial, it had narrowed to a suit against Tennessee Bank for Commerce in Nashville.

Nick contended that various corporate entities and individuals had stolen and/or misappropriated his ATMs. Nick also insisted that the Tennessee Bank for Commerce breached its contract with FNOP, tortuously interfered with his contracts with third parties, and failed to return ATMs belonging to him.

It took seven years, until August 2010, before we finally got our jury trial in Macon County. I handled the case, including some depositions, until April 2006, when I withdrew for health reasons. My next-door office neighbor, Frank Wilson, a fine attorney, then took over the litigation for the next two years. However, Frank became bogged down in 2008–2009, and Nick begged me to take over again. Nick is one of the most persuasive individuals I ever met. It is hard to say no to him. That is why he is such a good salesman. So in early 2010 I stepped back in.

What made it so hellacious is that there were many lists of ATMs floating around, each with many 10–15 digit numbers. It was enough to make me dizzy. How could one remember one list, much less three, five, or ten lists when compared to another list? It was very complicated litigation.

Further, Tennessee Bank for Commerce didn't believe it had done anything wrong, but Nick felt TBC was egregiously in the wrong and wanted at least a million dollars. The bank thought it had adequate justification when it reneged on loans earlier promised to Nick and FNOP. Nick claimed the Bank's actions had set in motion a chain reaction of numerous other problems he later had.

So the trial came down to eight hot, steamy days in August 2010, five days one week, three the next. TBC's attorneys protracted the litigation by objecting to virtually every question I asked our witnesses. Macon County Circuit Judge Tom Young did his best to keep the trial orderly. Yet he, too, was tested by all the objections and motions coming from TBC's attorneys.

Although we tried to be cordial and professional with TBC's attorneys, tension was so high by the end of the seventh day that I did something very atypical for me. After the judge and jury had left the courtroom, I said something less than flattering to my opposing counsel, coupled with a touch of profanity.

The next day, with the judge telling us that the trial would not go into a third week and he'd declare a mistrial if necessary, we ended up settling with TBC for $100,000. By this time, and given all the difficulties, Nick was grateful to get that much.

7

FALSELY ACCUSED BUT VINDICATED
SEVEN YEARS LATER

In late December 2007, David Clayton walked into my office and complained that false criminal charges for sexual abuse of a child had been filed against him in Pickens County, a rural, backwoods part of Alabama, northwest of Tuscaloosa.

David, a tall, handsome, but otherwise average-looking 48-year-old man, claimed he was the victim of retaliation by descendants of a pioneer Pickens County family who were upset that David had inherited 160 acres of land from the late Larry Craft, with whom David had had a relationship. David's sexual orientation made him seem, to some, prone to commit the type of crime with which he was later charged, namely sexual misconduct.

David was unwavering in his vehement protestations of innocence, so much so that even my usually skeptical paralegal Lynelle Howard became genuinely convinced that David had not done what he was accused of, putting his hands on a seven-year-old boy.

David insisted that a conspiracy existed between surviving members of the Craft family and a relative, the mother of the young boy making the false charges. A combination of jealousy over David inheriting family land from Larry Craft, ill-feeling toward their sexual orientation, and the backwoods culture made David's position very believable to me.

I hired an investigator from Tuscaloosa who persuaded me what David already knew—that he would never receive a fair trial in Pickens County. Therefore, in 2008 I filed a motion, with supporting affidavits, for change of venue. After granting the motion, the local circuit judge recused himself. So also did local district attorney Chris McCool.

The case rocked on and was finally set for trial in August 2010 before a specially appointed Judge Joseph A. Colquitt, a retired University of Alabama law professor known for being tough on criminal defendants. With the temperature outside the courthouse over 100 degrees, the trial took three days from August 2–4, with me grilling witnesses, including the mother of the boy, on cross-examination. On the third day, however, the trial was suspended because Judge Colquitt had a heat stroke and could not continue.

Therefore, discussions between Lynn Head, the very able Tuscaloosa assistant district attorney, and me continued for several weeks about what to do. Finally, it was agreed that a new supernumerary judge, John Karhh, would take over the case. Meanwhile, problems with jurors' schedules and other procedural issues led to a mistrial being declared in the still pending first trial.

Another year and a half passed. After a few telephone conferences with the attorneys, Judge Karrh also recused himself in late 2011. Finally, a fourth judge, retired supernumerary Clatus Junkins, still practicing law in his 70s, was appointed.

And then in January 2012 I received a letter from Lynn Head informing me that "The (alleged) child victim in this case has since reported that the allegations made by him previous to the indictment are false." She very professionally offered to dismiss all six charges against David, in return for a release. Advised that a civil judgment against the little boy or his mother would not be collectible, David reluctantly signed a release.

Months passed, with no order from the Court dismissing the case. In an April 2012 phone call, Judge Junkins balked at granting a dismissal. David was convinced that Junkins has personal ties with the original conspirators against him. In June 2012, I filed a "Motion to Dismiss Based on Contractual Agreement with the District Attorney's Office for Said Dismissal, or, In the Alternative, a Motion (for Judge Junkins) to Recuse Himself." Junkins denied my motion. I got gently "chewed" for suggesting the judge might be biased, but that was a small price to pay for standing up for my client.

More months passed. A couple of trial settings were continued, one due to surgery needed by Lynn Head. Finally, she convinced Judge Junkins to set a status conference in lieu of a trial, which he did, well in advance of a trial, on January 3, 2014.

David and I showed up for the conference in Tuscaloosa on a cold, first work day of January 2014. The now 14-year-old boy and his mother were upstairs ready to meet the judge to convince him about their not wanting to pursue the case. Reading the sincerity on Ms. Head's face, Junkins finally dismissed all charges—and everyone breathed a sigh of relief.

Justice delayed is often justice denied. In this case, it was seven years too late, but better late than never. The tragedy is that David Clayton was the real victim. For seven years he had false charges hanging over his head, and he had to pay a significant legal fee for his defense, costing him the value of much of his land.

Further, there would have been no pocket to collect from on a civil action against the boy or his mother, and in any action against the Crafts there would have been evidentiary issues, plus home-cooking in a backwoods county.

It was all totally unfair to David. A great miscarriage of justice cost him dearly financially and psychologically. While David was understandably embittered, I appealed to him to consider the basic tenet of forgiveness in the strained Christian faith that he still has.

8

Universities Saddled
with Employment Problems

I'll be the first to say that Auburn University is a great institution, academically and athletically, although not necessarily in that order. While it employs many enlightened people, there have been significant racial tensions, some bubbling beneath the surface, others in plain view.

Given my recognition as a civil rights attorney, it is no accident that many employment cases with racial issues involving Auburn keep coming to my door. These have included a steady stream of aggrieved faculty ever since my firm won federal court jury verdicts in two landmark cases in the mid-1980s. One was an age discrimination case on behalf of Drs. Milton Alexander, Winfred Shaw, and three other senior faculty. The other was a First Amendment case on behalf of six professors in the mechanical engineering department who had written a critical self-study of their own department that their department head and dean did not like. All were punished, five by being involuntarily transferred to other engineering departments.

Whatever happened to academic freedom?

It has helped in recent years that renowned Auburn City Councilman Arthur Lee Dowdell keeps sending people to me. Dowdell is no shrinking violet. He is also known as "Bishop" Dowdell, because he heads the New Testament Potter's House Full Gospel Church. Bishop is also a strong advocate for the healing ministry, a real interest of mine as well. We are good friends.

Bishop was famous in Auburn for removing Confederate flags from the municipal cemetery. I was present in late 2010 when he vigorously defended his doing so at an Auburn City Council meeting. He offended some people, but not me.

Tyrone Durrell and Seven Black Custodial Employees
Thus it was no surprise in October 2009 when Dowdell encouraged seven AU custodial employees, led by Tyrone Durrell, to come see me. After examining their complaints, namely that they were paid less money for

doing the same work as white co-workers, I helped them file a complaint with the U.S. Equal Employment Opportunity Commission in Birmingham. In January 2010, Dowdell and Durrell also lead a rally in front of Samford Hall, the main Auburn University administration building.

Durrell, a building specialist who worked in the AU student center, stated: "We're still hanging in there, but we're getting the rough end of the stick with harassment."

Dowdell, using a megaphone that echoed off the walls, stated, "in 1999 we stood on the same place and cried out with facilities workers . . . Eleven years later racial discrimination is still going on." Dowdell called for Auburn President Jay Gogue to meet with employees to resolve the claim within five days, or he would return with national civil rights leaders to continue their protest.

We slugged it out with Auburn University counsel on various evidentiary issues. After more noise during the first three months of 2010, Auburn University, led by its erstwhile general counsel Lee Armstrong contacted me, and together we worked out a satisfactory but confidential resolution. The clients were happy. I truly wish I could share the details, but an agreement prevents that.

NINE BLACK ATHLETIC DEPARTMENT EMPLOYEES

A few months later, in mid-2010, another nine employees from the athletic department, all African American, came to see me, again encouraged by Dowdell. Their leader was Curtis Chandler, accompanied by Antonio Floyd, Walter Hughley, Teresa Cigon, Eddie Mackey, Ernest Moss, Pamela Oliver, Sizzy Townsend, and Marquetta Williams. By June 2010, nine charges of race discrimination had been filed with the EEOC. Naturally, Auburn was not happy, but frankly the university deserved it after reorganizing its athletic department in such a way that it squeezed most of the few remaining black employees out of a job.

Working with the EEOC in Birmingham is frequently a prolonged effort in futility. The main problem is that the agency is overwhelmed and inundated by complaints from around the state; the EEOC doesn't have nearly enough investigators to pursue all the complaints.

Hence, by March 2011 there had been virtually no investigation, and no right-to-sue letter, which usually comes within six months. My clients were impatient, and understandably so. We filed suit under an alternative theory based on 42 U.S.C. § 1981, a Reconstruction-era law forbidding race discrimination in contractual relations. We reserved the right to amend a

Title VII claim, as an alternative theory, at a later date.

In civil discovery, I battled Auburn's intransigence until late August 2011. Paralegal Vicki Morrison helped me greatly, as did Bishop Dowdell. Just before Labor Day weekend of 2011, the case was confidentially resolved. All my clients were again smiling. Again, I wish more could be said.

With its outreach to star athletic prospects, especially for its major sports of football and basketball, Auburn University wants to avoid a reputation for racism at its school. Many of its top officials, including general counsel Lee Armstrong, are decent people who work hard to maintain that goal. Likewise, Dorman Walker, David Boyd, and Kelly Pate of the Balch and Bingham law firm in Montgomery always do a good job for their clients.

The problem is that Auburn University is just too big, and surprisingly too diverse, at least with all the strong egos running around. It's also hard to enforce good manners, racial sensitivity, and morality. Consequently, periodic outbursts and pockets of racism raise their ugly heads. This doesn't mean that my clients are always right, although most of them have proven to be. After representing a particularly difficult faculty member making claims of racial mistreatment (whose name I will not call), I came to see that Auburn University also has legitimate, non-discriminatory reasons for termination of some of its faculty.

EVELYN CRAYTON

Professor Evelyn Crayton of Auburn University's Cooperative Extension Service invited me to speak on campus to the Auburn Black Caucus in October 2011. It was great fun as I addressed a crowd of about 100 employees and students in a student center auditorium. In the crowd and sporting his white beard was Lee Armstrong, polite but with an ultra-serious look on his face. I took advantage of the occasion. Sounding a bit like a professor myself, I covered the many different types of illegal employment as well as free speech issues. To my surprise and delight, a two-page story with two photographs of me appeared in Auburn University's 2012 *Glomerata* yearbook.

Shortly afterwards, Dr. Crayton contacted me herself about a case of her own. She believed her prospects within Auburn University were not helped by inviting me to come speak. She alleged, first in her EEOC charge, and later in a lawsuit in the fall of 2011, that she had come under increasingly unfair scrutiny by two associate directors of the Extension Service. Dr. Crayton said that her judgment was being unfairly challenged, with unfair reprimands, and that her race played a significant negative role in the mistreatment.

Dr. Crayton, 65, was and is a super-impressive lady. She had brought considerable favorable national publicity and recognition to Auburn University in her field as a nutritionist. She didn't deserve the way she was being treated. She had good years left. But Auburn didn't see it that way.

Dr. Crayton alleged that after the departure of other well-qualified black Extension Service faculty, and her own impending departure, there were no longer any African Americans left in top administrative and supervisory positions at Auburn University's Cooperative Extension Service.

The noise we made was too loud or the merits of our case were too biting, because Dr. Crayton's case was soon satisfactorily "but confidentially" resolved as well, following a mediation. As with the other cases, I wish I could tell more. Dr. Crayton was happy.

A side benefit after the case was meeting Dr. Crayton's great son, attorney Kareem Crayton, a professor who taught voting rights law at the University of North Carolina, Chapel Hill. I wrote a letter to President Obama recommending attorney Crayton for one of Alabama's vacant federal judgeships.

FERN LIN-HEALY

After Dr. Crayton's case, I had yet another intense in-court battle representing Auburn University marketing department professor Fern Lin-Healy. She alleged that she was discriminated against on a racial or national origin basis. A well-educated Harvard grad with a pair of 800s on her SATs, young Dr. Lin Healy was of Chinese descent, but born in America. Her case was also "satisfactorily resolved" in January 2015, following a long deposition and other developments that played out for another two months before the case was dismissed in court.

DRS. FLOYD WOODS AND TSANHAI LIN

In 2015, I also had active cases representing two other Auburn University professors, Dr. Floyd Woods, of the horticulture department and Dr. Tsanhai Lin of the electrical engineering department. Dr. Woods, an African American, had a substantial race discrimination claim that I felt was quite meritorious. It was successfully resolved in 2015.

Dr. Lin's claim is based on his Oriental (Chinese) national origin. He has gone for years without a promotion from associate professor to full professor, while his Caucasian colleagues have zoomed past him. At this writing, his case was continuing into 2016, which is why I will say little more at this time.

Both Drs. Woods and Lin remain employed by Auburn. I have helped them guard their jobs.

THE DR. MARONI STORY

Tall, charismatic, and engaging, the native Californian "Dr. Maroni" was an Auburn professor who spread enough wit among his students that it sometimes got him into trouble.

When Dr. Maroni first came to see me in 2007, he was in his mid-50s and happily married to a lady psychologist. One of his female doctoral students, about 40, and also married, became infatuated with Dr. Maroni. We will call her "Bessie Brassell."

"Bessie" confided to Maroni about certain personal issues and was befriended by both Dr. Maroni and his wife. Maroni considered "Bessie" a close friend, and supported her career. Eventually, they developed a strong emotional bond.

When Dr. Maroni decided to end the friendship, the student retaliated, and, in Dr. Maroni's estimation, exaggerated their relationship to the Auburn EEO director, who filed formal charges against Dr. Maroni on the grounds of the professor-student relationship. In a later case, while cross-examining this Auburn EEO director, I got her to admit that she had always sided with the Auburn University administration in any lawsuit.

I was able to build a solid defense, based on violations of Auburn's procedures and the law. When the hearing finally arrived in early January 2009, we faced a faculty panel that included many feminists, including a notorious woman professor known as a man-hater. Dr. Maroni recognized that the deck was stacked against him from the beginning. I counseled Maroni to authorize me to issue a brief statement before the panel to dismiss his appeal on grounds of "constructive discharge" (i.e., resignation because of intolerable working conditions).

I subsequently filed a suit against Auburn University on various due process violations. Although a seasoned mediator was brought in to help Auburn and Dr. Maroni resolve the discord, the aggrieved student rejected every proposal. While I was successful in negotiating a settlement with Auburn that would have concluded the matter, again the aggrieved student, through a local attorney, intervened, and made financial demands against Dr. Maroni.

Hence, the battle morphed into more of a conflict between Dr. Maroni and the doctoral student, with Auburn University violating the confidentiality clause of the settlement agreement by disclosing it to the student's attorney.

The case was eventually assigned to Judge Mark Fuller, the same judge arrested for domestic abuse in 2014. As the trial was about to begin in

January 2010 (26 months after my first meeting Dr. Maroni), the opposing attorneys capitulated, and the case was settled.

Dr. Maroni was hired at a prominent Northeastern university, and has remained in contact. He is one of the many Auburn faculty members and employees I have successfully represented against Auburn University since the early 1980s. To Dr. Maroni and his wife, I wish them nothing but the best.

REPRESENTED OVER 300 FACULTY AND EMPLOYEES

It is no exaggeration that, beginning back in the early 1980s, I have represented or consulted with well over 300 Auburn University faculty members, including one dean and too many administrative employees to count. I've also represented quite a few students in cases ranging from race to sex, and wrongfully being charged with Honor Code violations.

I've also had a number of disability discrimination cases and sexual discrimination cases involving Auburn University. Early on, I also had many age discrimination cases, but the *Garrett v. University of Alabama in Birmingham* case that went to the U.S. Supreme Court stopped age cases against state institutions. In other words, the likes of our big 1986 courtroom victory in Opelika for Milton Alexander and five other Auburn faculty members could no longer be obtained.

A similar ruling makes it prohibitive to pursue a disability discrimination case against a state agency, unless they are receiving federal money. Auburn does. Thus, the federal Rehabilitation Act keeps Auburn straight on its disability cases. The Family Medical Leave Act (FMLA) also applies to Auburn. I've successfully used the FMLA many times against Auburn University and other employers.

I'm sure that Auburn's legal office and high executive ranks have a dim view of me, to put it nicely. But when I take the depositions of Auburn faculty members, I'm sometimes treated like a celebrity or hero. Please forgive my immodesty in repeating this, but these cases, and my representations of the many good faculty members and other employees, have made life more meaningful.

I still cheer for Auburn when they play anyone except a certain team from Tuscaloosa. My grandfather, the first Julian McPhillips, was on the University of Alabama's 1915 football team, when the sport was played more like rugby.

Roll Tide and War Eagle!

HUNTINGDON COLLEGE

I have also handled cases with many other colleges and universities, foremost of which have been Huntingdon College and Tuskegee University.

During Dr. Allen Jackson's last 12 years (1980–1992) as president of Huntingdon College, I had many disgruntled faculty coming to see me. In subsequent years, under new presidents, Huntingdon has seemingly had less turmoil in its faculty ranks.

The name that stands out in memory was Dr. Dick Johns, chairman of the religion department from 1985 to 1991. Dick felt that Dr. Jackson, as a Methodist minister himself, was setting a bad moral example as president of the Methodist-affiliated school.

Even after Dick and fellow minister-wife Louise Johns left the Montgomery area and moved to Long Island, New York, they remained friends of Leslie and me. Dick published in 2015 a book, *Broken Beyond Healing*, under the pen name of Richard Mosley. Though a novel, the book reveals the scintillating details of Dick's years at Huntingdon. To protect the innocent and the guilty, Dick has given everyone a fictitious name. I am referred to as "Richard McArthur," the author's attorney, quite a few times.

My dear friend Bobby Segall, who usually represents Huntingdon, also has a fictitious name, as do others I recognize. Bobby, and later his associate Shannon Holliday, were always pleasant to work with in resolving the claims of my clients against Huntingdon, and they did a good job for their client also.

Tuskegee University

I've had a number of cases with Tuskegee University faculty over the years, but I will only mention ones involving clients of the last five years.

In 2011, Dr. Leslie Porter, a highly ranked vice president and administrator, came to see me after he was unceremoniously forced out by the relatively new president, Dr. Gilbert Rochon, who had come to Tuskegee from New Orleans.

At that time Scott Golden, a former mayor of Wetumpka and more recently a missionary-law professor in Romania, worked for me for about one year. Scott was about 15 years younger than me. Together we worked out an excellent "resolution" for Dr. Porter, the terms of which were otherwise confidential

More recently, my law firm and I have represented Dr. Ali Abdel-Hadi, who said his Middle Eastern Arabic background caused him to experience national origin discrimination at Tuskegee. My associate attorney Chris Worshek worked closely with me in resolving his claims sufficiently to make our client quite happy.

Belinda Roby, a highly successful women's basketball coach at Tuskegee, came to see me after she lost her job in 2014. Tuskegee appeared to have a great gender disparity in its hirings and retentions, especially in its athletic department. Ably assisted by associate attorney Chase Estes, we raised Title IX and Title VII issues in a suit we filed in 2014. Finally, in 2015, with Tuskegee's new President Dr. Brian Johnson at the helm, we worked out a great resolution for her, with the usual confidential terms that all these academia settlements require.

The most recent client to come see me, in July 2015, was Tuskegee University's former dean of the College of Arts and Sciences, Dr. Lisa Beth Hill. Associate Chase Estes is helping me again. Dr. Hill also raises legitimate sex discrimination issues. Her case was successfully resolved at a mediation conducted by the seasoned Debra Leo of the Equal Employment Opportunity Commission on December 15, 2015. I've worked well with Ms. Leo many times over the last 30 years. Meanwhile, Dr. Hill was able to have an enjoyable Christmas and New Year's at her permanent residence in northern Virginia.

Troy University

One university whose name sticks out by omission is Troy University. I have had very few, if any, complaints from its faculty members over the years, either from the main campus in Troy or from its Montgomery campus. That says that either Troy must be doing something right or that Chancellor Dr. Jack Hawkins and top executive Ray Large have maintained a good relationship with their faculty.

Other Colleges and Universities

I have also represented faculty members from Auburn University, Montgomery; the University of Alabama in Birmingham; and even from the University of Alabama in Tuscaloosa. However, most of them were before 2005 and outside the time focus of this book. Some are mentioned in *The People's Lawyer*.

9

Chris Turner's Long Fight
Against Race Discrimination

Christopher Turner is an unsung hero in the latter days of the civil rights movement. Beginning in 1987 as a 22-year-old part-time firefighter for the City of Auburn, Chris developed the courage, humility, and fortitude to tackle a race discrimination hotbed that called itself the Auburn Fire Department.

Only as a result of a lawsuit did Chris become in 1991 one of the first black full-time firefighters for the City of Auburn. That was pursuant to a settlement agreement in *Hammoch v. City of Auburn*. Chris remained a Firefighter I for approximately seven years, whereupon in 1998 he was promoted to Firefighter II, with no pay increase.

Chris ambitiously took all the requisite courses and engaged in extensive training, such that he was certified to command at fires. By 1996, Chris became a station officer, assuming supervisory responsibilities, as assigned, at any of the four fire stations in the City of Auburn. As such, Chris had to interact effectively with team members, senior officers and the public. He also had to instruct, plan, lead, communicate, be safe, manage, and supervise, all leadership skills.

Chris had even served as an "acting lieutenant" from December 2011 through September 2013. Unfortunately for Chris, despite a number of applications for promotion, he was never promoted, not even to sergeant, let alone to lieutenant. Meanwhile, numerous white applicants with less experience and savvy were promoted over Chris. He had helped train some of them.

With Birmingham counsel, Chris filed a 2005 lawsuit that ended with a summary judgment against him in the Opelika federal court. It also caused considerable retaliatory bad will among the fire department bigwigs.

Chris came to me in early 2013, after filing four charges of discrimination in 2011–2012 for race, age, and unlawful retaliation. He had again been represented by Birmingham attorneys with whom he was dissatisfied, and so they withdrew. After research and investigation, I filed suit for Chris on November 27, 2013, and amended the suit twice in 2014. Mr. Turner's complaint set forth the following sordid facts about the Auburn Fire Department:

(a) every African American promoted since 1974 has received his promotion as the result of a lawsuit or pending lawsuit.

(b) no black firefighter has been hired since 1989 from the general public, and all firefighter positions have been filled through a so-called Student Program from Auburn University.

(c) 99 plus percent of the firefighters employed through the Student Program were white.

(d) Students in the Student Program were overwhelmingly trained by white officers.

(e) as of 2013, and for the past two years, whites continued to be overwhelmingly dominant in Auburn's Fire Department, in violation of the 1991 Settlement Agreement, which stated that the City may not discriminate in its hiring practices based upon race.

(f) Christopher Turner has wrongfully been denied consideration for promotion to lieutenant in the City of Auburn fire department, even though he was fully qualified for said promotion, and had served as acting lieutenant on numerous occasions.

From a public relations viewpoint, we received strong support from Auburn's lone black city councilman, Arthur "Bishop" Dowdell, who invited me to speak several times before the Auburn City Council. On one occasion, I urged all the councilmen to see the recently-released movie, *Twelve Years a Slave*, to understand the vestiges of slavery and racism, and how it still affected the City of Auburn.

Auburn defended its racist hiring and promotional practices by using their allegedly unbiased "Assessment Center" to prepare an allegedly "race-neutral" test. For some reason, Chris always landed at the bottom of the test-takers and was never promoted.

Admittedly, Chris's grammar was less than perfect, but questions on the exam were in less than grammatical English, and many of the white firefighters didn't exactly speak the King's English, either.

In September 2014, I took the deposition of Auburn's expert witness, Dr. Mark Foster. I got him to acknowledge several missing elements from the so-called race-neutral test as "significant shortcomings." They included: (a) no questions concerning geographical knowledge of the City of Auburn;

(b) a dearth of questions testing prior experience as an Auburn fireman; and
(c) the absence of any testing of physical skills.

Not long afterwards, the City of Auburn proposed a confidential resolution of all of Chris's claims. After considerable prayer, contemplation, and attorney-client communication, Chris deemed it in his best interests to bring the litigation to an end. A motion to dismiss was filed in October 2014.

Hopefully, the City of Auburn has learned from Christopher Turner's legal challenges. Hopefully, the Auburn Fire Department will see more blacks hired and promoted in the future. If that happens, Christopher Turner, as a civil rights pioneer, will be owed a debt of gratitude.

10

Black Belt Mayors in Need

During the last ten years, I've come to the direct legal aid of three Black Belt mayors and advised others. The three were: Whitehall Mayor John Jackson in 2007–2008; Union Springs Mayor John McGowan in 2009–2010; and Walter Hill, the mayor of Mosses in Lowndes County, in 2014.

Most mayors in Alabama, if and when they are sued, are covered by the Alabama Municipal Insurance Corporation (AMIC). That company not only provides an attorney at no cost to the mayor or city, but if a judgment or settlement is attained against the mayor, the AMIC covers it. Usually, however, there is no insurance to cover a mayor charged with criminal wrongdoing, even if the charge is false or wrongful.

Mayor John Jackson of Whitehall

Ironically, the first place outside Montgomery where I gave a speech as a young assistant attorney general in 1975 was Whitehall, a small "dot in the road" community about halfway between Montgomery and Selma. The original invitation was to Attorney General Bill Baxley, but he had a conflicting commitment and I drew the honor of speaking in his place. When Whitehall Mayor John Jackson came calling on me years later, I not only knew the location of his town, but I also knew the man himself, having met him in 2002 while I was campaigning for the U.S. Senate.

In 2007–08, the Alabama Attorney General's office, then under Troy King's leadership, had subpoenaed numerous documents from the town of Whitehall, as well as from Mayor Jackson. Leading the probe was the highly competent Assistant Attorney General Stephanie Billingslea, an African American female and Chambers County native who has sharpened her legal tools over years of statewide prosecutions.

The attorney general's office was looking for documents to show that when Whitehall created a gaming casino on Highway 80, Jackson himself had financially benefitted, or embezzled funds.

The Whitehall City Council, the Lowndes County Sheriff, and the town itself supported Jackson. Indeed, many of the town's citizens were his relatives. It turned out that some funds legitimately did go to Jackson to reimburse him for funds he had advanced or loaned to Whitehall, out of his own pocket, to get the bingo parlor project off the ground.

Fortunately, I eventually persuaded the Alabama Attorney General's office to back off. For a while, there was a relative peace and quiet, but then a federal investigator and the U.S. Justice Department started seeking the same information, motivated by informants from a rival political camp. I met with the same two prosecutors from the U.S. Attorney's office who successfully prosecuted Don Siegelman, namely Steve Feaga and Louis Franklin. I thought once again that we had helped Jackson to dodge a bullet.

Time passed, and Jackson moved on to another attorney, an African American from Selma. I don't know what happened, but one day I woke up to read in the morning paper that Jackson had pled guilty to some tax offense and would be spending the next year-and-a-half at the Maxwell federal prison camp.

I visited Mayor Jackson out at the Maxwell prison. He was in good spirits, seemingly at ease with the disposition of his case, and looking forward to getting out in months.

It may be that Jackson didn't cross all his "t's" or dot all his "i's," but in my opinion, the mayor went above and beyond the call of duty and spent money out of his own pocket to help Whitehall benefit from the bingo parlor on Highway 80.

I have always considered it a travesty of justice the way the Indian gaming and bingo interests in Atmore, Wetumpka, and elsewhere have been legally allowed to engage in a business that non-Indian Alabamians in Whitehall, Tuskegee, Birmingham, and Eutaw cannot engage in. These non-Indians are largely African American owners with many black employees. To me, the situation is a gross civil rights violation, but various legal efforts to challenge the Indians' special sovereignty and related benefits have so far been unsuccessful.

Meanwhile, the last I heard from Jackson, he was doing well.

MAJOR JOHN McGOWAN OF UNION SPRINGS

I first came to know John McGowan in the late 1970s or early 1980s. He was always a gentleman, with a spontaneous smile and kind word. I occasionally joked that maybe we are distantly related, despite our different skin colors, because I am descended from the McGowins of south Alabama.

My set spells the name with an "i," his set with an "a," but in earlier generations, spellings often got changed around.

John has come into my office multiple times over the past decades for consultation and advice. He also got me involved in annual events of the Nat King Cole Society that he helped to organize. I have also seen John at the mid-November "hog-killing time" barbeque feasts in the Bullock County countryside run by his distinguished first cousins in the Cox family, featuring most notably brothers Major and Hobson Cox. John and his cousins shared a common Caucasian grandfather.

I would also see John at Alabama Democratic Conference political events. After all, John was mayor of Union Springs, Alabama from 1984 to 1989, then he ran again in 2008 and was elected to another four-year term.

As John re-entered the mayor's office, he encountered hostilities from rival forces in the preceding administration and certain police officer allies with whom he had contract disputes. The city council also contained rivals, challenging the new mayor at every twist and turn. I've come to believe that life is often more challenging for mayors of small-towns than it is for those of big cities. I've seen rivalries and jealousies repeatedly disrupt small towns. Union Springs fit that mold.

Thus it came as no surprise when I learned that Union Springs Mayor John McGowan was arrested in the wee morning hours of December 26, 2009, after coming to the rescue of his stepdaughter who had been stopped by Union Springs police on a traffic offense. Awakened from a deep sleep by a telephone call about 2:30 a.m., John calmed his wife, jumped into his car, and drove the few short blocks from where he lived to where his daughter had been stopped.

Present at the scene were Union Springs police officers Nathan Williams and Gary Lewis. Now the officers had much bigger prey than McGowan's stepdaughter. Sgt. Williams subjected the sleepy mayor to field sobriety tests and judged his performance inadequate. Shortly thereafter, McGowan was booked for "DUI" and "obstructing governmental operation."

John contacted me in early January 2010. Given our long-term friendship, I quoted him a modest fee. I also gave him significant time. A non-jury trial was finally before District Court Judge Theresa Daniel on March 17, 2010. Testimony soon exposed the political skullduggery involved, and Judge Daniel found the mayor not guilty of obstructing government operations. However, despite the absence of a Breathalyzer test, but accepting the police officer's testimony about alcohol on John's breath and the allegedly poor field sobriety test results, Judge Daniel found John guilty of DUI. There may also have been political pressure on her.

An immediate appeal was filed to take the case before a jury in Bullock County. John suspected that a local jury would include people allied with his political opponents and others well aware the mayor had been a bartender and, frankly, was known for enjoying his drinks. Accordingly, Circuit Court Judge Bert Smithart granted a motion to change the venue from Union Springs to Clayton, in neighboring Barbour County.

The case was tried in March 2010 and ended in a hung jury. Afterwards, I negotiated with the District Attorney's Association in Montgomery, but hard-nosed prosecutor Brandon Hughes refused to back down.

After various pre-trial motions, the trial was reset for August 2010. We put together a strong and valiant defense. The mayor again took the stand. We expected a defense verdict until the prosecutor was allowed, over my objections, to call a surprise rebuttal witness who was closely connected to the mayor's political and police rivals.

This female witness (who will remain unnamed) concocted a highly prejudicial story against John, saying she had seen him out drinking at three different night clubs on Christmas Day night. John said this was flatly false, and we alleged perjury in a post-judgment motion. The truth, according to John and his wife, was that the mayor had retired early that night, between 9 and 10, after a big dinner.

Unfortunately, the surprise witness's statement was the last testimony the jury heard. It obviously swayed them. Ignoring the "presumption of innocence," and engaging in the more frequently used but improper "presumption of guilt," the jury found the John guilty of a DUI.

On August 2010, I filed a Motion for Judgment Notwithstanding the Verdict and for a New Trial, with three affidavits confirming the testimony was perjured, and that a verdict based on the same should be set aside. Unfortunately, on October 11, 2010, Judge Smithart denied the motion.

To provide fresh energy and expertise, I recommended that Mayor McGowan use a new attorney on appeal, namely my across-the-street attorney neighbor Bill Blanchard, a former president of the Alabama Criminal Defense Lawyers Association. He handles many appeals to the higher courts.

Unfortunately, Mayor McGowan was unable to pay the entire appellate fee quoted by Blanchard. Thus I later saw that a motion to withdraw by Blanchard was granted by the court. The conviction was upheld by the Alabama Court of Criminal Appeals.

Walter Hill, Mayor of Mosses in Lowndes County

One morning in February 2014, Walter Hill, the mayor of the small town of Mosses in Lowndes County, came to my office for legal help. He was not in trouble for anything he had done as mayor. Instead, it was his service as Lowndes County Emergency Management Agency (EMA) director from 2010–2012 that landed him most undeservedly in hot legal waters.

The "no good deed goes unpunished" doctrine and the axiom that "holding public office is an invitation for indictment" both rang true here. Walter grew up in Chicago, but, like many African Americans in the Windy City, he had deep roots in the South. In his case, in Lowndes County, Alabama. To escape a murderous crime environment victimizing his family in a Chicago neighborhood, Walter moved to Lowndes County in 1982. Given his humble and gentle personality, and genuine spirituality, Walter's leadership skills were soon recognized. He was appointed EMA director in 2004 by the Lowndes County Commission.

Part of the work of the EMA is to know "who's who" and "where they live." For various reasons, not everyone has a driver's license, especially the old, poor, and infirm. Walter was asked and authorized by the Lowndes County Commission and the Sheriff's Office to outfit the non-driver's license citizens with identification badges. That Walter did, with all the necessary identifying information.

Using a model supplied by the federal Homeland Security Office, Walter had ID badges made, with a State of Alabama emblem in an upper corner, which seemed appropriate to him. No one bothered to tell Walter that he needed permission from the Alabama Department of Public Safety to use the emblem.

Jealousies abound in politics, and a rival local interest stirred up this issue on Walter. Hence, he was forced to resign in 2011. Worse, on January 20, 2014, he woke up to discover the Alabama Attorney General's Office had secured an indictment against him. One count was for forgery in the second degree, a felony. Another felony count involved intentional use of his office for personal gain, yet another count was a misdemeanor of unintentional use of his office for personal gain; both were state ethics law violations.

The case was set for trial in April 2014 but was postponed until October. Associate attorney Chris Worshek helped me prepare and file a motion to dismiss both counts. The first count was challenged since there was no real forgery of a signature. The second count was challenged because Walter had not profited—the expenses of his agency in making the badges well exceeded the revenue generated.

Judge Terri Bozeman heard my arguments on October 6, 2014, but denied our motion to dismiss, which is generally what happens in criminal cases. Trial was scheduled for the next week. I was eager to take the case to court, despite the presence of an able assistant attorney general, Ternisha Miles, who would be representing the state. Ms. Miles had earlier offered to dismiss the felony charges if Walter would plead to the misdemeanor ethics law violation. I frankly and strongly counseled against accepting the plea, even though its unintentional misdemeanor nature would allow Walter's continued service as mayor of Mosses and would not interfere with any other activity.

In court on that October 6, Walter presented me with a letter I had not seen before. With his permission, I quote the following excerpt:

> After much prayer with family, friends, colleagues, church family, and the community of which I serve, I have prayerfully decided that in the event the Honorable Circuit Judge chooses not to dismiss, I will accept the state's unintentional misdemeanor plea.

As much as I wanted to try the case, the call was ultimately the client's, of course. So Walter pled to the unintentional use of his office, even though he made no net gain. The state's attorney had argued that any money received was technically a gain, even if the expenses were greater. While I believe a jury would have ruled in Walter's favor, the problem was that, with so many murder, rape, and violent crime cases ahead of us in Lowndes County, the court would not have reached Walter's case that session and maybe not even the next. The case would have bounced from one docket to another in a county where there are only two two-week felony criminal trial dockets a year.

Walter would have had to carry the charges as an albatross over his head for months, if not years. He had been elected a year earlier as president of the World Conference of Black Mayors, He was already in medical school part-time at prestigious Morehouse College in Atlanta. Walter had checked in advance and the misdemeanor would not be a problem with his school.

Nonetheless, the local *Lowndes Signal* newspaper and Channel 12 carried the story of Walter's conviction. The *Signal*'s article correctly quoted me as saying "it's a tragedy the case was brought in the first place . . . the travesty of it is that it was incited by jealous people in Lowndes County . . . and that he has done nothing (wrong) . . . he's one of the most honorable, decent, respectful persons I've ever met."

Walter's story didn't end in October 2014. Unrelated to the criminal case, in early November 2014 I saw Walter in the lead story on the 10 o'clock Channel 12 news (NBC). He was being interviewed following his home being hit by a fire bomb. It turns out that Walter had sent two law enforcement officers from Mosses to help fight illegal drug distribution in Lowndes County. Some thugs had retaliated. Once again, no good deed goes unpunished.

Walter and I remain good friends. He frequently attends our diverse Christ the Redeemer Episcopal Church in Montgomery and is highly appreciated by everyone in the congregation. He even preached to our church membership one Sunday in 2015.

In October 2015, Walter invited me to come to Fairfield, in the suburbs of Birmingham, to be the keynote speaker at the World Conference of Black Mayors. I immensely enjoyed the occasion.

11

Coach's Son Likes Dreadlocks

Blaise Taylor was the son of Auburn University's charismatic African American coach, Trooper Taylor. The father contributed significantly to the War Eagles' 2010 national championship football team.

One day in late 2010 then ninth-grader Blaise and his mother showed up at my office seeking help. Turns out that the basketball coach at Auburn High School, himself an older African American, didn't like Blaise's dreadlocks, and demanded that Blaise cut them, if he wanted to continue playing ball. Even as a ninth grader the swift and coordinated Blaise was one of the best players on Auburn High's team. But the coach called the shots and thought Blaise should conform.

Blaise, backed by both parents, considered the dreadlocks an inherently African American hairstyle. He showed me pictures of a white player allowed to play on the team despite his long blond, flowing hair. Case law confirms that it is just as illegal for one black to discriminate against another black on the basis of race, as it is for a white to discriminate against a black. We filed a lawsuit. However, based on early rulings, we could tell that the federal judge we drew was not sympathetic to our argument on the hair issue.

Amidst much publicity that neither the high school nor Auburn University enjoyed, we finally worked out a solution in January 2011 whereby Auburn High agreed to change its rules concerning hairstyles for players. It was a victory for Blaise and a positive outcome for those who dare to be different.

Fast forward three more years, and I read in a January 2014 edition of the *Birmingham News* that Blaise had accepted a football scholarship to play for the Arkansas State Red Wolves, where his father is now the new cornerbacks coach. Blaise turned down similar offers from Auburn, Nebraska, Memphis, and Harvard. I wish Blaise and his parents all the best in Jonesboro, Arkansas. Surely my brother Frank wishes Blaise had gone to Harvard.

I appreciate people like Blaise who march to the beat of that proverbial different drummer. My brother David did, and I often do. I also appreciate people who take on tough challenges to rectify injustices. Sometimes critics

will belittle motives or call the efforts "quixotic." Teddy Roosevelt's famous
words, which Don Siegelman loved to quote, said it in another way:

> It is not the critic who counts: The credit belongs to the man who is
> actually in the arena. Who strives valiantly: who errs, who comes short again
> and again: who knows great enthusiasms: who spends himself in a worthy
> cause: who at the best knows in the end the triumph of high achievement,
> and who at the worst, if he fails, at least fails while daring greatly.

Many of the people I have defended or represented as plaintiffs, described
in this book, fall into this category, including me. That is part of the thrill of
being a civil rights or trial attorney, taking on cases with difficult odds, and,
as with Blaise Taylor, bringing civil justice, and rectifying wrongs.

12

CAPITAL MURDER CHARGES
CAN INVOLVE INNOCENT PEOPLE

The first eight or nine murder cases I tried in the 1980s and 1990s resulted in either complete or partial acquittals. That included, famously, the cases of Arthurine Ringstaff in 1983, Dennis Heard in 1988, and Richard Lee Steele in 1994, all acquitted on capital murder charges, as well as of any lesser and included offenses.

In 1995, Bill Honey and I represented Alton Dandridge, who was acquitted of capital murder. Unfortunately, he was convicted on a lesser offense after a jailhouse con artist, with 23 previous felony convictions, escaped further prosecution of himself by fabricating a story that Dandridge had made an admission to him while the two were locked up together awaiting trial.

Skullduggery and shenanigans are not uncommon in criminal prosecutions. This contributes to a fair number of innocent people being convicted. That is why I am such a huge fan of attorney Bryan Stevenson and his Equal Justice Initiative (EJI) here in Montgomery. They have won the releases of a number of wrongfully convicted people, including the now-famous Walter McMillian who sat on Death Row for six years after being framed for a murder in Monroe County.

EJI also rendered indispensably helpful services in the eventual vindication of Alton Dandridge, though my former co-counsel Bill Honey, now in his 80s, deserves the credit for never giving up on post-judgment legal initiatives. On October 1, 2015, Dandridge was released from Kilby Correctional Facility after a review of fingerprint evidence determined Dandridge had never been involved in the 1994 death of Riley Manning. The Alabama Bureau of Investigation (ABI) had earlier falsely stated the fingerprints at the scene were Dandridge's. Additionally the jailhouse informant who said Dandridge confessed later submitted an affidavit confirming he gave false testimony to get a reduced sentence. Former Sheriff D. T. Marshall, then a Montgomery police detective, is the one who procured the false testimony from the jailhouse snitch, thus depriving Dandridge of 20 years of freedom—and letting the real murderer go free.

Sometimes law enforcement personnel themselves get charged with criminal wrongdoing. It is often deserved, and frankly needs to happen more frequently when excessive force, discrimination, or other misconduct is involved. Sometimes, however, it is unfair, as was the case of an officer south of Montgomery in 2007. Then I represented a White Hall town policeman, Jesse Johnson, in a Lowndes County trial, wherein Johnson was charged with vehicular murder and manslaughter for slamming into a lady at an excessive speed on Highway 80. Using precise testimony from accident reconstruction expert Larry Mann, we proved the lady's vision was obstructed by another oncoming car when she pulled from a side road onto Highway 80. Officer Johnson was acquitted on all felony charges.

THE EXTREME INJUSTICE DONE TO VANESSA GILL

Little did I suspect the trickery and deceit I would encounter when I first accepted the capital murder defense in Selma of Vanessa Gill in a December 2008 trial. Indicted 16 months earlier, but languishing in a hot Dallas County jail before trial, Vanessa was dismayed that her two earlier attorneys had withdrawn, one due to early onset dementia.

Vanessa was accused of putting her nephew, Curtis Cook Jr., up to brutally killing her husband with a baseball bat. She not only denied it, but the evidence was indisputable that she chased the masked attacker away from their carport and called the police for help.

The masked intruder indeed was Vanessa's nephew, Curtis Cook Jr., an ex-felon. In his first two statements after being arrested, he said nothing about Vanessa. However, in a third statement designed to save his own hide, the street-wise Cook claimed his aunt Vanessa had put him up to the assault.

Dallas County's population is overwhelmingly black. The victim Marshall Gill, the defendant Vanessa Gill, and her nephew were all black. Not surprisingly, we initially ended up with an all-black jury. But prosecutor Shannon Lynch, a tenacious white female attorney, pulled a reverse *Batson* challenge on me, which Judge Jack Meigs granted. (*Batson* was a 1986 case in which the U.S. Supreme Court established that potential jurors could not be excluded solely on the basis of their race.) That forced me to bargain with the prosecution to allow three whites on the jury, causing Vanessa Gill's jury to go from bad to worse.

The prosecution had clearly made a deal with the co-defendant nephew for his testimony, so I filed a "Motion to Reveal the Deal" which the State had with its star witness Curtis Cook Jr. While the trial court granted the motion, the prosecution falsely denied it had any deal. The deal may not have been in writing, but Cook's defense lawyer, a former prosecutor himself, well knew what a bargain he was getting and clearly helped negotiate it.

Meanwhile improper contact was going on between certain jurors and family members of the prosecution. When we called this to the Court's attention, the judge failed to probe further or ask relevant questions.

During the trial, over my objections, the trial judge allowed into evidence gruesome pictures of the deceased. This proved nothing, since Walter Gill's death was indisputable. Nonetheless, this greatly inflamed the jury, especially in closing arguments when Shannon Lynch starting flipping up the ugly photos while facing the jury with her back turned to me, hoping I wouldn't see.

Then, when the jury came back with a question during its second day of deliberations, Judge Meigs wrongfully declared that Vanessa Gill was in conspiracy with her nephew. Despite serious holes in his testimony, Vanessa's nephew had testified that his aunt put him up to the crime.

The jury returned a guilty verdict. Despite the capital murder charge, the State had decided not to seek the death penalty, so Vanessa was sentenced to "life imprisonment without parole."

My reaction was outrage and indignation, although I behaved myself in Court. I immediately filed post-judgment motions. I subpoenaed both prosecutor Lynch and Bruce Maddox, who had represented Cook, to find out more about the deal for his testimony, but Judge Meigs quashed my subpoenas. I subpoenaed the entire jury to find out more about improper contact with the pro-prosecution family members. Unfortunately, Judge Meigs released all the jurors from my subpoenas before I could address the Court on the matter.

Adding to the trickery, the prosecution waited long enough to allow my post-judgment motion to expire before sentencing the nephew. In late March 2009, Curtis Cook Jr. and his attorney met prosecutor Lynch in court. Cook pled guilty to a lesser offense of felony murder, not capital murder. Despite Cook's multiple prior felony convictions as a drug dealer, which ordinarily would have enhanced his sentence to life without parole, Cook amazingly got sentenced to life with the possibility of parole.

We filed well-researched and well-written appellate briefs before the Alabama Court of Criminal Appeals and the Alabama Supreme Court. Criminal conviction reversals are rare in both courts, and the judgment against Vanessa was affirmed in both courts.

So Vanessa Gill had now suffered the murder of her husband, had been wrongly convicted of instigating though not carrying out the actual murder, and the man who actually did the murder had received a lesser sentence than her own.

Within the year, however, what little conscience Curtis Cook Jr. had, or family pressure, must have gotten to him. Cook voluntarily produced a handwritten affidavit completely recanting his earlier testimony and confirming that he was pressured by both the prosecution and his own lawyer into giving false testimony.

Thus, Vanessa's second round of appeals began, beginning with a Rule 32 proceeding. (Under this limited legal vehicle, issues already argued before the state appellate courts cannot be raised again. There must be either new facts or new arguments.) I persuaded Montgomery attorney Landis Sexton, with payment from Vanessa's family, to take the lead. I reviewed and polished his briefs, which were excellent.

Despite the recanting of Cook's testimony, and all the other issues, the State courts affirmed a second time.

The first round of federal court appeals, now ongoing under a habeas corpus petition, is still in court. With the help of Peter Owuor, a native Kenyan who is not a lawyer but has excellent legal skills honed in immigrant detention, I wrote a good federal brief in the U.S. District Court of Montgomery. We filed it on October 4, 2013, more than two years ago at this writing.

The case was soon transferred to a federal judge in Mobile, because Selma (where the state circuit court trial took place) is in the Southern District of Alabama. The case has been assigned to one of the judge's law clerks and is still being worked on 27 months later, as the new year, 2016, arrived. Because Vanessa's loyal family regularly contacts me, I've called the Mobile federal clerk's office several times. I'm always told that "we are working on it." Vanessa herself remains locked up at Tutwiler Prison for Women in Wetumpka, Alabama.

FOR THE GUILTY, DEATH OR LIFE?

While I have represented a number of defendants who were innocent and were acquitted, and a few like Vanessa Gill who were innocent but still convicted, the fact is that many convicted of murder are guilty. And yes, they deserve to be severely punished. And yes, there are particularly heinous and gruesome murders, or mass murders resulting from shooting rampages or terrorist events.

Unquestionably, the perpetrators of the most awful crimes deserve the most severe punishment. In most of the United States—though not most of the world—that means capital punishment, the death penalty. (Although life imprisonment without parole is also a punishment for capital murder.)

But does that mean that we, as fallible human beings, are correct in meting out the death penalty? For a variety of reasons, I have long agreed with the growing number of Americans (now a small majority) who say no.

One thing I deeply agree on with my Catholic brethren is their high respect for life. In the view of many religious persons, "pro-life" extends not only to not killing an unborn child inside the womb, but also to not killing a live human being who committed the ultimate crime. Many Catholics, and many committed Protestants, believe that because of God's great respect for life, mankind should not be taking life. I agree.

Anti-death penalty advocates have a long list of reasons for opposing it. One is that it has never proven to be a deterrent to others committing the crime. Indeed, there is some evidence that use of the death penalty is counter-productive. Another big reason is the endless appeals of death penalty cases take a disproportionate amount of judicial time and money that could be better expended elsewhere in the criminal justice system.

Still another reason is that the death penalty is inarguably applied in discriminatory fashion against racial minorities and against poor people, regardless of race.

Finally, another huge reason is that innocent people are sometimes convicted. Our justice system is far from perfect. Many jurors ignore the judges' instructions about "the presumption of innocence." Instead, they are overwhelmingly guided by a presumption of guilt, which makes them feel psychologically better when they find someone else guilty—it is the jurors' part in fighting crime, and everyone knows how real and prevalent crime is. Perhaps for the same reasons, jurors are predisposed to believe police officers and expert witnesses for the state, even though such testimony easily can be just as wrong as that of any other witness.

Hence, no small number of innocent people have been convicted but later exonerated, such as Alton Dandridge and Walter McMillian, the two wrongly accused persons mentioned above. Further, there can be no worse "Crime of the State" than to execute an innocent person. But an increasing body of evidence proves that it has happened no small number of times.

All these are good reasons to eliminate the death penalty.

THE CASE FOR MERCY

Another reason to eliminate the death penalty is that sometimes an accomplice can be under the heavy-handed influence of a more dominant spouse.

Such were definitely the cases of Carla Fay Tucker in Texas and Judith Ann Neelley in Alabama. If Neelley, at age 18, hadn't complied with her husband's orders to commit a crime, she was certain she, and quite likely her children, would have been killed by her domineering and drug-crazed husband.

In Carla Faye Tucker's case, she was executed despite pleas from Pope John Paul II and evangelists Pat Robertson and Jerry Falwell, among many others to commute her sentence. The then-governor of Texas, namely George W. Bush, was campaigning for the White House at the time, and he pointedly ignored the cries that he commute the sentence. Bush's cynical response to reporters' questions about the case was to mock and belittle Tucker and say, "Oh, I want to live."

Alabama's governor, Fob James, to his everlasting credit, did much better in the Neelley case. In late 1998, as Judith Ann Neelley's date with the executioner was ticking down, I worked closely with Sister Helen Prejean (portrayed in the movie, *Dead Man Walking*) to convince Governor James to commute the sentence to "life imprisonment." Praise God, with his help, we were successful. On January 15, 1999, James commuted Neelley's death penalty sentence.

I have continued to represent Neelley at no charge in the 10 years since. I really can't explain why except that it has been like, at other times in my life, when I feel a tug from above and act on it.

I had listened to Neelley's appeal before the Alabama Supreme Court in 1994, while waiting my turn to argue another appeal. Her then-attorney, Barry Ragsdale, pointed out to the Supreme Court how sloppy and sleepy her trial defense attorney was, how Neelley was under the heavy influence of an oppressive husband, and how the jury voted for her to receive life imprisonment without parole. Unfortunately, the trial judge, Randall Cole of Dekalb County, overturned the jury's recommendation, and gave Neelley the death penalty.

After that, all governmental forces conspired to construe James's commutation to "life without parole," even though James's order said only "life." First, the Alabama Board of Pardons and Paroles secured a 1999 state attorney general's opinion that the commutation meant what it said, namely "life," not "life without parole." The parole board then informed Neelley that she could be considered for parole in January 2014, some fifteen years later.

Since Neelley was convicted in 1983, by October 2001 she had served 19 years. Accordingly, attorney Ragsdale sought a declaratory judgment in Montgomery County Circuit Court that, with time served, she was eligible for immediate parole consideration.

In July 2002, the Circuit Court said Neelley would be eligible for consideration, but not until 15 years after January 1999. Then in 2003, politically ambitious legislators passed Act 2003–300, which amended § 15-22-27(b) Code of Alabama to say that, henceforth, if ever any governor commuted a death sentence to life, it would automatically be "life without parole." Critically, language was added to the act making it retroactive to September 1, 1998.

It was obvious the legislature's retroactive application of the act was directed at and affected only one person, Judith Ann Neelley—the sponsoring legislators even called it "Neelley's Law."

I sent a letter to the Parole Board later pointing out the obvious, that the legislature's retroactive application of Act 2003–300 was an impermissible "Ex Post Facto" law, in violation of the U.S. Constitution. At first the Parole Board appeared to agree, and their enlightened attorney Greg Griffin (now a circuit judge) was in accord.

Later in 2013 and early 2014, upon being subjected to political pressure and a different attorney general's opinion in light of the 2003 law, the Parole Board said it couldn't consider Neelley's parole application.

Hence, Barry Ragsdale and I filed suit in February 2014 against the Alabama Board of Pardons and Paroles, seeking to have Neelley's application considered.

The attorney general's office is defending the suit vigorously, throwing all manner of technical defenses against us. We insist that both the U.S. and Alabama Constitutions prohibit this Ex Post Facto retroactive application of the law.

Barry Ragsdale is a brilliant attorney and is taking the lead. Like me, he is working without compensation. Together we have had to submit briefs, and respond to multiple motions. We hope to get a favorable ruling out of U.S. District Judge Keith Watkins in Montgomery. Even if Watkins does rule with us, it will be an uphill climb. Just getting a hearing before the Parole Board does not mean the board will grant parole.

Neelley has now been in jail for 33 years. She had a Christian conversion years ago, has a good record as an inmate, and has helped other inmates. Yet, given the politics of it all, the prosecutory forces and victims' organizations will do all they can to block her release.

13

No Joy in Troy

Troy, Alabama, is a great town in many respects. One of the early pioneer villages in the state, founded in 1838 and named after the ancient Greek city, Troy's greatest claim to fame is its dynamic university with extension campuses all over the world. The agrarian influence of Pike and the surrounding counties blends with its academic mantle, oozing cross-cultural tensions and conflicts. The famed civil rights icon John Lewis perfectly symbolizes the dichotomy. This native son of Pike County grew up in the area when it was completely segregated. Beaten unmercifully 50 years ago on Selma's Bloody Sunday, he is now in the U.S. Congress. A gracious senior statesman on an international level, a forgiving soul respected by friends and foes alike, he has been honored in recent years in his home county by the very university he grew up knowing he could not attend, because of his color.

It is out of this cauldron of history that five very interesting cases came to me in the last five years.

Edward Olanza Hardy v. Troy Police Department

Former City of Troy policeman Edward Olanza Hardy is an African American who had 19 years' experience in the Troy Police Department and had reached the rank of lieutenant. Ed arrived in distress at my office on September 13, 2012, bemoaning intentional race discrimination in his and other blacks' lack of promotions. We filed an EEOC charge in Birmingham that same day, citing a "pattern and practice of race discrimination" in the promotional practices of the Troy Police Department. Lt. Hardy made out a bold case against Troy Police Chief James Ennis. In retaliation, Hardy was challenged unfairly about a juvenile left unattended in a room used by the criminal investigation division. The investigation and Hardy's placement on administrative leave were raising uncomfortable issues of race discrimination in the police department.

After a couple of administrative hearings, amidst much publicity, the

City of Troy finally changed its tune and did something meaningful for Lt. Hardy. He resigned from the Troy Police Department but was otherwise all smiles. We are limited by a confidential agreement from commenting further, but I had a very happy client.

I have stayed in touch with Ed Hardy in the months and years since. The last I heard he was working with the Union Springs Police Department and doing well.

Suicide Death in the Troy City Jail

A second case involved the suicide by hanging in the Troy City Jail of Timothy Henderson, a white male, on January 29, 2013. As tragic, avoidable, and unnecessary as it was, I learned years ago that, when something like this happens, one just "keeps on going." I'm closely associated with the phenomenon, having lost my dear brother David to suicide in 1976. The pain for the immediate family is indescribable. The compassion I've developed for victims is genuine. I have used it to comfort many others over the years. No one likes to talk about suicide, but families everywhere have suffered from such losses.

Thus I was a natural source of help for Timothy's widow, Cille Henderson, to call upon a few days later. Her need was as much for a psychological counselor as for a legal technician.

This was not the first time I had been visited by a grieving pregnant widow of a man who hung himself in a city jail. The first was a 1981 case involving a young African American man. After working hard on a contingency basis and taking the case to trial before a Montgomery jury, Judge Joe Phelps directed a verdict against my negligence claim. Almost 30 years later, the male baby inside the womb at the time of his father's death came to see me at my office, hoping to discover more about the father he never knew. I shared what I remembered.

The outcome in the Timothy Henderson case was much better. In fact, after qualifying Cille as administratrix of her deceased husband's estate, I made a demand upon the City of Troy, and its carrier, the Alabama Municipal Insurance Corporation, for the maximum statutory limit for a municipality, namely $100,000.

The case for liability of the City of Troy shaped up quickly and well. Not all disgruntled ex-employees of municipalities come to see me, but quite a few do. I had only recently been in the Troy news with Ed Hardy's case. Accordingly, recently fired Troy city jail employee Chris Harvey called me. While I quickly informed her I had a conflict and couldn't represent her, she impulsively told me what had happened to Timothy Henderson, and how she had been made the scapegoat.

Harvey said that, following Henderson's arrest on January 29, 2013, he was transported to the Troy jail by local police. He entered the jail at 10:14 p.m. Henderson believed he was unfairly charged with disorderly conduct upon arriving. He was argumentative with the officers present. He was given jail clothes, but Ms. Harvey was unable to complete a medical screening before her shift-ending time of 10:30 p.m. This was just before Henderson was placed in the jail cell.

Hence Timothy Henderson received a sheet and blanket for his cell before a "medical screening" could rule him out as a "danger to himself." The protocol questions to prospective inmates included "have you ever tried to commit suicide, or are you thinking about it?" Had either answer been "yes," or had the inmate been determined to be drinking (which was true for Henderson) then the inmate would be denied a sheet and blanket, which can be tools for a suicide.

With the timing of change of shifts, no screening was done for Henderson. When checked at 10:46 p.m., Henderson was okay, but during the 40 minutes between that time and the next check at 11:26 p.m., he had hung himself with his sheet, and jail officials could not revive him.

Henderson had only recently told someone that, if ever he went to the Troy city jail again, he would hang himself. Jail policy requiring checks once every 30 minutes or less was violated. The 40-minute interval was enough time to kill himself. Policy was also violated, since Timothy's drinking should have kept him away from hanging materials, but that did not happen.

In my June 11, 2013, "Notice of Claim," we alleged that Troy was negligent in (a) not checking on Timothy Henderson in a 30-minute time frame, and (b) not giving Henderson a "medical screening." Both negligences, we said, caused or contributed to Henderson's death. The local newspaper, the *Troy Messenger*, was all over the story. It reported both the initial suicide and the subsequent legal action.

The maximum statutory amount recoverable under Alabama law was $100,000. Henderson's adminstratrix-widow Cille Henderson also claimed an unlimited amount under federal law. While a Settlement Agreement later entered into required confidential terms, including non-disclosure to media, a final accounting filed with the Pike County Probate Judge's office in August 2014 unavoidably revealed that the full $100,000 statutory amount was paid. No amount of money, however, can ever equal the worth of the life of an individual. Cille Henderson was placated but not satisfied about losing her husband.

JEANNA BARNES V. PIKE COUNTY COMMISSIONER

A third case I handled involving Troy public officials was also in the headlines of the *Troy Messenger* in 2013–2014. Jeanna Barnes, the Pike County Emergency Management Agency director, an employee of the Pike County Commission, came to see me on July 25, 2013, sharing the amazing story that a member of the Pike County Commission, namely a 60-plus-year-old African American, Charles Harris, had been sexually harassing her. It started more mildly in July and November of 2010 with words about her having a "sexy face" and being a "sexy hot mama."

Barnes at first brushed off and ignored the descriptive terms. After all, she needed to get along with her boss. However, on February 2, 2011, Harris grabbed Barnes from behind, leaned into her, and kissed her on the forehead. He then bragged to a companion, "This is my big baby." Numerous past complaints against Commissioner Harris for sexual harassment were subsequently discovered by Barnes. The Pike County Commission convincingly informed Barnes that it would make Harris stop, if she would not pursue the matter further. Two and a half years passed without incident.

However, a fourth incident on July 22, 2013, was simply too much. When Harris determined that no one was looking, he grabbed both of Barnes's arms so forcibly that she couldn't move. Harris then started kissing Barnes and forced his tongue into her mouth. He pressed his genitals and body against her body. She finally managed to escape, and Harris said, "Don't run off, and don't tell anyone."

Instead, she came to me. An EEOC charge was filed on July 25, 2013. Fruitless negotiations caused a lawsuit to be filed on September 26, 2014. The suit was widely reported by the *Troy Messenger* and on area television stations. Early attempts to mediate failed, due to health problems of opposing counsel. Finally, on January 26, 2015, the parties and attorneys met at my office with mediator extraordinaire Phil Adams of Opelika, who heard the competing claims and defenses. After an all-day donnybrook, Adams proved why he is so highly regarded. In a confidential agreement, the case was resolved.

It is always rewarding to have a happy client. This case fell into that category.

Churches in Distress

I had two more cases in Troy during the past five years, both involving African American churches. In 2010, it was New Mt. Pleasant Missionary Baptist Church. I represented the church against a group of three to four renegade deacons. A successful court ruling forced the deacons to return money and property belonging to the church.

Then, in 2014, big-hearted Myrtle Tolbert came to see me about a lawsuit she had already filed against the pastor and two deacons of St. Peter's Missionary Baptist Church in Troy. This case is discussed in a later chapter.

Bettye Messick v. Troy Regional Medical Center

Increasingly senior citizens are working longer and later, proclaiming that "60 is the new 50," and "70 the new 60." Indeed, I am in that group, having turned 69 on November 13, 2015, and thinking that 75 looks like a good time to retire or at least slow down.

Thus, I was sympathetic and careful to listen to senior citizen Bettye Messick in April 2015 when she shared her unfortunate circumstances.

The affidavit we prepared for her charge of age discrimination said she was a "70-year-old female of Caucasian descent, and . . . of sound mind and body." She had been in the nursing profession for 46 years, was an RN, and had been at the Troy Regional Medical Center for 15 years, mostly in a supervisory position.

Messick's performance reports were overwhelmingly good until she reached age 70 in May 2014, she stated in a charge filed with the Equal Employment Opportunity Commission in Birmingham. Such a charge is a necessary first step to obtaining a "right to sue."

In late June 2014, Messick passed out in the hospital dining room during lunch. She needed three units of blood to respond to severe anemia. Fortunately the problem was easily treatable, and she soon recovered. Unfortunately, although she was capable of returning to work the next week, the hospital kept her out of work until December 8, 2014.

In her charge, Messick said the hospital and Dr. Rick Gill acted as if she had a serious medical problem, which she did not; she was fully capable of performing all the necessary duties and functions of her job.

Although Messick did return to work for two more months, she was terminated on January 29, 2015. It was apparent that her age, more than her medical status, was the "driving factor" in the hospital's continuing efforts to get rid of her as an employee in 2014–2015.

She also alleged a pattern and practice of older employees at Troy Regional being treated less well than younger employees, and older employees being fired or forced into resignation.

An attempted mediation in September 2015 was unsuccessful. Once the right-to-sue is received, a draft of a lawsuit will be sent to opposing counsel. If that doesn't resolve the dispute, a suit filed in federal court will be the next step.

I BELIEVE THE CITY of Troy has many good people, both black and white. My hope is that, as their native son John Lewis models, they eventually will learn to forgive one another and will grow into the "beloved community" that Martin Luther King Jr. so often preached about.

14

CHICKENS COMING HOME TO ROOST

I can't tell Erin Griggs's story without commenting on some other well-known local Montgomery personalities, including former probate judge Reese McKinney, and his then right-hand man Patrick Murphy, the identical twin brother of former police chief Kevin Murphy.

Reese McKinney climbed the ranks of Montgomery politics and society. My first experience with him was in 1989, when he was the top assistant to Montgomery Mayor Emory Folmar. The Fitzgerald Museum was about to open in May of that year. Museum board member and local realtor Martha Cassels had already obtained clearance from the mayor's office for the Museum to open without a zoning variance. That was because we were a "house museum." At the last moment, however, Reese called and said there was a "change of mind," that we needed the variance, but not to worry, it should pass easily with the Board of Adjustment.

Unfortunately, it did not. It may have been a trap, getting us to go to the Board of Adjustment. After we had our public opening party in mid-May 1989, the Board voted 3–2 against us, which would have closed us down. The next day I filed a lawsuit in Montgomery County's Circuit Court, and ultimately we prevailed. But I had had my first learning experience about the trustworthiness of Reese McKinney.

After Reese served as Emory Folmar's right-hand man for many years, he became probate judge of Montgomery County. Probate judges in most Alabama counties are not required to be attorneys, and Reese does not have a law license. Yet probate judges make commitment decisions, and he wrongfully committed, in my opinion, two of my clients against their wills. One was a school teacher in her early 50s who was committed by her dementia-suffering 80-year-old mother because she was upset with her daughter for missing Sunday lunches. Another client was a tenant committed by his landlord, after a dispute between the two. In the first case, I got the teacher released from commitment. The second case resulted in a lawsuit we filed against the landlord, which ultimately settled for good money.

These cases furthered lowered my opinion of Reese McKinney. I did some research and found that the Montgomery County Probate Court was committing three to four times as many people as were probate judges' offices in the counties serving the other three largest cities of Alabama, namely Mobile, Birmingham, and Huntsville. I wrote a letter about this to the *Montgomery Advertiser*. I'm sure Reese wasn't happy about that.

I was not surprised when Erin Smith Griggs contacted me on May 17, 2011, complaining about being terminated by Judge McKinney as a probate office employee. The rationale for her firing was that she had allegedly "forged" the names of certain registrants to motor vehicle certificates at the office. She vehemently denied the charge.

Pat Murphy entered the picture as legal counsel for Judge McKinney. In May to June 2011, we had several conversations. Murphy said that, if Ms. Griggs tried to challenge her termination, then "criminal charges for forgery" would be brought against her. Naturally, such bullying threats got my dander up.

Ms. Griggs assured me that she hadn't signed anyone's name and certainly had not forged anyone's name. Ms. Griggs was entitled to an initial administrative hearing at Judge McKinney's office before proceeding to Montgomery City-County Personnel Board appellate stages. Murphy gave me the names of four witnesses, who would testify that documents, purporting to reflect their signatures, were not truly their signatures.

We had an administrative hearing on May 18, 2011, before Judge McKinney. One of the four witnesses didn't show up. Of the three who did, two were African American men, neither of whom personally knew Ms. Griggs, who is also African American. The third witness was a well-dressed and bejeweled white female, looking like she had come straight from the Montgomery Country Club.

At the hearing, both black men admitted the signatures on the disputed documents were their own, but "signed in a hurry," such that their faster signature looked different from their slower one. The white woman, on the other hand, disputed that the signature on the document was actually hers. Ms. Griggs, on the other hand, insisted she had never signed anyone else's name.

I figured that surely we had won this hearing. The independent witnesses were 2–1 in our favor, plus we had Ms. Griggs's own strong testimony, which should have counted the most.

But it seemed that Judge McKinney already had someone else ready to take Ms. Griggs's job. His mind appeared made up in advance. McKinney took the words of the well-dressed white woman over the two modestly dressed African American men.

Frankly, I still believe this was a strong case of race discrimination on Reese McKinney's part. Ms. Griggs could not afford my services any further, although she got low-cost, last-minute representation from another attorney shortly before the personnel board hearing. That attorney was unable to put much time in the case, plus the City-County Personnel Board is known for being stacked in favor of management. An unsuccessful outcome was pre-ordained.

Thus, when I heard that Reese McKinney had a credible challenger in Steven Reed for the election of November 2012, I was only too happy to help my young neighbor. I held a well-attended reception for him at my home, and paid for a picture advertisement of Steve and me together in the *Montgomery Advertiser* sports pages. In beating incumbent Reese McKinney, Steven Reed achieved justice for many people, including Erin Griggs.

Also unhappy with McKinney over his role in a sale of land to Hyundai was attorney Tommy Gallion. He has a strong personality and deep Montgomery roots. His opposition to McKinney contributed to his defeat.

At one point during the campaign, there was an exchange of competing columns, one by civil rights activist Morris Dees explaining why he was endorsing a white man and decrying reverse race discrimination. My column was a strong endorsement of Reed and rebutted Dees's reverse race theory.

Admittedly, McKinney had his share of friends and supporters, but there were many others besides Gallion and me unhappy with his actions in office.

In the end, accordingly, McKinney's chickens came home to roost when the incumbent judge was beaten by a political newcomer.

15

JUDGE NOT, LEST YE BE JUDGED

The biblical admonition, "Judge not, lest ye be judged," applies to most people. Alabama court judges, however, enjoy an exception, known as "judicial immunity," which allows them to get away with some forms of misbehavior. That exception, however, has had its limits since former Alabama Chief Justice Howell Heflin pushed through state legislation in the 1970s creating the Alabama Judicial Inquiry Commission.

That said, one of the toughest but most enjoyable challenges of my legal career was to defend Jefferson County Domestic Relations Judge Dorothea Batiste against charges brought against her by the Alabama Judicial Inquiry Commission. Of course, it was, to put it mildly, probably the least enjoyable challenge of Judge Batiste's legal career.

It started with a telephone call the first work day of January 2013. A follow-up visit with her that first Saturday helped me rationalize not flying down to Miami for the national championship Alabama-Notre Dame football game despite some free tickets having popped up at the last moment.

Batiste, or "Judge" as I usually call her, was charming, attractive, and witty. Unfortunately, she had been suffering from months of oppression, first at the hands of Scott Vowell, presiding circuit judge of Jefferson County, and then from the Alabama Judicial Inquiry Commission (JIC). Batiste easily looked 10 years younger than her mid-40s age, and her infectious laugh was endearing.

After studying the complaints filed against Batiste, it appeared they were stirred up against her by the presiding judge. Although Batiste does not claim to be perfect, I became convinced that she was a victim who had been bullied and treated to a different standard than her Caucasian "comparator" judges from Jefferson and other counties.

To say that an African American female Republican judge from Birmingham is an oxymoron is an understatement. African Americans in Jefferson County are 90 percent Democratic. Batiste, however, although she has maternal roots in Birmingham, grew up in Louisiana. Hence her Cajun surname.

Her maternal grandfather left Birmingham in 1957, after the KKK made a midnight visit looking for his teenage son. The family fled to Chicago.

Several years later, Judge Batiste's mother met and married a man from Louisiana. In 1972, the couple with their three children moved to Louisiana, and later had three more children. Judge Dorothea Batiste is one of these six children, whose various adult careers have included police officer, assistant to the DA's office, professional football player, ship's captain, and sales clerk.

How Batiste was elected to public office in Birmingham, Alabama, is a tribute to the efforts of many disparate elements in Jefferson County, working together at the grass roots, and to her own hard work and winsome personality. Further, her election in 2010 upset a favored African American Democratic female.

Thus, the Democratic establishment of Jefferson County was not thrilled with Batiste to begin with. That included the presiding judge, who was politically renowned for having led, as a one-time Court of the Judiciary member, the successful ouster of Roy Moore as Chief Justice in 2003.

WHEN I STARTED EXAMINING the many grossly unfounded complaints against Dorothea, I thought the situation was mainly political. I knew that Vowell's strong ties to the Court of the Judiciary gave him a greater credibility with the Judicial Inquiry Commission than Dorothea ever would have. Unfair, but true.

This credibility disadvantage was even worse, given that the JIC panelists were older, white males except for one middle-aged white female attorney and a token black layperson. There were no female judges, white or black, and no black judges or lawyers of either gender on the JIC. To say the deck was demographically stacked against Dorothea was an understatement.

The frivolousness of one litigant's complaint against Judge Batiste was that she spelled his name wrong on the caption of the pleading, even though the original incorrect spelling came from the complainant's attorney. Unfortunately, the presiding judge had convened with local attorneys stirring up complaints. Moreover, two of those lawyers died before the case against Judge Batiste came to trial.

In early April 2013, the exhausted Judge Batiste nervously made a reluctant bombshell revelation to me. She disclosed that, starting in 2011, the presiding judge became flirtatious with her. In her subsequent sworn statement to the Equal Employment Opportunity Commission (EEOC) in 2013, Judge Batiste stated that, although there were 38 judges in the Jefferson County Circuit Court System, the presiding judge personally came to see her at least once a week in her office, always closing the door behind him.

He would ask how she was doing, pay her compliments, and sometimes give her a hug. One day in April 2011, according to my client, Vowell came up to Batiste, placed his body in front of hers, then put his arms down by her waist, with his fingers just above her bottom, and, with his mouth near her ear, whispered, "Boy! You're a hot little thing, and you're looking good in that dress today." Batiste says she brushed him off and stood there in shock and disbelief. This inappropriate and unwanted attention was documented in Batiste's notarized EEOC statement.

Vowell denied these allegations. He has long had his own set of admirers, including some people who are close to me. I could feel the winds blowing both ways. I also acknowledge that Vowell has done many good things in the legal world, has contributed generously to charities, and has been a leader in his church.

Regardless, Batiste said that for the next year, well into the summer of 2012, Vowell continued to flirt with her and comment on how good-looking she was, while she continued to politely rebuff him.

Batiste's allegations were confirmed in the evidence of sexual harassment she shared with the Alabama attorney general's investigators as early as September 2012. This was four months before coming to see me in January 2013. Unfortunately, the attorney general's office told the Judicial Inquiry Commission about Batiste's complaints, and word of them traveled back to Vowell, whose former status on the Court of the Judiciary kept him well connected to the JIC. In retaliation, Vowell turned up the heat on Batiste, and the complaints against her increased considerably.

Again, the sequence of events and the allegations against Vowell were stated in the EEOC charge that Batiste filed in April 2013. As a domestic relations judge, Batiste was not an expert on employment law and can thus be forgiven for not understanding that the worst part of sexual harassment is the retaliation one later receives for not caving in. It's not the upfront "hands on," and "words spoken" parts, but the follow-up for not giving in to an aggressor's seductive actions and words. I've seen this in countless cases in my law practice over the years.

And wow was Batiste retaliated against, or so it appeared! We vigorously fought off approximately 10 complaints against her. The formal complaint from the JIC was reduced to only four counts, each saying Judge Batiste had misused her contempt power.

This brought us to the final stage, namely the Alabama Court of the Judiciary, the only state court higher than the Alabama Supreme Court.

In preparation, I took Judge Vowell's deposition and obtained a number of startling admissions. He could not articulate how Batiste had violated any of the Rules of Judicial Ethics. And as JIC Chairman Judge Ben McLauchlin famously stated:

> Judge [referring to Batiste], regardless of what comes of this proceeding, I would urge you to do a careful study of the law of contempt. *I think you have a misunderstanding of some of the aspects of contempt. A lot of judges do. It's sort of a difficult aspect of the law; and we don't deal with it as much as we do* some other aspects; and consequently we don't – just not as familiar with it as we need to be. [Emphasis added.]

In my pre-trial brief, with exhibits, we pointed out the greatly favored treatment that had been received by other judges from the JIC. One white female domestic relations judge in Jefferson County had issued contempt sentences to five litigants, each over 100 days and one as much as 325 days for non-payment of child support. A white male judge in Chilton County had sentenced a litigant to six months in jail as a contempt sanction. Yet no complaints were brought by JIC against either of these judges, even though JIC was well aware of their practices.

The TV and print media in Montgomery and Birmingham were all over Batiste's case. A week before trial, the *Montgomery Advertiser* printed a large article that was sympathetic to her.

Yet others in the legal establishment had a different view.

The three days of trial in the marble-columned chambers of the Alabama Supreme Court finally came to pass. It was like something out of the movies. Prosecutor-attorney Griffin Sikes was vigorously pursuing the case and wanted nothing less than Batiste's head—that is, he wanted her permanently removed as a judge. The least punishment Sikes would agree to without a trial was a 10-month suspension. That was unacceptable to us.

I brought in my law partner Kenneth Shinbaum to assist me with the more esoteric aspects of the case, and there were several. The high court judges were perched in their pulpit seats, 15 feet above the main floor. Sikes and I slugged it out. It became cantankerous. At one point, responding to one of Sikes's contentions, I made the mistake of looking at him, rather than at the presiding judge of the Court of the Judiciary, namely Michael Joiner. As a result, Joiner held me in contempt.

Ironically, I guess Judge Joiner was trying to show me how my client had too easily found people in contempt, without a hearing. Obviously, I had no hearing. But Batiste's cases were for non-payment of child support, or failure to appear as a witness when subpoenaed, not for *looking* at opposing counsel. Upon my request, Joiner lifted his contempt citation an hour later. I guess it did make me "slightly tamer."

At the end of the three-day trial, the Court of the Judiciary found that Judge Batiste had violated certain judicial rules by not granting a sufficient hearing before holding certain litigants or witnesses in contempt. She was suspended for only 90 days. But this was a "big victory," Batiste said herself, as she retained her circuit judgeship.

Judge Batiste was genuinely grateful for my help. On my advice, she elected not to pursue her EEOC sexual harassment complaint against Vowell. By then, in August 2013, Batiste was exhausted and suffering medical conditions that required some three months of treatment in hospitals and at home in Louisiana. The great tension from the JIC prosecution contributed significantly to her health issues, but the source of that tension was now eradicated. The 90 days off was actually a blessing that restored her health.

Vowell reached the mandatory judicial retirement age and left the bench in January 2014. In her first two years back on the bench, Judge Batiste has done well, with no complaints levied against her by the JIC. She has an excellent mentor in former judge Quentin Brown and a new presiding judge in Houston Brown. She is a decent, caring, and conscientious judge.

However, when a judge does domestic relations work, as Batiste still does, he or she can experience complaints from litigants who don't think he or she got enough of the disputed property, or custody of children. Therefore, Batiste can likely expect a complaint or two to pop up again. Notwithstanding, an article of her Christian faith is forgiveness. Accordingly, Batiste has forgiven Vowell for his mistreatment of her, wishes him well, and looks forward to more good years on the bench.

In late April 2015, Batiste was elected a board member of the pro-life Alabama Lawyers for Unborn Children. I, too, am a board member, and look forward to working with her on this good cause. On May 16, 2015, Batiste married her devoted Louisiana boyfriend, Alvin Young, in New Orleans. Along with paralegal Carlton Avery and law partner Kenneth Shinbaum and his wife Fern, I attended their wedding at the St. Louis Cathedral in Jackson Square. We all enjoyed the festivities.

I have represented, with good results, several other judges before the Alabama Judicial Inquiry Commission, including Dallas County Circuit Judge Richard "Dick" Norton of Selma and former Birmingham Municipal Court Judge David Barnes (now deceased).

Should I ever have to represent any more judges before the Alabama Judicial Inquiry Commission, at least I will have the pleasant duty of working with Rosa Hamlett Davis. Rosa was an assistant attorney general for more than forty years before going to work for the JIC. Indeed when I first showed up for duty on April 28, 1975, to work under Attorney General Bill Baxley, Rosa's office was immediately adjacent to mine. We've stayed friends over the years. Hopefully we'll work things out for any future clients of mine.

16

LAWYERS NEED HELP, TOO

It is a privilege and a high calling to defend other lawyers. Over the years I have represented many attorneys who had disciplinary issues with the Alabama Bar Association.

The general counsel of the Bar's disciplinary office is Tony McLain, a reasonable and seasoned barrister with broad knowledge of the pitfalls and potholes of law practice. I first came to know Tony while skiing at Big Sky in Montana in 1988, during an Alabama Trial Lawyers Seminar. Tony is ably assisted by attorneys Tripp Vickers and Jeremy McIntire, among others, including the veteran Bonnie Mainer.

I believe the Bar sometimes is overwhelmed with complaints, many legitimate. Further, it is not well-equipped to investigate improper solicitation of auto accident cases.

Lawyers have civil rights, too, and the old adage that "a lawyer who represents himself has a fool for a client" is particularly true in disciplinary proceedings. It is much better to have another lawyer assert your civil rights. That is especially so in a reinstatement proceeding, when being contrite, remorseful, and humble are necessary ingredients for a disciplined attorney seeking re-entry.

It is also true that a lawyer must be careful to avoid violating the disciplinary rules, not just to protect the interests of his client but to protect himself. While lawyers have an ethical duty to zealously represent their clients, they must avoid overzealous representation that offends judges, steps on too many toes, or steps on the wrong set of toes.

At the same time, a lawyer must have the courage or backbone to take on tough cases and take bold steps to protect the interests of his clients. In my law firm, I'm known for taking cases that most of my partners would turn down. This is sometimes wise, resulting in greater financial returns, and sometimes not.

However, my yardstick for taking a case is not just the "business interest" but the "justice interest." That is, an egregious injustice motivates me. The other side is that, before getting involved, like all attorneys I need to carefully assess how much time a case is going to take, as there is only so much room on one's plate, especially in plaintiff's law, which is predominantly my type of practice.

In 2013–2015, I represented two young attorneys after they had first received discipline from the Alabama State Bar Association. In both cases, I first handled an appeal to the Alabama Supreme Court. Both had 91-day suspensions, together with the public reprimand that goes along with it. In my opinion, both are fine young men and talented attorneys with potentially bright futures. Both have acknowledged their legal shortcomings.

They were willing for me to share their experiences and give my take on what happened.

TRENT GARMON

Trent Garmon of Gadsden was 28 at the time of his alleged solicitation offense in Etowah County in September 2011. I had represented his father Leon in disciplinary cases in the 1980s–1990s. Both father and son felt the Bar disciplinary panel's harsh treatment of Trent on a first offense went too far. Trent insisted his intention in calling the parents of a child killed in an auto accident was to refer them to a ministry experienced in helping such grieving people. The Bar called it an unethical solicitation.

Before I began to represent Trent, he had already turned down a Bar offer for a reprimand only in return for a guilty plea. Trent truly believed his motive was ministerial and not to get legal business. A bar hearing panel found him guilty and ordered him to serve a 91-day suspension.

Up to a 90-day suspension allows for immediate, automatic reinstatement. Any suspension of even one more day than 90 days requires a reinstatement hearing, the application for which can not be made until the suspension has run. After application, one must wait weeks or months more for a reinstatement hearing. Hence, the term "91-day suspension" is very misleading, because it can morph easily into 151 days, 181 days, or more.

Trent did well in his first reinstatement proceeding. He was genuinely humble and sorry. He was reinstated, subject to accepting a mentorship from a more seasoned attorney in Gadsden.

MARK OVERALL

The disciplinary case of Mark Overall of Dothan proved quite different. For one thing, instead of being a white Southerner like Trent Garmon, Mark is an African American Northerner. Mark's primary reason for being in trouble with the Bar was being late for court appearances, resulting in his being held in contempt by judges, or for other related disrespectful behavior. Part of Mark's problem was the lack of smoothness in his presentations to judges. Some considered him arrogant. Coming from his working class background of Buffalo, New York, Mark didn't have the easier rapport with judges or court officials that home-grown Southern attorneys either have or know how to cultivate.

In May 2013, Mark pled guilty to the Bar's disciplinary charges; he accepted a 91-day suspension, with a condition it be held in abeyance during a two-year probation. Mark initially believed he'd be back in the legal business in 91 days. He soon discovered otherwise. At his first reinstatement hearing, Mark represented himself. After the hearing began on March 19, 2014, he called me on one hour's notice to come and be a character witness for him. I dropped everything, dashed over to the Bar's office, and testified as Mark's only witness other than himself and one other person.

However, he had 10 supportive letters from local judges and nine more from respected attorneys. Yet the panel denied Mark's reinstatement. Suddenly another 365 days were added to the 6 months Mark had already been unable to practice.

After pursuing an unsuccessful appeal to the Supreme Court, Mark on his own filed two suits against the Alabama State Bar, one alleging race discrimination, the other a more general challenge to procedures. I later convinced him that his suits were counterproductive, and Mark dropped them.

Finally, one year later, or September 23, 2015, Mark had a second hearing, but I started representing him. He had the same letters from judges and attorneys, which were admitted and were highly supportive. Again, at his own insistence, Mark's only witness was himself. He sat on the witness stand for a grueling four hours and did his best to answer the panel members' questions. Unfortunately, after extended deliberation, the panel again voted against Mark's reinstatement. It will be another year before he is eligible for reinstatement. That seems very unfair to me. One of Mark's strongest local supporters, the Honorable Charles Price, the exalted but retired former presiding circuit judge of Montgomery County, was incensed.

I was surprised by the results, but not too surprised. Unfortunately, the Alabama Bar establishment was not ready to take Mark back.

I represented Mark pro bono, due to his tight financial circumstances. After being out of work so long, Mark didn't have the financial resources to pay for a transcript on appeal. Afterwards, Bar attorney Jeremy McIntire offered to help Mark with a roadmap for re-entry. Mark is considering that, but he is also considering moving further north, where he believes his views, appearance, and manners will be more acceptable than in Alabama.

That would be Alabama's loss, in my opinion. We need more attorneys like Mark, with the guts to take on tough cases against the establishment. Yes, he could use more polish and some mentoring. I offered to the Bar to provide mentoring to Mark.

I will continue to counsel Mark, at no expense. There are many junior attorneys out there like Mark and Trent, who are solo practitioners. They need counsel and guidance. Young lawyers in bigger, established firms have advantages. It is incumbent upon all of us more senior lawyers to help our younger brethren whenever we can.

The Alabama Bar Association has for years had a fine executive director in Keith Norman, and before him Reggie Hamner did a good job. I have recommended to Jeremy McIntire, and through him to Tony McLain, that a volunteer senior mentoring program be set up to help young lawyers in private practice who are unconnected with a big law firm. I know I'm glad to help, even at my ripe, young age of 69.

17

MISSIONARY BAPTIST CHURCHES IN CONFLICT

Somehow the word has gotten around central Alabama that I am the attorney to go to if you're in an internal church dispute, and need legal help. From the 1980s on, I've helped one side or the other in multiple cases. More often than not, they've involved Missionary Baptist congregations. This is a major denomination in the African American community.

A picture in the central hallway of my office building shows me standing beside my client Pastor Raymond Thomas in 2008, with a court order favoring him in his dispute with church deacons at Lilly Hill Baptist in Prattville.

Most recently, I worked with Missionary Baptist Church congregations in Tuskegee, Troy, and Montgomery.

GREENWOOD MISSIONARY BAPTIST CHURCH, TUSKEGEE

In the Tuskegee case, deacons Cornell Tatum, Charlie Hardy, Charles Lancaster, James Upshaw, and Lucius Fleming Sr. approached me in June to help them with a great divide that had developed between them and the pastor of their congregation, Greenwood Missionary Baptist Church.

Greenwood was a proud, older church, attended in its early years by Booker T. Washington. Unfortunately an irreconcilable dispute developed. We represented the overwhelming majority of the deacons, led by Chairman Tatum and Deacon Hardy. A majority of the congregation, the pastor, and the vice chairman of the deacons were on the other side, represented by Brian Strength, a local attorney. Strength filed suit against three of the deacons on behalf of certain church members.

The influential vice chairman leading the other side was Macon County District Judge Aubrey Ford. His close friendship with Circuit Judge Tom Young caused us to file a motion for Judge Young to recuse himself. Young denied the motion and ruled against us on the merits of the case, granting the other side a preliminary injunction. Shortly thereafter in August 2014, law partner Kenneth Shinbaum and I filed a petition for a Writ of Mandamus in the Alabama Supreme Court raising the issues of (a) lack of subject matter jurisdiction; (b) failure to join indispensable parties; and (c) failure of Judge Young to recuse himself.

The Alabama Supreme Court finally issued a ruling almost a year later, on July 10, 2015. It was apparent the case had stirred up strong but conflicting opinions among the nine justices. Chief Justice Roy Moore and Glen Murdock ruled in our favor, but the other justices were against us, with Tom Parker writing a long, concurring opinion. Parker turned our main point against us. Rather than agreeing with us that the Court lacked jurisdiction to resolve a religious dispute, he basically opined that our deacon clients lacked jurisdiction to challenge the church's removal of them from their deaconships.

Obviously, our deacons weren't happy with the Supreme Court majority's opinion. I urged the three deacons to try to resolve the case with the help of a seasoned Baptist moderator acting as a mediator. The last I talked with our clients, they were still considering their options but were undecided.

St. Peter's Missionary Baptist Church, Troy

The second church seeking my help was St. Peter's Missionary Baptist Church in Troy. Again, I represented the minority faction of approximately forty, led by Myrtle Tolbert, a 63-year-old woman with a friendly, expansive personality. She had already filed her own suit against the former pastor and deacons moving the church to a new location, over her strong objections.

After the parties had been in court several times, the judge finally ordered that a mediation take place. Troy attorney Thad Yancey generously agreed to conduct the mediation in his office at no cost. On the other side, the pastor's attorney, Joel Lee Williams, was a calming influence on his clients, namely the Rev. T. B. Moultry and certain deacons.

Property and financial issues dividing the parties were difficult to resolve. At the mediation, I suggested a two-campus coexistence, with a new associate pastor ministering to Ms. Tolbert's allies at the old location. Pastor Moultry would continue presiding at the newer building and would be senior pastor over all. For a while I thought the sides were too far apart, but finally, after praying with all parties and attorneys participating, the case settled.

My diplomatic skills have never been used to settle foreign entanglements, but they apparently work well in church disputes and did so in this case. Lingering issues have created some turmoil, but overall there is "peace in the valley." At least for a while.

Shiloh Missionary Baptist Church, Montgomery

The last but not least of the three churches was Shiloh Missionary Baptist

Church, coincidentally located in Montgomery only a few blocks from my home. In late September 2014, chief trustees Lee Sanford and James Long and head deacons Norman Williams and Jeffrey Reese visited me to share an amazing tale.

The preceding Sunday, the long-time pastor of the church, the Rev. Juan McFarland, disclosed from the pulpit that he was HIV positive as early as 2003 and now had AIDS. Furthermore, McFarland confessed to having had unprotected sex, inside the church facilities, with women of the congregation. On top of that, McFarland admitted to using illegal drugs and stealing church money.

Despite these confessions, Rev. McFarland astonishingly refused to step down as pastor. Once again I brought in my amateur rabbi and law partner Kenneth Shinbaum to help. We drafted several resolutions, which passed 80–2 the next Sunday. One resolution overturned a dictatorial constitution protecting the pastor. Another resolution removed McFarland as pastor. A third reaffirmed the authority of the board of deacons. A fourth established a search committee for a new pastor.

Nonetheless, amazingly and defiantly, an out-of-touch-with-reality McFarland refused to leave.

The following Tuesday, October 14, we filed suit for injunctive relief in Montgomery County Circuit Court. By then, the local, state, and national press were having a field day with the sensational story. Friends in West Virginia and California say they saw my picture in their newspapers in connection with stories about the case.

Montgomery Circuit Presiding Judge Charles Price set a hearing for two days later. Rev. McFarland was present, without counsel, and did not testify. Following presentation of evidence, Judge Price ruled that McFarland was out as pastor, and could not return to the church. Further, Price ordered McFarland to turn over his keys to the church as well as his church-financed Mercedes-Benz.

The news media was allowed inside the courtroom for the hearing. The case even made international news. This included an Italian camera crew and reporter, who interviewed me afterwards. Once again, Montgomery's name was sullied and tarnished.

However, Shiloh Missionary was able to do a clean sweep and is again functioning as a healthy, viable church.

18

Double Duty

How does an attorney get to do civil rights work for a client, and then perform a wedding ceremony for the same client? I call it "Double Duty," and I've had the great honor of doing it twice.

The first wedding was for my client Andy McCarter and his bride Kelly Liles in the spring of 2013. The second was for client Mark Boddie, whose case I handled from June 2012 to October 2014, but whose wedding ceremony was performed on March 23, 2014.

Best Buy Employees Seek Relief

Mark Boddie was the second of two Best Buy employees who came to see me in 2012 with substantial beefs about their employer. The first was Ravane Fall, a cheerful native of Senegal who became a naturalized citizen. He had a race and national origin discrimination case against Best Buy of Opelika, after he was wrongfully terminated.

Ravane was articulate, decent, and a well-educated product of Alabama's top private secondary school, namely Indian Springs School in Helena, near Birmingham. Half of Indian Spring's seniors every year are National Merit semi-finalists. Ravane, coincidentally, was a classmate of my nephew, Alex McPhillips.

The mistreatment of Ravane was serious enough that his case settled quickly. Typically, however, the terms were confidential, and I regret that I can say nothing more.

The good results for Ravane soon brought another interesting client with a Best Buy problem, namely Mark Boddie. At age 24, Mark was only three feet tall and weighed only 56 pounds, but he otherwise knew few limitations. Exceedingly bright and almost saintly in his cheerfulness, he could move himself around well in a motorized wheelchair.

Using a customized car, Mark drove himself places without assistance. When he came to see me in June 2012, he lived alone and could take care of himself. Seeing how well Mark managed his life would make most able-bodied citizens feel ashamed if they ever complained about any physical limitation of any type. He was and is an enormous inspiration to me.

Mark's unlawful employment discrimination case was based on violations of the Americans with Disabilities Act. What happened to him was ridiculous, and I was greatly surprised that Best Buy ever let it happen. It was to Best Buy's credit that it hired Mark in the first place, given his disabilities. Yet with Mark's winsome personality, he became the second-highest-performing salesperson in Best Buy's Opelika store. The company made plenty of profit off the hard-working, ever-smiling Mark.

Unfortunately, as reflected in public-record EEOC filings by Mark in Birmingham, the store manager, Peter Khun, needed extra money. He hit up his lower-level employee, Mark, for a personal loan. Over a period of time, and under pressure, Mark had loaned his boss $2,600, yet only $100 was paid back.

Mark complained to Best Buy's human resources department about what was going on, but nothing was done. Mark also talked to the assistant manager about what was happening, but the situation was laughed off.

Mark documented the occasions between April 2010 and April 2012 when he loaned money to Peter Khun. Mark felt quite pressured by his boss, who said Mark would benefit in various ways and could advance at Best Buy, despite his limitations.

The whole situation was unconscionable and shocking. Mark was also ridiculed by having his face, incongruously in a KKK hood, superimposed on a picture of a young child. Khun and another Best Buy manager told Mark he looked just like the photograph.

When Mark began trying to get his money back, Khun cut Mark's work hours from 36 hours a week to 22 hours. That's when Mark came to see me.

I filed Mark's charge with the EEOC in June 2012; two supplemental charges were filed in September 2012. I tried to negotiate with the same Atlanta attorneys who had represented Best Buy in the Ravane Fall case. This time, however, the company gave its attorney different marching orders against settlement. We therefore filed suit on May 13, 2013, in the federal district court in Montgomery.

Just as discovery was cranking up, the U.S. magistrate assigned to the case, Terry Moorer, agreed to mediate a resolution. The first attempt was unsuccessful. However, on Judge Moorer's own initiative, and to his credit, he called both sets of attorneys, got us into court, and under his persuasive influence, the case settled in October 2013.

Once again, the resolution included language of confidentiality about its terms. The exciting thing for Mark and his able-bodied girlfriend, Candice, was that they now had enough financial stability in their lives to consider getting married.

Knowing of my sideline involvement in ministry and my ordination with the Global Evangelical Christian Church denomination, they soon asked me if I'd perform their wedding ceremony. Having previously checked out the bonafides of my qualifications to do the same for an earlier client, as well as my office manager's son, I quickly agreed. Of course it was my joy and honor to do so, and I charged them nothing for the privilege.

Accordingly, on March 23, 2014, on a beautiful Saturday afternoon in Opelika, with a crowd of about 100 people present, I happily joined them together as man and wife. I'm sure I sounded like my ministerial father in the homily comments that I made.

Sadly, Mark Boddie passed away in August 2015. His death, according to his mother, Lisa Sizemore, was unexpected, sudden, and shocking, and no one knows the cause. Perhaps it was a heart attack.

While I mourn Mark's passing, especially at such an early age, I am thankful that I was able to help make his life richer in his last few years, and his life also encouraged mine.

BUCKMASTERS AND BLACK EXPO STAFFERS

Andy McCarter, a 28-year-old African American man came to see me on August 21, 2012, about a race discrimination claim against Buckmasters, the deer hunting-related media and retail conglomerate that began in Montgomery in 1986. Andy was unhappy about not being able to participate in a Buckmasters Expo at the Renaissance Hotel in Montgomery, only a week earlier.

The background reasons for Andy's unhappiness were set forth in an EEOC charge he filed himself in November 2012, but were repeated in greater detail in an amended charge I prepared for him in February 2013.

Both charges are public record, still on file with the EEOC in Birmingham. Andy is extremely bright, with a great personality, and was a good salesman. He was generally liked and appreciated by most of his superiors at Buckmasters. The problem was that the Buckmasters Expo overwhelmingly attracted an audience of white hunters. Many were "country whites," who apparently were considered by some Buckmasters managers as not receptive to Andy's profile.

Andy alleged that he was not the only black Buckmasters employee denied work because of his race. He also said that some people at Buckmasters were uncomfortable because of his interracial relationship with his fiancée, Kelly Liles, a white Buckmasters employee.

There was one very strong piece of evidence related to the racial nature of Andy's not working the Expo. However, given the confidential resolution of the dispute later worked out, I can't provide any further discussion of it.

Suffice it to say that Andy and Kelly were sufficiently pleased with the outcome. It helped them in several important respects. Accordingly, feeling more secure, they asked me to perform their wedding ceremony. As was the case with Mark Boddie, I considered it an honor and privilege and did so at no cost to the young couple.

MARK'S AND ANDY'S WERE pure civil rights cases, but they involved ministry not only in the legal work but certainly in the wedding ceremonies. Both cases were very satisfying to handle, from beginning to end.

19

A Good Samaritan or Not?

A Good Samaritan or not? That was the question bouncing around the airwaves, restaurants, and social media of Evergreen, Alabama, a country town 90 miles southwest of Montgomery, in 2014. Located in a county perhaps best known for its spicy Conecuh sausage, the locale has produced many colorful personalities.

None are more colorful, more homegrown, more controversial, and yet more beloved than James Leon Windham. In a local radio poll in April 2014, Leon was voted the "Greatest Good Samaritan" in Conecuh County, but also the "Biggest Son-of-a-Bitch."

Born on October, 20, 1946, Leon is only three weeks older than me. When I first met him in my office in October 2013, his long white, mangy beard echoed Santa Claus, minus the red clothes. Leon could also have passed for a Confederate veteran, but, if so, a kindly one with a heart for his local black brothers. His country wit and charm barely masked his superior intellect.

He was indeed known as Santa to local residents. For many years he collected toys and delivered them at Christmas to less fortunate children. In addition, he managed to get food to needy families. Leon also noted there was no Red Cross or similar organization available to assist in times of disaster. So he and his wife Tess established a free clothing locker for anyone in need due to fire or other loss or inability to cope.

Leon grew up in Conecuh County and after high school graduation in 1965 enlisted in the United States Navy. As an aircrewman, he served all over the world, including multiple tours in Vietnam. He served honorably for 28 years before retiring and moving back to Conecuh to care for his aging mother, upon a sibling's untimely death.

Many Evergreen citizens loved and cheered Leon for being a whistleblower against the wrongdoing of the Conecuh County Commission. Indeed, Leon was not shy about filing ethic complaints and citing Open Meetings Law violations against two of its commissioners, the red-faced Johnny Andrews and Commission Chairman David Cook.

Leon loudly blamed those two officials for inciting local yokel Terry Gray to file a Class C felony "Interference with Custody" charge against him.

Its roots were at the Conecuh County Animal Shelter in Evergreen, where Leon's wife Tess and Terry Gray both worked, where Gray's elementary school-age children were dropped off by a school bus at the animal shelter. Tess often helped to look after them. On April 8, 2013, the Windhams received word that the county commission was terminating Tess. At midday, Leon came by to see his wife, and an unfriendly exchange passed between Terry and Leon, who believed Terry was complicit in Tess's ouster.

About mid-afternoon Leon returned to pick up Tess at her scheduled get-off time and permanently remove her belongings. Upon arrival, Leon observed the two Gray children, a nine-year-old son and a five-year-old daughter, being dropped off at the shelter by the school bus. Father Terry Gray was nowhere around. Without the Windhams there, the children would have been left unattended. After waiting 10 minutes and making calls to county officials, including Commission Chairman Cook, the Windhams agreed it was unsafe to leave the children by themselves on the street in front of the shelter. Yet the Windhams needed to leave. So they took the children to their mother, divorced from dad Terry, at the Burger King two miles away.

Afterwards, commissioners Andrews and Cook met with Terry Gray, who was vengeful over the earlier altercation with Leon. They eventually accompanied Terry to a grand jury, and guess what? Leon was indicted for interfering with child custody, but not his wife, Tess. Leon was understandably livid that his Good Samaritan deed had been so wrongly construed and harshly punished. Given the absence of charges against his wife, and the commissioners' presence, the political nature of the indictment was blatantly obvious.

Trial was set for April 2014. Only a few days before trial the prosecution advised the defense that a videotaped testimony of the children existed. Although pre-trial discovery had been requested months earlier, this video, recorded in April 2013, made its appearance just before trial, along with the local district attorney's motion for a continuance. Leon, anxious to get his name cleared, opposed the continuance, and trial preparations continued unabated.

All the local judges had recused themselves, so Alabama Chief Justice Roy Moore appointed Judge Ashley McKathan of neighboring Covington County to preside. Preparing carefully the preceding Easter weekend, Leon and I showed up on Monday, ready to go. Yet District Attorney Steve

Wadlington secured a last-minute continuance. A new trial date was set for November 2, 2014.

Afterwards, Wadlington received so many irate letters from Conecuh County citizens challenging the prosecution that he withdrew. Attorney General Luther Strange's office was asked to take over the prosecution. Appointed to do so was the seasoned Stephanie Billingslea. Like her, all 12 jurors were African American, and like her, seven of the 12 were female.

I had preached to Leon about the importance of jury selection. He did not need much preaching. He was already on it. With his network of friends, Leon attained great intelligence on our prospective white jurors. About half were good, half bad. We struck the bad half, and the prosecution (with knowledgeable help from the county commissioners) struck our good half. And with an overall panel about 60 percent black, we ended up with an all-black jury. Leon later said that he and Tess had agreed that if they ended up with an all-black jury, that would not be a bad thing.

Not so.

Aided by associate attorney Chase Estes, we tried a good case, and even proved that Commissioner Cook had secretly paid Terry Gray at least $100 in cold cash, giving the appearance of a bribe and/or payoff. Gray admitted that nothing was asked of him in return. We also showed how the local detective investigator conducted a biased investigation, leaving out requested security videos from Burger King, and never reviewing the safety tape from the bus.

A big dispute existed over the admissibility of an audio-video tape, which I believe violated many rules of evidence. Assistant AG Billingslea assured the Court at the pre-trial hearing in late October 2014 that she would not be using it. Hence, Leon and I decided not to call an expensive expert to rebut it. That was a mistake.

Nonetheless, the all-black jury of seven women and five men obviously connected better with the younger African American Billingslea than it did with Leon and me, two 68-year-old Caucasian men. Billingslea interjected that I had somehow opened the door to the bad videotape, and Judge McKathan allowed it in, showing the young children looking victimized and scared.

I became worried when the jury, after initial deliberations, asked to have the tape replayed for them, and the judge allowed it. This video recording went against virtually every rule of proper testimony, with the two investigators asking leading questions and interjecting answers toward Corey Gray's testimony. All this was done with the children's father, Terry Gray, in the interrogation area, and his interruptions and corrections were allowed.

Also present was Corey's younger sister Bailey, who did not speak but added sympathy for the prosecution.

Long story short, the jury ruled against Leon Windham. But, as I told Leon walking out of the courthouse, this battle was far from over. The words were prophetic. A first set of post-trial motions was denied. With leadership help from Brewton attorney Kevin McKinley, a second set, challenging the improper out-of-county residency of one juror, was filed.

We had a hearing in early December 2014, and Judge McKathan granted our motion, leading to a new trial being granted—a victory of sorts, if not an acquittal.

It's been more than a year now, and no new efforts have been made to push the case to trial again. I believe that everyone was exhausted by the first trial, including the prosecutor's witnesses. It appears at this point the attorney general's office has bigger fish to fry.

William Shakespeare wrote a famous line that is often applicable, hopefully here. He said, "All's well that ends well." Nonetheless, during the preceding year, valuable lessons were learned.

20

BLACK LIVES MATTER

I have no problem saying "black lives matter" and saying it loudly. Yes, all lives do matter, as those pushing back on this issue have become fond of saying. But unfortunately racism is an epidemic in America, and way too many black lives do not matter enough, both to Caucasians and African Americans.

I admit that I have an affinity for immigrants and for African Americans. Accordingly, I have found joy, mission, and purpose in helping African immigrants, including Chichi Oji and her husband Success Jumbo of Nigeria, Peter Owuor and his sister Caroline Owuor of Kenya, and Caroline and Valentine Kemali and their extended family, also of Kenya.

Our first priest at Christ the Redeemer, Resurrected was the Reverend James Muriuki of Kenya. I have enjoyed helping him, his dear wife Jane, and their American-born children, Shalom and Reuben. All are quite talented. I've also helped Moses Semakula of Uganda and Niakour Fall of Senegal maintain their legal statuses. All of the above-named Africans are very smart people.

Hence, I was not surprised when, on December 11, 2014, I was visited by an exceedingly bright Dr. Emanuel Oranika and his wife Patience, both originally from Nigeria. Emanuel's Ph.D. is in urban planning and transportation systems, and he works for the Alabama Department of Transportation. Patience, an employee of the Alabama Department of Education, is nearing completion of requirements for an Ed.D. Both Oranikas deservedly became American citizens in earlier years. It is clear that in the process they learned much about the U.S. Constitution. So did their daughter, Jane, who was 17 and a senior at Booker T. Washington Magnet School when the Oranikas came to see me.

Given the then-recent tragedies in Ferguson, Missouri; Coney Island, New York; and Alexander City, Alabama, where innocent young black males had their lives snuffed out by heavy-handed law enforcement officers who suffered no legal consequences, young Jane decided to use her First Amendment free speech rights. She posted in the school hallway an 8x11-inch flyer, with an

American flag occupying much of the space and the bottom portion boldly proclaiming in capital letters and bold print: BLACK LIVES MATTER.

Rather than being commended for her initiative and sensitivity, young Jane found herself on the receiving end of school discipline with a suspension. An original one-day penalty morphed into a four- to five-day suspension, which was highly upsetting to both Jane and her parents.

Accordingly, on that same December 11, I caused a two and a half page letter to be hand-delivered to Montgomery County School Superintendent Margaret Allen and Dr. Quesha Starks, principal of Booker T. Washington, who had handed out the discipline. I cited the 1969 U.S. Supreme Court decision *Tinker v. Des Moines Independent School District*, 393 U.S. 503 as precedent.

I requested an immediate expungement of the suspension from Jane Oranika's record and a counseling of Dr. Starks about the First Amendment rights of students. I also requested that Jane not be harassed, intimidated, or retaliated against in any way. I further requested that Jane be allowed to make up classes and tests she missed and requested other relief.

I met face-to-face with Dr. Allen and her energetic attorney, Vernetta Perkins, a few days later, and then with Dr. Starks and her well-known attorney Lewis Gillis shortly after that. On December 23, 2014, I received a hand-delivered letter from Ms. Perkins certifying the following relief:

> 1. The suspension issued by the principal pursuant to the office referral dated December 4, 2014, is rescinded and we will facilitate the completion of all missed coursework, assignments and/or other projects.
>
> 2. The district will offer counsel to Dr. Starks concerning our expectations in handling issues of this nature.
>
> 3. The district will offer guidance to other principals and senior level administrative staff concerning our expectations in handling issues of this nature.
>
> 4. There will be no harassment or retaliation by any district personnel toward Jane Oranika or her parents pursuant to their challenge of this issue.
>
> 5. Should any future disputes arise, the district will work with the principal and the parents to ensure prompt resolution consistent with district policies.

I commend Emanuel and Patience Oranika and their courageous daughter Jane for standing up not only for the precious principle that all black lives matter, but also for reminding native-born Americans that the U.S.

Constitution's guarantees of freedom of speech (especially in matters of public interest) also matter.

Unfortunately, in April 2015, Dr. Oranika brought me proof that, months later, the suspension was still on Jane's record. I had to call attorney Vernetta Perkins. She was profusely apologetic and promised to clear up the discrepancy immediately. I understand that has been done.

21

LIBERATED FROM THE PUNITIVE
SEXUAL OFFENDER SYSTEM

One of the harshest and really most unfair aspects of penal systems in Alabama and throughout America is that of "sexual offender registration" laws. Once convicted, no matter how minor the offense, such as two teenagers engaging in consensual sex, one is branded for life with "SO"—modern-day scarlet letters. One becomes a lifetime member of a league of undesirables as untouchable as the lowest caste in India.

The onerous requirements of the sexual offender registration system in Alabama are excessively punitive and almost impossible to escape. Once so classified, one cannot live within 2,000 feet of a school or day care center, or be near minor children. One must also report multiple times a year to law enforcement and pay certain fees. Convicted sexual offenders may as well be lepers. No one wants them in their neighborhood, although many, like the two whose stories are told below, are actually decent people, who didn't deserve to be in the system in the first place.

A SEIZURE LEADS TO PRISON

Bruce Stolts, now 46 years old, suffers from about as many physical and mental ailments as anyone I have ever met. His frequent seizures have been especially disabling.

One day in 2005, a seizure hit Bruce while he was walking in Montgomery's Vaughn Road Park. In the grip of the seizure, without realizing what he was doing, Bruce exposed himself at a distance to a young girl; he had no actual contact with her. Bruce was arrested on a charge of "public indecent exposure."

A more aggressive defense could have gotten him a better outcome, but Bruce's court-appointed attorney negotiated a plea to a Sexual Offender II violation. Bruce received a four-year prison sentence, but given his medical condition he was out in two years.

Bruce's parents are dead, but Sandi Kerr made a deathbed promise to

Bruce's mother that she (Sandi) would look out for Bruce. Sandi and Bruce's mother were best friends since they began working together at Bruno's over thirty years ago.

Sandi, 63, is frail herself but sees me most Sunday nights at Christ the Redeemer Episcopal Church (see Chapters 35 and 36).

So Sandi and her devoted husband, Michael Kerr, 74, came to me for help. I explained the low odds of getting a pardon from the Alabama Board of Pardons and Paroles. But, bolstered by much prayer at church, and greatly assisted by associate attorney Chase Estes, we put together a good package for the Parole Board.

Most importantly, we persuaded two of the law enforcement officials to whom Bruce reported, Tracy LaChance of the Montgomery Police Department and Lt. Leigh Persky of the Montgomery Sheriff's Office, to testify on Bruce's behalf. Following the hearing on January 27, 2015, much to my surprise, the Pardons and Parole Board members acted like Bruce's case was unprecedented in having so much law enforcement support. I spoke first, pointing out all the extenuating circumstances, but the words of Ms. LaChance and Lt. Persky carried the day.

"Barely contained ecstasy" was the mood in the hearing room among Bruce, the Kerrs, Chase, me, and even LaChance and Perksy, when the chairman announced the Board's unanimous vote to grant Bruce Stolts a pardon, thus removing the sexual offender chains from around his neck. It was one of the sweetest victories ever in my law practice.

AN OLD OFFENSE UNFAIRLY CAUGHT BY A NEW LAW

Rick Thomas came to see me on June 7, 2010. He was extremely frustrated and upset. He was born in California in 1963 and grew up there as a youngster. In 1990, he had an unpleasant exchange of words with a female barely under 18. She filed charges against him.

To avoid the risk of a felony conviction, Rick pled guilty in 1990 to a misdemeanor offense under the California Penal Code 647.6(a) for "annoying or molesting a child." An alternative element of that statute's definition in California included molesting behavior, but Rick never touched anyone. At that time there were no sexual offender registration laws in California, Alabama, or virtually anywhere else in America.

In the mid-1990s, sexual offender registration laws started springing up like wildflowers in the United States and became a movement. Most states adopted such laws.

A retroactive application of a sexual offender law to someone convicted before the law was passed should be a violation of the U.S. Constitution's prohibition against *ex post facto* laws. However, a misguided higher Alabama appellate court ruled that such a law was not an extra penalty, but simply "a registration" requirement, as in "draft board registration" or "voter registration." So defined, the court reasoned that it was not a punitive measure, and therefore not ex post facto.

Rick moved to Prattville, Alabama, in 1998, and lived peacefully there for 12 years. He was never in trouble. He was working full-time and looking after his family, including his wife and children.

One day in 2010, Rick went to a pawn shop to buy a gun. The owner of the shop, Danny, surmised that it was a straw sale for Rick's brother, who was visiting with Rick from out-of-state. Danny called the Alabama Bureau of Firearms and reported the sale.

The ABF began investigating and found Rick's California misdemeanor offense, with the molestation word in it. Then a Prattville police officer showed up in Rick's neighborhood, proclaiming to everyone that Rick was a sex offender and a pedophile. The police arrested Rick for not registering, and he spent two days in jail. Meanwhile, Rick's mom was dying of lung cancer.

After Rick came to see me and I heard his circumstances, I checked the language of the California statute. The situation made my blood boil. Part of the reason was that Rick was living within 2,000 feet of a school in Autauga County. The Gestapo-like police effort forced Rick to move. The police said he could no longer visit with his daughter or family. Further, Rick could only visit his old house in Prattville, where his family still resided, for two days a week, when the school wasn't in session.

Rick was also required to add the words "sexual offender" to his driver's license. It was like the yellow star the Nazis forced Jews to put on their identification papers.

I did some fast research in both California and Alabama law and determined that lawsuits questioning sexual offender status had failed. The only way to properly challenge the situation was to file a petition with the Alabama Department of Public Safety (DPS). That we did.

We were assigned Montgomery attorney Chip Nix as a hearing officer at DPS. Chip is conscientious, sensitive, and a highly regarded member of Montgomery's bar. After hearing all the evidence from both sides on December 9, 2010, Chip ruled in our favor. Glory Hallelujah! Rick was vindicated and liberated from the jaws of an excessively punitive, unfair law. Rick and I celebrated his victory, but both of us had developed a great cynicism towards the misuse of Alabama's sexual offender registration laws.

The laws obviously have valid purposes for serious sex offenders, but as is often the case, there is much over-reach. Many harmless, productive members of society have been caught in its spider web, just as were Rick Thomas and Bruce Stolts.

22

Secretary to a King

Muttering that "No good deed goes unpunished," my dear friend Randall Williams stopped by my office on July 22, 2014, to share his burden. He had helped his famous friend Andrew Young, icon of the civil rights movement, only to suffer adverse consequences. Randall was not a happy camper.

And it was not the fault of the Rev. Dr. Young, the former right-hand man of Martin Luther King Jr., later mayor of Atlanta, U.S. congressman, and finally the U.S. ambassador to the United Nations under President Jimmy Carter. Young was only trying to fulfill the dying wishes of Dora McDonald, secretary to Dr. Martin Luther King Jr. before his 1968 assassination.

McDonald wrote a book about her work with and memories of Martin Luther King Jr. Titled "Secretary to a King," it remained unpublished upon her passing in 2007. In her will and testament, McDonald named Young as the "literary co-executor" of her estate, but she left her entire inheritance to a co-executrix, namely her good friend, Patricia Latimore.

A few years before her death, McDonald had signed a book contract with a Georgia publisher, Hill Street Press. But Hill Street ran into financial difficulties and in fact had offered to sell McDonald's contract to NewSouth Books, which publishes many civil rights-related titles. Randall is the editor of NewSouth Books; his partner, Suzanne La Rosa, is its publisher.

However, Randall and Suzanne declined to take on the McDonald project because they felt that it was not economically feasible, given the proliferation of Martin Luther King-related books that have saturated the publishing market in recent years. While McDonald's was a sincere and interesting memoir, it added nothing really new to the scholarship on King and would mostly appeal to McDonald's friends and colleagues.

Then Hill Street Press went out of business; the rights to "Secretary to a King" reverted to McDonald's estate. At the request of Ambassador Young, Randall agreed to print a limited 100 draft copies of the most current version of "Secretary to a King." The idea was to pass them out to McDonald's friends and colleagues. Randall and Suzanne deemed this a simple favor to Young; the $1,000 he paid NewSouth barely covered the out-of-pocket expenses for making the copies.

In recent years, Randall had successfully fended off over the phone two earlier sets of Atlanta attorneys, purporting to represent Patricia Latimore in claiming violation of her copyright. Unfortunately, in July 2014, a third attorney Ryan Isenberg, also from Atlanta, put together a fancy lawsuit claiming copyright infringement and conversion by NewSouth Books. Damages were unspecified, but copyright infringement laws allow damages to be escalated to a high figure, which NewSouth Books could not afford. Additionally, Randall was personally offended, as a matter of high principle, believing that he and his business had done nothing wrong.

On Monday, December 1, 2014, at an Alabama State University breakfast, I spoke with Andrew Young, sitting at the head table. He was the guest speaker. When I mentioned the case, a deep frown appeared on Dr. Young's face. Fortunately Dr. Young, his daughter Andrea, Connie Curry, Randall, and his partner Suzanne LaRosa all provided me with pertinent and helpful affidavits to use in Randall's defense.

Thus, on a cold Saturday morning of January 17, 2015, Randall came over to my Old Cloverdale home. Together we organized a number of evidentiary exhibits, and cobbled together a solid Motion for Summary Judgment. I filed it a week later.

On February 2, 2015, I received a phone call from attorney Isenberg of Atlanta. He had seen our summary judgment motion. He was now singing a different tune. He was ready to surrender. Ryan said that if NewSouth Books and Randall Williams would waive any rights to Dora McDonald's book, he would dismiss his lawsuit.

No problem. Neither Randall nor NewSouth Books ever claimed any copyright or other rights to Dora McDonald's autobiography.

Randall was overjoyed with the outcome, to put it mildly. Randall did ask me to extract some additional language in a Stipulation of Dismissal by Ms. Latimore, which Isenberg agreed to. That language was as follows:

"Plaintiff (Latimore) forever withdraws any claims that respondent (NewSouth Books) infringed copyright or otherwise acted wrongly with regard to the manuscript and book, *Secretary to a King*."

I put a fair amount of time into this defense, but not an excessive amount. I gladly did it *pro bono* for my good friends Randall and Suzanne. Their "quid pro quo" was that they would put extra time and energy into helping me develop *Civil Rights in My Bones*.

23

THE KING OF REWARD ZONE POINTS

Jarvon Cubitt was a bright and personable 26-year-old African American of Cuban ancestry when he came to see me in May 2014. He had made his way up the corporate ladder as Best Buy's top salesman at its Opelika store during the preceding seven years.

Unfortunately, on May 9, 2014, Jarvon was indicted for first degree theft of property for "exerting unauthorized control over lawful United States currency, the property of Best Buy Company, Inc., having a value in excess of $2,500, with the intent to deprive the owner of said property in violation of § 13A-8–3 Code of Alabama."

Basically, Jarvon admitted he had used Reward Zone points that had been abandoned by customers with no desire to use them. Further, no customers complained about any missing points. Best Buy's policy manual said the points had no cash value by themselves, and could not be redeemed for cash. They could only be used to lower the price of a purchased item.

Further, there was nothing in Best Buy's policy manual that specifically prohibited the use of abandoned points by an employee. Although Jarvon acknowledged that his doing so may have been naïve and questionable, he maintained that he thought he had a right to use the unclaimed points and did not knowingly intend to steal. An element of the crime of theft is that an individual must "knowingly" commit the crime.

Further, Jarvon maintained that his purchases through unclaimed points created profit for Best Buy that would not have existed had the points remained unclaimed. Jarvon's managers and supervisors had plenty of opportunity to see his using points, but they had never objected until Jarvon purchased a refrigerator at an extremely discounted price.

In June 2014, I filed a Motion to Dismiss, making many of these contentions, but Judge Jacob Walker denied it. After a couple of continuances, the case was called for trial on March 16, 2015. Associate attorney Chase Estes accompanied me to Opelika for trial in the Lee County Circuit Court. I could see, during the jury selection process, that we were not going to have a good jury. I took a chance, with my client's consent, and did something I've never done before—I offered to Assistant District Attorney Gentry Jackson that we drop our jury demand. She agreed to do so, thus cutting the time of the trial in half. The Court heard approximately two days of testimony from multiple witnesses, including Jarvon himself.

After the State and I had both rested, I filed a Motion for a Directed Verdict of Acquittal or in the Alternative for Dismissal of Charges Based on Failure of Evidence to Meet the Definition in the Indictment. Basically, I argued that the Reward Zone points did not, and could not, meet the definition of "currency" as the indictment expressly stated that it did. I said that "if the D.A. lives by the sword of the indictment, he must also die by it."

Judge Walker had seemed impressed with what I was saying and gave both sides two extra weeks to file memoranda in support of, or against, my motion. I filed my memorandum of March 30, 2015, and the State responded three days later.

I anticipated a favorable ruling, but on May 4, 2015, to my great surprise, Judge Walker put together a seven-page opinion and adverse order. With a twisted logic, and overlooking the plain English meaning of the words of the indictments, the judge found Jarvon guilty of theft of property in the first degree.

I've associated my partner Joe Guillot to work with me on preparing a strong brief on appeal. Associate attorney Chase Estes is assisting us.

Meanwhile, Jarvon's sentencing was June 2, 2015. Even though Jarvon Cubitt received a probationary sentence, he does not want this theft conviction on his record. Jarvon is absolutely right to appeal. Hopefully, we'll convince the higher appellate court.

24

VIRGINIA COLLEGE'S ARBITRATION NOOSE

O ne of the most dastardly violations of civil rights in America today is the outrageous "arbitration noose" which employers, colleges, credit card companies, car dealers, franchise eateries, and others force upon their employees, students, and customers.

Most Americans still have no idea how cut-throat and unfair arbitration is and how deceptively powerful interests use it to the detriment of most consumers or workers. Arbitration simply makes double and triple victims of aggrieved employees and damaged consumers. Unfortunately, legislators owned by corporate interests and Republican-dominated courts have no guts to stop the practice.

Applebee's Restaurant is one of the worst perpetrators of heavy-handed arbitration tactics. It denies its employees the right to meaningfully contest employment discrimination based on race, sex, age, and disability. How does it do so? By sneaking an arbitration clause by them when they first come to work. It's essentially a contract of adhesion. You can't get a job unless you agree.

My firm is currently representing an older African American female, Loraine Fortson, in an involuntary arbitration. Applebee's has an enormous advantage in arbitration because it can repeatedly choose an arbitrator, whereas Ms. Fortson most likely will never have reason to select more than one American Arbitration Association arbitrator in her lifetime.

Ditto with most car sellers. You can't buy a car unless you agree to the substantial repression of your consumer rights by arbitration.

Why is arbitration so bad? First, it frequently imposes excess costs on a plaintiff—win, lose, or draw. Worse, you get a biased arbitrator, rather than a more neutral judge. Arbitrators have an enormous incentive to rule in favor of a corporation if he or she ever wants to get hired again at an hourly rate in the $250 to $400 range. That is because the corporate interest is likely to come back and choose them again and again. Conversely, there is no incentive, other than professional integrity, for the arbitrator to rule for an individual, who likely will be a one-time participant. Accordingly consumers and their lawyers have zero confidence in the fairness of an arbitrator.

Another problem is that arbitration too often allows a dispute to get dragged out over a much greater period of time that could end up being years. Justice delayed is justice denied!

Being lyrically blunt, arbitration causes an employee, consumer or student to be "used, bruised, contused and abused."

One of the worst perpetrators of the civil fraud of arbitration, in my opinion, is Virginia College, an educational institution based in Alabama and operating in other states.

Virginia College should be ashamed of itself. Any publicity about its problems was initiated by Virginia College itself by its open and public refusal to treat its students fairly. I saw and heard Virginia College's Montgomery campus president, Madeleine Little, denying on WSFA TV in September 2015 that its college professor had ever sexually harassed Brittany Tyus. Accordingly, she opened the door to what is said further in this chapter, in response. We, of course, gave our version publicly, and nothing more has been added here.

For starters, its name seemingly is trying to play on the good name of the University of Virginia, a highly prestigious school with which Virginia College has no association whatsoever. Of course, most of the public doesn't know that, so naive students get suckered into Virginia College's spider web.

I've represented at least five female students in 2015 alone who've been badly taken advantage of by Virginia College. That includes two U.S. military veterans, Brittany Tyus, 24, of Selma, an ex-Army veteran with 14 months' service in Afghanistan. Another is Jazmine Williams, 26, of Montgomery, an ex-Marine who spent nine months in Iraq. And there are Mildred Williams, a disabled but competent cosmetology student, nursing student Deana Gray, and Rekita Jackson, a student at Virginia College on a substantial federal loan for which she has not received the full benefits.

How have they been ripped off?

Brittney Tyus, an attractive young veteran with some PTSD issues from Afghanistan explosions, was repeatedly sexually harassed by her professor, Dr. Edward Davis. She has numerous witnesses to confirm the harassment. However, Virginia College ignored it all until Ms. Tyus filed her suit, where-upon Dr. Davis was no longer employed.

Jazmine Williams, on the GI bill like Ms. Tyus, simply had the audacity to ask Virginia College President Madeleine Little why she (Jazmine) had not received the school books and teacher hours due her as part of her government-paid $56,000 tuition. The president took offense to the question, and summarily, without a hearing, "disenrolled" Ms. Williams. What happened to due process?

Mildred Williams (no relation to Jazmine) filed suit, via an earlier attorney, pursuant to the Americans with Disabilities Act, because she was kicked out of school due to a modest mental health issue that didn't prevent her from attending class. Mildred is now being represented by my law firm.

Deana Gray, the oldest of my clients at age 44, was also sexually harassed and treated badly in other ways. She was a witness also in federal court for us on Brittany Tyus's challenge to her arbitration agreement.

Rekita Jackson, who has obligated herself to many thousands of dollars in federal loans, discovered that much of what the federal money was supposed to buy for her was not delivered by Virginia College, constituting a major rip-off.

What do all five of these female students have in common? The answer is that none had a clue they were being hog-tied by arbitration agreements. Not only that, but they never even signed an arbitration agreement. They were all deemed to have "assented to arbitration," whatever that means, when they enrolled as a student.

Unfortunately, the nine Republicans on the Alabama Supreme Court have upheld a doctrine of "assent," as opposed to "consent." Again, what does it mean to assent? It means that, once you partake of a service by anyone such as Virginia College, you obligate yourself to an arbitration clause, whether you sign it or not, and whether you know about it or not. How un-American, how un-democratic, and how unsavory!

In court on August 2, 2015, Ms. Tyus vehemently insisted that she never signed anything, did not authorize anyone to sign anything for her, and was never told by anyone there was an arbitration clause. Ditto for Jazmine Williams and Deana Gray, with their similar experiences. Yet, Judge Keith Watkins, in an order and opinion issued on August 4, 2015, stated that he was troubled by the thin veneer of an arbitration agreement, but felt bound by the 2015 Alabama Supreme Court decision in *American Bankers Insurance Co. v. Tellis*.

In the *American Bankers* case, the Supreme Court of Alabama said insurance policy-holders were bound by an arbitration agreement they didn't know about and didn't sign. The rationale was that once they partook of the services of the insurance company, they were hooked. Judge Watkins said that this Alabama case had a binding effect on him in the federal Tyus case. In the related lawsuit of Mildred Williams, Judge Paul Greene felt bound by the Tyus ruling of Judge Watkins.

And so the dominoes continue to fall against consumers. And innocent students and consumers, like a bug trapped in a spider web, have their civil rights crushed.

I consider arbitration not only a gross violation of civil rights. We in America, even those in the power structure of the legislature and judiciary, should be ashamed. That is because arbitration has rendered innocent victims powerless to contest outright fraud, illegal employment practices, consumer rip-offs and other sinister ills.

Just before this book went to press, the claims of two of the five plaintiffs, namely Brittany Tyus and Mildred Williams were "confidentially resolved." Therefore, I will say nothing more about their cases.

Nonetheless, the U.S. Congress needs to pass a law to correct the arbitration fiasco perpetrated upon the consuming public. However, given the powerful forces that wrongfully support arbitration, such legislation is not likely to happen any time soon.

25

WILDCAT VERSUS TAMEDOG

O ne of the most interesting clients I have represented is Steven Clayton "Wildcat" Thomason, a late-40s African American gentleman
of many talents.

With his long, straight black hair and an ancestry including Irish and
American Indian forebears, Clayton, as he is more formally known, exudes
charm and intelligence. He is a gifted home repair contractor, an accomplished
singer with a jazz band, and a legal buff who has successfully represented
himself in court.

Clayton is also a widower raising two teenage daughters. I frequently tell
him this is his greatest and highest avocation. That doesn't keep this handsome fellow from spreading his charisma among a diversity of attractive
woman, ranging from young to middle-aged, and consisting of a variety of
ethnic backgrounds.

The "Wildcat" nickname stems from Clayton's singing routine, which
can often be seen on the *Harriott* riverboat cruises on the Alabama river. His
band includes guitarists Frank Gray and Atiba Dudley and drummer Unika
Newsome. All are also members of our Christ the Redeemer church jazz band.

Clayton first came to see me for legal advice and help. In a humorous
moment, I suggested he might want to adopt the alternative nickname of
"Tamedog" and similarly tame down some of his many legal initiatives. Since
then, my relationship with Clayton has grown to include roles of both pastor
and friend. Clayton sometimes comes to Christ the Redeemer Church, and
he needs to come more often.

I remember once waiting with Clayton in Elmore County Circuit Court
for a judge to come to the courtroom. In that span, I was prepping him for
his legal defense, while alternately listening to him, and responding pastorally,
about a deteriorating girlfriend relationship. When the case was continued,
we retreated to my car, and had a good, long prayer about his social life.

Clayton does sometimes struggle between the "Wildcat" and "Tamedog"
sides of his personality,

The first several cases I helped him with arose in Montgomery County. One involved a suit by Clayton against a woman who failed to pay her bill to Clayton because she said he was not registered with the Alabama Homebuilders Licensure Board. This was just an excuse to avoid paying a legitimate bill, because she had no complaint about the quality of his work.

Clayton had initially filed the suit himself. However, the ancient adage that a lawyer who represents himself has a fool for a client may be all the more true when a non-lawyer is representing himself. So I entered an appearance for Clayton and cleared up his allegations with an amended complaint. We pursued aggressive discovery, and in the end I wrangled a decent settlement for Clayton in Judge Johnny Hardwick's courtroom.

I also got two sets of criminal charges dismissed against Clayton in Montgomery County District Judge Troy Massey's courtroom. This was no small accomplishment as the dismissals came over the protests, overruled by the Court, of the District Attorney's Office and the Alabama Homebuilder's Licensure Board, which initiated the charges in the first place.

Meanwhile, despite Clayton's claim of exemption due to the grand-fathering provisions of a Washington County license, I convinced him to go ahead and apply for his homebuilder's license, just to get that agency off of his back. Clayton did just that, submitting his application in June 2014. The licensure board kept coming back to Clayton for more information, all of which we provided, but which delayed his approval.

Unfortunately, before the board could grant him his license, it dug up a spurious new complaint from a lady in Millbrook. Ignoring our evidence to the contrary, the board put Clayton's application on hold. So there we were again, duking it out. My letter expressing great indignation and breach of an agreement in Judge Massey's courtroom was mild in comparison to the missile Clayton himself unloaded on them. Clayton, who loves to draft his own lawsuits in his own name, put together a classic, alleging all manner of bad faith, due process violation, and breach of anti-trust laws. I was only advised of this pleading "after the fact." Clayton also named as a defendant Montgomery County District Attorney Daryl Bailey. Bailey is a friend of mine and has helped me and can help me more on other clients' cases. Thus, I had a conflict and could not be Clayton's attorney, on that case anyway.

Later, after a ruling against Clayton by Elmore County District Court Judge Glenn Goggans, my wildcat client, without checking with me first, added Judge Goggans as a party defendant on various constitutional grounds. My understanding is that a judge's immunity is absolute for anything done in court. For that reason, and for conflict reasons, I was all the more constrained not to be Clayton's attorney in that case.

I am now representing Clayton in Elmore County Circuit Court on an appeal of his Elmore County District Court conviction. A jury trial has been requested in the Circuit Court. Clayton's big lawsuit against the Homebuilder's Board has now been removed by the defendant to federal court, where Clayton continues to represent himself.

Clayton still comes to Christ the Redeemer Episcopal Church occasionally, but not often enough, in my opinion, for his overall well-being. Notwithstanding, our friendship remains strong, given its multi-faceted nature.

Regardless of whether Clayton leans more towards the "Wildcat" or "Tamedog" side of his nature, this able fellow not only remains my good friend and client, but he spurs me on in my civil rights work. After all, that's what I've done for Clayton, protecting his "civil right to work without oppressive, governmental interference."

26

Dothan Police and Fire
Departments Challenged

Challenging an entire police department is not new for me. I did it successfully back in the mid-1980s with the Montgomery Police Department. I tried two cases against the MPD two weeks apart in 1986.

The first case challenged the system of promotional practices under former Mayor Emory Folmar. I was assisted by co-counsel Alvin Prestwood, now deceased. Our cause of action was not based on race, sex, age, religion, or disability, but solely on Emory's wrongful practice of choosing all cronies as bodyguards, and then promoting them to the highest ranks of the MPD, including chief. It violated due process, Alvin and I said. Fortunately, a great federal judge, Myron Thompson ruled in our favor, although it took three years and three months before we received a ruling.

The second case involved my representing a former MPD officer, Steve Eiland, who wrote an unflattering poem about Mayor Folmar, whom he had nicknamed "Emory Amin." The poem was posted on the MPD's elevator door. Emory didn't like it and Steve lost his job. My good friend Vanzetta McPherson, a future magistrate judge, asked if she could help me on the case. I gladly said yes. A bomb threat on the day of the trial stirred sympathy for Emory, and a jury ruled against us. Notwithstanding, Vanzetta, artfully articulate with her pen, took the lead on an appeal to the 11th Circuit, which reversed and ruled in our favor.

My police brutality cases have challenged police departments, but those cases primarily involve one or two officers, not the whole department. Nonetheless, I have learned much about police procedure and protocol over the years.

The Dothan Police Department

Accordingly, I was primed when an African American female and former Dothan police officer, Raemonica Carney, came to see me in August 2015.

Raemonica earlier had an attorney from Birmingham, who withdrew in early January. She had spent the next seven months consulting with outstanding employment law attorneys in Alabama, Georgia, and Florida, but all turned her down. Raemonica came to us at a time when I already had too much on my plate. I was therefore hesitant about such a highly involved undertaking.

Doubting at first that I'd take the case, I asked associate attorney Chris Worshek to join me in the library, as we politely listened to the demure and well-spoken Raemonica. She had worked for the Dothan Police Department for 14 years. She had done well in many aspects, including developing software on computer applications that helped the DPD nab criminals.

Yet Rae, as she is sometimes called, described a culture in the Dothan Police Department that was overwhelmingly racist and sexist. There were very few women in the Dothan Police department and very few blacks.

A black male DPD captain, Ivan Keith Gray, had filed a similar EEOC charge in the same year, 2013, that Rae filed hers. He was much more fortunate in his drawing of judges, as he received the afore-referenced Myron Thompson, the only African American federal judge left in Alabama, and a fair judge for plaintiffs in civil rights cases. Raemonica, on the other hand, had drown Keith Watkins, a decent and intelligent judge, but one whose white Republican background reflects a more conservative philosophy on such cases. Indeed, Judge Watkins's track record is that he rarely denies summary judgment for defendants in race discrimination lawsuits. This is bad news for civil rights cases and African American plaintiffs.

Captain Gray had already successfully defended a summary judgment motion by the City of Dothan and had reportedly received a settlement offer well into six figures. However, a 100-page brief and thousands of pages of exhibits had been filed against Raemonica by super attorney Stephanie Wells of Birmingham. Even worse, Rae's already extended deadline to respond was about to expire.

However, there was something very persuasive and sincere about Raemonica, now an active duty Army officer stationed at Fort Knox in Kentucky. The more I looked at her facts, the more I knew she had been wronged. Figuring into my consideration was that Dothan had recently won the dubious award of being "the most redneck city in Alabama," probably something many of its police officers considered an honor.

I also knew from representing two other African Americans with legal problems in Dothan, namely Sanjanetta Barnes and attorney Mark Overall, just how harsh the City of Dothan's officialdom, including judges and police, can be on blacks. What had happened to Raemonica failed the "smell test."

So Chris and I told Raemonica, after determining she could meet the reasonable attorney's fee quoted, that we would make a limited appearance for the purpose of filing a motion to get a continuance of the summary judgment deadline of August 25 and the trial deadline of October 20. If the court granted that motion, then we would enter a full appearance, respond to the summary judgment motion, and represent her at trial, assuming we defeated the motion.

A few days later, Magistrate Judge Paul Greene granted our motion to extend the summary judgment response deadline to September 25. The trial date was extended to February 2016.

Thus, I had to spend significant portions of all three days of Labor Day weekend working on Raemonica's case. I had Rae meet us that Sunday night at Christ the Redeemer Church. From there she followed Leslie and me back up to our Lake Martin place and spent the night. The next morning at 7 am, we were both up, and we went next door to my brother Frank's lake house to work in the quiet, while my children, grandchildren, and wife gradually woke up and made noise at our home. For the next five hours we made tremendous progress, nailing down a first draft of a long evidentiary affidavit from Raemonica. That afternoon Raemonica drove back to Fort Knox.

Chris and I worked hard for the next three weeks. The heart of our brief said that, although Rae's DPD responsibilities had substantially increased over the years, she received no additional compensation and no promotions, while white male employees were promoted quickly and were paid more. Rae also said she had been harassed by white male employees, while upper management turned the other cheek. She described a hostile working environment that became increasingly hostile when she started voicing concerns about the rights of minority citizens.

Raemonica also offered strong proof that she was treated unfairly in employment-related exams, when compared to white employees. Even firearms testing was erroneously scored against her, to her detriment.

What got her in the most trouble, however, was when she posted comments on Facebook intended for her close personal friends. She commented how another minority police officer, out of Los Angeles, had raised legitimate issues of constitutional rights abuse by the police. Unfortunately, that officer went berserk and shot and killed other officers. Raemonica decried and abhorred the killings but suggested they would not have occurred in the first place if the Los Angeles Police Department had been more race-sensitive.

Somehow, Raemonica's posts got into the wrong hands and made it to the Dothan police department. The white officers were upset and Corporal

Carney was suspended for two weeks and then placed on probation.

Meanwhile, white male officers had made Facebook postings very critical of blacks. In January 2015, one white Dothan officer posted an ugly picture of President Obama, calling the president a two-faced liar and hypocrite. Yet the DPD did nothing to discipline those officers.

Soon thereafter the Dothan police department got the excuse they were looking for to terminate Raemonica. She came home late one evening and was off duty when she had a dispute with her fiancé. There was no physical abuse or even verbal threat by Raemonica. In fact, it was her fiancé who opened the door of her police car and reached in and grabbed her. The two later made up and were married.

However, a set of white police officers showed up at her house and later lodged an internal complaint that was used to terminate Raemonica.

We said the actions against Raemonica constituted a classic violation of her First Amendment right to free speech. We also said it was related to her Title VII race discrimination claim.

On September 25, 2015, Chris and I filed a 38-page brief in opposition to the summary judgment motion. We also filed two lengthy affidavits from Raemonica, affidavits from other witnesses, the deposition of Captain Gray, and Gray's entire summary judgment response in Judge Thompson's court. We also referenced Raemonica's deposition and all exhibits the City of Dothan filed against her.

We also filed a Motion to Amend the Complaint to assert a 42 U.S.C § 1981 cause of action left out by the first set of Raemonica's attorneys. Had that cause of action been asserted, we wouldn't have been so restricted by the timeliness requirements of the Equal Employment Opportunity Commission, because the City of Dothan denied it ever received the plaintiff's EEOC termination charge prepared by her earlier set of attorneys. Unfortunately, the court denied the amendment, because it was long past the deadline for such amendments.

On January 28, 2016, Judge Watkins released a 61-page opinion granting summary judgment to the City of Dothan.

Finding in favor of Dothan that Raemonica's first attorneys never filed her wrongful termination charge with the EEOC, even though one existed with Raemonica's signature on it, Judge Watkins found her race case to be untimely and thus ineligible for relief.

As to Raemonica's free speech case, the judge ruled that she spoke out on a matter of public concern and did so as a private citizen (all helpful rulings for her). However, in the critical "balancing of the interests" test,

Judge Watkins found that the City of Dothan's interest in maintaining order and morale among its police force (allegedly greatly upset by Raemonica's postings on Facebook) was greater than Raemonica's right to free speech. In doing so, Watkins ignored all the anti-Obama racial slurs of the white police officers, and held Raemonica to a higher standard.

We respectfully believe Judge Watkins was very wrong, and that his ruling has further contributed to the gross watering down of free speech rights. Post-judgment motions are being worked on. At the end of January 2016, plaintiff Raemonica Carney had not yet signaled to us, as her current attorneys, whether she will appeal the decision to the 11th Circuit in Atlanta.

OTHER ISSUES IN THE DOTHAN POLICE AND FIRE DEPARTMENTS

In my opinion, Dothan has a problem with the way it treats minority citizens. I refer particularly to its wrongful arrest and mistreatment of Sanjanitta Barnes, a young African American female reporter for Channel 4, who was arrested for disorderly conduct because she dared question a policeman who stopped her while she walking home.

I also refer to attorney Mark Overall, a young African American male, who was held in contempt by a local circuit judge, after Mr. Overall questioned the judge's ruling.

However, former Dothan firefighter Sam Tew, a middle-aged white male client of mine, is proof that Dothan doesn't just pick on blacks and females. In the mid-1990s, Tew blew the whistle on a Dothan battalion fire chief who over a five- to seven-year period was selling hundreds of assault weapons, including AK-47s, and other illegal firearms while on duty at the city's Westgate Fire Station.

Proving that no whistle-blowing goes unpunished, Tew was arrested for an alleged violation and wrongfully terminated. In the years since then, Tew says he has been subjected to 20 false arrests, was exonerated on 17 of them, and found not guilty on the other three. In addition, Tew was assaulted by the Dothan police nine times, incurred over $100,000 in medical bills, and suffered numerous other wrongs. Tew has a hard time grasping that the statute of limitations has run on most of his claims, and he keeps going to the Dothan City Council meetings seeking justice. Meanwhile, I help him when I can.

Based on the above, Dothan needs to shape up, in my opinion.

27

The Law Firm Family

Icould not have handled the foregoing legal cases and controversies without solid assistance from my law firm. That includes not only my fellow lawyers, but especially my office manager and bookkeeper, our paralegals, secretaries, receptionist, runner and server of process. How did it happen that the law firm I started in 1978 grew to what it is today?

As already discussed, I ran hard for attorney general of Alabama in 1977–78, finishing second in a nine-man race in unofficial statewide tallies compiled by the Associated Press and the United Press International. I was 5,000 votes ahead of Joe Fine, president of the Alabama Senate, and campaigning hard during the first week of the runoff in September 1978. Then I received one of the great shocks of my life when the official tally came in. Suddenly I was 5,000 votes behind, with Fine's totals going up and mine proportionally down, in six counties.

I pursued a challenge for a week. However, faced with posting a $200,000 bond, with the runoff itself only a week later, I faced up to the futility of contesting an election that so obviously was stolen. Reluctantly but necessarily, I abandoned the challenge.

What then was there to do? After spending a week in Cancun, Mexico, with Leslie, my answer was "start a law practice." That is what I did in late September 1978 with the kind and generous Tommy Gallion persuading me to come into the building at 516 South Perry Street, then owed by his parents-in-law. While Tommy and I maintained our separate accounts, we practiced law so closely together on so many cases from 1978–82 that we were defacto partners. In 1982, I bought the 10,000-square foot, three-floor red brick building from Tommy's in-laws. Beautiful interior woodwork remains from the original 1870s house. Tommy moved on to new quarters, but I'm still here 38 years later, enjoying the location.

For the first two months, Leslie served as my secretary while our one-year-old daughter, Rachel, crawled around on the floor. In November 1978, I hired 17-year-old high school senior Regina Lee, still in school, to be my first legal secretary. Eagerly answering the phone and enthusiastically banging away on my old typewriter, Regina helped me launch a law practice that surprised even me at how well we were doing by the end of 1978.

Client Carroll Puckett, with insurance, real estate, and securities licenses, but all suspended, came in to see me in late 1978 and early 1979. I quickly got all three licenses restored, and Carroll, impressed by my prowess, soon thereafter became my hardworking legal assistant. Carroll stayed with me until 2006, and often had his wife Betty and son Paul assisting him. Carroll was with me at several special moments and assisted me in many cases from the late 1970s through the mid-2000s. I'll always be grateful to Carroll and his family.

Jim Debardelaben became my first associate attorney in 1981, and another year after that he was a partner. We had some great cases together. I became godfather to both of Jim's sons, but following a divorce in 1990, Jim wanted a change of scenery and moved on. We remain good friends.

My next law partner and friend was Frank Hawthorne Jr., an aggressive former assistant district attorney. We became known as McPhillips Debardelaben & Hawthorne until Jim left in 1990.

Meanwhile, Kenneth Shinbaum became the next associate in 1986, and then William Gill thereafter in 1988. Mary Goldthwaite came on board as an attorney in 1992, and Allen Stoner in 1993. Mary and Allen, like Frank, were former assistant district attorneys, and knew their way around a courtroom.

Frank came to me in 1993, and said that his father, Frank Hawthorne Sr., a partner at Balch and Bingham, had just turned 70, mandatory retirement age for that firm. Young Frank wanted to leave to practice with his father for a few years, which I especially could understand. Frank and I remain good friends today.

The very able paralegal Lynelle Howard came to work for me as my personal assistant in 1987, remaining until 1996, when she moved to Colorado. Lynelle returned again in 2007, and remained with me until April 2013, when she retired for health reasons. Mary Goldthwaite accurately described Lynelle as being "fiercely loyal" to me.

Mary was herself a "fiercely competitive" lawyer and advocate during her 14 years with the firm, from 1992–2006. No one worked harder, and she scored some great victories, especially in a Title IX sexual harassment case against the Selma Public School System, following multiple incidents of sexual harassment by a teacher against students. Mary is now doing well as an assistant attorney general for the State of Alabama.

The 1990s were halcyon years for my law practice. Aaron Luck, Jim

Bodin, and Joe Guillot came to the firm as junior lawyers in 1994, 1995, and 1997, respectively. They are partners today.

Associate attorneys Kay Dickey, Alfred Norris, Karen Sampson Rogers, Elizabeth Spear, and Allison Highley practiced with the firm in the 1990s–2000s, as did "of counsel" attorneys Bill Honey and Gary Atchison. Even former secretary Regina Lee came back in 1994–2000 as an attorney, mostly in domestic relations. Charlie Hawthorne also did a good job for us as an associate attorney in 2013–2014.

Kay Dickey, also a sister church leader at Christ the Redeemer, once remarked to me around 2003 on a trip back from an out-of-town legal case: "Oh, Julian, you've lived such a charmed life." I replied, "Oh yes, I've been blessed, but I'm not sure about charmed." I added that I lost a dear brother to suicide, a mother to Alzheimer's, and a father to surgery I had begged him not to have. I also painfully broke my leg twice in one wrestling season, experienced a minor depression in 1966 as a result, and had an attorney general's runoff spot stolen from me in 1978. I was also the victim of a successful sabotage in the runoff of my U.S. Senate race in 2002. And Kay's comment came three years before I experienced a more severe depression in 2006.

Yet I admit that I have been exceedingly fortunate in my life and career. I try to give God all the gratitude, credit and honor that he deserves.

THERE WERE TWO SUBSTANTIAL challenges to the firm in the 2000s, but with God's help, we weathered them both. The first was my U.S. Senate race, discussed fully in the second edition of my earlier book, *The People's Lawyer*. Somehow all the lawyers who began with me before the campaign began in 2001 were still with me when it ended in June 2002 (even though Mary Goldthwaite and Karen Rodgers were having babies during that period).

The very talented and hardworking William Gill left on his own accord in 2004. William helped the firm achieve in January 2003 the biggest settlement we ever had, in a Macon County case. It was my case, too, involving a major personal injury and products liability claim against Ford and Firestone. We miss William.

The firm's ship sailed on well enough from mid-2002, after the Senate race, until early 2006, when suddenly another big bump, a major depression caused by a mis-diagnosed thyroid condition and an excessively strong medication (see Chapter 37), slowed me down. All the partners, especially Kenneth, and the other attorneys helped cover for me during the rough period from April to July 2006.

Transitions of personnel in the office were part of that difficult 2006. In February, before the depression had gotten bad, my good friend and paralegal Sim Pettway left to take a job with the Alabama Democratic Party. Sim remains a good friend today. The Pucketts, including my long-term right-hand man, Carroll Puckett, left involuntarily in May. I experienced much anguish over the tough decision Kenneth and I jointly made to let Carroll go. That included his part-time team of wife Betty and son Paul. In those days, Carroll was frequently away from the firm. It seemed inevitable. Still, Carroll had been a close friend, and this severance exacerbated the depression. (Carroll later sued me and the firm, but the case was dismissed on our motion for summary judgment.)

Meanwhile, attorney, partner, and friend Karen Rodgers decided on her own to leave in August to found her own one-attorney firm, with her father as office manager. Attorney-partner Mary Goldthwaite, after working with me for 14 years, left us in September to transition to the Alabama attorney general's office.

Fortunately, the worst of the depression was over just in time for the remaining five partners, Kenneth Shinbaum, Aaron Luck, Jim Bodin, Joe Guillot, and me to restructure ourselves into the firm name of McPhillips, Shinbaum, Luck, Bodin & Guillot. We decided to restructure the firm in a way that gave all partners a greater share of the profits and a vote in the management. This restructuring, and the shedding of other employees and attorneys, helped assure the long-term survival of the partnership, now called McPhillips Shinbaum, LLP, consisting since 2006 of the five partners. We became a sleeker ship, enabling us to sail through the troubled national economic waters of 2008–11, when other law firms were going under.

A REAL STAR OF our operation, and an unsung hero who I sometimes call the "Mother of our Firm," was hired in 1996. I'm referring to Amy Strickland. She started as my paralegal, but soon became office manager, bookkeeper, and computer guru. When we expanded to advertising in 2003, she developed a new talent as our advertising manager. Amy is exceedingly loyal, has great common sense, and is very helpful in talking down subrogation claims and in bargaining astutely with providers of office supplies, services, and advertising. She, too, was very helpful during my depression.

Bless Amy's heart. She has had her own struggles with health issues, especially skeletal ones, but she goes the extra mile, working even when in pain. She is a prayer partner, and we both are praying for her improved health. I once gave her a scriptural sign, now hanging on the wall behind her desk, that accurately describes her: "Blessed are the Peacemakers."

Most people who know Kenneth Shinbaum, my loyal partner of almost 30 years, now 63, would say we are personality opposites, extrovert and introvert, although we share common values. I often joke that Kenneth sees the problems in cases, while I see the possibilities, and we balance each other out. What makes Kenneth an "unsung hero" for me is that he goes around the law firm helping all the lawyers, including me, with our cases. Every now and then, Ken also lands a "big fish" that especially helps the firm financially, and he adds plenty of smaller fish to the cash flow.

Aaron Luck, now 48, my next partner, was once the wrestling champion of Great Britain and comes from a professional Marine family. His deep-voiced persuasiveness and dogged pursuit of a case makes him an effective negotiator. He's put together some big settlements. Aaron and I have a special bond, going back to 1994, when I prayed for him when he had a bad migraine. It immediately disappeared and has not come back in the years since.

Next in line is partner Jim Bodin, also 48. My bond with him strengthened in 2000 when I helped him find his adopted son, Jon Eric, through the same lawyer in Birmingham who ten years earlier handled the legal papers for my adopted son David. Jim is also good at negotiating a personal injury case up for settlement. Jim tends to handle the most narrow range of cases, mostly auto accidents, slip and falls, and other personal injuries, of all the attorneys in the firm. He is well-organized and methodical.

Jim and I were defending a client in a criminal felony case in the Lee County Circuit Court in Opelika in September 2001. The first day, on September 10, had gone well for us. The next day, September 11, as we driving back to Opelika from Montgomery, I received a call from Leslie saying that an airplane had hit one of the World Trade Center towers. We got to Opelika and resumed trying the case before the jury. However, Judge Jacob Walker then revealed to everyone what happened with the second tower. He declared a mistrial because some of the jury members might have family connections with people in the towers.

Jim and I hightailed it back to Montgomery. When we got there everyone was in an uproar. I'll never forget the experience of togetherness in the law firm, as all twenty of us gathered together in the Oak Room on our ground floor, had prayers together for our country and all the victims, amidst tears, and just watched the television reports.

Last but certainly not least among our attorneys, Joe Guillot, 61, is a great lawyer, good person and loyal partner. Number 1 in his graduating class from Jones Law School, Joe had the advantage of extra maturity and

Leslie and Julian at Lake Martin—2014.

Left: Louise and Frank McPhillips on the edges, with Julian and Leslie in middle and Rev. John Alford in chair for President Obama's speech in Selma—2015. Right: Nephew Dixon McPhillips and Uncle Julian McPhillips in New Orleans, May 2015.

Top: Grace Lunsford, Rachel Plucker & David McPhillips – Thanksgiving 2013. Right: Jay and Rachel McPhillips Plucker, with their son Jude and daughter Laurel.

Son David and Julian McPhillips at National College Wrestling Tournament, St. Louis, Missouri, 2015.

Christ the Redeemer Episcopal Church members having Christmas dinner together, December 2015.

Mr./Mrs. Success and Chichi Jumbo, and son, Success, Jr. during Christmas, 2015.

Right: Leslie and Julian at nation's capitol, Washington, D.C., for Barack Obama's Inauguration, January 2013. Below: Corbett and Grace Lunsford in front of Church of Our Saviour, Chicago, 2014.

Leslie and Julian McPhillips in Ephesus, Turkey, during Pilgrimage, 2012, following in the steps of St. Paul around Greece and Turkey.

Right: Julian in Havana, Cuba, with Cuban ladies— February 2015. Below: Leslie and Julian sitting in Cuban rickshaw taxi.

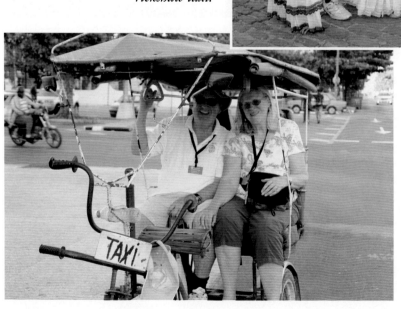

Top: Grace McPhillips Lunsford and Leslie McPhillips on the red carpet at Cannes Film Festival, May 2015.
Bottom: English Canon Andrew White (center) at Healing the Nations Conference in Charlotte, North Carolina, October 2015, with David, Leslie, and Julian McPhillips.

Family reunion December 2013, in Santa Fe, New Mexico, for the 50th wedding anniversary of Sandy and Charlie Pitre. Present were all 49 descendants of Eleanor and Julian L. McPhillips Sr. and the Pitre, Williams, and McPhillips branches of the family.

Good friends Steve and Teresa Stearns joining Julian and Leslie for dinner in Princeton, New Jersey, November 2015, during Princeton-Yale game. Steve, a former Princeton football captain, was recruited by Julian from Montgomery in 1979–80 and now lives in Connecticut, where he is a stockbroker and Teresa is the Yale Law School librarian.

THIS PAGE, TOP RIGHT: Dr. Ivan Watts, Dr. Evelyn Crayton, Julian McPhillips, and Tanja Matthews pose for a picture after McPhillips' presentation. THIS PAGE, BELOW: Julian McPhillips shares his expertise about employee rights to a captivated audience. OPPOSITE PAGE, TOP LEFT: Dr. Pambanisha Whaley, Dr. Evelyn Crayton, and Shirley Scott-Harris discuss the topics brought up at the civic engagement event. THIS PAGE, TOP RIGHT: Dr. Evelyn Crayton addresses the crowd. -Photos by Taylor Henderson

Above: The Auburn University yearbook, Glomerata, *devoted a full page to Julian McPhillips meeting with and speaking to the black faculty caucus and leaders in October 2011.*

Above: Dr. Tonea Stewart with Leslie and Julian before Civil Rights Commemoration—January 2016. Below: Julian with Mayor Walter Hill of Mosses, Lowndes County, Alabama, 2015. Walter is also president of the World Conference of Black Mayors.

Top: Julian with Andy McCarter and bride Kelly Liles, after performing their wedding ceremony in the spring of 2013.
Bottom: With Mark Boddie and Candice Waldrop, after Julian conducted their wedding ceremony on March 23, 2014.

Above: Right, Julian's client Nick Autrey (of the case from Hell), with, left, Auburn attorney George Blake, in 2010.
Below: Julian with Adrin Russell and family on Lake Martin pontoon boat, 2015.

Above: With client Alton Dandridge after his vindication and release from wrongful murder conviction, November 2015. Below: With client Dimple Patrick, former nurse at Baptist South hospital, and associate attorney Chase Estes, 2015.

Left: With client Judge Dorothea Batiste at her wedding rehearsal dinner, New Orleans, May 2015.

Above left, inset: With client Clayton Thomason, aka "Wildcat" or "Tamedog," 2015.

Above right: Willie Thompson, executive director of the Scott and Zelda Fitzgerald Museum, May 2013.

Left: With Arthur Lee "Bishop" Dowdell, who has referred many cases to me, 2010.

Pictured with fellow attorney Bobby Segall, paralegal Carlton Avery, and associate attorney Chase Estes working on Emerson Crayton Jr. case, 2016.

Mark McDonald (head of the Georgia Trust for Historic Preservation) presenting a Zelda ancestral family bible to Leslie and Julian at the Scott and Zelda Fitzgerald Museum, December 24, 2015.

Julian with (top) paralegal Carlton Avery and (left) friend Randall Williams at the Selma-Montgomery march reenactment in March 2015.
Below: With Mr. and Mrs. Dan Harris at political reception hosted by Julian and Leslie McPhillips, May 2015.

Top: Julian with Terri Sewell, her mother Nancy Sewell and aunt at Terri Sewell's initial swearing into Congress, January, 2011. Center: First Lady Michelle Obama with Leslie and Julian at reception in Birmingham, 2012. Bottom: With former First Lady and current presidential candidate, Hillary Clinton, in December, 2015.

discipline as a retired Air Force Lieutenant Colonel when he graduated from law school at the age of 43. Upon retirement from the military, his general praised Joe for his "keen intellect." Joe handles a broad range of cases, and backs Amy up admirably with his bookkeeping talents.

Like Kenneth and me, Joe not only does personal injury cases but works in employment law (representing mostly plaintiffs) and criminal cases. Social security law is also a specialty for Joe. In fact, no one else in the firm does social security law. Joe has a military precision, thoroughness, and no-nonsense approach. He has been especially good lately with criminal cases and criminal appeals. Joe is also on the board of directors of the Montgomery Area Community Organization on Aging (MACOA), the organization that does so much to help needy seniors.

Now, in 2015–16, we have two additional associate attorneys, Chris Worshek and Chase Estes, and 15 employees altogether, counting the partners.

Chris is a retired Army captain. He spent seven months in Iraq in the waning days of that war. Chris's father has been a Christian missionary in Uganda. Chris is the oldest of five brothers. Quiet-spoken, he is married to a brilliant lawyer-wife, Dee. They have two daughters, and at this writing Dee was expecting their first son in February 2016. Chris, with keen organizational skills and accuracy, has also worked up some good settlements on both the personal injury and employment areas of our firm.

One thing all six of us married lawyers (the five partners and Chris) have in common is that we are loyal to our wives and good fathers. This keeps us out of trouble and helps maintain stability in the firm.

Our youngest and newest associate attorney, Chase Estes, was born in 1988. He is 42 years younger than me, virtually young enough to be my grandson. Chase is a high school valedictorian from Athens, Alabama, who did well both at Auburn University and Jones Law School. Chase also has a great sense of humor and flatters me by laughing at some of my bad jokes. Chase has developed a special skill for helping me prepare briefs and letters in our employment cases.

I must thank two other outstanding attorneys, Elizabeth Spear and Allison Highley, for the significant contributions both made to the firm. Elizabeth was with us a little longer, about three years, and Allison about two years, during 2004–2007. Both had excellent minds, and good work ethics. I wish them nothing but the best. Another good attorney who worked with us first as a paralegal, and then as an attorney, from 2010 to 2012, was Lakeisha Griffin. She insisted on going out on her own. I hope she is doing well.

The employees in the firm must like it here. Paralegal Page McKee, reporting directly to Aaron Luck, has been with us for 18 years. She began as a receptionist in 1997. I've always appreciated her sweet spirit. Paralegal Patricia Williams, working more directly with Joe, has been with us 15 years, paralegal Jennifer Lee, assistant to Jim, has been with us 10 years, and paralegal Stephanie Murray, right arm to Kenneth Shinbaum, has been with us four years.

Runner/ investigator Kaylon Jenkins, who also doubles as firm chaplain, has been helpful with both clients and employees spiritually. He has been with us 18 years. While the employee benefits include health, disability and life insurance, as well as retirement contributions and a good vacation and sick leave schedule (better than many law firms), there must also be a dynamic within the firm that works.

I also speak a good word about Lindsey Segrest, our receptionist of the past seven and a half years. Her position is very important to the firm. She's the first to receive incoming calls, and to route them to the correct attorney. She must also greet clients coming in to the receptionist desk, and respond to miscellaneous requests from attorneys and the office manager. She has also helped me with the important tasks of addressing and stuffing large mailouts, copying, faxing, sorting the mail, and watering the plants.

After loyal Lynelle left in 2013 for health reasons, I had a talented paralegal, Denise Bertaut, until she left in February 2015. Since then I have had the devoted and enthusiastic Carlton Avery. Carlton, 32, is different in three demographic respects—age, ethnicity, and gender—compared to my previous personal paralegals, mostly middle-aged Caucasian females. Carlton is excited about his work, and I am excited about him. He has a good sense of humor and great future ahead, if he keeps his good attitude and winsome demeanor intact.

My dear wife Leslie is very much a part of our law firm family. She frequently substitutes as a receptionist and sometimes helps on special errands. She also drives me on many longer trips, thus enabling me to work on papers and make calls en route.

Likewise, long-time friend Sandra Long does substitute paralegal work, and is poised to cover the firm's receptionist desk when Lindsey leaves in February 2016 to have her baby.

THE RECESSION OF 2008–2011 was a tense time for many law firms. Three fairly large firms, all based in Birmingham, but one with a prominent Montgomery office, "imploded." By that I mean that their expenses in the preceding, more productive years had gotten to be fairly high. When many of their corporate clients started experiencing financial pressures in 2008, these corporations looked for ways to cut back their own expenses, including legal expenses. Thus some law firms were left struggling. Some went bankrupt, others went out of business.

Fortunately, our firm survived fairly well. That is because, as reflected in what I am correctly quoted as saying in the coffee-table book *Montgomery and the River Region Sketchbook* (Indigo Publishing 2002) by Mary Ann Neeley:

> We are the People's Law Firm. We don't present any big corporations or insurance companies; we don't represent any agencies or departments of State, and we don't represent the city or county of Montgomery. We just represent the people who have problems with them all.

This flow of average, ordinary clients has served our firm well. We are known for handling employment law cases, personal injury and auto accident, general civil litigation, police brutality, administrative law, and criminal defense. One partner handles worker's compensation cases, another social security cases. Nonetheless, we have our own internal tensions, as do all law firms, between attorneys handling different type of cases. We are also challenged, as are other firms, about when, where, and how to advance expense money. The answer to this depends on a complicated equation that takes in the likelihood of success, the amount of recovery expected, and the client's own resources, or lack thereof. It is an inexact science, and sometimes a lawyer can be burned. Other times lawyers do well.

I am more often willing to take chances on cases than most of my law partners. This, too, can produce tension. Generally, none of my partners want to handle police brutality cases, like I do. For them, there is not enough money in it, and too many defenses. Nonetheless, I handle a fair number of them, with the help of the firm's two associate attorneys, Chris Worshek and Chase Estes, my primary paralegal, Carlton Avery, and loyal office manager Amy Strickland assisting.

Reflective of this line of cases is the picture of an early American Indian in our central hallway, which states "To give dignity to a man is above all things." This is a central theme in our law practice.

My law partners Kenneth Shinbaum, Joe Guillot, Aaron Luck, and Jim Bodin are all hardworking and conscientious. Oddly, it seems the older partners work the longer hours, but that is probably because the younger ones have a higher percentage of personal injury cases. I recognize that, as partners, they are their own bosses. After so many years, they want to run, and are entitled to run, their own show, especially so long as their monthly production numbers in attorney fees are sufficiently high.

Thus, my management style is "hands off" with my partners, but fairly "hands on" with my individual cases. I enjoy the attorney work more than the management work I do. Collegiality between our firm's partners is important, as is a harmonious relationship with our clients. After a restructuring in September 2006, the three younger partners (Luck, Bodin, and Guillot) all obtained a percentage of the partnership and a vote in firm decisions, which they didn't previously have.

I still have the highest percentage vote in the firm, and fellow senior partner Kenneth Shinbaum has the next. Nonetheless, we try to reach consensus on major firm decisions. Sometimes this can be awkward and aggravating, but it is essentially democratic. I try to set a tone, and maintain a vision, but that doesn't always work.

IN APRIL 2003, OUR firm started advertising for the first time, thus joining about six other firms or lawyers in the Montgomery plaintiff's world who did. Unfortunately, or fortunately, our budget for advertising has grown. There are different opinions among the partners as to what kind of advertising to pursue, how much to pay, and where to advertise, but we usually work it out.

I maintain that the advertising is primarily to help us with our personal injury cases, where the competition is stiff, and is really not needed at all to help us on our employment and civil rights cases, which overwhelmingly come in due to my own reputation.

Most notably, there was the famous football TV ad in which I completed a pass to a paralegal receiver, while dodging insurance company tacklers. The public absolutely loved it, and the Alabama Bar Association (Gil Kendrick and Tony McLain) approved it. The first weekend I ran it in early 2004, it brought in a big case with a six-figure settlement value. A decade and more later, it is amazing how many people Amy Strickland (our advertising manager) and I run into who still talk about the football ad and would love to see it again. But some of our younger partners encountered snide comments from the defense bar. That made them question the ad, or think it was not sophisticated enough. Amy and I wanted to revive it, but persistent opposition from the younger set has kept it shelved.

There was one other famous ad involving me taking down and pinning a 300-pound high-school wrestler. It ran with a great public reaction for a few months. It was colorful, funny, but made a meaningful point. Yet it met the same resistance from my younger partners and got shelved. Eventually tamer ads were constructed that still had public appeal, though probably not as much as the more colorful ads. However, internal comity within the firm is worth preserving.

Especially popular with the public has been the TV ad involving the young girls talking about "how at McPhillips Shinbaum, we are family." I was asked by many in the public if any of the girls were my granddaughters. The answer is no. One was the daughter of partner Aaron Luck, one the daughter of paralegal Page McKee, and one the granddaughter of paralegal Patricia Williams. Patricia by the way, is the only one in the firm older than me. She has always done a good job and is our firm's photographer.

It was simpler in the old days, and much less expensive, before we started advertising in 2003. In those days, I was in the T.V. and print news more often and was very active politically. All that helped generate business. It still does somewhat, but we now call it "public relations."

Thus, our firm has developed many of the attributes of a family. That is not to say we don't have disagreements and competing strong views. My regular memos to the firm are meant to be inspirational and encouraging to our lawyers, but they sometimes may be received differently. I've often said "we must work together, and help one another." I also say "we will rise or fall together, sink or swim together." So far we're swimming well enough, thanks be to God. That doesn't mean we can't improve our work habits, work product, and intake of clients.

A motto in clear view in the men's bathroom on the central floor of our law office building, and in my inner office quotes the prophet Isaiah:

> . . . those who hope in the Lord will renew their strength. They will soar on wings like eagles; they will run and not grow weary; they will walk and not be faint. — Isaiah 40:30–31

Those ancient words are as timely today as they were 3,000 years ago, and they inspire me and others "to keep on keeping on."

All in all, I personally see the law practice as a combination of professional work, business methods, and ministry. They are interrelated. To be successful or effective, long-term, all three must harmonize. I also see law practice as a hobby. That way, I don't mind spending the extra hours on it that I frequently devote in evening hours and on weekends.

Part III

Family and Personal Life

28

OUR CHILDREN AND OTHER FAMILY

Although I have many interests, as the chapters of this book reflect, I nonetheless consider my top priority to be my children and family, including especially my dear wife Leslie. If you, the reader, consider this too much of an inside story, or too spiritual in nature, feel free to skip over to the subsequent chapters. Otherwise, read along.

"One born in the '70s, one in the '80s, and one in the '90s," I humorously proclaimed on the U.S. Senate campaign trail in 2002, referring to our three children, Rachel, Grace, and David. If Leslie was with me, I would add the crack, "If you ask me, about this decade, I'll tell you it ain't over yet." Amidst the responding rumble of laughter, Leslie would add, "Oh, yes it is."

Leslie grew up as one of four children, and I was one of five. We both know how much fun big families can be. Hence after Rachel's birth in 1977, and Grace's in 1981, we were quite disappointed that child number three was miscarried in 1985, in the third month. The same thing happened again in 1987 with child number four, also at the third month. David's coming to us via adoption when he was one day old in October 1990 was the clearest case of divine intervention I've ever seen. A third miscarriage for Leslie occurred in 1993. Hopefully we'll see these miscarried three children in heaven someday, and they'll have much to tell us. I discussed these momentous developments at more length in *The People's Lawyer*.

Of course, our experience with each child has been very different, as is the case with most families. Rachel, at times, was like "raising an angel." No doubt it helped that Rachel received much gentle attention from Leslie's governess Martha Farias, brought up from Brazil by Leslie's parents in 1977 –78, while Leslie and I campaigned around Alabama when I was seeking election as attorney general of Alabama.

RACHEL SANDERSON MCPHILLIPS (PLUCKER)
Rachel was the direct result of prayer Leslie and I enjoyed on Christmas Day 1976, when Leslie informed me her fertility moment was perfect. God

knew what he was doing. He sent us someone very special. Rachel's sweet spirit is indelible but unmistakable.

Rachel was on the shy side, growing up. Although tall for her age, she was young for her class. She was a natural "good, older sister."

Rachel is so much like her mother Leslie—tall, blonde, and blue-eyed. Their personalities are also remarkably similar. Rachel is also a team player, very supportive, and the glue of her family, all of which is like her mother. Accordingly, Rachel is adored by her husband Jay and her children Laurel and Jude. We adore Leslie and also adore Rachel.

Rachel has been an incredibly good mother to her children, and she continues to be a loyal daughter and sister.

Rachel has been a great schoolteacher for going on sixteen years, ever since she graduated from Elon University in North Carolina in 1999. Although only an average student at St. James School in Montgomery, Rachel graduated cum laude in elementary education from Elon and had a 4.0 average in getting her master's degree in education at Samford University in Birmingham. She is now a seasoned and much-appreciated teacher at Randolph School in Huntsville, where her daughter gets an excellent education and her son soon will. In fact, Rachel is head of the math department at Randolph's middle school and helps run math tournaments.

Her husband, Jay, works with the U.S. Army Corps of Engineers. Leslie and I have much enjoyed our periodic trips to Rachel and Jay's home over the last nine years (2006–2015), first to Helena, in Shelby County, and later to Huntsville. We've also enjoyed frequent weekend visits with them at the McP Retreat, our Lake Martin place. They've enriched the tapestries of our lives. We thrill over having more time with the grands.

GRACE BURTON McPHILLIPS (LUNSFORD)

Grace came into this world on January 8, 1981, in a whirlwind of three important events in a 24-hour period. First, Leslie and I signed the contract on the home we still occupy. Secondly, that night we got together and named our beloved church "Christ the Redeemer." Last but not least, Grace was born. A blaze of glory, all three!

Grace showed early signs of being outgoing and fearless. In 1987, on a week-long Salmon River raft trip in Idaho, Grace and I frequently scooted down the river together over the rapids in a "funyak." At one point Grace jumped off a forty foot cliff—with assistance, or shall we say she was thrown—into the river. The next year, 1988, Grace rode a camel in Morocco, while her older sister watched from the sidelines.

I was involved, and Leslie more so, with both girls in Brownies and Girl Scouts in the '80s and early '90s. Grace was full of personality at an early age, an actress in bloom. It was a natural step for Grace to develop into the leading stage persona that she did at St. James School. It also followed naturally that when given the opportunity to name the St. James School theater after Grace, I accepted the challenge. Grace loved it. It may have helped inspire her later towards the limelight.

Elon University was for Grace, as it was for Rachel, a wonderful choice, yet in a very different discipline. It was musical theater for Grace, elementary education for Rachel. Little did Grace realize that, in the fall of her senior year, she would meet the young man, Corbett Lunsford, who would become her husband two years later in 2004. Corbett, at the time an accomplished pianist with Chicago's "Second City" touring company, fell head over heels for Grace, oozing with her mother's good looks and charm.

I tell Grace and others that she got a special ingredient from me, called "moxie," for lack of a better word. Drive, ambition, and a sense of wanting to make a difference, together with compassion and ample intelligence fuel Grace's machine. She graduated magna cum laude from Elon in 2003, and started a singing group, the Sweet Signatures, which still exists twelve years later.

Along with Rachel, Grace was raised in an enthusiastic Christian faith. I know that it has given both girls additional backbone, and a moral compass.

Grace moved to Chicago in the fall of 2003. Her musical theater and singing talents morphed into movie-acting and movie-making skills. After appearing in several smaller films, beginning with *The Apartment* (2006), she moved up to feature-length films. Grace not only was the lead actress but also executive producer of *The Other One*, which can be found on Amazon and other retailers. She plays a schoolteacher wounded in a school shooting in which her husband was killed. Grace's character then returns to her childhood home, and the main action occurs when she has to look after her grumpy mother who is struggling with dementia. There are also two human ghosts in the film. This movie won great recognition at many film festivals.

Meanwhile, Grace continues to produce and act in other films. Her passion project with Zelda Fitzgerald is entitled "Beautiful Little Fools," a mixture of modern times and the historical Zelda, driven by the lead character.

Grace and Corbett have been to many film festivals, including Sundance in Utah and Cannes in France, where in 2014 Grace walked the red carpet in connection with her short film, *Eclipse*. In 2015, Grace was asked to speak on a panel, "Women Achieving in Film," and she persuaded Leslie to accompany her to Cannes. They had a wonderful mother-daughter trip.

Contemporaneously Grace has encouraged her husband Corbett to develop his home improvement business, which makes homes more energy-efficient. Corbett has now expanded into training people to improve homes with "The Building Performance Workshop." Corbett also wrote the book, *Home Performance Diagnostics*.

For the first ten years of marriage, Grace deliberately held off having children, but in 2015 we were delighted to learn that she and Corbett were expecting their first. They also moved in November 2015 from Chicago to Tampa, where Grace gave birth in February 2016 to Nanette Lillabelle Lunsford. By April 1, 2016, Grace, Corbett, and the baby were expected to be on a tour of twenty cities around the U.S., pulling a "tiny house" behind them, promoting Grace's films and spreading the Gospel of Home Performance with a tour called "Proof is Possible." Eventually they plan to settle in Atlanta, where they'll not only be closer to Grace's parents in Montgomery and Corbett's parents in Tampa, but much closer to the McP Retreat at Lake Martin, which they very much enjoy.

DAVID LARSON McPHILLIPS

Much has already been written in *The People's Lawyer* about the miraculous way in which David came to us and how his significant impact was experienced in our family. I have written more about David which I hope to incorporate into another book about him someday.

Suffice it for now to say that David's coming to us in 1990, and the way he came to us, was transformational for our family, not only for me, but for the three girls as well.

On the Thursday before Memorial Day weekend, 1990, I was sitting at my office desk, sharing with paralegal Carroll Puckett about the special Bible verses Leslie and I had been reading every night since January that year. The verses were given to us in January 1990 by healing evangelist Mahesh Chavda, a modern-day prophet, who said that, if we read these verses together daily, and said our prayers fervently, we'd be surprised about adoption opportunities coming that year. This was 1990, following Leslie's preceding five years of infertility, including two miscarriages during the last half of the 1980s. We agreed to do what Mahesh suggested. There was nothing to lose.

Mahesh was right. A first adoption opportunity came in March 1990. A late-30s lady had an out-of-wedlock pregnancy she wanted to give up for adoption. We arranged to have the woman taken to an expert for a sonogram. The prognosis was a 90 percent chance for a girl. With two girls already at home, Rachel, Grace and Leslie thought we should wait for the chance of a boy. So we passed that opportunity up.

Back to Carroll Puckett. At the precise moment I was telling Carroll (the only member of my staff so informed) about the Bible verses, I received a telephone call from a young grandmother. She was only a little older than me, and had a married son and daughter-in-law coming up from Pensacola that weekend to have an abortion in Montgomery. The young married couple, I later learned from the grandmother, had first sought an abortion at three months pregnant but didn't have enough money to pay for it. Both her husband and she were out of work, and they already had a nine month old daughter. This time, at five months, however, they had the money and had an appointment at a Montgomery clinic.

The "anything but coincidental" timing of the telephone call from the grandmother was "proof positive" of divine intervention. It was like handwriting on a wall. It still blows my mind 25 years later. There was no other way but God's involvement. The chances of coincidence were infinitesimally small.

I asked the grandmother how she happened to call me. She didn't know. She said that somehow she opened the telephone book, and somehow her finger landed on my name. This was out of hundreds of attorneys in the Montgomery telephone book. Yet the grandmother didn't know me from Adam's housecat. Nonetheless, I accepted her invitation to come out to her home two days later, to give information about a private adoption alternative for the young couple, who, the grandmother said, was firmly committed to having the abortion. Carroll Puckett went with me, but I did most of the talking. Strengthened by the Holy Spirit, I shared reasons for the couple not to have the abortion, and go the adoptive route.

Somehow the young couple changed their mind. I took the mother to the same sonogram expert as before. Once again, however, the sonogram indicated the baby was going to be a girl. Meanwhile, shortly thereafter, the first adoption possibility from March was born a boy. Leslie and I quickly agreed we weren't going to make the same mistake twice. We therefore set it up that, in the event the baby was born a girl, she would go to a childless couple in Birmingham, namely Sue and Michael Staff. Sue was my brother David's widow, four days older than me, at that time almost 44. At that age, Sue was not likely to conceive. Adoption was a brand new idea to the Staffs, but they got excited quickly. We truly believed the baby would be a girl, and the sonogram expert would not be wrong again.

In June, Leslie and I traveled around Israel as part of an educational study group based at St. George's College, Jerusalem. We had special prayers in Bethlehem, Nazareth, and Jerusalem for the future child of our family, although we didn't know who, what, or when. We were joined in that effort by our Christ the Redeemer rector Mark Tusken and his wife, Vicki.

I'll never forget the call on October 4, 1990, from adoption attorney Rick Wyatt in Birmingham. "Julian," he said, "are you sitting straight in your chair? That baby we all thought was going to be a girl has been born a boy. What's more, I am going to deliver him to your home tomorrow at 1:30 p.m." This was 3:30 p.m., the afternoon before, giving us only 22 hours notice.

I raced home and told all three girls, as Leslie was bringing Rachel and Grace home from school. Their jumping up and down for joy is emblazoned in my memory forever. The expression on Leslie's face was priceless . . . dumbfounded, but happy. The daughters couldn't believe their good fortune. We were all praising God.

The many truly amazing experiences we all had with David in his single digit years is recorded in *The People's Lawyer* and won't be repeated here. Suffice it to say we all had great fun together, especially when traveling.

And then David hit his teen years. At that time Leslie and I started learning what it's like to have a challenging child. A couple of times in 2006–2007, I had to put unfriendly wrestling holds on David, to let him know who was calling the shots in our house, and that he was going to school, whether he liked it or not.

Substance abuse, drugs, and alcohol were a part of David's surrounding teen culture, and he was no exception. After the seventh grade, David transferred from St. James School to Montgomery Catholic. He transferred to a boarding school, Stony Brook School in Long Island, New York, for his ninth-grade year in September 2005. He didn't make it past February 2006. At that point David transferred back to Catholic.

David made many good friends at Catholic and urged me to start a wrestling team there, which I did in 2007. However, in his senior year, feeling pressure and remembering how much better he was doing in summer school at the Sylvan Learning Center, David pulled out all of his persuasive points and somehow convinced Leslie and me to let him transfer back to Sylvan in October 2008, for the balance of his senior year.

After graduating from Sylvan in the summer of 2009, David enrolled in Shelton State Junior College in Tuscaloosa. He shared an apartment with his two best friends, Peter Carl and Adam Benedict. That was a mistake. Partying was the main thing David and Adam did, and both dropped out before the year was over. Peter, son of a Marine colonel, somehow stayed and transferred the next year, as had been David's plan, to the University of Alabama.

The partying and substance abuse ushered David into one of the roughest periods of his life, ending up in May 2010 with a three-week recovery program at the Friary in Gulf Breeze, Florida, near Pensacola.

By the fall of 2010, David was off to Belize in Central America, as part of a Youth with a Mission training program. It was also great recovery for him. After three months of discipleship training in Belize, David was off to the Philippines for two more months. These experiences shaped David for the better, as did five months with his sister Grace in Chicago in 2011, upon his return to America. David finished 2011 with a final internship leg of his YWAM training under Mahesh and Bonnie Chavda of North Carolina. That experience was a great boost for David, who received his discipleship training certificate from YWAM in early 2012.

After a year and a half home with us, January 2012–July 2013, while taking courses at Troy University Montgomery and working as a pizza delivery man, David decided he wanted to experience the dormitory-style life of a college student, this time at a Christian university. Through his own online discovery work, David found Anderson University in South Carolina. He transferred to Anderson in August 2013, and has been there ever since, proudly standing on his own two feet. It has been a great experience for David, maturing and motivating. He entered his senior year in August 2015.

David is no longer just a "C" student. He has racked up some A's and B's in his School of Christian Studies major. His immediate professional goal is to become a youth minister. After that, David wants to go into missionary work. Helping others is in David's DNA. We are grateful to God that it is.

As to All Three Children

David looks like a third pea out of the same pod, when compared to Rachel and Grace. They've enjoyed a symbiotic relationship, I like to say, with the girls developing their mothering skills. David has also benefitted in myriad ways. Overall, all three have been far more joy than difficulty. Helping them with their challenges is part of a parent's responsibility and adds meaning and purpose in life. All three of our children, like their parents, are still "works in progress," and we enjoy them immensely.

Other Family

Parents: Much has been written about my dear parents, Julian L. McPhillips Sr., and Eleanor Dixon McPhillips. They were the best. They couldn't have been better, in my opinion. Their lives inspired and helped many, including all their children. The four-volume manuscript of their autobiographical "The Drummer's Beat" is a fascinating read.

Brother David: In 1976, the number of my parents' surviving children was reduced to four. The loss of my dear brother David was tragic, and the suicidal nature of it deepened the pain. David and I grew up 20 months apart in age, talking each other to sleep at night. We shared hopes, dreams, ambitions, and confidences. He was every bit as good a student as I was and graduated in 1970 from one of the best small colleges in America, Williams College in Massachusetts. Unfortunately, David got caught up in the counterculture movement of the Vietnam War era, and drugs contributed to his psychological illness. To help my own healing, I have sponsored scholarships in David's name at his two high schools, first at Indian Springs School, near Birmingham, and the other in Montgomery at the LAMP program, begun at Sidney Lanier High School, and continued by its LAMP successor entities. Due to God's great mercy and loving grace, I will see David again in heaven someday. We'll have lot to talk about. I expect he'll be among the first to show me around. I might add that the coming of my son David in 1990 greatly helped me in the healing process. I am certain it helped my Mom and Dad as well. Thank you, Lord.

Sister Sandy: Born in 1942 and my only older sibling, Sandy has always encouraged me greatly. She's now a widow in Sante Fe, New Mexico, with two married children, spouses, and seven grown grandchildren. She had a great 51 years with her husband Charlie before he died in December 2014. The family had an awesome memorial service together in Santa Fe, only one year after Sandy and Charlie celebrated their Golden Anniversary.

Sister Betsy: My sister Betsy, born in 1949, now lives in Chesapeake, Virginia. Growing up, she was the third of the "three musketeers," the moniker my parents gave to their three children born in a three-year span, 1946–49. Betsy was married to Johnny Williams for 25 years and is now divorced, but has 10 wonderful grandchildren from her four married children. She is active in the Little Gym business in the Virginia Beach area.

I love and admire both my sisters greatly.

Brother Frank: Born in 1954, brother Frank was the only one young enough to go to India with my parents in 1966 and live long-term in Calcutta. He graduated from Harvard University and Virginia Law School, and married Louise Jones. They have three fine sons, Jamie (a Washington, D.C. lawyer), Alex (a Google executive), and Dixon (an assistant director in high-budget movies). All three, like their father, are Harvard grads.

Frank, a senior partner at the Maynard Cooper law firm in Birmingham, is considered by many to be one of the leading bond attorneys in Alabama. We are next-door neighbors at our Lake Martin cottages and have enjoyed each other's families over the years. I love and admire Frank and his family greatly. Frank and Louise also have a heart for civil rights, as do my sisters. Credit our parents. The acorns didn't fall too far from the trees.

Sister-in-Law Sue: I still consider as a sister-in-law, Sue Staff, widow of my brother David. Sue was a wonderful wife to David while he lived. She was also dear to my parents, siblings, and me. She remains so. A few years later, Sue married Michael Staff of Birmingham. Both Sue and Mike remain close to Leslie and me. Of course, we shared in the great adoption deal of 1990 that led us to getting our son, David, and the Staffs their daughter, Rebecca.

Leslie's Siblings: Leslie had a good relationship with her father and was a good "big sister" to her three younger brothers. That made me think Leslie might better (than other women) understand my male idiosyncrasies or "machoisms," to coin a word. I was right. Given that Leslie and I see one another as "two halves of one whole," it is appropriate that I mention her three younger brothers, Mark, Craig, and Keith Burton. Mark, three years younger, was decent when sober, but his alcoholism caused his premature demise in 2011. We still pray for him twice daily. Her middle brother Craig, five years younger, is the more like Leslie and their father. A level-headed solar engineer, he has two fine sons, Clark and Paul, and a very considerate wife, Sandra. Leslie's brother Keith, ten years younger and in Utah, became a grandparent sooner than Leslie, from his daughter Elizabeth, and later again from his son Adam. Leslie also has two sharp stepbrothers, Tom and Mel Aden, both graduates of MIT, and both residents of the San Francisco Bay area. She also has a dear stepsister, Dr. Marilyn Aden of Chicago. All three are the children of Leslie's father's second wife, Mary Jo Aden, a widow who married widower Clark Burton in 1985.

Leslie's parents: The dear Eva Mae Larson Burton, a nurse behind the lines in France during World War II, died in 1983 from pancreatic cancer. Leslie's father, Clark Burton, an international banker who raised his family in Brazil and Argentina, lived another 21 years, before passing in 2004 at age 85.

Wonderful Uncles, Aunts, and First Cousins: We have had wonderful uncles in Dave Dixon (1923–2010, my mother's brother) and my 92-year-old Uncle Warren McPhillips (1923– , dad's brother) of Cullman, Alabama. David was married to Aunt Mary Dixon, still living at 86 in New Orleans. Uncle Dave, my mother's only sibling, was a very special uncle, and a wonderful male role model. Founder of the New Orleans Saints football team and, known by many as "Father of the Superdome," Uncle Dave especially doted on me in my toddler years of the late 1940s. He inspired me for the rest of his life.

Our deceased Aunt Sarah Frances McPhillips, like my mom, was an Alzheimer's victim, but at a much earlier age. She had an infectious laugh, inherited by her children. A widower for many years, Uncle Warren remains a dear patriarch to my siblings and me. An avid golfer, Warren's fifth hole-in-one came at the age of 87.

Both sets of uncles and aunts had great children, our only two sets of first cousins. That includes Uncle Warren and Sarah Frances' two sons, Warren Jr. and John, and daughters Francie, Libby, Mary Morrow, and Emily. It also includes Dave and Mary's three Dixon sons, Frank, Shea, and Stuart. They also have many fine grandchildren, and Uncle Warren has many great-grands.

A special word for cousin Frank Dixon, only four years my junior. What a lifesaver in political campaigns. In August–September 1978, in the last stage of my campaign for attorney general of Alabama, my brother Frank, the earlier manager, had to return to law school. So cousin Frank Dixon came up from New Orleans and took over, providing a steady hand I needed. Again in June 2002, in the last few days of my race for U.S. Senate, Frank Dixon came up again and energetically worked my Birmingham boxes. Thank you, both brother Frank and cousin Frank. I'll always be grateful.

Discovering Other Cousins: I continue to discover cousins all the time, especially in Montgomery, Mobile, Birmingham, and Cullman. An 88-year-old bicycle-riding second cousin once removed, David Davidson Sanderson, just moved to Montgomery in 2015 to live near his 91-year-old sister, Katherine Sanderson Campbell. Katherine's son, David Campbell, is the long-time official photographer for Alabama State University. Third cousins, we are great-great grandsons of the original Rev. David Davidson Sanderson Sr., 1820–1891, co-founder of Stillman College in Tuscaloosa.

I also discovered a fourth cousin, Susan LeSage. Well, she discovered me. She works for the City of Montgomery and is descended from a sister of Rebecca Frances Moore (1840–1871), a great-great grandmother of mine who lived in Covington County, Alabama. Susan's and my great-great-great-grandfather, the Rev. John S. Moore, was an early Methodist minister in Alabama.

I also have a slew of McPhillips- and McGowin-related cousins all over Alabama. That includes local Bradley Arant attorney Bill McGowin, a fourth cousin, once removed. In that regard, we are typical of many other Alabamians. We are all a part of the family of mankind.

Leslie and I pray for all of our above-mentioned family, immediate and extended, twice daily, in the morning before work, and at night before bed.

COUSINS ARE GOOD TO HELP LEGALLY

Uncle Warren and Aunt Sarah Frances McPhillips had a great family of six children, one more than Mom and Dad. In the late 1950s, we all lived in Cullman and often enjoyed weekends together at Guntersville Lake as one big family. Their beautiful daughter, Libby, 2 weeks younger than me, was "the cutest girl in town," and made me wish relationships with first cousins weren't illegal. There were three other daughters, of whom Francie was the oldest and Emily the youngest. Tragically, Mary Morrow, their fifth child born about 1955, didn't get enough oxygen at birth. This left her disabled mentally. She could communicate well enough, but was limited in vocabulary and analytical skills.

As Mary Morrow grew older, she became qualified for Social Security and Medicaid and lived in a group home in Birmingham. One day in 2007, I received a telephone call from John McPhillips, the younger of the two sons of Uncle Warren. John, along with his older brother Warren Jr. of Atlanta, had become co-guardians of Mary Morrow. They informed me that their sister had developed a legal problem. The Alabama Medicaid office was after Mary Morrow to repay more than $30,000 in health-related Medicaid benefits.

The problem arose because Mary Morrow had earned too much money, Medicaid said, from sacking groceries. Allegedly, that income, plus her Social Security, meant that Mary Morrow made too much to receive Medicaid, and thus must reimburse the State $30,000 plus.

It was my joy and privilege to help Mary Morrow. Since she was family, I didn't charge a dime for my services. There was no small amount of work involved, but John and Warren Jr. helped me piece together the facts. In the end we had a hearing at one of the State office buildings in Montgomery before Administrative Law Judge Tori Adams-Burke. We laid out Mary Morrow's case, not only that her receipt of the benefits was inadvertent, but that someone at St. Andrew's Church in Birmingham was at fault in not advising her of the problem.

Thanks be to God, and to an enlightened judge, the ruling was in Mary Morrow's favor. She was spared having to pay back this large sum of money, which she didn't have. Her brothers wanted to compensate me, but I still refused. Finally, I relented to them making a $1,000 contribution to the construction of Montgomery Catholic Preparatory School's Pope John Paul II Fieldhouse. Mary Morrow was always one of my parents' favorite nieces, and she is very much loved by all the extended McPhillips' family, including me.

CLOSING THE BOOKS ON THE FAMILY BUSINESS

It was also my privilege to help Uncle Warren McPhillips legally as he closed down King Pharr Canning Company's operations in Uniontown, Alabama, in 1978–80.

Speaking of King Pharr, the McPhillips family business from 1946 to 1976, many of us gathered in Cullman on December 19, 2014, at the old King Pharr plant grounds to dedicate a historic marker (see Appendix B).

It was a cold day, but highly meaningful to all of us. My brother Frank and his wife Louise popped up from Birmingham, while Leslie, David, and I drove up from Montgomery. Cousin Warren McPhillips Jr. drove his father Uncle Warren over from Zebulon, Georgia. Cousin John McPhillips and his wife Linda, still residents of Cullman with three grown sons, hosted a reception. Three of Uncle Warren's daughters made it to the dedication, namely Francie, the oldest, Mary Morrow, and Emily. Only cousin Libby and my sisters Sandy and Betsy were too far away to be present.

We had a strong feeling that day, however, that my parents, grandparents Poppy and Ibby, and Aunt Sarah Frances were all looking down from heaven and smiling.

29

Traveling with Leslie

Civil rights may be in my bones, but Leslie is in my heart.

"She's like my American Express card, I won't leave home without her," I said resoundingly, but with humor referring to my dear wife Leslie. At that time, in 1988, she and I and our daughters Rachel and Grace were traveling in Portugal, Spain, and Morocco. Leslie's Portuguese from her native Brazil, her Spanish from having lived in Argentina and working in the Mexican branch of a New York bank, and her French, learned from two years of high school in Switzerland, were exceedingly useful in those three countries.

In the summer of 1985, before David was born in 1990, we took Rachel and Grace to England, Scotland, and Wales. The trip for Grace, 4, was a breeze, but the first night in St. Albans, England, Rachel, 7, was upset that her room was down the hall from us, not immediately adjacent. Grace laughed about it. The four of us had an awesome time, nonetheless, exploring ancient ruins, beautiful valleys and lakes, and singing "you take the high road, and I'll take the low road, and I'll get to Scotland before ye."

I admit that all this traveling may seem extravagant to some. Certainly I've been fortunate financially in my law practice, and Leslie brought resources into the marriage. With us, it has been a matter of priorities, the knowledge that we live only once and that the maxim that you can't take anything material with you to heaven is unquestionably true.

These travel adventures and sometimes misadventures, both with and without our children, have enriched our marriage and journey in life together. It may sound like a lot of traveling, but it has been done in bits and pieces over the nearly 43 years Leslie and I have known each other. It's far from an everyday thing. And some of the travel was before we met one another, yet I have to unapologetically admit that travel is in our blood.

In 1986, Leslie and I made a three-week trip to Asia. The main part was traveling in mainland China as it was just beginning to reopen to the West. We not only visited Peking, Shanghai, and the Great Wall, but also thrilled to see the terra cotta soldiers in Xian. One memorable moment involved a passenger still running down the aisle as a Chinese plane was taking off.

On the way back to the American mainland, we had enjoyable visits in Hong Kong, Japan, and Hawaii.

In May 1989, we left our daughters home for the first time while we went on a long overseas trip, as we joined a People-to-People Ambassador trip to Hungary, Poland, and Czechoslovakia. This was especially exciting because the Iron Curtain in all three countries was caving in. There were approximately 20 attorneys and their spouses in our group. While we didn't meet the presidents of these countries, we met the next level of officials, all top-level cabinet members (see Appendix 7).

One of the momentous outcomes of this Eastern European journey was our joining with fellow team member Bill Navarre of Michigan to visit a church in Prague. This was where healing evangelist Mahesh Chavda had led a crusade only three weeks early. The church's minister was still dumbfounded by how masses of people, some born blind, some born lame, others with dread diseases, were healed. It sounded biblical and made us to want to meet Mahesh, which we did three months later in Atlanta. Leslie was seeking healing in her reproductive organs, and Mahesh sounded most interesting.

Prague, by the way, is a beautiful city whose ancient architectural splendor has not been damaged much by either World Wars I or II.

Of course Leslie is fun to travel with, because she's beautiful, interesting, a responsible and knowledgeable traveler, and, when the kids were with us, an excellent mom, keeping them safe and intact. Our son David was not born until October, 1990, but after auspiciously entering the world, he attended weddings with us in New Orleans six weeks later and in San Francisco at the age of six months. In June 1991, at eight months old, David spent two weeks with us in Alaska, the last week on a cruise of the Inland Passage. His joyous expressions and noises lit up the previously serious faces of some fellow travelers on a cruise ship.

The '90s and first half of the '00s were full of trips with the kids, but Leslie was always the not-so-secret ingredient making things happen. Or she stopped bad things before they could happen, when appropriate. In 1992, we took all three kids on a round trip of the Dakotas, Nebraska, and Missouri, completing for me a goal of visiting all 50 states. In 1993, it was a trip around France, especially in the Chateaux country of the Loire Valley. In 1995, we cruised the Mediterranean, with stops in Italy, Greece, Egypt, Cyprus, and Israel. As you can imagine, we have colorful pictures and stories of all these ventures.

All throughout the '80s, '90s and '00s we made numerous weekend trips to a condo at the Gulf Shores Plantation or our Lake Martin cottage. The lake place, known as the "McP Retreat" was virtually an extension of our Montgomery home, especially on good weather weekends, since the two homes are only a 45–50 minute drive apart. With some inheritance received in 2011, Leslie greatly polished and expanded our five-bedroom, three-bath lake cottage. It has been used for many family reunions, vestry retreats, celebrations, and even a 2005 planning session by national leaders of Benin for the next election in the small African country.

To begin the 1995 Mediterranean cruise, Leslie, Rachel, Grace, David, and I flew to Rome. After enjoying many wonderful sights in the Eternal City, we traveled to Assisi, home of St. Francis, which was greatly moving. Finally, we boarded the Italian cruise liner *Costa* in Naples. We stopped first in Pompeii and observed the amazing aftermath of the eruption of Mt. Vesuvius in the first century. Afterwards, we floated across the Mediterranean to Egypt, where we landed in Alexandria, and enjoyed the pyramids in Gaza. We also had a special day-long trip by private car around Israel, stopping where David slew Goliath, where Jesus was born in Bethlehem, and seeing much of Jerusalem. We then stopped in Cyprus and the Greek islands, before returning to Italy.

In 1997, the five of us savored a cruise of the Hawaiian Islands. One morning, David and I hit the fishermen's jackpot on an excursion boat. We were two of five fishermen who together landed a 12-foot, 800-pound blue marlin. Framed pictures of this trophy fish adorn several Montgomery restaurants and can be found in *The People's Lawyer*.

During the winters of the '80s and '90s, we made annual week-long trips to the Rocky Mountain ski county, including numerous resorts in Colorado, Utah, Idaho, Montana, and Nevada. Our summer outdoor trips included week-long river raft trips down the Salmon River in Idaho in 1987 and 2001. The first trip was with Leslie and Grace (Rachel opted to go on a gentler Mississippi River steamboat trip with her grandparents). The second trip was a father-son excursion with David, as a break from my U.S. Senate campaign. I wrote a column for the *Montgomery Advertiser* about the 1987 trip (see Appendix 8). Both trips were hosted by my Tonsmeire cousins from Mobile.

During the 1980s, we went on a couple of Caribbean cruises, the first around 1983 with the Alabama Trial Lawyers Association, the second in 1987 with growing daughters Rachel and Grace. In 1996, we took young David with us on a cruise that started in New York but went up the east coast of Canada to Nova Scotia and New Brunswick. Especially memorable was seeing a museum with artifacts from the *Titanic*.

For the week between Christmas 1997 and New Year's 1998, we enjoyed a ski trip to Chamonix, France, in the Alps. Leslie took us all to see her high school at Chateau Brilliamont in Lausanne, Switzerland. It was on this trip that a young lawyer from North Carolina, Calvin Cunningham III, helped relight my political fuse. It almost resulted, four months later, in my receiving an uncontested Democratic nomination for the U.S. Senate, to challenge incumbent Richard Shelby. The press described him as an 800-pound gorilla. In the end, my mother and fellow trial lawyers supporting Shelby talked me out of it.

In June 1998, following an anguished decision not to run for the U.S. Senate, Leslie, Grace, David, and I took off on a trip to South America. There we visited and encouraged Christian missionaries in Chile, Peru, and Bolivia. Thanks again to Leslie for her language skills. I made the trip as a trustee of the South American Missionary Society (SAMS) of the Episcopal Church. It was an honor to serve on its board from 1994 to 2000.

Our Silver Anniversary was in 1999. To celebrate 25 good years of marriage, Leslie and I took all three children on a cruise to Norway and its beautiful fjords, reliving part of our honeymoon journey in 1974 to Norway, Sweden, Finland, and Russia. The anniversary cruise was full of wonderful moments, awesome scenery, and great family times. The first trip was by land, the second by water.

The next few years involved my helping Bill Bradley run for president in 2000 and then my own run for the U.S. Senate in 2002. Accordingly, Leslie and I stayed closer to home. That summer of 2000, Leslie, Grace, and David accompanied me to the Democratic convention in Los Angeles, as a member of the Alabama delegation. Our family enjoyed seeing Disneyland, Hollywood, and other landmark southern California sites.

For the Christmas week of 2001, the five of us escaped to Bermuda for a wonderful one-week family vacation. In 2002–2003, recovering from the election and enjoying Grace's graduation from Elon, we enjoyed good domestic trips to New Hampshire and North Carolina.

In 2003, Leslie and I flew to southern Spain, took in coastal sites, including Picasso's hometown, and enjoyed Gibraltar. We then got on a cruise ship to the Madeira Islands off Portugal and traveled down to the Canary Islands, due west of Africa.

The next big family trip, and virtually the last that just the five of us took together was our 30th Anniversary celebration trip in June 2004 to Germany, Austria, and Switzerland. There were many highlights, but enjoying one another's company was, as always, the best part. Grace was on the phone most of the trip with her fiancé, Corbett Lunsford. They were married in August, only two months later.

From 2004 onward, our trips were more often just the two of us, although frequently with David. With Grace in Chicago and David in New York at Stoney Brook School, we made frequent trips to those metropolitan areas. That included attending five-year-cycle reunions at Princeton in 2003, 2008, and 2013, and in New York City for Columbia Law School reunions in 2001, 2006, and 2011. Another set of five-year reunions of my Sewanee Military Academy Class of 1964 took place in Tennessee, from 1979 to 2014.

An especially meaningful trip was one Leslie and I made in late July–early August 2005, when we traveled to Benin, formerly named D'Ahomey, when it was a French colony. (I was familiar with the name from collecting stamps in the 1950s.) It is located immediately between Togo and northern Nigeria. The eight days we spent in Benin were quite an adventure. On August 1, we witnessed an impressive Independence Day parade in Cotonou, the capital. Leslie and I spoke in French with most of the natives, and were surprised at how conversant we were. I even preached in French in two different churches.

Our journey was part of the Alabama-Benin Reconciliation Movement, organized by former Prichard, Alabama, Mayor John Smith, who was assisted by the Rev. John Alford, my close friend, then president of the Montgomery SCLC chapter. Tuskegee Mayor Johnny Ford, then president of the World Conference of Black Mayors, was also a leader of our delegation that included State Agricultural Commissioner Ron Sparks, Mayor James Perkins of Selma, State Senator Hank Sanders and his wife Rose, also of Selma, and Bishop Leo Lewis of Miracle Deliverance Church in Montgomery.

Benin was the last part of Africa from which slaves ever came to America (and into the Prichard area near Mobile). This was on the eve of the Civil War, 50 years after Congress made illegal the importation of new slaves into America.

We also personally met and talked with both Benin's president and the chief justice of the Benin Supreme Court.

Thanks to our great local guide, Chichi Oji, we traveled around Benin, seeing Porto Novo and Ouidah (from which captured slaves were shipped). One time we had a driver take us to Ganvie, a floating village on a lake. We had a memorable, harrowing experience on a slow-moving, narrow dirt road on the way back to Cotonou, when our taxicab driver lightly bumped into a motorcyclist, while semi-parked in a slow-moving line. The motorcyclist became very angry and demanding. It was pitch black except for headlights.

I slipped our driver a $20 bill to appease the motorcyclist. It may have saved us all.

Fights between local Beninese were not uncommon. An earlier guide named Vincent explained how he was one of 11 sons and 12 daughters born to his parents. The daughters were all still alive, but he was the only son still living. The other brothers, he said, had killed each other in voodoo disputes. Vincent credited his conversion to Christianity as the reason for his survival.

In November 2005, Chichi called us from Africa, and said she was coming to America, and wanted to know if she could stay with us for a month. We said yes, but it ended up being four months, January–April 2006. Chichi, a highly committed Christian, became like a member of the family. In 2013–2015, she, her husband Success Jumbo, and their new baby were members at Christ the Redeemer Episcopal Church. They are among our best friends. We are happy to help them in various ways.

The travel bug had bit me even before I met Leslie. To improve my French, I spent the summer of 1965 in France, primarily in Saint-Malo, but traveling by mobilette through other parts of the country. The summer of 1967 I returned to research my Princeton thesis topic on the "Role of the French Communist Party in the Resistance Movement" against the Nazis. I was based in Paris. Later I traveled with my brother David, en route to India, stopping in Germany, Greece, Lebanon, and Iran on the way.

After five weeks in India, David, my sister Betsy, and I stopped off in Bangkok, Thailand; Hong Kong, Japan, and Hawaii, traveling back to the U.S. That summer of 1967 was also our first trip to California, but we approached it from the Orient. We took in both San Francisco and Los Angeles before flying to Dallas, where Betsy and I were godparents at our niece Lynwood's baptism.

The summer of 1968, also en route to India, I spent three weeks traveling with my brother Frank around much of Western Europe. He was only 14. I was 21. We had a ball, including several significant misadventures. The worst, in Switzerland, we called "Basel my Kasel'" as we fled Basel in the middle of the night, avoiding "ladies of the night" knocking on our bedroom door.

Following three arduous years of law school at Columbia University in New York, I celebrated finishing the New York Bar exam by spending one month in the western United States, camping out with my brother Frank all over the Rockies.

Immediately afterwards, when Frank went back to school, I took off on a month-long journey to South America. A diverse schedule took me to Columbia, Ecuador, Peru, Chile, Argentina, Brazil, and Venezuela, in that order. Traveling was cheap in those days, and I stayed in inexpensive quarters like youth hostels. I flew back to New York in late September 1971 to begin work at the Wall Street law firm of Davis Polk & Wardwell.

Leslie also developed the travel bug at an early age. Hers was certainly influenced by her growing up in South America, and mine by my family living in India from 1966–69. After our June 1974 honeymoon in Scandinavia and Russia, we used the same American Express travel discounts to tour the African continent in 1975 (seeing Egypt, Kenya, Tanzania, South Africa and Angola) before stopping off for a week in Brazil.

Among the highlights of that African continent trip were: (a) catching Pharaoh's plague in Egypt, after drinking lemonade near the Pyramids; (b) almost getting charged by an elephant convoy in Tanzania, closely following lions, and defending against orangutans in our Kenyan "Treetops" bedroom; (c) enjoying the beauty of Capetown, South Africa but revulsing at the signs of Apartheid; and (d) stopping briefly in Angola after a plane just before us had been shot at, and guards at the airport had loaded rifles pointed at us. We flew the short distance from Africa to Brazil, which was a homecoming for Leslie. I met some of her best friends. In Brazil, I received a telegram from my mother that I had passed the Alabama bar exam, which I had taken two months earlier in Montgomery.

Tales of my drowsiness at inappropriate times and places in far-away continents make for good humor at my expense. The further away from home I get, the more relaxed I become. One embarrassing moment in Rio de Janeiro involved my becoming so relaxed that I briefly fell asleep at the dinner table. We eventually made our way back home to New York in late April 1975, before driving down to Montgomery to establish a new home.

We had fun traveling together to several Central American countries: Mexico in 1978; Honduras in 1994; Costa Rica with the kids in 1997–98; Belize in 2010; Panama in 2012; and Cuba in 2015. Amidst many adventurous stories, Leslie's Spanish helped open doors and keep us out of trouble.

The most inspiring trip spiritually for us was our three-week journey to Israel in June 1990. Accompanied by Mark and Vicki Tusken, we were part of a 35-person group that was about 40 percent American, 40 percent Australian. While in Israel, and not yet knowing of David's coming to us, the four of us had special prayers in Jerusalem, Bethlehem, and Nazareth for the future child of our family.

Also, while in Israel, I'll never forget the titillating feelings five of us felt upon descending feet first into Lazarus's tomb. The Holy Spirit came over us super strong when an Australian priest, his wife, an Irish priest from Egypt, and Leslie and I together sang "Alleluia, Alleluia, Give Thanks to the Risen Lord." Additionally, our walk through knee-high water in Hezekiah's tunnel was exhilarating (see Appendix 9).

That same summer of 1990, just before David was born, we had two more inspiring domestic trips. One in mid-summer was to Indianapolis, Indiana, to attend the World Conference on the Holy Spirit and Evangelism. We were accompanied by six others from Christ the Redeemer Episcopal Church of Montgomery. Of the 25,000 participants, a fourth were Episcopalian, half were Roman Catholic, and the final fourth consisted of others. We saw some amazing miracles of healing, especially in the nondenominational room led by John Wimber.

A few weeks later, in Rocky Mountain National Park near Estes Park, Colorado, Leslie's Burton clan joined together with the Aden clan of her father's new wife Mary Jo Burton, after widow married widower. Especially memorable was a climb up Long's Peak, over 14,000 feet high, with Leslie's stepbrothers, Tom and Mel Aden, and Mel's wife Betsy. It was one of the most physically exhausting moments of my life.

One of the most enjoyable trips was the summer of 2010 when we took a cruise of the Great Lakes. Starting in Toronto, we sailed first onto Lake Ontario. We made it through the locks of Niagara Falls, and then out to Lake Erie. From there, we went up the Detroit River and locks into Lake Huron, and eventually to Lake Superior. Particularly enjoyable were all the Canadian sights as well as Mackinac Island in the Upper Peninsula of Michigan. The only Great Lake not visited was Lake Michigan, but we've done that several times from Chicago. We ended up in Minnesota, and made our way to St. Paul, where we saw many of F. Scott Fitzgerald's haunts from his childhood and youth.

A great spiritual highlight was a two-week pilgrimage in October 2012 around Greece, with a brief excursion to Ephesus, Turkey, following in the missionary footsteps of St. Paul. We started in Athens, went to Corinth and Phillipi, then up to Macedonia, and back down to the Greek islands, including Patmos, Rhodes, Mykonos, Crete, and Santorini. Led by Archbishop Robert Duncan of the Anglican Church of North America and professors Leslie Fairfield and Mark Stevenson of Trinity Seminary, Ambridge, Pennsylvania, our tour group of 50 enjoyed an exciting and educational journey.

Perhaps the most exalting trip, as far as pure adventure and the beauty of the landscape, was the trip to Antarctica in January–February 2014. Seeing all the penguins, seals, and whales among the snow, ice, and deep blue water was awesome. At both ends of the trip, we enjoyed Argentina and Brazil, especially Buenos Aires and the magnificent Iguasu Falls (see Appendix 10).

More recently, in February, 2015 a first-ever trip to Cuba was highly stimulating . . . seeing the big island before it is swarming with American tourists and businesses (see Appendix 11).

We've also enjoyed two week-long trips to Ireland, one in the summer of 2011, the other in 2015 (I made a solo trip to Ireland in 1968, five years before meeting Leslie). The latest trip was a part of the International Fitzgerald Conference, as were earlier trips to France in 2000 and 2011, and to Switzerland in 2004. We also hosted an International Fitzgerald Conference in Montgomery in November 2013. Inspired, I wrote most of this chapter during my first night in Dublin, Ireland, on July 3, 2015. The shadows of all those great Irish writers, including James Joyce, who lived near our hotel, stir one's blood, including this would-be writer.

We had long planned a two-week trip to India for January 2016, to visit Calcutta and West Bengal, places where my family lived in 1966–68, when Dad was director of the American Peace Corps in India. My mother worked with Mother Teresa there. We were to travel up the sacred Ganges River and stop at the "Sisters of Charity" location where Mother Teresa's ministry was headquartered. We also planned to take in New Delhi, the Taj Mahal, and Agra. But we received a last-minute cancellation of the trip by the Chicago company organizing it. There were problems on the Indian end with the boat we were scheduled to ride on.

So we opted instead for a week-long voyage in the Caribbean aboard a Wind Star sailing vessel. Starting in Barbados, we traveled to St. Lucia, Grenada, the Grenadines, St. Vincent, and other islands. The India trip is being re-offered for November 2016, the month I turn 70. If good health for both of us remains, we may give it another chance.

In 1973, with an American Express discount, I traveled very inexpensively to New Zealand, Australia, Tahiti, Guam, and Micronesia. Leslie, however, has never been to that part of the world. I arrived in Tahiti on a Pan Am plane and left a few days later on a Pan Am plane. Tragically, just after I arrived, a third Pan Am plane crashed in the ocean, killing everyone on board. That is how my mother and wife first met one another, over the telephone, comparing travel schedules I had given them. Worried sick, they rejoiced when they discovered I was not on the crashed plane.

Travel is sometimes quite daunting and is not for the "faint of heart." Between mechanical issues and weather delays, flights are delayed or cancelled, and travel agents make booking mistakes. Security checks today can also be a hassle. Our last time returning from international travel into the

Miami Airport, we found ourselves behind a thousand people in long lines snaking to customs kiosks. As usual, I could use more patience.

Mark Twain famously wrote, "Travel is fatal to prejudice, bigotry and narrow-mindedness." Leslie and I very much agree. We've come to love different cultures and different views. We all share a common bond of humanity. We are all children of God.

Certainly traveling itself is not a civil right, but it has often replenished my scattered resources. Over the years it has also renewed my energy and vision for work in the civil rights field and everything else.

30

THE FITZGERALD MUSEUM

I t is natural for a civil rights attorney to have an interest in history, literature, and museums. Surely F. Scott Fitzgerald and his wife Zelda would make the connection, and approve of it. After all, the Fitzgerald Museum in Montgomery is the only museum anywhere in the world dedicated to either of these internationally renowned literary icons. This was a huge shortcoming, which was set right in 1986–1989.

At that time, Ernest Hemingway had four museums, including ones in Key West, Florida; outside Havana, Cuba; in Forest Park, Illinois; and Sun Valley, Idaho. Edgar Allen Poe had three museums: in Philadelphia, Baltimore, and Richmond.

Most literary buffs would say that Fitzgerald is at least the equivalent of Hemingway, if not more outstanding. According to an Oxford University of England study in 2000, *The Great Gatsby* is the second most widely read novel in the world. Only James Joyce's *Ulysses* is ahead, and *Tender is the Night* by Fitzgerald ranks 26. Fitzgerald is quoted by speakers far more often than Hemingway. Only Mark Twain is quoted as much. Fitzgerald's almost 300 short stories were popular entertainment for the American public in the 1920s–'30s. Fitzgerald also coined the phrase "the Jazz Age," and his novels and short stories chronicled the era.

Zelda Sayre Fitzgerald was also a novelist, and an artist, and has recently experienced a resurgence of interest in her life. Four books were published about her in 2013, one from an Italian author, and two more in 2014.

This colorful twosome is absolutely unique as a couple impacting the literary world.

Civil rights legal work involves patching things up. It helps to have an interest in history and a little skill in writing. It also helped that Leslie and I only lived two houses down from what is now the Fitzgerald Museum, in Montgomery's Old Cloverdale neighborhood. We also wanted to see the historic nature of Felder Avenue preserved.

Other Fitzgerald board members are also dedicated to civil rights. That includes three with a connection to historically black Alabama State University, only one block away down Dunbar Street. I refer to former ASU history department chair Dorothy Autry, English department chair Jackie Trimble, and public relations man, Ken Mullinax. It also includes our executive director Willie Thompson and his wife Silvia Giagnoni, dedicated to helping immigrants. In fact, it includes most of our board, including my dear wife Leslie, and especially Lori Boone, Randall Williams, and Janie Wall. Janie lives just across the street from the Museum. As a talented landscape architect, she keeps the grounds impeccable and beautiful.

Anita Folmar, Montgomery's one-time first lady, proclaimed to me in the 1990s, upon seeing Virginia Durr's name, my name, and others on the board: "You're a hotbed of liberals." Maybe we are, or have been. I don't believe either of the Fitzgeralds would have objected. After all, their only child, Scottie Fitzgerald Smith, was a well-known liberal politically and a supporter of liberal causes.

Speaking of Virginia Durr, back in the late '80s and early '90s, she responded quickly when a few Montgomerians claimed they were Scottie's special friends and said Scottie wouldn't have approved of the Museum. Virginia shot back that they were only jealous and wanted to be "keepers of the flame." Virginia was in a position to know. Besides, Old Cloverdale neighbor and early board member Bob Bogard and I talked with Scottie about the idea only a few months before she died. Scottie told us that while she wasn't the proper person to head such a project, she was pleased to know Bob and I thought it a good idea.

It has been almost 30 years now since that fateful December 24, 1986, day when Leslie and I bought the house at 919 Felder Avenue to keep developers from tearing it down. It was an 8,500-square-foot mansion when the Fitzgeralds lived there for only six short months in 1931–32. Then, during the Great Depression, it was subdivided into four apartments. The Museum gradually grew from occupying one apartment, to being spread out now into the two first-floor apartments, a total of almost 5,000 square feet. We've come a long way from the "modest museum" that columnist Rheta Grimsley Johnson described in a 1999 editorial.

In May 2014, we celebrated the Silver Anniversary of the 1989 opening of the museum. We are on our way, if not already there, to becoming a "world-class museum." After all, we regularly have visitors from nearly every continent. Increasing numbers of Alabamians are coming also.

How did this all happen?

It has helped greatly in the last several years to have a dynamic duo of an energetic young executive director in Willie Thompson and a charismatic director of development in Shawn Sudia-Skehan of Atlanta. Both have contributed enormously. Thompson, bubbling over with ideas, and increasingly knowledgeable of all things Fitzgerald, spearheaded the Museum's doubling its size. Thompson envisions a long-term commitment on his part, and not merely because his great-grandfather dated Zelda during their teens at Sidney Lanier High School, before F. Scott met her. Indeed, Willie is more inspired by the Fitzgeralds' colorful legend and their influence on America's culture. Willie has captivated the Museum's increasing number of visitors, cajoling them with comparisons between Scott and Zelda of yesteryear and Brad Pitt and Angelina Jolie of today.

Willie also retains the skills he employed when he was his fraternity's social chairman at Washington and Lee University. He puts that talent to good use in organizing the Museum's biggest annual event, a fund-raiser called the Gala, in early May. It is a festive, kick-up-your-heels recreation of a 1920s jazz party. It's a lot of fun, usually attracting 300–400 people. Willie puts his electronic savvy to work, broadcasting Museum news on social media as well as more conventional news outlets.

Thompson, still in his early 30s, draws upon an even younger set of volunteers and paid assistants to keep the museum lively. His primary assistant, 27-year-old AUM graduate student Deric Sallas, says, "I like working here to present another side of Montgomery, both to the younger generation and a national/international audience." Deric ran the Museum's Christmas party on December, 12, 2015, while Willie was vacationing in Italy with his wife Silvia's family, but sending regular emails back across the Atlantic.

Shawn Sudia-Skehan once famously asked Leslie and me why we were so committed to the Museum. Besides my usual response about living close by, I told Shawn that it had "become a hobby and a 'labor of love.'" Shawn's quick reply was "Oh Julian, that's not enough. It must be a passion." While she and I shared a hearty laugh at that, Shawn was serious, and her comment reflects the passionate style she brings to the Fitzgerald Museum. We have benefitted enormously from Shawn's assistance as director of development.

Shawn, in her early 60s but with the energy of someone in her 30s, draws on her professional experience in the nonprofit field. She has worked closely with our board of directors in developing our vision and mission statements, and we continue to draft our business plans. She and Willie are also organizing a series of programs for our local community, supporting interests important to both Fitzgeralds during their lifetimes. While programs under Zelda's track focus on art, those for F. Scott focus more on writing.

In recent years, Shawn has also donated many artifacts, memorabilia, photographs, and publications to the museum, as well as the stamp collection that Scott and daughter Scottie started in Paris in the late 1920s. Many of the rarely published photographs Shawn has secured for the Museum depict all three Fitzgeralds in private, joyful moments. Shawn has also reframed our collection of original Zelda paintings, with many prints authorized by Zelda's granddaughter Bobbie Lanahan to Zelda's Art Gallery.

Equally committed to keeping Fitzgerald's work alive, Shawn has also donated a complete collection of the author's appearances in the *Saturday Evening Post* and *Esquire* magazines. She expects to augment the Museum's library with her personal collection of F. Scott Fitzgerald's appearances in such other historical magazines as *Shadowlands, Hearst's International, Bookman, American Mercury, The Dial, Colliers, Liberty, The Smart Set,* and *Scribner's.* These resources are already attracting Fitzgerald scholars as well as amateur enthusiasts.

When Fitzgerald died in 1940, he left some 300 books in his personal library. Using Princeton's list of these books and their publication year, Shawn has begun replicating his collection with the same titles published in the same year. Furthermore, Shawn hopes eventually to replicate the list of books the author compiled for Sheilah Graham in her *College of One.* In addition, Shawn is working with the Museum to obtain documentaries and other audiovisual presentations left by those who knew the family, to create a media center for scholarly research on the Fitzgeralds.

I laugh when I think how Shawn recently had to twist the arm of Princeton University rare books librarian Dan Scemer to obtain a fascinating 1960s documentary, *Marked for Glory*, featuring Andrew Turnbull and Scottie Smith talking about Scott and Zelda. Shawn was ecstatic about it. I had to sign an agreement on behalf of the Museum to hold Princeton University harmless from anyone's legal claims.

We're also excited that the *Princeton Alumni Weekly* assigned top journalist Barksdale Maynard to do a feature story, and hopefully a cover story, about the Fitzgerald Museum. After all, Fitzgerald is Princeton's greatest literary light, and his Class of 1917 is coming up on its 100th Anniversary. The *PAW* has a circulation of about 48,000. Thus, such an article should help the museum immensely.

While the Museum continues to seek what the late Fitzgerald scholar Mathew Bruccoli called "bait" when we first started organizing the museum in 1987, Shawn has helped us enhance the museum itself by donating display cases and fittings for our exhibits.

As much as they've inspired us in recent years, the Museum has been far more than a "Shawn and Willie" show.

I gently remind people that we're not holding up either Scott or Zelda as "role models," although they are obviously great models of creativity. Indeed Fitzgerald's literary works and gifts of writing have encouraged me personally to write, and to write better. Yet, my motivation for doing the Museum is not because we both attended Princeton. In most other respects, our lives have been very different.

We still maintain the long-time goal we had when we first opened the museum in 1987, namely establishing a literary colony in the two apartments on the top floor. There emerging writers could live and develop their art as writers.

I encourage Fitzgerald enthusiasts to see the 1988 video produced by former WSFA-TV anchor Bob Howell, which captures the spirit and motivation behind the Museum's creation in 1986–89. That video is still quite popular with tourists and fans, some 28 years after it was made.

I wrote most of this chapter in spare moments at the F. Scott Fitzgerald Society's international conference in Waterford, Ireland, in July 2015. The biennial conference took place for five days in Waterford and added an extra day in Cork. The conference actually began with two days in Dublin. This Irish trip was also a good vacation, allowing Leslie and me to enjoy a good time together. I caught my breath from my work as a civil rights attorney and trial lawyer back home.

The vice president of the Fitzgerald Museum, Dr. Kirk Curnutt of Troy University Montgomery, was largely responsible for running the conference. Kirk is also the longtime vice president of the Fitzgerald International Society and is well-respected in international literary circles, in part also for his work with the Hemingway Society.

We began Sunday morning, July 5, 2015, breaking bread in Dublin with two of the Fitzgeralds' grandchildren, Bobbie Lanahan and her brother, Samuel Lanahan. It was a stimulating breakfast. They appreciate our efforts, and we appreciate them.

Meanwhile in Waterford, such leading Fitzgerald scholars as Scott Donaldson, retired professor of William and Mary College; Jackson Bryer, professor emeritus of the University of Maryland; and professors from England, France, Germany, Japan, and America analyzed Fitzgerald literature and lore. Kendall Taylor, a Zelda biographer, was an engaging participant, reflective of her work.

This was the sixth International Fitzgerald Conference Leslie and I have personally attended, out of 13. The first was at Princeton in 1996; then in Nice, France in 2000; in Vevey, Switzerland in 2004; followed by Paris and Lyon in 2011; Montgomery in 2013; and in 2015 in Ireland. The venues for the Fitzgerald literary conferences alternate from one side of the Atlantic to the other, every other year.

Montgomery's international conference in November 2013 was a huge success, attracting several hundred participants from five different continents, showcasing not only the Museum, but Montgomery's many other historical attractions. An opening night event involved lovely St. James School girls dancing, à la Baz Luhrmann's 2013 *Great Gatsby* film adaptation, amidst a marching band that electrified the evening.

From its beginning in 1986–89, the Fitzgerald Museum has been far more than a shrine for Scott and Zelda. What has excited me the most is to see it become an instrument for literary revival rather than a mere shrine for Scott and Zelda. At least in Alabama, and sometimes well beyond, we've encouraged good writing with the annual Fitzgerald Museum literary contest for area high school and college students.

On September 28, 2015, the Museum held a reception celebrating the winners of its 27th annual contest. Present were most of the winners, their teachers, and their parents. First, second, and third place award winners in both the college and high school short story contests won $250, $100, and $50, respectively. Each winner's teacher received $50. Previous contest winners have already emerged as professional writers. We expect more to do so in the future.

Four days earlier, on September 24, 2015, Fitzgerald's 119th birthday, we held the Museum's first annual seminar for neophyte writers. We brought in distinguished Mississippi writer Mary Jo Tate, author of *Critical Companion to F. Scott Fitzgerald: A Literary Reference to His Life and Work*," to lead a workshop at the Museum. Tate's sessions included "The Composition of a Masterpiece: How F. Scott Fitzgerald Wrote and Revised the Great Gatsby"; "The 5 P's of Publishing: How to Plan, Pen, Polish, Publish, and Promote your Book"; and "Getting It Right: How to Polish Your Writing."

Speaking of encouraging writers, Leslie and I enjoyed housing English biographer Sally Kline for several months in the basement apartment of our home, two doors down from the Fitzgerald Museum, while she worked hard on an impressive biography about Zelda. Sally shared several Fitzgerald insights with us.

No organization stimulates the arts in Montgomery—written and visual—more than the Fitzgerald Museum. Its annual literary and art contests, its highlighting of Zelda's paintings, and the popularization of and access to Scott and Zelda's novels, short stories, letters, documents, and artifacts have benefited our city, state, and even the world.

The Fitzgerald Museum has been administered by the McPhillips Shinbaum law firm since December 1986, when Leslie and I purchased the house. In the 30 years since, all the official functions of the Museum, from secretary, treasurer, president, and attorney have been volunteered by our firm, which has also absorbed thousands of dollars in out-of-pocket costs.

Unfortunately, the Montgomery business community has only a modest appreciation of the museum and appreciates even less my firm's help. Apparently, this is because I am a civil rights attorney. I remember my late friend Henry Leslie, at the time president of Union Bank, saying he pushed in the early 1990s for our firm's recognition by the Montgomery Area Business Committee for the Arts (MABCA) but that others in the organization did not like my politics and voted it down.

In the 25 years since, we've never been recognized by MABCA. That organization consists mainly of business leaders patting each other on the back. But perhaps that is why we've received little assistance from the Chamber of Commerce and business leaders. They should support us strongly for bringing in so many tourists and Fitzgerald aficionados from Europe, Australia, New Zealand, Asia, and all over the Americas, who would not have come to Montgomery otherwise.

I exempt from that statement, however, business leader Jimmy Lowder, who has been very generous to the Museum. I also exempt Montgomery's Mayor Todd Strange and the Montgomery City Council and Montgomery County Commission. When the Museum hosted an International Fitzgerald Conference in November 2013, Mayor Strange, the city councilmen, and county commissioners were all very helpful. Especially helpful was County Commissioner Dan Harris.

The Museum has several unsung heroes. One is the saintly and eccentric Janie Wall, whose landscape architectural talents have dressed up the outside gardens. Another is Martha Cassels, who ran the Fitzgerald Museum's literary contest for the first 25 years and was recently recognized by the City of Montgomery for her long-term advocacy for and support of the literary arts. Martha also manages the two upstairs apartments in the Museum building. Board member Brian Miller also ran the contest for a year, with assistance from board members Annette Clifford and Jackie Trimble. Dr. Trimble, chair of the ASU English department, recently assumed leadership of the literary contest.

Board member Al Steineker, a caterer, has generously contributed thousands of dollars worth of delicious food over the years to our annual galas.

As mentioned earlier, Dr. Kirk Curnutt of Troy University, Montgomery, has made heroic and myriad invaluable contributions to the Museum over the past 20 years.

Amy Strickland, my law office manager, has also been exceedingly valuable to the Museum as treasurer and secretary since 1996. She quietly pays all the bills, makes the deposits, and does all the accounting and tax-related work. At the annual galas, she collects the money from the silent and live auctions.

We're also delighted with our new secretary, Carlton Avery, whose youth (32), gender (male) and ethnicity (African American) add to the diversity of our leadership. Carlton's enthusiasm, wit, and hard-working ethic are contagious.

Last, but far from least of the unsung stalwarts, has been my life partner Leslie McPhillips. She frequently covers for Willie as a tour guide, and is constantly sprucing up the Museum's gardens. Leslie has also given generously of her own financial resources to meet maintenance and rehabilitation needs of the building and grounds.

Our newest board member, Vicki Morrison, also a faculty member at Troy University Montgomery, and a former paralegal of mine, brings new energy and organizational skills to help us with fundraising, especially among the International Society membership.

Board member Brian Jones helps us with publications and grants from his employer, the Alabama Department of Tourism, and board member Kyle Gassiott has benefited us over the Troy University public radio station he operates.

Two other great but recent board additions enhancing the Museum have been Rick Anderson, former chairman of the English Department at Huntingdon College, and Diane Teague, a popular personality and widow of Barry Teague. Another younger board member, Dr. Lee Murphy, lives only four houses down Felder Avenue from the Museum, and gives us inroads into the medical profession.

Lee was a classmate and good friend of my actress daughter Grace at St. James School. I should not omit what Grace has been up to in the Fitzgerald world. Influenced by the museum as she grew up in our home two doors down from the museum, Grace has long been intrigued by the legend and spirit of Zelda.

Also a movie producer, Grace completed a colorful script several years ago about Zelda, and has been trying to garner the financial support necessary to produce a movie with the working title, "Beautiful Little Fools." The script features a modern-day Zelda Stone, who moves to Montgomery with her auto executive husband. The contemporary Zelda discovers the story of Zelda Fitzgerald and begins to encounter similar experiences, which are juxtaposed in creative flashbacks with the Zelda of old. The Fitzgerald Museum will benefit greatly when this movie is completed and shown.

Late in 2015, the museum became the beneficiary of two great Sayre family artifacts. The first, given to us in October by former board member John Napier, now 91, and his wife, Cameron, was a beautiful saber from the Spanish-American War that belonged to Zelda's brother-in-law Newman Smith, who was married to Zelda's sister Rosalind.

The second artifact was a large, leather-bound circa 1850 family bible from Zelda's maternal Machen branch of the family. The donor, former Montgomery resident Mark McDonald, now living in Atlanta, is head of the Georgia Trust for Historic Preservation. Matt is well-placed and interested in helping the museum more. He and Shawn Sudia-Skehan have already gotten together to plan future initiatives.

The board has recently implemented two important developments. First, the Museum created a new national board of advisers. This will help us draw leadership support from all over the U.S. and beyond. Second, the Museum established a new annual award: the Fitzgerald Museum Literary Prize for Excellence in Writing. In January 2016, the board named Kim Cross, the 39-year-old Alabama author of *What Stands in a Storm,* as the inaugural winner of the prize. Her book is a dramatic, gripping nonfiction tale of three days of tornadoes in April 2011 that killed 324 persons across the South, including 240 in Alabama. Future winners will probably include one fiction and one nonfiction winner. This literary contest and prize also should enhance the Museum's reputation nationally.

As it heads toward its 30th year, the Scott & Zelda Fitzgerald Museum is poised, and purposed, for a long run.

31

WRESTLING IN MY BLOOD

I f civil rights are in my bones, wrestling is in my blood. The two arise from the same wellspring and often jive together. Indeed, going into the courtroom in front of a jury is similar to stepping into a wrestling ring in front of a crowd.

The comparisons may seem more psychological than physical, but they are both. In not only in the ultimate drama of the fight, but the self-disciplined preparation before the battle, there is much in common. I've often thought my years of amateur wrestling did as much to prepare me for civil rights cases as did my three years in law school. Just in a different way.

I first got involved in wrestling as a high school sophomore to help my football playing. I was a starting guard on the Sewanee Military Academy (SMA) varsity team as early as my ninth-grade year, while 13 years old. Wrestling must have helped. I treasure the letter I received in 1963 from Bear Bryant about playing football at Alabama. As an SMA senior, I was a 190-pound guard on offense and a linebacker/end on defense. I was humbled to be recruited by three Ivy League football teams, Princeton, Yale, and Dartmouth.

My interest in wrestling soon surpassed my affection for football. Inspired by heroic coach Bill Goldfinch, I was fortunate to first learn the martial art in my last three years at SMA, 1961–64. Four more years of wrestling at Princeton (1964–68), and seven with the New York Athletic Club (1968–75) infused the sport into my blood and bones—quite literally, if you count breaking my right leg twice as a sophomore while wrestling at Princeton in 1965–66.

The first break was at a Christmas season tournament in Charlottesville, Virginia, in December 1965. I was wrestling a 6'5", 275-pound University of Virginia heavyweight who outweighed me by 85 pounds. I was ahead 8–1 with less than a minute to go in the match. Suddenly the big guy kicked back when I had my shoes firmly planted. Something had to give, and it was the fibula bone above my ankle. It sounded like a gun had been shot, with the loud break. Paramedics rushed out, inflated a temporary air cast around my leg, and hauled me off on a stretcher. Fortunately, the young heal quickly. Six weeks later I was wrestling again and went undefeated in four straight matches before breaking the leg again in practice 10 weeks later.

Both breaks were excruciatingly painful, but in my 14 years of competitive wrestling, those were my only serious injuries. Not counting the Virginia forfeit, I lost only one dual meet match in my four years of wrestling at Princeton. As a 191-pound junior, I also upset the No. 1 and No. 3 seeds in the 1967 NCAA wrestling tournament at Kent State University in Ohio. The next year *Amateur Wrestling News* listed me as a pre-season All-American.

My mother punned in the summer of 1966 in Birmingham that my leg injury "might turn out to be a lucky break." She was proven correct two years later in May 1968, when the physical exam officer of the draft board in Newark, New Jersey, looking at an x-ray showing a two-centimeter widening of the mortise joint in my right ankle, gave me a temporary I-Y military deferment, good for six months. The papers must have gotten lost after that, as I was never called back up for another physical, and thus I was not drafted for the Vietnam War that I opposed on numerous grounds.

I resumed wrestling too soon after the first break. After the second one, the doctors told me I should never play football or wrestle again. Despite a minor depression after the second break in 1966, I took the physician's advice on the football, but not on the wrestling. In my junior year, I had to tape my right ankle all season, but my only collegiate dual match loss that season was 5–2 to Lehigh's ace wrestler, Ron Ries, an Ohio State champion, whom I had beaten 5–2 as a freshman and defeated again as a senior, 7–2.

The latter 1968 victory against Ries propelled Princeton to its first win in more than 30 years over perennial Eastern champion, Lehigh University. It was neat being carried off the mat by my teammates. The 1968 Princeton yearbook said I flashed a patented "B'ar" grin. The expression was a play on both my accent and the real "Bear" of Alabama, football coach Paul Bryant, in that era.

It wasn't just the personal satisfaction of repeatedly winning the Ivy League championship, individually and as a team, that kept me going at the sport in my post-graduate years. Instead, it was the sheer fun of wrestling. I developed greater techniques. That included over-the-head lateral throws to pin someone in a single move, and a leg-wrestling style used to pin an opponent with a guillotine move.

Before I knew it, besides coaching undergraduate wrestlers at Columbia College, while attending Columbia Law School, I was wrestling with the

New York Athletic Club team, where I was fortunate to contribute to several national championships in AAU (Amateur Athletic Union) wrestling in the 1970s. At 215 pounds, I won the Eastern AAU heavyweight title for the NYAC in 1971 and 1973, despite my 220-pound weight class being combined with the unlimited division both times. This pitted me against larger guys, some weighing 260–280 pounds, in my championship bouts.

In 1972, at the National Wrestling Olympic Try-Outs finals in Anoka, Minnesota, I was the last one eliminated in my 220-pound weight class. In my first year of working with a Wall Street law firm, I wasn't training hard for the Olympics. If only I had trained more seriously, maybe I would have made the team. A nice dream, but a big maybe.

I also placed fourth in the National AAU's in 1973. I was in a lot of tournaments in those days, winning the Metropolitan New York Championships several times in Long Island, Westchester County, and Manhattan. At the NYAC, we were "America's team," wrestling against teams from the Soviet Union, Turkey, Iran, and the championship teams of all the major U.S. military branches. It was exhilarating. I was having a ball.

Perhaps the most pivotal long-term decision I ever made arose in the context of the Eastern AAU championship March 30–31, 1973. Earlier in the week, I had been invited by Bob Wise, a fellow associate attorney at Davis Polk on Wall Street, to come to a party he and his roommates were throwing at his Upper East Side Manhattan apartment on Friday night, March 30. I gave him a tentative "maybe" response, due to the wrestling tournament conflict. Fortunately, the three matches I wrestled at the New York Athletic Club in the preliminary rounds were fairly easy, all resulting in pins. I therefore walked the 20 blocks from Central Park South to the party and made my "rendezvous with destiny."

Who should I meet that providential night but my future bride, then known as J. Leslie Burton. She was statuesque and knockdown beautiful. I couldn't help drifting quickly over to where she was standing. Interesting conversation about her being from Brazil transpired. I had been in Brazil only two years earlier and thus engaged Leslie easily in conversation on that topic.

I was unable to convince Leslie to come see me in the Eastern AAU semifinals or finals the next day at the NYAC. It was my second Eastern championship in three years. She didn't know me well enough at that stage. Nonetheless, our mutual interest grew quickly. In two to three weeks, Leslie was at the Grand Ballroom National Dancing championship in Miami, where she won first place. The same weekend I was in Cleveland, Ohio, at the National Wrestling Championships, winning matches but not the tournament.

Although we were in different sports, Leslie and I quickly realized we had much in common, and things skyrocketed. She went with me to my fifth class reunion at Princeton in June 1973, which was apparently a telltale sign of future commitment. Prophetically, we were married in Wellesley, Massachusetts, in June 1974.

A sad footnote cannot be omitted. The young lawyer who invited Leslie to the party that night was a Princeton classmate, whom I did not know beforehand, named Charlie McCrann. Twenty-eight years later, Charlie was on the 100th floor of the first of the World Trade Center towers hit by a plane on September 11, 2001. Mercifully, Charlie probably perished instantly. In the years between our 1973 meeting and 2001, I had come to know Charlie better, mainly at five-year cycle Princeton reunions. Coincidentally, Charlie was a roommate at Yale Law School of Alabama's U.S. District Judge Myron Thompson. Myron presided over a memorial service in Manhattan for Charlie in October 2001. I was unable to attend that service but in November 2001 saw Charlie's widow and teenage children in their Village home in SoHo. Their eyes were glazed from having cried so much they couldn't cry anymore.

By the spring of 1975, and a year into our marriage, Leslie and I decided to return to Alabama. In February that year, I flew down to Alabama, did a six-day study blitz at my parents' Lake Logan-Martin place, due east of Birmingham, and took the bar exam over three days in Montgomery. By mid-March, we flew to Cairo, Egypt, to begin a tour of the African continent, including Kenya, Tanzania, South Africa, and Angola. At the end, we stopped off in Brazil, on the way back. While in Rio de Janeiro, I received word that I had passed the Alabama Bar exam.

After returning to New York and pulling our belongings behind us in a little red Vega, we arrived in Montgomery in April 28, 1975, whereupon we stayed briefly with Clifford and Virginia Durr, out at their famous Pea Level home in Wetumpka. For me, it wasn't the first time living in Montgomery.

Back in June, 1962, Mom and Dad and their five children arrived in Montgomery for a two-year adventure, as Dad began his new career as a priest at the Episcopal Church of the Ascension. Ironically, I was the only one of the seven not to stay full time, finishing up at Sewanee Military Academy. Yet, I was the only one who ever returned. Little did I suspect, in 1962–64, that eleven years later in 1975, Montgomery would again be my permanent home for over 40 years. Little did I realize there would be ample opportunity to continue my interest in wrestling.

It was in those earlier years, in fact 1962–63 that I helped coach the first wrestling team that Sidney Lanier High School in Montgomery ever had.

This was during the Christmas holidays when I was home for three weeks. Somehow Lanier's first wrestling coach, the famous football mastermind Billy Livings, heard about me and invited me to come help coach his first team. After all, Livings knew nothing about wrestling, and I was a three-year veteran of Sewanee Military Academy wrestling. I always enjoyed the workouts and the opportunity to teach young fellows how to wrestle better.

This was a harbinger of things to come. After returning to Montgomery in 1975, I helped coach wrestling at Jeff Davis High School from 1976–77, before running for attorney general of Alabama in 1978. In the early and mid-1980s, I helped coach Robert E. Lee High's wrestling team. (In 2015, I ran into a former Lee heavyweight, Anthony Brown, who went on to play football at Auburn in the '80s. Anthony told me he had used on the football field at Auburn one of the takedown techniques I taught him on the wrestling mat at Lee High.) In the late '80s, I also helped coach the Carver High wrestling team.

By the early 1990s, word had gotten around the greater Montgomery area about my interest in wrestling. Hence, Coach Trent Miller of Prattville, starting a wrestling team there, and another coach in Wetumpka, starting a team there, persuaded me to assist financially the beginnings of their respective programs. Trent nicknamed me the "Johnny Appleseed of wrestling" in the greater Montgomery area. Trent himself later became known as the "dean" of high school wrestling in the Montgomery area."

Meanwhile, my son David was growing up in our home. I took every chance to wrestle with David either in the backyard or the bedroom. David seemed quite interested in the sport. I wanted him to have a team at St. James School to wrestle with, so in 1997, in anticipation, I anted up a six-figure amount to triple the size of the St. James fieldhouse. A wrestling room occupied one third, a weight room a second third, and the locker room the original one third. I also purchased a wrestling mat, uniforms, and head gear, and helped them find their first wrestling coach, Dale Harris. St. James insisted on naming their new facility the McPhillips Fieldhouse.

In 2005, David transferred to the Montgomery Catholic Preparatory School. They didn't have a wrestling team, either. David put his persuasive touch on me again. Thus in 2007, I committed $250,000 over five years to build Catholic a fieldhouse and start a wrestling team. I declined the naming honor and said I wanted the new building named in honor of my hero, Pope John Paul II. Catholic was only too happy to oblige but insisted on giving the wrestling room my family name. This was to honor the four generations of Catholic McPhillipses in Alabama from whom I am descended, beginning with my Irish immigrant great-great grandfather James McPhillips, and ending with my father, Julian L. McPhillips Sr.

David was a member of Catholic's first wrestling team and in fact was its first captain. I helped coach the team in its first season, 2007–08, and even wrestled fairly vigorously, at age 61, with the high school boys. Fortunately, I suffered no injuries and surprised wrestlers young enough to be my grandson. After all, I was 44 when David became my son in 1990.

St. James School has also honored me by naming its annual wrestling tournament after me since 1998. I hand out the trophies every year and continue to support that team as well.

I was excited to see the St. James wrestling team win the Alabama State Championship for 1A-4A teams in 2013. I've also been thrilled to see one of Catholic's wrestlers, Zack Van Alst, rip off four straight state championships, starting in the seventh grade, when he defeated a senior and junior in the final rounds. An all "A" student with two seasons yet to go, I believe Van Alst would make a great recruit for Princeton, Penn State, Iowa State, or Cornell.

I've also enjoyed helping Huntingdon College get its first wrestling team started at the intercollegiate level. It is also the first college team in Alabama since Auburn unwisely shut down its SEC championship team in 1976, thanks to then head football coach Pat Dye wanting more weight-lifting space for his football players.

I've been greatly encouraged by Mike Moyer in Pennsylvania, executive director of the NCAA Wrestling Coaches Association, to support collegiate wrestling, especially in Alabama. Towards that end, I've also attended wrestling championship tournaments in St. Louis, Iowa, Philadelphia, and again in St. Louis. David went with me to the last tournament in March 2015. The 2016 NCAA tournament is scheduled for Madison Square Garden in New York City, and I have long held tickets for it.

I could go on and on about the many great benefits of high school and collegiate wrestling for those who genuinely devote themselves to the sport. One develops good habits of self-discipline and the exercise from practice rids one of bodily tensions. One learns to confront fear and/or aggressively rid oneself of it. One learns to stay far away from alcohol, drugs, cigarettes, and foods that are not good for you. One learns how to become a tough-minded optimist. One develops self-confidence from knowing he can defend himself, if necessary, without guns and knives, thus learning how to make things happen more peacefully.

That relates to my latest wrestling-related venture in April 2015 when

Phillip Brooks, a special ed teacher and head wrestling coach at Lee High School, came to see me for legal help. I prepared for him the articles of incorporation for a "Peace on the Streets Training and Tutoring Center, Inc." program. This brainchild is designed to get kids off the streets and away from shooting each other. Instead, they are being taught by Coach Brooks to wrestle peacefully. I pray that this program will grow and save some lives.

In conclusion, I must say that a wrestler's training temperament, together with sufficient spirituality and reverence for God, are most helpful for meeting the challenges of life. For me this has included being a civil rights attorney and a trial lawyer. That truth is deep in my blood and bones.

None of the above is to say that wrestlers, being human, don't experience the problems of everyday life. They do, as happened to five-time state champion Hayden Countryman.

THE COUNTRYMAN FAMILY

Given my love for amateur wrestling, it wasn't long before I developed a great friendship with the Countryman family of Prattville. That included the father Cline and mother Cindy, about thirteen years younger than me, and their three sons, Tyler, Jordan, and John Hayden.

I helped the Prattville wrestling team get started around 1990 with financial and moral support. Accordingly, I quickly developed a solid friendship with its coach, Trent Miller and even personally worked out with the Prattville team as late as my early 60s. When I started a wresting team in 2007 at Catholic High, it was Coach Miller I called for a recommendation for the first Catholic wrestling coach. Trent said he had just the right person in mind, namely Tyler Countryman, the oldest of the three sons. Tyler, the tallest of the boys at 6'2", was moderately laid back, but dedicated to the sport. He had finished third in the Alabama 6-A Wrestling Championship in his weight class, an outstanding accomplishment. But Tyler's father was a state champion, and so were both his two younger brothers.

While Tyler did well coaching for Catholic in its first five seasons, it was his younger brother, Hayden, with five straight state championships in his weight class, who made the biggest splash. In fact, Hayden was a legend before he graduated from Prattville High School. In his senior year, Virginia Tech offered him a scholarship. Hayden was also a good student. He could handle the academics, but he couldn't handle being "beat out" by someone else for the starting position in his weight class.

So Hayden came back home. As wonderful as Cline and Cindy are as parents, Hayden's return sent him in a downward spin. Although enrolled at AUM along with his two older brothers, and staying active with a local wrestling club, young Hayden moved into some negative circles and behavior. One night Hayden and a friend were at the home of another friend. Booze was plenteous, and in poor judgment as they were leaving, they picked up a jug of coins, worth a few hundred dollars, that was sitting on a porch. Criminal charges were filed, but pre-trial diversion led to all charges later being dropped.

Another time a girlfriend complained that Hayden threw a beer can at her face, bruising her. Hayden said it was an accident. With negotiation, and mutual reconciliation, the charges were also dropped.

As Hayden's attorney, I tried to counsel him generally, and even prayed with him. His parents and brothers were doing all they could to help. In March 2012, however, while intoxicated again, Hayden took some muscle relaxer medication. The combination was nearly fatal, but Hayden was revived. He should have learned from that mishap, but unfortunately did not.

In September 2012, a telephone call informed me that Hayden was dead. My heart sank, as did the hearts of thousands of relatives, friends, and acquaintances. Given Hayden's notoriety as a five-time state champion, his death was big headline news, at least in the local sports pages.

Apparently, the same combination of alcohol and muscle relaxer drugs was fatal this time, although unintentionally so.

Leslie and I attended Hayden's funeral at First Baptist Church of Prattville. It was highly inspirational. Many were in tears. The Countryman family held up as best they could, but they were all terribly wounded. Middle son Jordan was especially unable to control his emotions.

In the months afterwards I have had occasional contact with both parents, and with Tyler. Prayer was frequently a part of it, especially with his mother. There is a deep desire among parents and siblings losing a family member at a young age to make something more meaningful out of it and honor the one who left too soon. I know that personally from my similar experience in losing brother David at age 27, in 1976.

I join with the host of Hayden's many friends in praying that Hayden is receiving the best in his greater life beyond the grave. I trust that Hayden has been basking in God's awesome love, mercy, and grace. I also wonder if Hayden has found time to challenge one of the angels to a wrestling match, like the angel who wrestled with Old Testament patriarch Jacob.

Hayden's family and many friends hope to see Hayden again someday, when their turn comes to enter new life beyond the grave, that place we traditionally call heaven. I share their hope.

32

Others Who've Influenced Me

This chapter includes a few heroic personalities and friends, not adequately commented upon in previous chapters, who have inspired and influenced me in personal ways that I want to share.

Heroic Individuals I've Personally Been Inspired By

The following are known nationally or internationally. I know them personally and consider each to be a personal hero.

Bill Bradley: He was a senior at Princeton when I began as a freshman in 1964–65. He was 1st team All-American in basketball all three years and won the 1965 Sullivan Award as the Most Outstanding Athlete in America in all sports, professional or amateur. Bradley was also a Rhodes Scholar, New York Knicks professional basketball player, and three-time U.S. Senator from New Jersey. In 1999–2000, I chaired Bradley's Alabama campaign for the U.S. presidency. Bradley's personal integrity, spirituality, keen intellect, and hard-working habits inspired me at Princeton and have continued to inspire me in the years since.

Jimmy Carter: My favorite president of my lifetime, Carter has inspired me in many ways. The way he was elected president in 1976 encouraged me in my 1978 campaign for Alabama attorney general. Under tough circumstances after the Watergate scandal, Carter restored integrity to the world's most powerful office. Carter invited Leslie and me to the White House to have dinner with him (ostensibly to keep competitor Teddy Kennedy from luring me away) after I was elected a Carter-pledged delegate from Alabama for the 1980 Democratic National Convention in New York. We had also attended his 1977 inauguration. Carter's post-presidency, in terms of service to mankind worldwide, is the most impressive of any former president. The graceful, dignified, and faithfully confident way Carter shared his late-stage cancer and excitement about a new adventure in eternal life has encouraged me and many others.

Wernher Von Braun: People marvel when I tell them how well I came to know America's greatest space scientist, the man most credited for putting America on the moon. This also allows me to mention (with my wife's consent) his dear daughter, Iris Von Braun, whom I dated in 1969–71. Iris spent a week with me in New Orleans in 1970, celebrating Mardi Gras, staying at my grandmother's house. She invited me on two long sailing trips with her and her father, one in the Chesapeake, the other on the Potomac. On one trip, I questioned Von Braun extensively about what he knew as far as what was happening to the Jews in Germany in WWII. Von Braun was a young man working in the caves of Peenemunde, Germany, developing the V-2 rocket during the war. He confirmed that he knew very little and never knew how bad it was. However, Von Braun's range of knowledge on a wide variety of other subjects reflected the Renaissance man that he was. I will always cherish fond memories of Iris and her father, Dr. Von Braun, as I called him.

David F. Dixon: Founder of the New Orleans Saints of the NFL, father of the New Orleans Superdome, founder of World Championship (or pro) tennis, and founder of the United States Football League, this naturally creative genius was my mother's brother and only sibling. So he was my uncle, and all we McPhillipses were very proud of Uncle Dave. Dave doted on me in my toddler years of the late 1940s and when I worked at a New Orleans law firm in 1969. Dave made it to all our family weddings through 2006. I enjoyed sitting next to him in his home as the Saints finally won the Super Bowl in 2010. Eight months later, at age 87, he went home to be with the Lord.

Mahesh and Bonnie Chavda: No one has influenced Leslie, me, and our children more positively since 1989 than Mahesh and Bonnie Chavda, world-class healing evangelists. Mahesh was originally from Kenya and born of East Indian parents, while Bonnie was from New Mexico. As discussed earlier, Mahesh played a big role in the way our son David came to us. As will be discussed later, the Chavdas have also inspired Leslie and me in the healing ministry and at Christ the Redeemer. Mahesh and Bonnie's worldwide ministry, based in Charlotte, North Carolina, has helped thousands receive God's healing touch.

Canon Andrew White: This native Englishman, 18 years my junior, has had an extraordinary life involved in the dangerous but badly needed reconciliation work. He has mediated between Palestinians and Israelis, Muslims and Christians, Shiites and Sunnis, and frequently travels from England to the Middle East, to Nigeria, and occasionally to America. At the bare minimum age of 33, White became Canon of Coventry Cathedral, and served as the director of its International Center for Reconciliation. Andrew helped broker peace in Bethlehem when the historic Church of the Nativity (built over where Christ was born) was taken over by terrorists. For years White has served as the Anglican Vicar of Baghdad, where he was once kidnapped. I met White at a Healing the Nations Conference (sponsored by Mahesh Chavda) years ago, and I saw him there again in October 2015. White's fearless Christian witness, at great personal risk, is a huge inspiration. You cannot put down his autobiographical *My Journey So Far* and earlier book, *The Vicar of Baghdad.*

20TH-CENTURY HEROES WHO INFLUENCED ME GREATLY

I didn't know the following personally, but they nonetheless have significantly impacted my life in various ways.

Helen Keller: As a child growing up in Cullman in the 1950s, I read three Helen Keller biographies, each progressively more advanced. My mother gave me the books. Little did I know that the house in Montgomery I'd end up living in, from 1981 to the present, is the very house that Keller herself frequently visited because her sister, Mildred Keller Tyson, owned it from 1923 to 1960. Helen Keller was a worldwide champion of the deaf and blind, traveling all over Europe, and to Australia and Japan, promoting the cause of helping people with either disability. In addition, in the 1920s she championed women's rights and worker's rights. In the 1930s, she was also an outspoken opponent of Jim Crow laws.

Mother Teresa: Until the 1970s, this Nobel Peace Prize-winning saint of a lady was not well known outside Calcutta, India, where she worked. In earlier years, in the late 1960s, my mother worked closely with Mother Teresa in Calcutta while my father was the American Peace Corps director in India. The way Mother Teresa and her Sisters of Charity went around Calcutta ministering to the sick, dying, and homeless was Christ-like, or angelic. Mother Teresa also had a heart for the unborn. My own mother was thrilled and inspired to be with Mother Teresa and her sisters, as they helped the downtrodden and destitute.

Eleanor Roosevelt: Along with her awesome husband, four-time President Franklin Delano Roosevelt, Eleanor Roosevelt rendered enormous service to the homeless and the disenfranchised. She championed worker's rights and, of course, sparked the role of women in politics, including in voting. I am fortunate to have in my house a framed photograph of Eleanor Roosevelt on her 60th birthday. This original picture was so precious to FDR that he kept it—along with an original photo of himself on his 60th birthday at the White House—in his desk at his Warm Springs, Georgia, estate. Both photos were found in a secret panel of the desk, which was purchased by Charlotte Payne, a real estate broker in Scottsboro, Alabama. She gave the photos to me in appreciation of the good result obtained on her case in 1983 (see Chapter 1).

Pope Francis: I am overwhelmed and deeply touched by his leadership to the world. An example of humility and kindness, his Christ-like spirit has touched people of all religions, ethnic groups, nationalities, and ages. His "who am I to judge" comment and forgiveness toward sinners comment are sparking reconciliation. Pope John Paul II was also a great hero (I named a fieldhouse after him), but Pope Francis's wonderful example has caused me and many others to reexamine our priorities. Pope Frances is largely responsible for the rapprochement between Cuba and the USA. His trip to the United States was sensational. Hopefully, his words to Congress will be taken seriously by both parties.

Scott and Zelda Fitzgerald: While I've never considered either to be a role model, I must concede that both have influenced my life greatly. It was quite by accident, as explained elsewhere, that Leslie and I became involved in the world's only Scott and Zelda Museum. The two icons are literary giants, and their legend and writings still captivate a large domestic and international audience.

Barack Obama: Of course, Obama's first election to the presidency in 2008 was near-miraculous, and seemingly divinely inspired. Obama pulled us out of 6,000 Dow Jones territory under George Bush, and tripled it to 18,000. Obama's courageous ending of the ill-advised Iraq War, yet fearless and successful pursuit of Osama bin Laden and fight against terrorism, are all heroic. Obama's Affordable Healthcare Act was badly needed and has helped many people. His continued fight for social justice and against gun violence and the senseless killing of innocents in America deeply touches me. I agree with Obama that we need much better gun control. Obama's treaty with Iran helped to avoid a third world war. The hateful attacks against Obama are highly political, often racist, and usually misguided, but they are less than what Abraham Lincoln endured, and Obama has handled it well. I have been dismayed however, by his failure to commute Don Siegelman's lengthy federal prison sentence. In Alabama, we've also suffered from Obama's failure to appoint badly needed federal judges, and he took too long to appoint the highly qualified George Beck as U.S. Attorney for the Middle District of Alabama.

Jack & Bobby Kennedy: I'd be remiss not to include them. Jack Kennedy inspired a whole new generation of us Americans coming of age in the '60s. His instituting the Peace Corps influenced my family greatly, as we ended up in India in the late '60s. The JFK Assassination caused great remorse, and yet highly motivated me (see Appendix 4). Bobby Kennedy picked up the fallen torch. I know that neither was popular in the South, due to their pushing integration in the schools, but they added political muscle to an inevitable movement, especially civil rights, which I have embraced and cheered.

Pope John Paul II: Well before Francis, this Pope also inspired me greatly. He had a wonderful ecumenical outreach not only to Christians besides Catholics but also to people of other faiths. During WWII in Poland, he risked his life helping Jews escape from the Nazis. His example of bringing forgiveness in prison to the Serbian who attempted to assassinate him was a mind-blowing example of Christ-like behavior. This Pope is such a great hero of mine that, when given the chance, I named a newly constructed fieldhouse after him at the Montgomery Catholic Preparatory School.

George McGovern: His example of moral courage in standing up to power in a war gone terribly awry, was enormously inspirational to me in the early 1970s. He further exemplified that the highest form of patriotism can be to stand up to and speak out, when your country is doing wrong. Of course, it takes a great democracy like America and freedom of speech guarantees under the U.S. Constitution to do this. George McGovern influenced my whole family. Mom and Dad, fresh back from living in India, became McGovern's leaders in Alabama. Dad was the chairman of McGovern's presidential campaign in Alabama and he and my brother Frank represented Alabama for McGovern at the 1972 Democratic National Convention in Miami. That was gutsy, because most Alabamians saw McGovern differently. I became co-chairman of Taxicab Drivers for McGovern in New York City. He remains a great hero for me.

Franklin Delano Roosevelt: The greatest American president of all time, say many historians. He led us through the Great Depression and World War II. Although he died one year before I was born, he has enormously inspired and influenced me. His 20th-century presence qualifies him for this list.

Teddy Roosevelt: I can't leave Teddy out, since he, too, was a 20th-century figure. Teddy, with all his energy and dynamism, despite physical disabilities, has also influenced me, even though I was born three decades after his death. His tough-mindedness, environmentalism, and rough-rider persona, and his famous quote about being in the arena, have been most inspirational to me during my lifetime.

Woodrow Wilson: If I mention the two Roosevelts, I must include this great president. Certainly his two terms in office, through the 1910s, were well before my day, but I've always been inspired by his international-mindedness (influencing mine) and moral rectitude. During my four years at Princeton, I heard about Wilson all the time, because he was president of Princeton University only two years before he became president of the United States. The Woodrow Wilson School of Public and International Affairs at Princeton gave me a grant in 1967 to research my thesis topic in France. An interesting footnote is that my wife Leslie's paternal grandfather, John Reginald Burton, was Woodrow Wilson's presidential campaign manager in New York state in 1916. He was also secretary of the Democratic National Convention that nominated Wilson that year.

Dietrich Bonhoeffer: This great German theologian-martyr risked life and limb standing up to the excess of Nazi Germany, including its persecution of Jews, one of whom was his long-time girlfriend. Bonhoeffer's book, *The Cost of Discipleship*, with its accurately descriptive title, has positively influenced me and countless others. I have read several books by and about Bonhoeffer.

Billy Graham and son Franklin Graham: Billy Graham, now 97, has evangelized the world with the Gospel, with great results. He has also written a number of persuasive books that have touched me. This counselor to many presidents has been an enormous influence for good. His son Franklin, with his Samaritan Purse efforts, has brought badly needed supplies to places torn by war, famine, and disease, and inspires me as well.

OTHER GREATS WHO HAVE INSPIRED ME IN LIFE'S JOURNEY

This section does not include my wonderful parents, who are discussed in Chapter 1, or my wife and children, who've been the greatest good influence, but they are written about especially in Chapter 28 and other chapters. So also have been many other good friends, many of whom are talked about in other chapters of this book, including my law partner, Kenneth Shinbaum and Joe Guillot, paralegal Amy Strickland, and colleagues and mentors Bill Baxley, Tommy Gallion, and Bobby Segall. My brothers Frank McPhillips and David McPhillips, my sisters Sandy Pitre and Betsy Williams, and my Uncle Warren McPhillips have also been very positive influences, and special time is also devoted to them also in Chapter 28. Uncle David is discussed above.

Julian Byrnes McPhillips and Lilybelle McGowan McPhillips: My Dad's parents. Grandfather "Poppy," as I called him, was on the University of Alabama football team in 1915 (when the sport was more like rugby). I have a Gold Elocution Medal he won that same year while in law school. Poppy became a soldier in the First World War, and in the 1920s he founded

McPhillips Shrimp Company, headquartered in Bayou La Batre. In 1946, with my Dad and Uncle Warren, Poppy founded King Pharr Canning Company (see Appendix 2). Poppy was like a second father, attended my college graduation at Princeton in 1968 when my parents were too far away in India, and, as mentioned earlier, helped me campaign for Alabama attorney general just before he died in August 1978. More assertive and outgoing than my father, Poppy was probably more like me in personality than my father was. My grandmother "Ibby," from a distinguished McGowin heritage, was a wonderful lady. She greatly loved and inspired her 11 grandchildren, including me.

Stuart Sanderson Dixon and Frank Dixon: My mother's mother ("Stu" as we called her) sparked us all with her generosity, contagious kindness, and "50 cents an A" rewards. Stu was a really huge influence on all of us for the better. Her husband, Frank Dixon, is the only grandparent I never personally knew, since he died in 1937, before I was born. Grandfather Dixon founded the Great Southern Box Company, which later merged with Continental Can Company. The stock he left my grandmother paid for all eight of her grandchildren's college educations, including mine at Princeton. I look forward to meeting Grandfather Dixon in heaven someday.

Petronilla McPhillips and Lula Belle Graham McGowin: These great-grandmothers, both on Dad's side, influenced me positively, including on the issue of potential longevity. The first lived until I was 12 and she was 83; the second until I was 19 and she was 95. Petronilla ("Mare," as we called her) descended from early Spanish settlers of Florida, including Governor Don Manuel Gonzalez, and from a French explorer and Choctaw Indian princess. My other great grandma, called "Mamoo," regaled me with stories of Civil War veterans and knew me well into my college years."

Doug Carpenter, and his father, Bishop C. C. J. Carpenter: These men, son Doug and father, the Bishop, inspired me greatly over the years in my walk in faith. They were the two people most responsible for my going to Princeton to college. I treasure four letters I received from Bishop Carpenter written in the 1960s when I was a cadet at Sewanee Military Academy and a student at Princeton. Doug, his son, counseled me during my depression, and encouraged me the most in my leading the restoration of Christ the Redeemer Episcopal Church; at 83, he remains a good friend in 2016. We've also been Camp McDowell friends for 60 years.

Bill Goldfinch: He was my highly inspirational English teacher and wrestling coach at Sewanee Military Academy, in Tennessee, 1961–1964. Getting into amateur wrestling has been an enormous blessing for me and others whom coach encouraged (see Chapter 31). He was the first teacher to encourage me to read F. Scott Fitzgerald's novels, *This Side of Paradise* and *The Great Gatsby*. This was a foundation to my later interest in and efforts with the Scott and Zelda Fitzgerald Museum.

Steve Stearns: Certainly the most outstanding male I ever recruited from Montgomery to Princeton (Terri Sewell is the top female), Steve went on to captain the 1983 football team, achieve a 4.0 average, and do many other outstanding things there (Princeton '84). Steve married the beautiful Suzanne O'Sullivan (Princeton '83), and they had a dozen good years together before she died of cancer in 1995, leaving Steve with a young son and daughter. Now remarried to Teresa, the Yale Law School librarian, Steve is my and Leslie's stockbroker, based in Connecticut, and has done a good job. We stay in frequent contact on a multitude of business and personal matters. Adopted at birth, Steve's great example inspired us to adopt our son David.

Cliff and Judy Fenton, Chicago; Tim and Ilia Smith, San Francisco, and Walter and Mary Bliss, New Jersey: We were all at Princeton and Columbia Law School together in the mid to late '60s and early '70s. Although they were two years ahead of me at Ole Nassau, I knew Tim ('66) through Chapel Deacons and Walt ('66) through football. I didn't know Cliff ('65) until later. However, all four of us couples became great friends at Columbia and in New York in the late '60s and early '70s. We summered together at the Hamptons in '72–'73 and went to each other's weddings. In 2007, we began an annual tradition of three-day weekend reunions in far-flung parts of the U.S., including twice in Alabama. It is amazing how we spark one another, mostly with wit and humor. We're all still happily married to the same wives, more than 40 years later, and enjoy our families.

Carol and Mike Jones, Montgomery: About 10 years younger than me, this African American husband and wife are dear friends of Leslie's and mine. We share a lot spiritually. I've often preached at their Unity Divine Church. Carol and I host a television interview show called "Conversations with Carol and Julian" which is surprisingly popular on cable television late Saturday and Sunday afternoons. The theme is religious. Good at concrete work, Mike has also paved the driveway at Christ the Redeemer Episcopal Church.

The Right Reverend Frank and Hurdis Bozeman: The Bozemans have been a great inspiration to me since I met Frank in 2001, in the early part of my U.S. Senate campaign. Frank appreciated and encouraged my civil rights work and got me to be on the board of directors of his Global Evangelical Christian Church seminary and denomination. In January 2003, Bishop Bozeman insisted on ordaining me and SCLC National President Charles Steele as ministers in the Global Evangelical denomination. I've represented the Bozemans individually legally, have preached numerous times in their churches, and have prayed for their healings several times, with good results.

The Right Reverend A. L. ("Arthur") Dowdell: Bishop Dowdell, head of the New Testament Potter's House Full Gospel Church denomination, and a long-time City Councilman of Auburn, has had a spirited but multi-faceted relationship with me. As mentioned earlier, Bishop frequently refers civil rights and other cases to me. We share a strong interest in the healing ministry and have done things together in the spiritual, political, and legal realms.

Courtney McKoy, Arab, Alabama; Don Weaver, Deatsville, Alabama; and John Shaw, Montgomery, Alabama: All of these fellows were born in the same year I was, in 1946. We were childhood friends growing up in Cullman. Courtney and his parents and siblings were similarly aged to my parents and siblings. We all frequently vacationed together in the late 1940s and early 1950s in Daytona Beach, Florida, and Gulf Shores, Alabama. Don Weaver, my next-door neighbor in Cullman from 1953–59, was a great athlete and independent-minded and inspired me in both regards. John Shaw was the catcher and my battery-mate on the Cullman County Little League All-Stars. I've stayed in touch with all three over the years, especially Don and John in the Montgomery area, and I see Courtney when I get up to Cullman or Huntsville.

Bishop C. Fitzsimmons Allison of Georgetown, South Carolina: One of the great theological scholars of the 20th century, and in 1959–61 a seminary professor of my father's at St. Luke's Seminary, Sewanee, Tennessee, and youth minister to me in Sewanee, Dr. Allison, or "Fitz" became a close friend over the years. He performed my sister Betsy's wedding in Alexandria, Virginia, in 1969, and counseled Leslie and me on marriage in 1974 in New York City, where he then ministered at Grace Episcopal Church in the Village. Fitz later became the Episcopal Bishop of the diocese of South Carolina, his native state. Fitz was at his best combining brilliant scholarship with deep Christian commitment. His book, *The Cruelty of Heresy*, is a classic and influenced my faith. Fitz also helped counsel me during my depression in 2006. He is doing well at almost 90 in 2015, the last time I spoke to him in October 2015.

Barbara McElroy, Princeton '81, Birmingham, Alabama: She is listed both individually and as a representative of 100 or more others I've recruited for Princeton University, my alma mater, from 1976 to 2015. I first met Barbara when she was a 16-year-old at Robert E. Lee High School, where she graduated in 1977. She's now a talented 55-year-old advertising executive in Birmingham, with a son headed to law school. Barbara also provides the leadership and spark for many Princeton-in-Alabama causes, including bringing the Princeton Prize in Race Relations to Alabama. Barbara's positive influence on many others, including me, makes my recruiting efforts well worth the effort. She is reflective of other Alabama recruits with whom I have a close relationship over the years, including Susan Price '81, Farris Curry '83, David Sawyer '87, Shannon Holliday '89, and Rick McBride '93.

Fred Billings, Princeton '68, and Bill Potter, Princeton '68: They are listed both individually and as representatives of the approximately 800 members of my class of 1968 at Princeton. I stay in touch with Fred, a retired doctor from Baton Rouge, and Bill, a still active attorney in Princeton. Other influential '68 members were Lew Retrum of Cleveland, Tracy Mott from Memphis, Stanley Bynum and George Lynn from Birmingham, and Steve Pajcic from Jacksonville, Florida. Many classmates, including fellow wrestling teammates Paul Arnow from Arizona, Warren Huffaker of Maryland, and Pete Detweiler from North Carolina have moved on to greater life beyond the grave.

Jay Carlisle, Hudson, New York, and John Siebold, Milwaukee, Wisconsin: In the late 1960s and early 1970s we were all counselors to Columbia College undergraduates while pursuing our studies at Columbia Law School. At that time both were a great positive influence on me. They have remained friends over the years and in different ways they inspire me.

Father William Wilson: Originally a Catholic priest and missionary to Bolivia, and a great friend to both my parents, William has become a good friend of mine as well. He and his wife, a missionary doctor 10 years younger, married when William was in his 50s, and at 60, William adopted two children. William reflects the life of Jesus more than almost anyone else I know. His recent book *Pathways to Union with Jesus*, has been very meaningful to me.

Bob and Jeannie Graetz: Heroes from the mid-1950s when their all-black Lutheran church and adjacent parsonage was bombed, these two Caucasian leaders are what I call "walking, talking national civil rights monuments." Bob was an original member of the seminal Montgomery Improvement

Association, along with Martin Luther King Jr.; Jeannie was with him in that ministry. This gentle twosome, in their advanced ages of 87 and 85, greatly inspire the entire Montgomery civil rights community. They are especially beloved at Alabama State University. They have inspired me also by their broad-minded emphasis on Montgomery's becoming a "Beloved Community." The Graetzes are also close neighbors who frequently visit our house and Christ the Redeemer Church. They are wonderful role models.

THIS LIST IS BY no means exhaustive. There have been many other teachers, friends, relatives, fellow attorneys, and others who have very positively influenced me in life's journey.

33

THE POLITICAL GENE

My political gene came naturally. Mom and Dad were very comfortable in relating to people, most of the time. Mom especially had a contagious enthusiasm. I am the proverbial acorn that didn't fall far from the tree.

But the political gene didn't pop up in my earliest years. At Sewanee Military Academy I was not an elected class officer, although I was a cadet officer. Frankly, I was too caught up in the demands of the academic, athletic, military, and religious worlds. Although I was one of the youngest in the class (after skipping from the sixth to the eighth grade) no one ever tried to bully me. That was partly because I was one of the biggest and probably the strongest in the class.

Ditto at Princeton. Our class was full of former student body presidents and class presidents. I never bothered to seek office. Wrestling, academics, religious life, and a little social life were all I had time for.

But something different happened at Columbia Law School from 1968–1971. Together with the civil rights movement and the anti-war movement of that era, the Columbia years honed me into a more politically conscious person.

The chairman of the Columbia Law School Senate was the student body president. As a first-year student concerned about the Vietnam War, I was elected to the Student Senate. Then, in the first semester of my second year, the existing chairman resigned for personal reasons. Surprise, I was elevated to replace him, because the "radicals" (mainly against the Vietnam War) and "the conservatives" (who liked my manners) came together and unanimously agreed to my election. Suddenly I was enjoying a degree of personal popularity that had escaped me at both Sewanee and Princeton.

Between fall 1969 and spring 1970, I was caught up in the so-called "soapbox conspiracy" at Columbia Law. What this essentially amounted to was student leaders like me standing on a soapbox in the hallway, and speaking out for a greater student voice in the governance of the law school.

Then, in early May 1970, President Nixon invaded Cambodia, thus widening an already deeply unpopular war. Four hundred U.S. colleges and universities went on strike, protesting the war's expansion. That included Columbia College. Our law school students were mostly older, but the overwhelming sentiment was to join the strike in solidarity with other students in America.

That all happened quickly, but the looming decision of what to do suddenly propelled Dean Michael Sovern and me to debate before an expanded, triple-size classroom of 900 students and faculty. I have never felt more exhilarated. Somehow impassioned words flowed from my mouth. Others later told me I was articulate and inspired. I know that I was highly motivated.

The vote was overwhelming in favor of the strike. But in a meeting afterwards. Dean Sovern warned that if I didn't help him work out a compromise to allow students who wanted to take their exams on time to do so, I might not be back the next year myself. Notwithstanding the threat, I thought that, democratically, everyone should have a choice. Hence, we did work out a resolution. About 15 percent of the students were allowed to take their exams on time in May 1970. As for the other 85 percent, we could either take the exam home for the summer and get a pass-fail grade, or come back in the fall, and take the exams for the grades.

In May 1970, we had the second big million-person anti-war march on Washington in seven months. The first was in November 1969. I had become a bona fide activist as chairman of the Columbia Law School Coalition Against the War. We didn't do anything illegal, but we did everything else we knew to express our patriotic opposition to a war we strongly believed was illegal and contrary to the country's best interests. The war would ultimately claim 58,000 American lives, millions of Southeast Asian lives, and trillions of wasted dollars, and it tore America apart domestically. Indeed, on the domestic side at this time, in 1970, four students died at Kent State and four more at Jackson State in Mississippi in incidents related to anti-war protests.

All of a sudden, politics was in my blood and bones. I began to see it as a tool to accomplish greater public good and rectify wrongs. I was hooked, although, as the war came to an end, my focus was directed more towards civil rights, with my parents, Virginia Durr, and Bill Baxley encouraging me in that direction.

I had been greatly inspired by the passions of Eugene McCarthy and Bobby Kennedy in opposition to the Vietnam War in 1968. However, George McGovern's campaign in 1972 took my political interest to an even higher level. Hence, I worked hard as co-chairman of "New York City Taxicab Drivers for McGovern" in 1972. What a joy!

Meanwhile, Dad was chairing the McGovern campaign in Alabama, with great assistance from Mom. Coincidentally, I first met Don Siegelman in 1972 in my parents' home as Don worked under Dad as campaign coordinator of the Alabama McGovern campaign.

Jimmy Carter was also an enormous inspiration to me when he charmed the country in 1975–76 to become first the Democratic nominee and then president of the United States. Some people kidded me about the similarity of my green and white campaign colors when I ran for statewide office in 1978. Carter, in the auspicious work of his post-presidency, has motivated me even further.

Mom and Dad were pleased when I went to work for Alabama Attorney General Bill Baxley from April 1975 to June 1977. Although a little nervous when I decided in 1977 to run for attorney general in 1978 to succeed Bill, my parents campaigned all over Alabama for me in their camper, called the "Mom and Pop Machine."

However, the response of my 80-year-old grandfather, Julian B. McPhillips, was, "Your father has already lost one son, he doesn't want to lose another." That was not enthusiastic encouragement, but he was just speaking his mind and knew I was old enough, at 31, to make up my mind. Hence my loyal and devoted grandfather, "Poppy" as I called him, campaigned hard for me, especially around Mobile. We spent much wonderful time together that year riding around Mobile, as I soaked up his stories about who lived where, and who did what. He died in August 1978, one month before the election.

What happened in my Alabama attorney general's race in 1978 and my U.S. Senate campaign in 2002 was fully discussed in second edition of *The People's Lawyer*, and I won't repeat it all here. However, former Democratic party chairman Joe Turnham, who ran twice for the U.S. Congress and lost, articulated it best when he said "you may be called by God to run for public office, but that doesn't mean you're called to win." His words have much meaning for me.

Meanwhile, I have been elected to the Alabama delegation to the National Democratic Convention three times, in 1980, 2000, and 2012, and elected multiple times to the Alabama State Democratic Executive Committee, on which I still serve. I also did much to help Ron Sparks in his race for the Democratic nomination for governor, which he won, as well as in the general election, which he lost.

I have remained politically active in another way by helping other candidates. In 2012, I had a joint reception for three Montgomery County candidates: Tiffany McCord, running for circuit clerk; Steven Reed, running for probate judge; and Troy Massey, running for district judge. I went on television endorsing McCord and did a strategic sports page ad for Reed. Massey and McCord won by landslides, and, as described in Chapter 15, Reed defeated incumbent Reese McKinney.

More recently, in the 2015 Montgomery mayoral race, I endorsed Dan Harris, my long-time tenant and the vice-chairman of the Montgomery County Commission. I also held a reception for and substantially contributed to his campaign. Of course, the incumbent Todd Strange won reelection. I respect Mayor Strange and recognize that he has done much to help the City of Montgomery.

I am now content to help others who are philosophically compatible in their political races. I have empathy for the difficulties they encounter, including raising money. I've also supported Democratic candidates for president from George McGovern on up to Bill Bradley and Barack Obama. At this writing, Hillary looks like the best of the bunch. She did well enough in the October 2015 debate with four men to deter Vice President Joe Biden from entering the fray. Hillary also handled herself with acuity, dignity and grace in the Congressional Benghazi hearing.

It's not just Hillary's impressive resume as First Lady, U.S. Senator, and Secretary of State that wins my support. It's also my belief that Hillary has a heart for the little guy. I wish she were better on abortion, but for children and adults "outside the womb," Hillary is the most "pro-life" and "pro civil rights" of any of the candidates. I especially appreciate her courage and insight in speaking out for greater gun control in America. Given all the massacres of innocent civilians, this is an important issue for me, and for our country.

Joe Biden might make a fine President, but the wear and tear on him, physically and emotionally over the years, has taken its toll. I also appreciate the many issues, especially of income inequality, raised by Bernie Sanders but his self-proclaimed socialist tag will make him difficult to elect. The Republicans, as usual, while including some decent people in their midst, are too bellicose for my taste, and too unsympathetic to civil rights for my liking. I find Donald Trump's angry, accusative style especially distasteful, and I believe he would do America great harm in high office. Ted Cruz's harshly anti-Obama and anti-Affordable Care Act stand, covered in opportunistic sanctimoniousness, is even more unattractive.

Of all the Republicans, I find Ohio Governor John Kasich and Dr. Ben Carson the most attractive. Jeb Bush would be a stronger general election candidate, but his more moderate stands and personality seem out of touch with Republican extremists.

At this writing, I don't know who the Republicans will nominate. However, Hillary has a nationwide lead for the Democratic nomination. She also has a strong chance to become our first female president. Given all her experience and intelligence, she should make an excellent president.

SURELY "POLITICS AIN'T BEAN bag," as former Speaker of the House Tip O'Neill was fond of quoting from Mr. Dooley. Yet, unfortunately, the public perception that politicians are corrupt detracts significantly from what is otherwise a noble pursuit. There are many good, inspired people in politics, motivated for worthy reasons, and sacrificing personally for a greater public benefit. Of course, there are others with bad motives or egos run wild.

Politics and law are closely interwoven. Accordingly, if I am going to successfully pursue a career as a civil rights attorney and trial lawyer, as well as a museum president and lay minister, it behooves me to have a political gene. But please keep me in your prayers!

I would be dodging a sensitive bullet not to comment on the split between the two factions of the Alabama Democratic Party. I refer to the Joe Reed-Nancy Worley faction and the Mark Kennedy faction. I get along well with both, and wish that both, in the interests of electing Democrats statewide and stopping the Republican onslaught, could forgive and make up. Humility and reconciliation are as valuable in politics as in any other walk of life. So also are courtesy and respect. We can all do better.

Ideally, everyone should be involved in politics at some level, if only to vote. I am greatly concerned about impediments to voting that have been created in recent years. That includes Governor Bentley's attempt, due to lack of legislatively enacted funds, to close down driver's licenses offices in certain poorer counties of the state. Since identification photos are required at most voting booths, this would adversely affect the African American vote, because more African Americans live, disproportionately, in those counties. I applaud Congresswoman Terri Sewell for standing up against Bentley's efforts.

The biggest enemy that Democrats and Republicans have is not one another, but public apathy. Also a challenge is to maintain "an informed citizenry." That comes not only from better education but also from good, honest, and independent journalism. The press has historically been called the "fourth branch of government" because it helps to keep the other three straight and honest. If that is to remain true, the U.S. media needs to get on the stick.

34

Don Siegelman and
Other Political Prisoners

I must also comment again on my contemporary and friend, former governor Don Siegelman, who was much more successful at politics than me—and more successful than anyone else in Alabama history, if you consider that he is the only person who has ever been elected to all four of Alabama's top political offices—secretary of state, attorney general, lieutenant governor, and governor.

It's a no-brainer to say that I wouldn't trade being elected to all four top state offices if I'd known the price would be federal prison, away from my family, for seven long years.

There is nothing worse, in my opinion, in the legal or civil rights worlds than to be prosecuted for political reasons. Yet it happens all too often in modern-day America, and in recent years, under highly political Republican prosecutors, it has been happening way too much. The most blatant, "stink to high heaven" obvious case of politically motivated prosecution is what happened to Don Siegelman in 2006. It continues to stink 10 years later (see Appendix 9).

Looking at what happened to Don, I think "there but for the Grace of God go I." I could just as easily have done what Don did and think I had done nothing wrong. I strongly believe that both Don and Richard Scrushy were wrongfully convicted. First, there was "no quid pro quo," and Siegelman's actions did not benefit his own pocketbook or his political campaign. Instead, it promoted the lottery vote, which, had it passed, would have greatly enhanced public education in Alabama.

To begin with, Don should have been reelected governor of Alabama in 2002. But Don, perhaps more egregiously than what I experienced in 1978 in the Alabama attorney general's race, had his 2002 governor's election stolen from him. As everyone knows, or should know, it happened in Baldwin County, where, as Governor Wallace used to say, the votes were "recapitulated." And Don went from being a narrow winner over

Republican nominee Bob Riley to being a narrow loser.

Don has repeatedly said, "It was theft, pure and simple," and I and many others absolutely believe him. Don did what he could to challenge the fraud, but the attorney general's office was also in Republican hands, as were the local judicial offices in Baldwin County. As with George Bush's theft of Florida votes in the 2000 presidential race, there was too much power to protect wrongdoing, and the Republican forces coalesced quickly to protect their ill-gotten gains.

Since I was a candidate in a state election race myself in 2002, I frequently passed Don on the campaign trail. I was always impressed about how organized and how inspired he was. Don was also an incumbent governor. Most of the time he got the respect he deserved; sometimes he did not. Don, like me and other white Democrats, had to deal with the underlying racism, sometimes subtle, sometimes obvious, of the white-flight voters into the Republican Party of Alabama.

As a disclaimer, let me disclose the extent of my relationship with Don Siegelman. It goes back a number of years.

I first met Don in my parents' Woodland Drive home in Birmingham in the spring of 1972. My father had been named chairman of the George McGovern presidential campaign in Alabama. I was co-chairman at that time of Taxicab Drivers for McGovern in New York City but was home in Alabama for a weekend visit. I not only met Don, named by Dad as the state coordinator of the McGovern campaign, but also his first wife, an attractive young red-headed girl; Al LaPierre, another McGovern campaign worker; and Louise Lindblom.

We were all much younger, and very idealistic, including my parents, who were only 52 at the time. Don and I were born in the same year, 1946, and were thus in our 26th year. I immediately recognized a kindred spirit. We were all fired up against a war we considered immoral, illegal, and against America's best interests. A war that had already taken hundreds of thousands (eventually into the millions) of innocent Southeast Asian lives. A war that eventually cost the lives of 58,000 of America's best young men. We honored the patriotism, courage, and sacrifice of America's soldiers, yet we challenged the arrogant, misguided power of America's president and top generals.

Although our candidate would suffer a catastrophic defeat nationally, we McGovernites had a special bond. At the Democratic National Convention in Miami, my father and Siegelman were greatly dismayed when Morris Dees, McGovern's national fundraiser, told them "you are just wasting your time in Alabama." Morris may have been technically correct—the margin of

McGovern's defeat was great in Alabama—but my father, Don, and other Alabamians were working hard for McGovern. They didn't like being put down so sharply and abruptly.

My loyalty to my father was great, and remains so even in his death. My loyalty to Don grows out of their close political relationship, which remained a friendship between them until Dad went home to heaven in February 2001.

After I returned to Alabama in April 1975 to work for Attorney General Bill Baxley, it wasn't long before I reestablished contact with Don, then executive director of the Alabama Democratic Party. As such, Don was working very closely with party chairman Bob Vance, later a federal judge before his assassination in 1987. The heroic Bob, a member of St. Luke's Episcopal Church in Mountain Brook, where my father was rector from 1964–66, remained a good friend of Dad's for many years thereafter.

Before I became a candidate myself in 1978, both Don and Bob gave me a helpful written opinion confirming my eligibility to meet the five-year residency requirement for qualifying. I had been back in Alabama full-time for only two and a half years. But while I was away in New York, I had maintained enough indicia of residency, including draft board registration, family, home, and church membership to meet the residency requirement. This countered what fellow assistant attorney general Bill Stephens, himself contemplating a run for attorney general, was saying. Don researched the issue and wrote the opinion, and Bob signed it. I was grateful.

All the ex-McGovernites were excited again, at least in Democratic circles, about Jimmy Carter's being elected president in 1976. That spirit helped spur a record number of candidacies for statewide political office in 1978. There were five serious candidates for governor (the three B's—Baxley, Beasley, and Brewer—plus Fob James and Sid McDonald). There were twelve serious candidates for lieutenant governor, which was won by my friend George McMillan) and nine for attorney general, counting me. Don, with great support built up within the Democratic Party, was easily elected secretary of state.

Don did a good job during his subsequent two terms, building that office up into much more than it had ever been before.

Meanwhile, in the same eight-year period, 1978–1986, I had a meteoric rise in my law practice that included many groundbreaking and precedent-setting cases. During one week in 1986, I was on WSFA-TV news six days out of seven, with five different cases.

Many politically-savvy people were saying that, after eight years of Charlie Graddick, I was the strong favorite for the Democratic nomination for attorney general, if I wanted to seek the office. At that time, the Democratic nomination was tantamount to election. The Republican party statewide was very weak; the reverse is true today, thirty years later.

The problem was that I was having so much fun in the private sector, earning many times more than the attorney general, and enjoying my two young daughters and my beautiful wife, Leslie. We were also still trying to add a third child.

So in 1986, Don, in a politically savvy moment, came to me and said "Julian, I am thinking about running for attorney general, but I won't do so, if you say you're going to run." I'd already thought about it enough to give Don a quick response, which was "Thanks, but no, I'm not running." So Don ran, and with a good statewide organization, he won. In a sign of times to come, the governorship was won that year by Guy Hunt, who was Alabama's first Republican governor since Reconstruction.

Four years later, Don ran for governor, but he lost the Democratic nomination to Paul Hubbert. Hubbert then lost the general election, unfortunately, in my opinion, to incumbent Guy Hunt. Jim Folsom Jr. was elected lieutenant governor, and two years later ascended to governor, when Hunt was convicted of a felony and removed from office.

When Don ran for lieutenant governor in 1994, I supported him, as did many others, and he was elected. That gave him four years to build the successful foundation for his 1998 governor's race, when he beat Fob James in the general election. I supported Don, but so did a majority of those voting in a state where white voters were turning increasingly Republican. It was quite an accomplishment for Don to win in that changing environment.

Shortly after assuming office, in January 1999, Don, however, did something I greatly disagreed with him on. That is, in an appeal to voters who support the death penalty, Don blasted former Governor James for having commuted to life imprisonment the death penalty sentence of Judith Ann Neelley (see Chapter 15). I agreed with most of Don's other initiatives, but not that one.

Another McPhillips fan of Don's is my dear brother Frank, one of the founding attorneys of Alabama's distinguished law firm of Maynard Cooper and Gale. Frank became a top independent advisor to Don. I've heard Don make many glowing comments about Frank's help.

After Don had his 2002 reelection bid stolen in Baldwin County, he started working hard to lay a foundation to retake the governor's office in 2006.

And that's when the Republican big-wigs started getting out their knives and guns, and the skullduggery became thick and big-time.

Attorney Tommy Gallion reports that in 2001-02, he received a telephone call from his long-time friend Winton Blount III, son of the famous Red Blount. Tommy was a Republican, so Winton invited Tommy to join a group of other Republicans meeting with Karl Rove at a local law firm.

Winton informed Tommy that the Republicans were setting up "Operation 2010." They were getting Leura Canary appointed U.S. attorney, and she would prosecute Democrats and their supporters. Blount further said that Congressman Bob Riley was running for governor against Siegelman, and that Siegelman would be indicted in the middle of the next election cycle.

Blount added that the Republicans' goal was to control by 2010 the Alabama legislature, the Alabama judicial system, and the constitutionally elected offices, from governor on down.

Tommy's reply was, "Winton, this is crazy to use the federal prosecutorial system to indict political enemies. Count me out."

As we have seen, the Republican goals became a self-fulfilling prophecy reflected not only in the Siegelman prosecution—further facilitated by the appointment of political hack Mark Fuller as federal judge—but in the election of Republicans to all state constitutional offices and all nine Alabama Supreme Court judgeships. And there were the subsequent politically motivated prosecutions of gambling magnate Milton McGregor and of numerous Democratic state legislators.

Tommy reminded me that Bob Riley aide Bill Canary (Leura's husband) was not only connected in Washington to Karl Rove, but also to Jack Abramoff, and Michael Scanlon, who went to federal prison for racketeering related to controlling Indian casinos. Tommy added that Bob Riley got his political money from Indian casinos.

Starting in 2004, the Republican U.S. Attorney in Birmingham, Alice Martin, wrongfully lodged baseless criminal charges against Don. They were so stupid I can't even remember what they were. After a favorable evidentiary ruling from U.S. District Judge U. W. Clemon, and a persuasive opening statement from Bobby Segall, the U.S. attorney's office voluntarily dismissed the case.

But not to be outdone, Alice's sister politico in Montgomery, U.S. Attorney Leura Canary, decided she would use the U.S. government's resources to take an even better shot at Don. She conducted an investigation that stretched out over more than a year, amidst many press reports, suggesting that Don was about to be indicted over unknown misdeeds as governor.

The whole investigation, and indeed the entire prosecution, was rotten to the core for several reasons. First of all, Canary was the wife of the right-hand political aide of then-governor Bob Riley, seeking another term in 2006. Riley had barely beaten Siegelman in 2002 on the stolen election results, and did not want another contest with him.

It is naïve beyond belief for anyone to accept Leura Canary's statement that she was constructing a "Chinese wall" between her and the prosecution team. I have great respect for Louis Franklin and Steve Feaga and their legal skills, as the top-notch prosecutors they were, in handling the case. However, it has leaked publicly that Canary orchestrated behind the scenes and perhaps even indirectly orchestrated some of the press coverage.

To help make a case against Siegelman, the prosecution lassoed in Richard Scrushy. The founder and former CEO of HealthSouth Corporation, Scrushy was a client of mine, and, in my opinion, he is a decent and much misunderstood person. He had only recently been acquitted of federal fraud charges in Birmingham after a six-month trial. Many of the executives under Scrushy had pointed the finger at him while working out favorable pleas with the prosecution. However, Scrushy was well represented by a defense team led by Jim Parkman of Dothan and Donald Watkins of Birmingham. I helped on some lesser legal issues with the press.

After Scrushy was acquitted in 2005, some people in the public, and probably federal prosecutors in Birmingham and Montgomery, believed Richard's billionaire resources unfairly helped him achieve his acquittal. So what if they did? He was acquitted. The government also had enormous financial resources, plus extortionist threats of "worse consequences," to force co-defendants to plead guilty, testify against others, and avoid trial.

Nonetheless, Scrushy's reputation was sullied by the Birmingham prosecution. Roping Scrushy into a Siegelman prosecution lowered Don Siegelman's prospects for acquittal due to the "guilt by association" factor. Motions to sever the cases were denied, so the two powerful defendants, Siegelman and Scrushy, were tried together, in a well-sprung trap for both.

In Judge Mark Fuller, Siegelman had the most unfair federal judge in the country, one who had a personal grudge against Siegelman. Fuller bent over backwards to hurt Don at every twist and turn, while trying to project an image of professional impartiality.

Sometimes Fuller's bias was undisguised. Before he was appointed to the federal bench, Fuller, while district attorney of Coffee County, reportedly had a bad experience with Siegelman and continued to resent it. The *Montgomery Independent* reported that after Siegelman was convicted, Fuller was seen in his chambers with a big smile on his face. The seven-plus-year sentence Fuller gave Siegelman and Scrushy in 2006 was brutal considering the charges they were convicted of. Fuller also had them put into chains in the courtroom after the verdict, and led out in great indignity, without allowing them to speak with their family members.

And for what? Scrushy served on a state Hospital Certificate of Need Board and reportedly asked Siegelman to extend his tenure, although there was no proof of this, since both Siegelman and Scrushy elected not to take the stand. Further, Richard had served on the same board under three previous governors; he thought he was doing Don a favor by continuing to serve on a board that oversaw health care needs for the public good.

Siegelman, on the other hand, got no money personally for the contributions construed by the prosecution as a bribe, nor any contribution for any reelection campaign. What happened was that two large contributions of $250,000 each (one from HealthSouth; the other from a Maryland corporation) helped pay off the advertising debt for an unsuccessful lottery campaign that Siegelman had pushed as governor. And what would the lottery legislation have done, had it passed? It would have provided lots of money to public education, which is why Siegelman was trying to get it passed in the first place.

The prosecution's evidence was pathetically weak. There was no evidence of a "quid pro quo"—that Siegelman ever told Scrushy he'd give him a CON board reappointment—in return for the contributions. Never mind that little detail. Judge Fuller's prejudicial charges to the Siegelman-Scrushy jury helped make the connection.

It also came out after the trial that two members of the jury, both reportedly Auburn professors, were emailing each other back and forth during the trial, contrary to judicial instructions that forbade jurors from discussing the trial until deliberations began, and then only in the jury room. Yet Judge Fuller denied defense post-trial motions to explore that tainting of the jury process.

Richard Scrushy served his sentence in 2012 and is living in Houston, Texas, trying to rebuild his life. But Don Siegelman was out on bond for a few years while his appeals worked through the federal court system. When the appeals were denied, he was returned to prison and, unbelievably, remains in federal custody as of this writing in early 2016.

Don has had an excellent appellate team. Several superb amicus briefs have been filed on his behalf at the U.S. Supreme Court level, with one currently signed by 116 former state attorneys general, both Republican and Democrat, from forty-six states. All are supporting Siegelman's appeal. But all Don's appeals have been denied, and Siegelman continues to languish in a Louisiana federal prison, far from his family, where he apparently will be until the summer of 2017.

It is especially aggravating that the federal judge, Mark Fuller, who gave Siegelman such an unfair playing field and such a harsh sentence, has now been chased off the bench in disgrace, because he was arrested in Atlanta in August 2014 for beating up his wife in an Atlanta hotel room. Fuller's cases were taken away from him that month, but he refused to resign, and he continued to draw his $200,000 annual judicial salary for another year. Finally he did resign because he was under pressure from his fellow federal judges to do so and because U.S. Congresswoman Terri Sewell had announced that she was bringing impeachment proceedings against him.

Of course, I feel so strongly about how badly Don Siegelman has been treated that I have written publicly about it several times (see Appendix 12). Yes, Don's civil right to due process has been denied at every level.

Don has an army of devoted supporters, including long-time friend Bobby Timmons, head of the Alabama Sheriff's Association. However, I am deeply touched by how devoted and tireless have been his children, daughter Dana and son Joseph, in working for Don's release. I met with Joseph in Birmingham in November 2015 to plan further legal strategies. Joseph shared that at that moment his father was in indefinite isolation as a discipline for the great sin of speaking by telephone to a radio station.

At that time, Joseph was reluctant to go public, believing it might hurt his dad. Five weeks later, after Don remained "completely and utterly in isolation" with no contact with anyone, including family, Joseph went public. The next day, December 11, 2015, front-page stories in the *Montgomery Advertiser* and *Birmingham News* publicized this tortuous injustice.

The next day my wife, Leslie, found the radio interview on the "Free Don Siegelman" Facebook page (also available at free-don.org). I listened to it. All Don did was speak the truth, that he was a political prisoner. Nothing different from what he had been saying for years. Don said nothing disrespectful about or critical of the prison, warden, or anyone connected.

My blood boils over all this. Has America become like the old Soviet Union, as described in *The Gulag Archipelago*? This is a legitimate question, and it must be answered.

A footnote: In 2013 I sent Don a $250 check to help with canteen expenses. The check went to the proper Federal Bureau of Prisons address made for Siegelman's benefit. The cashier's check came from First Tuskegee Bank, where it was issued, and that check was deposited into someone else's Cleveland, Ohio, account. The check never got to Siegelman. It was obviously embezzled. I reported this to the Bureau of Prisons in Iowa, to the prison itself in Louisiana, to U.S. Attorneys in Iowa and Alabama, and to the U.S. Justice Department. Yet, two years later, I've not gotten a single response to any of my complaints or demands for action. It's like, "Who cares? We are the federal prison. We keep thieves here, but we've learned how to steal also. What are you going to do about it?" It discourages me sending anything more to Siegelman. That must be what the prison and legal authorities want to accomplish by stealing the money.

I greatly share the Siegelman family's frustration, and want to do anything legitimate to help, and help soon. I hope this chapter helps.

Others Have Been Politically Prosecuted

As everyone who follows the news should know, many people have been prosecuted for political reasons. On the other hand, for similar political reasons, people who ought to be prosecuted, especially in law enforcement ranks for wrongfully shooting and killing innocent civilians, escape the same.

I believe this is true in Alexander City where the policeman who wrongfully killed Emerson Crayton Jr., an unarmed 21-year-old African American, has the local district attorney as his biggest defender. This echoes what has happened all over the United States in police misconduct cases.

In Montgomery, an especially egregious political prosecution took place in 2011, when the Republican Leura Canary was still in office, causing Milton McGregor, owner of Victoryland Dog Track and Casino, and numerous legislators, to be indicted for alleged bribery or attempted bribery.

Fortunately, McGregor was well-heeled enough to hire a top defense team of Joe Espy and his sons, plus Bobby Segall and Shannon Holliday of the Copeland Franco firm. Bill Baxley was hired by another defendant, and Susan James was hired by someone else.

After a long first trial of about six weeks, State Senator Quinton Ross was acquitted of all charges and dismissed as a defendant. The other defendants were acquitted of most of the hundred or so charges, but there was a mistrial on one or more charges with each of them. At that point the federal prosecutors should have dismissed the rest of the case. Instead, they insisted on retrying the remaining defendants on the unresolved count. A few weeks later, the remaining defendants were all acquitted.

It helped for those defendants to have a fair judge in Myron Thompson, one of my heroes. If Siegelman had had Thompson, there surely never would have been a conviction. I feel certain Thompson would have thrown out the bribery charges on preliminary motions before the case went to a jury.

35

LIFE IS A CIVIL RIGHT

I was in Dublin, Ireland, on July 4, 2015, riding in a taxi with Leslie to attend a scholarly James Joyce presentation sponsored by the biennial International Fitzgerald Conference. Suddenly a traffic jam developed, as 20,000 people wove their way down main thoroughfares past Trinity College, en route to Merrion Square. To make it to our destination on time, we exited the taxi.

I soon discovered the march was part of a Rally for Life that had begun earlier. I joined in the parade with delight, Leslie by my side. My heart soared with emotion, as I realized how deep my commitment remains to the pro-life cause.

That commitment has cost me dearly over the years. It has also brought me great joy from my one and only son, David, saved twice from an abortion before he was born. As described earlier, the first time his biological mother, a young married woman, three months pregnant, was at a clinic but neither she nor her unemployed husband had the money to pay for it. The second time, at five months pregnant, the young couple had the money, but God used a paternal grandmother to intervene.

Many skeptics or secularists scoff at the notion of Divine intervention. Most of my Christian friends, especially in the Catholic, Baptist, and Pentecostal worlds, nod their heads in agreement. Even many of my fellow Episcopalians and brethren in the Methodist, Presbyterian, and Lutheran denominations agree that Divine intervention occurs, and may acknowledge that it happened in David's case. Yet others of a more liberal ilk smile benevolently at my story, but they wonder why such intervention doesn't occur more regularly, or fairly and reason that therefore it must not occur at all.

God's work is in a realm way above the intellectual capacity of any of his earthly creatures to understand. Yet God sent us his only son, Jesus, to explain God's nature to us. God also enlightened us with Old Testament prophets and New Testament apostles. Jesus upheld the sanctify of life greatly in his teachings and commandments, but his many healings represent that principle as well. Jesus also had strong words about how little children should be treated.

And how has my pro-life commitment cost me? First, it unquestionably cost me the Democratic nomination for the U.S. Senate in 2002, which I should have won without a run-off, as discussed in *The People's Lawyer*. It has also strained relations with some close friends and extended family who view the issue differently.

I freely admit the obvious, that the whole abortion issue is very controversial, probably more so than any other issue in American politics today, including gay rights and same-sex marriages. It is not politically correct to write this chapter. I am not against contraception or prophylactics. I am far removed from those who react otherwise. It's just that abortion involves more than one life. There is a second very precious life involved, with a heartbeat and brain wave so strong at five weeks that if in an adult, the law wouldn't allow the removal of life support.

I also realize, unfortunately, that my pro-life views weigh against another freedom, namely that of a woman and a man to have unprotected sex, without risk as to the consequences. In an ultra-secular, "anything goes" world that many live in, the pro-life view may seem backward, or puritanical. The freedom to abort is a civil rights issue to some.

Thus, if there is a conflict between two civil rights, how do we resolve it? I say, after much prayer, discussion, and study that the "civil right to life" should be greater than the "civil right to convenience." Yet, in saying this, I am savvy to what the U.S. Supreme Court has decreed as the law of the land in *Roe v. Wade*.

I recognize the life of the mother as a legitimate exception, but that is a rare one. Further, if President Jimmy Carter's exceptions stated when he was campaigning, to include rape or incest only, were extended, that would still eliminate 99 percent of the abortions in America. Of course, there is a collateral issue as to when rape may have occurred.

I frequently quote a famous ACLU lawyer out of New York, Nat Hentoff, who is both Jewish and, last I heard, atheist. He is also very pro-life. Contrary to the pro-choice (really pro-abortion) stand of most of his ACLU brethren, Nat has concluded that the scientific evidence of life inside the womb is so great that, as a matter of integrity, he cannot be otherwise than pro-life.

Our son David came to us in October 1990, saved from an abortion in May that I talked his biological mom out of. In God's honor, I gladly paid the cost of about $1000 per month, through Christ the Redeemer Episcopal Church, for two billboards in strategic locations around Montgomery.

One said "'Abortion Stops a Beating Heart'; call Sav-A-Life" and gave the telephone number. The other had a similar message. People at Sav-A-Life told me that many young, expectant mothers came to see them in the 1990s, strongly considering abortions, and changed their minds.

Of my civil rights friends who've questioned me on this issue, almost all are white liberals. Yet sadly, the African American community has also lost many babies over the years, negatively impacting its political clout. The holocaust of the 42 years since *Roe v. Wade* was issued in 1973, has cost Americans as many as 59 million lives.

The obvious difficulty from a civil rights standpoint is that some activists claim that, since it's a female body involved, only women should have a say-so. That fallacy ignores that half of unborn babies are male and that some fathers want the child even when the mother does not. It also ignores the truth that the only problem with pro-choice is that it is absolutely no choice for the one life really at stake, namely that of the unborn child.

I was educated at Ivy League universities and began my serious dating life while living in New York City from 1968–75. The Big Apple is known by some as "Sin City" for its anything-goes sexual revolution of the early 1970s. I came out of Manhattan in 1975 with the natural, self-protective view that pro-choice seemed the only reasonable position. Even when I ran for attorney general of Alabama, I confirmed to liberal activists that I was pro-choice, and I was.

My change began about ten years before David came to us, starting in the early 1980s. Influenced by pro-life activists like Merrilly and David Brewer at our new Christ the Redeemer Episcopal Church, and influenced further by a young female high school student saved from an abortion, I began to question my earlier views.

If there is a conflict between a young child's right to live (even if the child's still in the womb) and a young woman's right to abort, which right should govern? Obviously once the child is outside the womb, to take its life is considered murder. Some states even call it a "double murder" if a pregnant mother is shot and killed.

An abortion should not be minimized, dismissed, and compared to simply another miscarriage. In the latter case, it is simply Mother Nature at work. As already mentioned, Leslie has had three miscarriages, each at three months. This was painful for her and me. In the book *Heaven Is for Real*, a young boy who almost died described seeing, before returning to his earthly body, a miscarried sister he never knew he had. Maybe Leslie and I will meet our unborn children in heaven someday.

I detest the use of the word "fetus," because it denigrates the unborn life to the status of an "it," or a blob of unwanted flesh. That's where the blindness is involved.

It is a blindness akin to those, in the days of slavery, who considered a black person to be no person at all, or $3/5$ of a person, and not a life worth protecting. Maybe that's why my black friends are more sympathetic to my pro-life stand. I remember at the Democratic Convention in Charlotte in 2012, Fred Gray Jr., son of the distinguished civil rights icon of the same name, told me how pro-life he was.

Most of my pro-life legal work was in the 1990s. That included my nationally famous 1998 case of *Anonymous v. Anonymous*. The Alabama Supreme Court first established the right to appoint an attorney as a guardian-ad-litem to protect the life interest of an unborn child. Judge Mark Anderson, who appointed me, agreed that, if under Rule 17(c) of the Alabama Rules of Civil Procedure, a guardian-ad-litem could be appointed to represent the "property interest" of unborn children in estate proceedings, then why couldn't an attorney be appointed to represent the "life interest."

It has been very gratifying in the '90s and '00s to have been directly involved in several legal cases that saved unborn children. Several years ago, about 2010–11, I was in Tuskegee University's Kellogg Center eating lunch between morning and afternoon sessions in Macon County Circuit Court. A Caucasian lady sitting with two African American women at an adjacent table came up to me and said, "You're Julian McPhillips, aren't you?" I answered yes. She then replied, "Oh, you don't know what a hero you are to me. You saved my grandson's life." I asked how, and she reminded me of a case several years earlier, around 2007–08, when I helped a 17-year-old girl and her boyfriend (the grandmother's son) file child abuse papers in Elmore County Court that helped stop the teenage mother's parents from forcing her to have an abortion the next day.

By the way, one of the African American women also thanked me for keeping her teenage son out of prison on trumped-up charges. I forget what happened with that client in Macon County Circuit Court that day, but I'll never forget the genuine gratitude of those two ladies.

I have been active on two pro-life boards. One was long known as NOEL, or "National Organization of Episcopalians for Life," on whose board I served from 2000–12. It's now called Anglicans for Life, which includes both Episcopalians and denominational Anglicans. Another board since the early '90s that I remain on today is Alabama Lawyers for Unborn Children. I've enjoyed supporting Democrats for Life and Students for

Life, both growing organizations, and both headed by females.

The president of our Alabama Lawyers for Life board is a young white female, Susan McPherson. A newer member of our board is Judge Dorothea Batiste, an African American female. Both are from Birmingham. The other four board members are Caucasian men, Dean Johnson of Huntsville, Dick Browning of Mobile, Paul Spain of Birmingham, and me of Montgomery. Thus, we have the demographics and geographic areas of Alabama covered. Our membership roster includes hundreds of attorneys statewide.

Throughout the first decade of the 2000s, I had several more legal proceedings that helped save lives of unborn children. I've never charged money for such pro-life cases, because I am always overwhelmingly honored and privileged to be so involved.

Further, the refrain of many pro-choicers that the pro-life movement is spearheaded by men is simply untrue. Anglicans for Life, a national organization, has long been headed by a female, Georgette Forney. In her early years, Georgette had an abortion. It so troubled her that the only way she gained peace was to be active in the pro-life movement. Georgette has been especially vocal in leading the "Silent No More" movement among women who've been pained, anguished, and sometimes severely injured by abortions.

In 2007 I wrote a column for the *Montgomery Advertiser* agreeing with the need for a new law prohibiting partial birth abortions. Yet my work in the pro-life arena seems to have receded until 2014–2015 came along. In the summer of 2014, the Alabama Legislature passed a law codifying the right of guardian-ad-litem for an unborn child. Then, suddenly that year, national and international media swept down upon me for interviews and debate participation. In September 2015, Al Jazeera News was the first, putting me in a panel debate before an international audience with three female co-panelists, two pro-choice, and one pro-life.

Shortly afterwards in October 2015, MSNBC sent an attractive Italian female reporter and her cameraman to follow me into the courtroom and church; and engage me in an extended interview about guardian-ad-litem appointments for unborn children and the pro-life cause (See MSNBC/Julian McPhillips).

Not to be outdone, *The Daily Show* with Jon Stewart, based in New York, called me for an interview in late November 2015. They were willing to fly me up, but, given the value of time and a crowded schedule, I let them come down. With star reporter Jessica Williams coming, my dear Leslie and daughters Rachel and Grace urged me not to do the interview, due to the show's known ultra-leftist stand and tendency to cut and paste editorially to serve an ultra-liberal position. I did the interview anyway (see Daily Show/Jon Stewart/Julian McPhillips). For the most part, I received positive reviews from friends, acquaintances and strangers. That included a lady from Indiana, unknown to me, who wrote the *Montgomery Advertiser* to say how impressed she was.

Then, in January 2015, MSNBC did another interview (see again, MS-NBC/Julian McPhillips), and in February 2015, the Christian Broadcast Network did its first interview (see CBN/Julian McPhillips). I continue to receive positive comments, but critics are probably too discreet to comment, especially since I am not running for office anymore.

I know that some who read this chapter will not like it. Nonetheless, I consider my pro-life stance to be a part of my Christian witness. I do not apologize for that. Realizing *Roe v. Wade* legalized the procedure, with some limitations, my deal, so to speak, is to try to educate and encourage others to see that pro-life is far and away the best "choice" to make for many reasons.

One big reason is that there are millions of childless couples who want to adopt, as we did. Further, if the mom fighting the abortion issue elects to keep her child, then we, as a society, must be there for them. In this regard, I believe the Democratic Party, after birth, is more pro-life, with its greater support of a range of social services for families.

I was touched by Pope Francis's 2015 comments expressing forgiveness toward those who've had abortions. This was not an endorsement by any means but an expression of the orthodox Christian position that Jesus's death on the cross was a sacrificial act that paid the sin debt for all mankind. I hope the Pope's kind and conciliatory comments will be helpful in the public debate.

While the controversy will continue to swirl, and while more educated professional people, single and married, may elect not to have children, I believe a growing, emerging consensus of Americans has now come to see abortion is what it is, the deprivation of human life from innocent children. To extend a phrase from our dear Dr. Martin Luther King Jr., the long arc of justice seems to favor all future unborn. Yet, until that time, many precious lives may be lost to the altar of convenience and choice.

36

THE DEPRESSION

Time heals most things. If this book had come out in 2010, five years after the second edition of *The People's Lawyer*, this chapter would be closer to the top. As I approach the 10-year mark since this life-challenging event occurred, the whole episode has faded. Thank goodness, and Thank God!

Increasingly, however, not only among clients coming to see me but also among other lawyers and acquaintances, I see the heavy and costly hand of depression. I therefore think I'd be highly remiss not to share my own experience. I hope something in this chapter will be helpful to someone.

How did circumstances develop in 2005–06 that sent me tumbling into a bad depression, the worst four months of which were April–July 2006? The worst illness of my life? Worse than the excruciating pain of breaking my leg twice ten weeks apart. My son-in-law Corbett Lunsford was the first to speculate this might be a "spiritual attack." He was right.

While I'm not into numerology, I can only wonder about the coincidence when this depression first sunk its fangs in February 2006. It was exactly 40 years earlier, a biblically significant number, when I experienced a minor depression in February 1966.

The number *40* also signifies a wilderness experience—it was the number of days Jesus spend in the wilderness fighting temptation and the number of days Noah was in the ark. It was also the number of years Moses was in the wilderness with the Israelites before they reached the Promised Land.

My first depression came when I broke my leg the second time in the same wrestling season, as a sophomore at Princeton. Afterwards doctors told me that I should never wrestle or play football again. My identity as an athlete and self-esteem as a person took a beating. For the remainder of the second semester of 1966, a heavy cloud which I could not shake hung over me. But I was functional, attended classes, and returned to Birmingham the summer of 1966, where the depression lifted. So I thought a depression was a mood disorder . . . until I discovered quite differently 40 years later.

The depression that rocked me in 2006 was a dog of a darker color, with sharper teeth. At first, I didn't recognize where it came from, thinking the accumulated pressure of two tough back-to-back federal criminal trials was taking its toll. The first in November 2005 involved George David Salum, a former Montgomery policeman, whom I had come to genuinely like.

I could see and feel the deep anxiety in Salum's eyes. He had served Montgomery well as a uniformed cop for almost 20 years. Then he helped a friend obtain classified police documents that exposed another officer's bullying behavior. I felt the case for Salum was winnable, despite having drawn an ultra pro-prosecution judge in Mark Fuller. The hard-fought trial lasted most of a week and ran into late Friday night. The jury was repeatedly deadlocked. Judge Fuller then used a "dynamite charge," which usually helps the prosecution. After the first such charge, the jury remained deadlocked. Some jurors lived as far away as Dothan and Phenix City. Judge Fuller threatened to have the jury come back on Monday, November 11, Armistice Day, a national holiday. The jury finally caved in, finding Salum guilty on one count, although not guilty on others. My emotions were stretched.

Thus, when I came into Dr. Teresa Allen's office the following Tuesday for my annual blood work, my thyroid rating was high, though it probably was only temporarily elevated. Rather than being in the median 3s, which is perfect on a TSH rating scale of 0.5 to 5.5, my thyroid rating had moved up to 4.49.

Dr. Allen, an osteopath but not an endocrinologist, told me in late January 2006, a full two and a half months later, that she had been worrying about me since my blood results of November. She said that, if my thyroid kept going up, it could cause me serious problems, including "brain fog." So she prescribed a medication called "Nature Thyroid" and instructed me to take one 200 milligram tablet daily. Thinking it was like another vitamin, I naively took it.

It proved devastating.

Soon I noticed I was getting nervous, hypersensitive, and jumpy. I found myself waking up at night on cold February mornings, feeling heat on the thyroid gland in my neck. Inexplicably, I was also perspiring on the top of my head on a cold night. Midway through the three weeks of taking the pill, I attended a prayer meeting and found it difficult to throttle my emotions. It finally dawned on me that the medication must be causing this. Dr. Allen was off on a trip, not available to consult with. So I stopped taking the pills—"cold turkey," as the term was later described to me, not a good idea.

The medication caused my thyroid to swing sharply downward to 1.9, much too quick a drop. So I finally consulted an endocrinologist, having just discovered that thyroid problems were their specialty. The endocrinologist shook his head, informing me that my earlier 4.49 was well within normal range. He added that I never should have taken any medication, especially something so powerful as 200 milligrams daily of Nature Thyroid. Another doctor, who became a client several years later, told me the medication was so strong it could have caused me to have a heart attack or a stroke.

Nice to discover that after the fact.

Now I understand better how the depression, creeping up on me after getting off the medication, made me feel like a heart attack or stroke might be coming any day. I also began to irrationally personalize the pain of others seen on TV, or viewed elsewhere.

In late February 2006, our family took a ski trip to Sante Fe, New Mexico, and visited with my sister Sandy. Already an inner transition was setting in, including a loss of appetite. When my future son-in-law, Jay Plucker, asked my permission in Sante Fe to marry Rachel, our oldest daughter, I found it difficult to control my emotions. Ditto upon driving home from the Birmingham Airport in late February, when son David shared his negative feelings about returning to Stony Brook School in New York. David drew his finger across his neck signaling what he would do to himself if he didn't come home. I wasn't willing to take the chance.

I plodded away at the office during March 2006, advising and representing clients as well as I could. Nonetheless the bleariness, or dreariness, of life was beginning to take its toll. I was seeing things through a lens of dead, brownish colors, rather than the green, blue, or more vibrant hues usually framing my vision. I had also backslid spiritually, without realizing it.

I eventually got back in touch with Dr. Allen. She was sympathetic and prescribed a medication helpful for people with epilepsy. She said it had helped some folks snap out of depression. She thought it might do the same for me. But it didn't help at all.

My sister Sandy and others suggested an anti-depressant, Lexapro, prescribed by my family doctor. It worked well for her. I tried it, but it so activated my mind that I couldn't sleep for two days straight. Later, my general doctor, to calm me down, countered with a little Xanax. But the drowsiness it caused was hard to shake. After that, no more Lexapro, no more Xanax. The depression worsened, exacerbated by three counter-medications that didn't work.

In late March 2006, my long-time friend and loyal law partner, Kenneth Shinbaum, and very devoted office manager, Amy Strickland, came over to my house one night. They visited me while I was in bed. Leslie was also present. We all decided it would be wise for me to take off some time from the firm. However long that might be was undecided. I would stay at home for the time being.

Gradually, the wheels of time ground down to the slowest pace I had ever experienced. And the dullest. Life in good times was a zoom and a joy, but depression made it dull, with a gray tone. Nonetheless, in mid-April, with help from Paul and Carroll Puckett, I completed my annual tax returns. Due to a drop in my productivity the depression was causing, I gave money back to the firm out of my own pocket, to meet the firm's retirement obligations.

Distorted by the quicksand of depression, I started envisioning the law firm caving in without my rainmaking capabilities involved. Panic occasionally waved its ugly head. In April, I tried handling a few cases, but then I backed away and turned them over to other lawyers in the firm. When Amy visited me at the house, I shared a fear that our firm might collapse. Thanks be to God, and the loyal support from the office, that didn't happen. Kenneth and the other law partners, especially Joe Guillot, Aaron Luck, and Jim Bodin, stepped up to the plate and pinch-hit for me. Amy deserved special credit for keeping a level head. So did my dear wife Leslie.

One major source of tension weighing me down was representing Tyrone White, an African American Auburn policeman. We believed Tyrone was framed for accepting money in return for minimizing, or not giving, tickets. A number of witnesses, all black, testified to being coerced by federal agents into lying about Tyrone. I even had a great witness statement recorded between Tyrone and a complaining party, reflecting that the complainant was making things up. In the fall of 2005, with investigator Billy Smith and paralegal Sim Pettway present, we voluntarily played a recorded interview with a witness to the U.S. attorney's office. We hoped it would cause prosecutors to step back and dismiss the case. How naïve! Instead, one prosecutor construed certain language in the tape to be helpful to the government. Unfortunately, I didn't hear directly from the U.S. attorneys that they wanted the tape until two months later.

By that time Tyrone, who had taken the tape home with him, inadvertently erased it. So now, with the prosecutor wanting it, and us explaining that Tyrone didn't have it, the prosecution insinuated that Tyrone had intentionally destroyed it. The next thing I knew, Billy Smith, Sim Pettway, paralegal Allison Highley, and I were all being subpoenaed by the U.S. attorney's office to provide testimony before a criminal grand jury concerning what we knew about our client's missing tape.

The thought that I, or any of my staff members, might be forced to stand in front of a criminal grand jury and give testimony against a client was anathema. In my opinion, it would have been highly unethical to do so. Further, a prosecutor before a grand jury has the power to obtain a criminal contempt ruling from a nearby federal judge against a witness refusing to testify. That could have jeopardized any of us. My staff members, except for independent investigator Billy Smith, were starting to feel paranoid about this, seeing draconian possibilities. Comparisons to what happened to TV celebrity Martha Stewart came to mind. That didn't help my depression one bit, instead feeding its twin sister of anxiety.

Also stimulating my paranoia was seeing how badly the U.S. Attorney's office was crucifying Don Siegelman and Richard Scrushy over something I didn't even think was a crime. Both men were friends of mine. It reinforced the image that these Republican prosecutors were persecuting high profile Democratic figures. As a well-known, successful attorney myself, a candidate for the Democratic nomination for the U.S. Senate in 2002, I fit the bill as a pretty good target myself.

My team quickly filed a motion to quash the subpoenas served by the U.S. Attorney. Yet federal magistrate Susan Russ Walker denied the motion, forcing us to appeal to the 11th Circuit. We did so anxiously, knowing well about that court's pro-law enforcement rulings.

Meanwhile, despite the weight of the anxiety and depression, I was level-headed enough to retain two good local attorneys to represent us. I first consulted my dear friend Bobby Segall, the best attorney in Alabama, in my judgment. Bobby referred me to attorney Ron Wise for help on the criminal defense part. I also retained former Republican-appointed U.S. Attorney Jim Wilson, now in private practice, to speak diplomatic common sense to the federal prosecutors.

The combination of Ron Wise and James Wilson was what the doctor ordered. Prayer coverage also helped greatly. In the end, the U.S. Attorney's office backed down from the subpoenas, if the four of us, that is, Billy, Sim, Allison and I would give individual depositions. At least our counsel Ron Wise and James Wilson would be present for each deposition.

Our attorneys represented us well, making timely objections. None of us got into any trouble. Unfortunately our client was later indicted for obstruction of justice in his accidental erasing of the tape. I considered that harassment enough, because I strongly suspected that the U.S. attorneys had made and retained a copy of the audiotape from the earlier voluntary meeting in their office in the fall of 2005.

Wanting my client to have the best representation possible, and not be handicapped by my depression, I filed a motion to withdraw from further representing Tyrone White, citing a potential conflict and health reasons. The Court granted the motion. A seasoned and competent criminal defense attorney, Russ Duraski, took over the case. I refunded Tyrone's $10,000 fee, which he promptly paid over to Duraski.

Heart-warmingly, and reflective of Tyrone's good character even though he was later convicted on some of the charges, Tyrone sent me a wonderful letter on October 5, 2006, thanking me for all I had done to help him. Tyrone stated that he had "great faith in Russ Duraski. He is almost as good as you (smile)."

Fast backwards to April 2006. We avoided the grand jury with good lawyering and much prayer. Yet the dilemma exacerbated my depression, caused in the first place by an overly strong medication. We still had a residual anxiety that something in our depositions might be misconstrued, leading to potential legal trouble down the road.

In late April 2006, giving in to, and placating, my dear wife Leslie, I finally consented to her driving me up to see a psychiatrist in Birmingham, former Episcopal priest Larry DePalma. He was recommended to us by our good friend, the Rev. Doug Carpenter of Birmingham. I remember meeting with Dr. DePalma in mid-April in his office. Leslie, Doug, and I were all present. The psychiatrist asked me to rate, on a scale of 1 to 10, how I was feeling. I gave him a "3," even though inwardly I felt the true number was lower. I feared the psychiatrist might try to commit me somewhere if I gave him too low a number.

In late May and early June 2006, Leslie had me accompany her on a week-long road trip to Virginia to tend to her father's estate. We also saw my sister Betsy in the Virginia Beach-Chesapeake area. My depression was embarrassingly obvious. I found myself covering my eyes at a movie. I had trouble talking to anyone, though I was rational. During that trip we received word that the 44-year-old Dr. DePalma had died from a heart attack.

It was this psychiatrist-reverend who, after our first and only meeting, recommended that I take Cymbalta, prescribed in a dosage amount I cannot remember. What I do remember is that this anti-depressant was dangerous and very counter-productive. For the first and only time in my life, it made me think about the unfathomable, namely doing something to myself. I know that my brother David had been goaded by anti-depressants when he drove into a Mountain Brook garage in 1976 and killed himself with carbon monoxide poisoning. It occurred to me, however, that if I ever attempted something, I would mess it up, as David had in his first attempt in the summer of 1970, maiming his brain with carbon monoxide poisoning in an Alexandria, Virginia garage. As a result, David lost his short-term memory and damaged his balance and speech, the combination of which was tremendously disabling.

Never before in the two earlier months of depression had I entertained such thoughts. This was unnerving. An Auburn psychologist had given me a test in the early 1990s and remarked afterwards that I was the most secure person she had ever met. But here in May 2006, especially after taking a second and third Cymbalta tablet, I was thinking of how I could do myself in. Unbelievable, in hindsight. And very humbling. It helped me understand better how others can develop such thoughts and, unfortunately, sometimes act on them.

Fortunately, I never attempted anything. Despite a very strained spirituality, or separation from God, I retained enough sense to fall on my knees, and say, "Lord, help me. I can't handle this. Please help me." The prayer support of others also buttressed me.

And God did what he is best at.

Therefore, maybe it was divine insight, mixed with common sense, that caused me to do something else with the Cymbalta tablets that Leslie was riding herd on me—following doctors' advice—every day to take. She was always asking, "Have you taken your pill?" I would answer, "Yes, I have taken it." I just didn't tell her what I did with it. What I was doing, however, after taking the pill from the bottle, was putting it into a sock and hiding it in my chest of drawers.

Thus, for the first and only time in my life, I was deceiving Leslie. I knew she meant well, reminding me so vociferously every day about taking the pills. My will to survive, however, was greater than my thoughts to the contrary. It was only in September or October 2006, when I was doing better, that I told Leslie what I had been doing with the tablets. At that point, she grabbed the sock, removed the pills and flushed them down the toilet. Good riddance! Cymbalta was the worst of the anti-depressants.

The months of June and July, leading up to Rachel's August 5, 2006, wedding were difficult. Some days I'd go in the sunroom at home and just stare endlessly for hours, wondering how long I could continue to endure it. I got dragged by Leslie to a couple of wedding receptions, one at my brother Frank's house in Birmingham in June, the other in July at a fancy house in Mooresville, near Huntsville. I did my best to "fake it," perhaps taking a cue from my mother's graciousness when she was in the early stages of Alzheimer's. But people who hadn't seen me in a while were amazed to see how much weight I had lost. There was also a personality change. I had gone from my usual extroverted self to a reserved, introverted person.

Indeed, at Grace's wedding in August 2004, I had weighed a fairly muscular 245 pounds. By the time Rachel's wedding arrived two years later in August 2006, I was down to 185 pounds, having lost 60 pounds. I looked like an older man, much older than two years earlier, and frankly older than I now look a decade later. Losing a lot of weight and becoming gaunt will do that for you. The loss of appetite was caused by the depression. If Leslie hadn't been pushing me to eat something, death by starvation was around the corner, she believed.

So Leslie was the major hero in keeping the consequences from becoming worse. Once, passing me on the stairwell, she screamed, "I married you for better or worse and this is worse!" That caused me to chuckle. When I shared the episode at Leslie's 60th birthday party one and a half years later, the 135 people present roared with laughter. They could relate to what I said. I never received any institutional treatment, because Leslie was there for me. I also give my daughters Rachel and Grace and son David much credit. I thanked Rachel, and later asked her forgiveness, for the disconcerting atmosphere my depression was causing in the months before her wedding. Rachel, like her mother, is exceedingly level-headed, and replied that her only concern was my health.

Grace, bless her heart, flew down to Montgomery from Chicago in late July 2006, two weeks before the wedding . . . to help out, but her special mission was to encourage me and cheer me on. She succeeded, and I will always be grateful.

And dear David! He kept it together, too, although he was at a critical, transitional age of 15, and at the time, dealing with confusion and a minor depression of his own. We hung in there together! Leslie knew that my driving David to school and picking him up was therapeutic. And it was.

As a word of inspiration to others suffering depression, one tactic that helped me was to write notes . . . sometimes one page, sometimes several pages, to express my thoughts. I really didn't show them to anyone, except occasionally to Leslie. This helped me endure the anxiety and boredom of the depression. I have 20–30 such notes, stashed away in a manila envelope, placed in a 2006 album.

No doubt, I was the beneficiary of great prayer. It blew me away when the Reverend Fred Shuttlesworth, hero of the Birmingham civil rights campaign, came to my home in Montgomery not once, but twice, during the summer of 2006 to pray with me and encourage me. Dr. Shuttleworth appreciated my work against police brutality. I'll never forget his words "Julian, it's o.k. to be depressed; just don't let it become despair."

This showed me, and role-modeled to me, the pastoral side of Fred Shuttlesworth that many people did not know. He and I had grown close during my campaign for the U.S. Senate in 2002. He not only campaigned for me around Birmingham but he traveled with me on a bus tour of the Black Belt. Also on that trip were Martin Luther King III, my daughter Grace, and Sarah Chavda, daughter of Mahesh and Bonnie Chavda.

Other key prayer warriors who helped me in this spiritual battle were neighbors and civil rights heroes Bob and Jeannie Graetz and dear friend Rev. John Alford, who sparked Shuttleworth's coming. I'll always feel that my son-in-law Corbett Lunsford's aunt and uncle, Ellen and Art Sanborn, were exceedingly helpful in their prayers, especially at Lake Martin after Rachel's wedding.

Wonderfully, Bishop Fitz Allison of South Carolina, a seminary professor of my father's at the University of the South in Sewanee, and a long-time friend, was most helpful. Most importantly, supporting me in prayer were Leslie, Rachel, Grace, and David, the immediate family. Thank you, Lord.

In late July 2006, a week before Rachel's wedding, Leslie, Grace, David and I drove up to Charlotte, North Carolina, to visit with dear friends Mahesh and Bonnie Chavda, the world-class healing evangelists. Their prayers truly blessed us all. My siblings Sandy, Betsy, and Frank also supported me with their prayers and kind concern, for which I was grateful.

The wedding weekend of August 4–6 finally arrived. It was a wonderful occasion and the catalyst for my recovery. As with Grace two years earlier, I walked Rachel down the aisle. What a lovely bride she was. Jay was also a handsome groom. Leslie and I gave Rachel away. That night, at the reception, I spoke to the crowd. Although it was difficult, I finessed it as best I could. Others said I did fine.

With that spark, I thought, "Hey, come hell or high water, I am going back to the office and just gut it out." And that's what I did . . . with great help from Leslie and Amy, and enormous help from God. Surprisingly, the highest fee totals in August for any attorney in the firm came from me. Yet there were emotional pangs and concentration challenges. All was not yet well.

It wasn't until mid-October 2006 that I shed the final vestiges of the depression. I wanted to make a deal with God, but I wasn't sure how to do it. So I called up my good friend, Dr. Fitz Allison of South Carolina, and asked him if it was possible to make a deal with God. Bishop Allison first replied that he didn't think so. Then I reminded him, "Didn't the Old Testament Israelites enter into a covenant with God, and isn't a covenant essentially an agreement?" Bishop Allison replied, "Well, yes, you are right."

So I wrote a letter to God on October 12, 2006 (no stamp was needed), and I freely reprint it below, hoping it might help someone else.

October 12, 2006

Dear God:

I want to make a deal with you. A deal for you to heal me, to heal the fluttering sensation I feel in the back of my head, and to heal an overall sense of oppression or depression, returning joy to my life.

The deal is this. If you will heal me, I will devote the rest of my life, far more than ever before, to doing your work on earth. That is, spreading the Good News of your salvation through Jesus Christ, and trying to glorify you in my life's work, whatever I do. Also, I will follow more energetically Christ's principle of serving others, and helping those in need around the world.

Is this too much to ask of you, Lord? I hope not. You know how many modern day saints and average ordinary Christians I have had praying for me. That includes my devoted wife Leslie, and devoted daughters, Rachel and Grace.

Some bad things I thought would happen have not happened, and some good things I didn't anticipate have happened. I thank you, Lord, for all of this. But I can't enjoy or take advantage of these blessings if I don't have good physical, mental and spiritual health to enjoy it with.

So please, Lord, grant me this favor, this blessing. I will keep my word. You can count on it. I will share this with some other key Christian friends of mine, to make sure they hold me accountable, to make sure I keep my word.

Your son,

Julian

The devoted "pray-ers" also included my dear son David, he later reminded me. I couldn't thank him enough. After writing this letter, I felt the remnants of the depression lift. Beforehand, I could still feel a "swirling sensation" occasionally in the back of my head, and sometimes a pain in my heart area. I literally felt all that lift and go away, and now, as I write this nine years later, none of it has come back.

It's mysterious how that happened, but the realm of the spirit is a domain of mystery and wonder. And it is the habitat of God.

Within weeks afterward, sometime in November, I openly shared my battle with depression in a TV interview conducted on the program "Conversations with Carol and Julian" (I am the "Julian"). I had earlier thought this was a show primarily seen in the black community. But afterwards I had two local white attorneys contact me, Don Gilbert, a lobbyist, and Darren Hendley, a municipal court judge. Both said how helpful and inspirational to them seeing that interview had been. Don had experienced depression, fairly severely, as he gained 70 pounds while taking medication fighting cancer. It was most gratifying to hear from them both.

I was 59 when the worst year of my life hit me. Until that point, I thought I had escaped the mid-life crisis. Actually it was just delayed. It was a huge test of faith and learning experience for me, the kind of education one can never get from books. It can only be learned the hard way. During its worst, I wasn't sure if the depression was ever going to lift, or if I was ever going to recover. It was like being stuck in a hole with no way to get out, or in quicksand. Many nights, when I said my prayers before going to sleep, I asked God to take me up to heaven if I didn't wake up. But I always woke the next morning. Thank you, Lord.

By mid-November 2006, when I turned 60, I'd been fully well for over a month. I was already gaining my weight back. I was running again every day. It was almost as if the depression had never happened. I wasn't burdened by memories. I celebrated my 60th birthday in Montgomery and again in Chicago with Grace, Corbett, and other long-time close friends, the Rev. Mark Tusken and Cliff and Judy Fenton.

Ironically, but characteristically for me as well as for most who experience depression, some good (or "silver lining") came out of the awful experience. Besides the law firm slimming down, which helped us better sail through the recession years of 2008–11, I also gained a greater compassion and empathy for the many people suffering depression. The number is huge. I read a *Newsweek* cover story in September 2006 which said about two-thirds of the CEOs of major corporations in America end up experiencing depression. There are many different kinds of depression. Mine, as physicians later diagnosed, was overwhelmingly caused by the excessive thyroid medication.

Also, the type of clients I have are often susceptible to depression: people losing a job, sometimes after 20–30 years with the employer; people unjustly charged with crimes they didn't commit, or for which they have a good explanation; people suffering a serious physical injury, which causes the body chemistry to change; people who have taken a prescription medication, as I did, that was too strong for them. Some clients have come to me in a deep or disabling depression. I have been better able to help them, because of my own experience. Empathy is stronger than sympathy.

I understand these people much better now. I was one of them. I can literally feel their pain. And the client can tell, especially when I briefly share my own experience, as I sometimes have. While my own battle was humbling, and embarrassing at times, it was never shameful because it was not a character issue but an illness—an illness that has become all too common in America today. And a dose of humility is good for the soul. It reminded me of the famous biblical truth that "it is in our weakness that God's strength is made perfect."

I get along fine today with Dr. Allen. She is completely forgiven. She meant well, but was simply outside her field in dealing with a thyroid issue. While her medication was the main cause of the depression, it was worsened by the anti-depressants I was subsequently prescribed. Dr. Allen is an osteopath and good in that field. Her prolotherapy has helped me and many others (see Appendix 10). She is also a very good person, a friend, and has a heart for her patients. I still consult her on muscle and joint issues.

I have also found my experience helpful when I pray for people with depression, migraine headaches, gout, or other maladies, including cancer. It is a great joy, and a great honor from God, and for God, when some of these people look at me afterwards and ask, "What did you do?" Some have even been fortunate enough not to return to the particular illness he or she had before they came to see me and we prayed. What a joy. To see God's holy spirit still healing people today is an awesome wonder and privilege!

I haven't touched any medication since May 2006. My good health that returned in October that year has remained. While I personally am very "anti-medication," I recognize that it can be helpful to some. However, for many others, as it did for me, medication often causes more harm than good.

It would be trite to leave it with Shakespeare's phrase that "all's well that ends well." I remain enormously grateful to God. He didn't cause my depression, but God allowed me to experience and endure its pain. With the Holy Spirit sparking the prayers of others, and sparking my faith, healing did come. In the process, God honed and shaped me into a better tool in his hand. I accept his challenge to remain as such.

37

THE RESURRECTION OF
CHRIST THE REDEEMER

"Let the glory of the Lord fill this house," I ring out, in challenge to the congregation at the beginning of our 6 p.m. Sunday services at Christ the Redeemer, Resurrected. In return, people respond enthusiastically with the same words: "Let the glory of the Lord fill this house." These words are handwritten by Mahesh Chavda on the front of our church bulletins (see Appendix 3).

Led by a four-member African American jazz band, we then get off to a rousing start, bellowing out "Come, Now Is the Time to Worship." On other Sundays we may start with "Open the Eyes of My Heart, Lord" or "We Are Standing on Holy Ground." We also get high spiritually on such traditional hymns as "Holy, Holy, Holy, Lord God Almighty," or "I Sing a Song of the Saints of God."

Another special hymn we enjoy is "Alleluia, Alleluia, Give Thanks to the Risen Lord." This reminds me of being inside Lazarus's tomb in Jerusalem in 1990, when five of us crowded in and sang the hymn, which echoed around the close-knit chamber.

We also enjoy singing together "As the Deer Pants for Water, So My Soul Longs After You" and "These Are the Days of Elijah." Other favorites include "Amazing Grace," "Michael, Row the Boat Ashore," "Sanctuary," "Let There Be Peace on Earth," and "Swing Low, Sweet Chariot."

We may be small in number, ranging from a usual high of mid-20s on down to the high teens. Yet we get high and lifted up spiritually every Sunday by these praise and worship songs and hymns.

Recently, we've even taken to singing "Onward, Christian Soldiers." There was a time when I considered the song too bellicose, especially during the days when we were protesting the Vietnam War. Yet how well do I remember my five student years from 1959 to 1964, when I marched to church every Sunday morning up on that cold Sewanee Mountain to the tune of "Onward Christian Soldiers." At Christ the Redeemer, Resurrected

THE RESURRECTION OF CHRIST THE REDEEMER

we consider this hymn appropriate because of the famous words of St. Paul about spiritual warfare: "We struggle not against flesh and blood, but against powers and principalities of this dark world and against spiritual forces of evil in the heavenly realms." Ephesians 6:12.

The resurrected version of Christ the Redeemer has brought back a few of our former members, including Michael and Sandi Kerr, Janie Wall, Lewis Underwood, mother-daughter Ann and Cindy O'Ferrell, and Leslie and me.

We've also attracted a new set of people. We're about half black and half white, with the occasional Korean or two. This tri-racial group has included at times as many as seven nationalities—Kenyan, Nigerian, Scottish, German, Korean, Brazilian, and, of course, American (the largest group).

Among our most active members are Nigerian immigrants Success Jumbo, his wife Chichi, and their one-year-old son, Success Jr., our youngest member. Leslie and I met Chichi in Benin in 2005. Success handles the electronics part of our ministry on Sunday evenings, using Power Point to project on the wall the entire service of prayers, songs, and scriptural readings, which everyone can easily read. ChiChi became an American citizen in 2011. She expects her mother to arrive soon from Benin and also to become a member.

Another amazing member, Steve Watkins, in his 40s, was a homeless veteran when he first visited CTR in the summer of 2014. Today he would tell you he is completely transformed, with a special-education teaching job, a decent apartment, and a great love for Jesus as Lord.

Linda Reynolds and Peggy Gelpi are both Caucasian and in their early 60s. Life experiences and health issues have challenged them both. However, thriving on the healing ministry of CTR, they realize that in their weakness, God's strength is made perfect. They, too, have been enormously renewed by CTR.

Our jazz band consists of Frank Gray and Curke Dudley on guitars, Unika Newsome on drums, and Isaac Harris on a piano. The talented four frequently play on the *Harriott II* riverboat, along with singer Clayton "Wildcat" Thomason (see Chapter 25), who also attends our services.

Like other churches, Christ the Redeemer had its struggles in its earlier years. The 1980s and 1990s were largely glory days. I remember that co-founder Hunter Flack Sr. (who gave the five acres of prime Montgomery real estate for the church) and I had a friendly dispute over the 10th of Hunter's 10 charismatic tenets he wanted Christ the Redeemer to adopt. I was okay with the first nine but had a problem with the tenth, which said "I believe in the eternal happiness of the saved and the eternal punishment of the lost." I referred to the Good Shepherd who leaves the 99 sheep who are found to go looking for the one who is lost." I added that Jesus, as the Good Shepherd, could find the one who is lost."

The good ol' days lasted until the last Sunday of January 2005, What happened on that date, and the ensuing struggle of 2005–06, led to Bishop Henry Parsley declaring an involuntary dormancy upon CTR in January 2007. I say more on this below. For the next half-dozen years, Leslie and I explored and frequently enjoyed other options for worship. However, I kept longing for the best part of Christ the Redeemer. Eventually, after a lot of prayer and persistence, the church sprang again from its dormant, but far from dead, roots.

On April 28, 2013, we re-opened with an African priest and 37 congregants. Spirited praise and worship music raised the roof and echoed through the sanctuary, as it still does. For a seasoned civil rights warrior, the worship refills my cup weekly. It renews my energy for the next week's challenges.

How WE BECAME THE resurrected CTR is quite a story, some parts of which Alabama Diocesan leaders would prefer I not tell. But it is a history worth preserving. If this is not your cup of tea, then skip to another chapter. I will understand.

Leslie and I were among the 30-plus Montgomery-area Episcopal Christians who came together in the fall of 1980 to form a new Episcopal church. Leslie and I had been members since 1975 at the Church of the Ascension, the Episcopal church where my father began his priesthood in 1962. On January 7, 1981, at the home of Ted and Betsy Copeland, the nascent group enthusiastically agreed upon a name, splitting the difference between those favoring "Christ the King" and those preferring "Our Redeemer." Christ the Redeemer it was!

Christ the Redeemer was evangelical and charismatic, with a strong emphasis on the healing ministry, and exalting praise and worship music. The attire was more informal. Except for our wonderful and frequent interim minister Vernon Jones and his wife, Lillian, we were virtually all Caucasian, though from varying socio-economic backgrounds. From the beginning, Methodists, Baptists, Catholics, Presbyterians, Lutherans, and persons from non-traditional backgrounds, including Pentecostal, frequently joined us and contributed to making us an ecumenical church, different from most of our sister Episcopal churches in Montgomery.

To our great delight, four major healing conferences led by Mahesh and Bonnie Chavda took place at Christ the Redeemer in 1994, 1996, 1999, and 2003. I enjoyed chairing each conference, working with many other

Montgomery area religious leaders of various denominations or non-denominational backgrounds. CTR was packed to its maximum, 400-plus each time. An off-site conference held at the Governor's House motel attracted close to 1,000 one night.

Our first rector, coming in June 1981, was a former businessman, the Rev. Fred Pinkston. He, wife Carolyn, and their three sons will always occupy a special place in our hearts. Fred left in 1985. For the next year we were blessed with the Reverend Vernon Jones as interim rector—he was the first African American Episcopal priest in the Alabama diocese.

Starting in 1986, we enjoyed an eight-year term with the best priest Christ the Redeemer has had, Mark Tusken, who was assisted by his wife, Vicki, and their two young boys. Air Force chaplain Dave Bena was a great priest assistant. By 1994, Mark's last year, after quadrupling both the congregation and the worship space with a new sanctuary, the congregation peaked at 400 members, with two morning services. We even had a "double dose" praise and worship service at 6 p.m. for those wanting more. But Mark moved to Illinois in 1994, and the congregation began to recede.

For the next year, our interim priest was again the dear Reverend Vernon Jones. He was accompanied by the renowned Reverend Forrest Mobley, originally of Destin, Florida, but who in the mid-1990s ran a marriage enrichment center on Lake Martin, 40 miles north of Montgomery.

In 1995, CTR attracted the talented Coleman Tyler, a gifted preacher and musician, and very committed to the Lord. Coleman's wife, Susan, and three kids blended well into the strong family orientation at Christ the Redeemer. We were not surprised, however, when Coleman accepted a call to a much larger church in 1999, returning to his native Virginia.

Another year under Rev. Jones's interim leadership passed, and finally in 2000, the Reverend Doug McCurry became our next priest. His helpful wife, Cathy Sue, and their four boys continued the charismatic and evangelical theme.

In 2003, a major controversy within the Episcopal Church hit the entire national body like a ton of bricks. That occurred when openly homosexual Gene Robinson, accompanied by a young man as his "significant other," walked down the aisle and was consecrated Bishop of New Hampshire. The consecration required the approval of a majority of other bishops in the national Episcopal Church. Many priests and lay people were in an uproar all over the country. Many left the Episcopal Church. No one at Christ the Redeemer was happy about it, but most of us, at that time in 2003, did not feel that leaving Christ the Redeemer would serve any good purpose.

Nonetheless, Reverend McCurry, encouraged and abetted by certain CTR lay members, including a conservative retired Air Force colonel, announced on the last Sunday of January 2005, that he was leaving Christ the Redeemer (for which Doug professed positive feelings). Mainly, he said, he was leaving the national Episcopal denomination. Three-quarters of the CTR congregation, seeming to have rehearsed it, stood in unison and declared they were leaving with Doug.

Soon thereafter, the Reverend John Michael Van Dyke, at the socially prominent Church of the Ascension, announced that he, too, was leaving the Episcopal Church. Episcopalians locally were torn. Even some families, mainly at the Ascension, split, some leaving, others staying.

These departures were unintentionally aided and abetted by Alabama's Episcopal bishop, Henry Parsley, who maintained too tight a control of the priests in his diocese. How did Parsley do this? By not allowing McCurry, Van Dyke, and other priests to join an emerging network of conservative priests who were opposed to clergy with same-sex orientation. Admittedly Henry was a bishop in difficult times. However, had he not insisted on such tight control, and had he been more diplomatic, accommodating, or understanding towards conservatives in the diocese, the splits at both CTR and the Ascension could have been avoided, in my humble opinion.

Henry, however, was running for presiding bishop of the Episcopal Church, USA. He had voted against Robinson's consecration, a conservative but necessary vote to maintain his bishop's office in Alabama. Notwithstanding, Henry was trying to reach out to the many liberal bishops in America, because he was competing with liberal female bishop Katharine Jefferts Schori for election to the highest office of presiding bishop in America. By taking a tough stand against the conservative Alabama priests, Henry hoped he would show the more liberal bishops nationally that he supported the gay priest movement nationally. At least that's how it appeared to me.

Hence, after the last Sunday of January 2005, Christ the Redeemer was reduced in number to about 40 members, uncertain about how long they would remain. My law partner Joe Guillot and his wife, Maria, the Murrays (John, Carol and Elizabeth), Pam Long, and newcomers Jack and Dolly McLemore were among the stellar remnant. For the next eight months, until September 2005, octogenarian priests came on Sundays, paid to "do communion and preach."

Finally, in about September 2005, a 47-year-old priest right out of St. Luke's Seminary in Sewanee, Tennessee, the Reverend John Paul Thompson, was assigned to us by Bishop Parsley. John Paul meant well, but he primarily read his sermons from the pulpit, without looking up. John Paul also had trouble getting along with women in the church, although my wife, Leslie, as senior warden, was an exception. Once, coming from an adjacent building, John Paul chastised Carol Murray, our keyboardist, for practicing her music too loudly. That did not sit well with the sensitive Carol.

We struggled on for a year under Thompson. Unfortunately for me, part of this time, from April to July 2006, was complicated by the serious depression I described earlier. I went to church but lacked my usual, outgoing personality. It was a struggle.

Finally, in October 2006, Bishop Parsley came to CTR to meet with Leslie as senior warden, the remaining three vestry members (Sandi Kerr and the McLemores), myself, and the Murrays. By then the Guillots and Pam Long had left the ever-dwindling remnant. At the meeting, Bishop Parsley, perhaps unintentionally, but nonetheless greatly upset Leslie by acting as though he had never heard many things Leslie had been telling him over the phone in recent months about CTR. Carol Murray exploded and announced she was finally leaving the church. Leslie felt compelled to support Carol, and, without checking with me first, announced her similar intention. I felt compelled to support my wife, although I never said I was leaving the church.

The last two months of 2006 and the first few weeks of 2007, Leslie did not attend CTR, but I frequently did. She was exploring an emerging Anglican Church in Montgomery, Christchurch XP, and I joined her in looking. Then, on the last Sunday of January 2007, Bishop Parsley swept down from Birmingham and misled Sandi Kerr and the McLemores, the three remaining vestry members, into signing dormancy papers. I was there, and witnessed it. Seven years later, I obtained affidavits from all three, confirming how badly they were deceived by Parsley, how they were subjected to duress, and how they didn't know what they were signing.

Nonetheless, as Henry later in 2007 explained to me over the phone, the "dormancy" did not mean CTR was being closed permanently. It only meant "closed for a period of time," after which it could be reopened. I didn't know what or whom to believe. "Dormant," however, is synonymous with "sleeping." Indeed, in French the word "dormer" means "to sleep."

As much as we loved CTR and felt we were still members, Leslie and I were disgusted by the turn of events. We acknowledged to ourselves, "Oh heck, let's try out some other places." And so we did, attending briefly Christchurch XP and then the Holy Spirit Anglican Church in Prattville under Alan Reid's leadership between 2007–09.

Finally we attended the First Methodist Church in Old Cloverdale from 2010–13, especially its 6 p.m. service at the former Cloverdale Junior High School. We especially loved the Reverend Lawson Bryan, First Methodist's kindly head pastor, who mixes humor with serious content in preaching a good sermon. We also enjoyed getting to know Bishop Paul Duffey, who came to our home for dinner once.

These other churches were good places to worship and meet new people. We also visited some Catholic churches. But gradually, in me more than in Leslie, the feeling began welling up inside that we were missing something special that we used to have at CTR. I felt a silent hand guiding me toward its restoration.

Leslie had made it clear to me that she didn't want to attend any Episcopal church as long as Henry Parsley was bishop of the Alabama Diocese. But Parsley announced his pending retirement in 2010, and by August 2011, the suffragan bishop, McKee Sloan, was elected bishop. We were hopeful.

On August 15, 2011, I wrote Bishop Sloan, congratulating him on becoming the new head of the Episcopal Diocese of Alabama. I also let him know that certain members of CTR wanted to see the dormancy lifted and the church reopened. Receiving no reply for three months, I wrote Bishop Sloan again on November 11, 2011. No reply again, so I wrote again on January 10, 2012, and said, "I would appreciate the courtesy of a reply."

In all this, I strongly felt the nudging of a Silent Hand, and complete peace.

As more time passed, I telephoned the diocesan office, and arranged to have "Kee," as the new bishop insisted on being called, stop by to visit us in our Montgomery home late Sunday afternoon, January 29, 2012. While Bishop Sloan was noncommittal, he seemed to listen carefully. I made it clear in a letter of January 31, 2012, that we didn't want to interfere with the larger Korean Methodist congregation that was meeting at CTR on Sunday mornings. We instead wanted to have a 6 p.m. evening service. Bishop Sloan confirmed, in answer to my questions, that the diocese had no plans to sell the property.

More months passed. I wrote Bishop Sloan again on June 25, 2012. No answer again. Then another two letters in August 2012. Still no answer. I told Bishop Sloan that two former CTR members were in poor health and wanted to have their funeral services at Christ the Redeemer, when the day came. I also said, "If the Episcopal Diocese of Alabama does something with the Christ Redeemer property other than the original purpose of its benefactor, that would violate not only a legal trust (for which there is a legal remedy) but far worse, it would violate the Spiritual and Divine purposes for which the Church was originally formed." Again, the Silent Hand continued to nudge me.

Still no answer. Therefore, on September 28, 2012, I addressed a letter to Bishop Sloan entitled "Demand for a Return of Diocesan Church Property to Christ the Redeemer Episcopal Church." The letter referred to all my previous correspondence. I also referred to the original 1982 deed from the J. Hunter Flack Foundation. I said the original dormancy initiative was completely Bishop Parsley's and that "dormant" does not mean "dead."

On October 16, 2012, Bishop Sloan finally wrote me back, thanking me for my "continuing faithfulness to our Lord and to His Church." He apologized for not answering earlier letters and assured me that his "mother had raised him better than that." Otherwise, Bishop Sloan dodged the issue altogether, with pleasant wishes to both Leslie and me. He did not answer anything. Thus, on October 22, 2012, I wrote the Bishop back again, requesting a response to the concerns expressed in my preceding six letters.

In response to my November 9, 2012, letter to Bishop Sloan, I received a November 20, 2012, letter from the new assistant bishop of the diocese, the Right Reverend Santosh Marray, stating that "the future of Christ the Redeemer Episcopal Church is in active discussion in diocesan administration."

Christmas 2012 passed without further reply from Bishop Sloan. So, on January 9, 2013, I wrote both bishops, confirming my contacts with the local Korean Methodist pastor, and further confirming that no conflict existed with the Koreans for our projected 6 p.m. Sunday service.

Still no response. So on January 24, 2013, I wrote both bishops again, imparting a hodgepodge of legal and spiritual points. I also attached a support letter from former rector Mark Tusken, now in Geneva, Illinois.

Still no more reply. Therefore, on February 21, 2013, while the Episcopal Diocesan Convention was meeting at St. John's Church in downtown Montgomery, I had my son David hand-deliver a letter to Bishop Sloan. I referred the bishop to the most recent issue of the *Alabama Episcopalian*, and quoted his own points as reasons why I was trying to engineer the resurrection of Christ the Redeemer Episcopal Church.

That same day, while meeting with a client in my firm's library, my secretary rushed down the hallway and said, "Julian, the bishop is on the phone and really wants to talk with you." I picked up the telephone. The bishop, sounding almost frantic, said, "Mr. McPhillips, when can we meet with you?"

Accordingly, a meeting date and time were immediately set for March 7, 2013, in Birmingham. I brought with me my dear better half, Leslie. We met with Bishop Sloan, the Reverend Rob Morpeth, and chancellor-attorney

Maibeth Porter. After opening and ending with prayer, Bishop Sloan finally agreed to allow us to restart services at CTR. It was quickly agreed that the reopening date would be April 28, 2013.

Meanwhile Leslie and I, on our own initiative, met with the executive committee of the Korean Methodist Church, which had been using CTR's property since before the 2007 dormancy. All were very pleasant, though they surprised us when they said that our coming back was a surprise to them. That was because, in January 2013, the diocese had offered to sell to the Koreans the entire property at a high price, in the millions. We, too, were floored, because Bishop Sloan, at our January 2012 house meeting, told us the diocese had no plans or intention to sell CTR's property.

Anyway, with a few tweaks and facilitating conversations, on March 26, 2013, Bishop Sloan wrote me, stating: "Before the Diocese considers taking any action regarding the dormancy, we need to give your worship services time to develop and mature."

Meanwhile, I heard from our former frequent interim priest, the Rev. Vernon Jones, by then almost 90, that Episcopal priest James Muriuki, originally of Kenya, might be available to help administer communion and our services. I met with Reverend Muriuki; he felt inspired and agreed to help.

Former CTR members Sandi and Michael Kerr and Janie Wall could hardly wait to get started again and have provided much leadership. Other former members participating have included Ann and Cindy O'Ferrell and Lewis Underwood, but we are otherwise a new set of folk. Shirley Broadway, a strong believer in the healing ministry and an ordained minister, has also become a part of us.

On April 28, 2013, the resurrected, reborn version of Christ the Redeemer Episcopal Church kicked off. As stated earlier, 37 people attended our reopening. Afterwards we often had not as many people, but we still had a healthy number frequently in the 20s. Retired 73-year-old Methodist minister, the Reverend Hamp Kicklighter, also a client of mine, agreed to help as well. Civil rights hero and retired Lutheran priest, the Reverend Bob Graetz, and his wife, Jeannie, honored us by attending our grand re-opening and expressing their support. So also did the Reverend Al Perkins and his wife, Virgie. Perkins is a senior but still active Episcopal priest; he was in seminary with my father when I babysat his kids in 1959–60.

Our initial band consisted of former CTR members Bruce and Debbie George, now members of Immanuel Presbyterian Church but free to do music for us on Sunday evenings. We paid the Georges, Muriuki, and

Kicklighter modest amounts for their assistance, money collected from offerings. Otherwise, the expenses were minimal.

In 1992–94, CTR members, and not the Diocese of Alabama, had paid for all the buildings and burned the mortgages. By 2013, the Korean Methodists were paying the Diocese $4,000 monthly rent, plus maintenance and utility costs. The Diocese was still responsible for major maintenance. The Koreans' rent was later reduced to $2,000 monthly, when their attendance lessened after a popular minister moved to California.

During our first year back, 2013–2014, the Reverend James Muriuki was our primary priest. He also did communion. His great theme was the wonderful Love of Christ. Hamp Kicklighter emphasized his "Cost of Discipleship" insights from the pulpit. It wasn't long, however, before I preached every third Sunday. I was asked by Father Muriuki to be one of the trio, notwithstanding my lack of an Episcopal ordination.

Preaching, whether from the pulpit or to a jury, actually came naturally to me. I can recall many of my father's sermons, right off the top of my head. A theme I shared at Christ the Redeemer was that the healing ministry is still alive and well, because Jesus is still alive and well. I quoted Hebrews in saying that "Jesus is the same yesterday, today, and forever." He is Lord of all.

The Anglican bishop of the South, the Right Reverend William Wilson, a former Catholic missionary to Bolivia and a close friend to my parents, also helped us restart CTR. He came twice on special Sundays in 2013 to preach and serve communion. I gave out copies of his inspirational book, *Pathways to Union with Jesus*, to CTR members as Christmas gifts at our 2015 Christmas party.

It is my hope that the Episcopal and American Anglican branches of the Anglican community worldwide will someday reconcile as sister entities of the same denomination.

I AM ORDAINED BY the Global Evangelical Christian Church denomination due to my civil rights work, not because of any seminary training. This denomination is overwhelmingly black. In the last few years (2011–15) I have spoken as a guest preacher to at least 10 African American congregations, especially at funeral services, but at a multitude of other occasions.

When I became administrator and lay minister at CTR Resurrected in April 2013, Janie Wall, a close neighbor and dear friend of Leslie and me, became the assistant lay minister. Like me, Janie shares inspired messages to the congregation on Sunday nights. Leslie handles the altar guild work, assuring that song books and prayer books were available for services. I get the weekly bulletins printed up.

Leslie, Janie, Hamp Kicklighter, and I met at our request with the bishop's office in January 2014. Hamp got lost on his way, arrived 45 minutes late, and brought an attitude that did not sit well with the two bishops and others present. The "powers-that-be" were still not yet ready to lift the "dormancy status," they said, although Bishop Sloan readily agreed we were a "vibrant congregation."

We continued through the winter and spring months before finally meeting in May 2014 with a committee of 12 to 13 priests and lay leaders at the Alabama Diocesan Office in Birmingham. They called themselves the "Committee on Evangelism and Church Growth." Leslie, Janie, Steve and Marie Hixon, and I represented CTR. We were surprised by the crowd occupying the other three-quarters of a long table. Nonetheless, we acquitted ourselves well, because the committee voted to lift the dormancy status and treat us as the equivalent of what was formerly called a mission church, but now a "worshipping fellowship."

The summer of 2014 brought substantial changes to the leadership. In June, Hamp Kicklighter, already holding back because we wouldn't agree to let him take over the church leadership, died. Shortly thereafter Rev. Muriuki announced that he had accepted a call to pastor a congregation in southern Illinois.

Meanwhile, a young 29-year-old associate priest from Montgomery's St. John's Episcopal Church, the Reverend Daniel Cenci, who had been attending some of our services, offered to become our priest. This was gladly accepted. Daniel got Bishop Sloan to encourage another young priest, 34-year-old Matthew Grunfeld, rector at the small All Saints Episcopal Church of Montgomery, to assist him. Between the two, they covered the sermons and communion services as well. I was happy to be relieved of my preaching duty, though I continue with more administrative and pastoral duties, not to mention my full-time work as an attorney.

It was not until September 15, 2014, a year and a half after we reopened, that we finally had a service attended by Alabama's Episcopal Bishop McKee Sloan. Forty-seven people were present. We finished with a covered dish supper in the narthex. Bishop Sloan seemed pleased to see the crowd, including our four African American musicians.

Services continued well through the fall and early winter, 2014–2015, with Daniel and Matthew alternating the priestly duties. For the first time since 2005, CTR had a Christmas Eve service in 2014. Although many people were visiting families out of town, we still had a core of 15 people present. Most of our services range from about 15 to 25 participants.

Just before Christmas 2014, Daniel informed us that he had accepted a call from a small North Carolina church in the eastern part of that state, near his wife's family. Daniel was an enormous blessing. We miss him, although Matthew stepped in and did an excellent job as our sole priest.

We entered 2015 with a strong foundation laid, based in a solid belief of God the Father, Son, and Holy Spirit as the Way, the Truth, and the Life. We celebrated the second anniversary of our resurrection on April 26, 2015, with a spirited service and potluck dinner afterwards. Twenty-five worshipers were present. I am excited about CTR's future and the impact it is already having through inreach, outreach, its healing ministry, and other exciting moves of the Spirit.

Matthew Grunfeld, however, accepted a call to move to Florida in late November 2015.

WE'RE HAPPY TO BE sharing space with the Korean Methodists. Although Christ the Redeemer, through the Episcopal Diocese as trustee, owns the church building and the grounds and therefore pays nothing for its use, the Korean church is larger and uses the church's sanctuary on Sunday mornings and the parish hall throughout the week. The Koreans also pay the diocese a good rent, which has been used for new carpets, driveway repairs, etc. Most importantly, to have the Koreans worshiping at Christ the Redeemer is a good evangelical use of God's property, serving two congregations.

Leslie, our son David, and I enjoyed worshiping together with the Koreans on Christmas morning 2015, as did Shirley Broadway. It felt almost like Pentecost with our beautiful church having familiar Christmas carols being sung in Korean. I could barely repress tears of joy. The Koreans also recognized and thanked us, in front of their entire church body.

The praise and worship music on Sunday nights at CTR, infused as it is by the Holy Spirit, truly lifts my spirits for the rest of the week. It has the same effect on many others in our congregation. It is with me when I go jogging, and even when I am in court. Civil rights work becomes easier when the Lord is helping you carry the load. The opportunities for pastoral assistance, from prayers for healing, to pro-bono legal help, to modest financial assistance, make for a multi-faceted ministry. The stated goal in our weekly bulletin is that "we should all be lay pastors, one to another," and we are. With or without a priest present, we are a body of the Lord Jesus, whom we love deeply.

I tell people who already have another church in the morning to come and be a part of our "Double Dose Society." That is, continue going to your morning church, but get a double dose of the Holy Spirit in the evening. We are also good at the 6 p.m. hour for other Christians leaving Montgomery for the weekend but who can be back by late afternoon Sunday.

A fair number of my legal clients worship with us. That includes Linda Reynolds, Lothar Donde, Steve Watkins, Angela Donner, Stacy Whitehurst, Bruce Stolts, the Jumbos, and three of our four musicians. This is an extension of my pastoral ministry. I make very little financially off of their cases, which are often pro-bono, so economics is not an incentive. Nonetheless, Christ's words about helping to get one's "ox out of the ditch" does motivate me.

On a broader note, I hope to see all the churches in Montgomery, as well as elsewhere in the world, abandon the cultural "spirit of religiosity" which often causes division and discord. My father, the priest, said it a different way, "that a church should not be a country club for the righteous but a hospital for sinners."

Meanwhile, with personal initiatives to other Montgomery area Episcopal churches, I am trying to get CTR to be more a part of the local Episcopal family, and less separatist than in the old days.

We need to emphasize more what we have in common, the central nuggets of Christianity. Foremost is the love of God for mankind, as his creatures, and especially that love as revealed by his only son, Jesus our Lord, who gave us the road map for eternal life. Jesus even told us to "love our enemies." That, of course, is not easy. It takes an indwelling of the Holy Spirit to make it happen. Seeing more clearly the grace of God and "life as gift," to quote the renowned late Reverend John Claypool, are part of this spiritual orientation.

At Christ the Redeemer, we believe that if we develop a personal relationship with a living Jesus as Lord, then his grace, forgiveness, reconciliation, compassion, charity, and unselfish love will well up within us and inspire us, to become a part of a new Great Awakening. That awakening is much needed nationally, and is already happening. In turn, greater peace, joy, meaning and purpose in life flow to those who participate.

In early November 2015, CTR's long-time member and thrice-interim rector, Vernon Jones, went home to be with the Lord, joining his dear Lillian, who predeceased him by a year. All of us at CTR owe a great debt of gratitude to this Christ-centered couple.

With our priest Matthew Grunfeld having just departed, I preached at Christ the Redeemer on Sunday, November 29, 2015, the first Sunday of Advent. Before a congregation that included Lutherans Bob and Jeannie

Graetz, I talked about the four candles of the Advent wreath, symbolizing hope, love, joy, and peace. I added that all these qualities are in Jesus, our Lord, Redeemer, and Savior, and that's why we should all be excited about the coming of Christmas. I also gave Martin Luther credit for starting the Advent wreath with its meaningful candles.

In Matthew's absence, the Reverend David Peebles has been presiding over Holy Communion and preaching while we look for a permanent rector. David's full head of hair, with little gray, makes him look younger than his 54 years. He is originally from Memphis and was a space engineer in Huntsville before going to seminary.

David came to Montgomery in 2000. He spent five years as associate priest at St. John's Episcopal and the last ten years as rector at Grace Episcopal Church in Pike Road. David was serving as a supply priest at Christ the Redeemer on Sunday evenings when this book went to press. He looks good to me. We'll see.

Nonetheless, given the temporary absence of a priest, we encouraged members of CTR to worship at alternative venues on Christmas Eve and Day. Hence, Leslie, David, and I enjoyed a Christmas Eve service at our sister small Episcopal congregation, Church of the Good Shepherd. On Christmas day, as previously stated, we worshiped with the Korean Methodists.

Whatever happens, I am at peace that God the Father, Son, and Holy Spirit will continue to guide and inspire us, as we continue to honor and share the Gospel of the One whose name adorns and inspires our church.

38

The Healing Ministry

D o I believe Jesus performed all the healing miracles described in the gospels and many more? Absolutely. Do I believe Jesus is still performing healing miracles today, by and through the Holy Spirit? Absolutely. Do I believe the disciples and apostles of biblical times continued the healing miracles, including in succeeding generations, up through present day times, and that miracles of healing are still being performed? Absolutely.

While this subject does not fan flames of controversy like the abortion and same-sex issues, nonetheless there is a great diversity of opinion among contemporary people. It is not just Pentecostals, charismatics, and spirit-filled Christians who embrace the healing ministry. A surprising number of average, ordinary folk have encountered the healing touch of God and know it.

Many others, including highly religious leaders of mainstream denominations, believe God heals providentially in his own good time, but they do not believe God does so suddenly or dramatically. They limit God to not intervening to cure serious illnesses and to not taking away disabilities. This includes bishops, priests, ordained ministers, and other top ecclesiastical leaders in the Baptist, Methodist, Presbyterian, Episcopal, Lutheran, Church of Christ, Church of God, and Catholic worlds. The mentality is that you just live with the hand that is dealt you.

Indeed, it sometimes seems that too much religious knowledge is an impediment. Even worse is the obstacle of religiosity which is a cultural phenomenon drawing on one's own sense of spiritual sufficiency.

As my experience has grown and deepened in this field, I have learned that a genuine humility, embedded in an awareness that "God's strength is made perfect in our weakness," is an important foundation to such a ministry (2 Corinthians 12:9).

The "healing ministry" is a generic term that could broadly apply to either a slower, providential healing or the more sudden and dramatic type. For the purposes of this chapter, my focus is on the latter. It is not an art or a science, because it is not in the realm of the five senses. Instead, it involves a "sixth sense," accessed through faith and prayer.

Yet, contrary to what skeptics and cynics contend, the healing ministry does not involve a "turning on or turning off of God," like the turning on or off of a water faucet. That is because, as my healing evangelistic friend Mahesh Chavda loves to say, "Only God is God." He alone resides in his realm, He alone calls the shots, and He alone has the knowledge of the bigger picture, which includes why some people are called home early, and others not, and why some are healed in their earthly bodies, and others not.

Ultimately, the greatest, biggest healing of them all is when we leave our earthly body and enter into our heavenly body. A mystery, yes, and a wonder, yes, but thanks be to God and his awesome mercy, grace and love, it is true.

Agnostics, atheists, skeptics, and some Christians may protest that such a ministry cannot be real, because it violates their own sense of fairness or notion of what a just God should be like. The obvious problem with that reasoning is that it puts us in the upside-down position of "defining God." The reverse is true. God, as the great creator of the universe 15 billion years ago, is both Creator and Definer. He defines us and our humanity. He has given us the New Commandment and the Great Commandment, and most importantly, God gave us Jesus Himself to show us the way to abundant life. This life is the beginning of a much greater life beyond the grave.

A big part of living life well is learning how to communicate well with God. It makes all the difference in the world. Praying, combined with faith, opens many doors, and helps one navigate through, or around, the potholes, pitfalls and snares of life.

I also believe that the peace and joy which comes from a healthy relationship with the Lord are worth more than gold or silver.

How did I get so interested in the healing ministry? As I described in two previous books, *The People's Lawyer* and *The History of Christ the Redeemer Episcopal Church,* it gradually developed over time. The greatest catalysts were: discovering my father's private involvement in it; meeting and being inspired by Mahesh Chavda; experiencing Christ the Redeemer Episcopal Church; reading certain books about the healing ministry, most notably, the Bible; and praying myself with and for other people and seeing great healings as a result.

This is an interest my dear Leslie and I have grown in together. Indeed, as mentioned earlier, Leslie's need for healing led us to Atlanta in 1989, to meet

Mahesh, whom we had learned about when we visited a church in Prague, Czechoslovakia, three months earlier. The story is told in *The People's Lawyer*.

The German-born Czech minister's description of Mahesh's crusade was jaw-dropping: People healed of blindness, lameness and dreaded diseases, etc. So many people healed at one time. It was biblical in dimension . . . like Jesus was walking around again, as He did 2000 years ago.

At one of Mahesh's subsequent 1989 services in Atlanta, Leslie and I both experienced the spiritual phenomenon of being "slain in the spirit," and our eyes were opened. Our young rector at Christ the Redeemer, the Reverend Mark Tusken, drove over to Atlanta the next day and experienced the same.

All of a sudden, Christ the Redeemer Episcopal Church was "all abuzz." Shortly thereafter, in September 1989, a great lady from Seattle, Washington, Darlene Sizemore, came to Christ the Redeemer and, lo and behold, it was more of the same—spectacular healings, and people being slain in the spirit, right and left.

Our friendship with both Mahesh and Darlene grew, and so did our enthusiasm for the healing ministry. I soon learned more from Mom about the number of times Dad had prayed for parishioners or others with cancer, only to see the cancer go away. Dad had not told me, largely out of humility and the related concern that no one think that Dad was claiming credit for anything. To Dad, and to me, and to Leslie, all honor, credit and glory goes to God himself, and to God only.

This is why I have been reticent to share my own experiences in this realm. I did share some, however, in *The People's Lawyer*, and will share more here.

To further confirm the legitimacy of this realm, and of the healing ministry, I did no small amount of research. This included books written by or about Katherine Kuhlman, Dennis Bennett, Frances MacNutt, Emily Gardner Neal, Ruth Heflin, and Benny Hinn. Of course, Mahesh Chavda, to the largest extent, his dear wife, Bonnie, and Darlene Sizemore were our greatest inspirations, especially because we came to know them so well personally.

Darlene led crusades at Christ the Redeemer in 1989 and 1992, but at a ripe age in her 70s passed on to the heavenly realm in 1993. God must have needed her up there. Mahesh Chavda, born the same year (1946) as me, stirred Montgomery by leading major healing conferences at Christ the Redeemer in 1994, 1996, 1999, and 2003. Amazing healings took place all four times, and people still talk about it.

Our family friendship with Mahesh and Bonnie deepened in 1998 when their son, Ben, came to work with me in my law practice. Their daughter, Sarah, also worked in my U.S. Senate campaign in 2002. In subsequent years, including a strategic visit with Mahesh at his home in July 2006 when I was fighting depression, and usually once every year or so after that, Leslie and I have popped up to Charlotte, North Carolina. There, at his Healing the Nations Conference Center, and sometimes at a church in Atlanta, we've continued to be inspired by Mahesh and Bonnie. Our most recent sojourn to Charlotte was the weekend of October 16–18, 2015. Our son David drove up from Anderson University in South Carolina to join us.

MY PERSONAL WITNESSING OF the healing ministry includes the time in 1994 when I prayed for my law partner, Aaron Luck, who was enduring a painful migraine headache that had been plaguing him every other week. The migraines not only went away immediately but haven't come back in the 21 years since. I recently asked Aaron to reconfirm this point.

The list goes on and on. There was a mayor of a small town in south Alabama whose son was plagued with debilitating headaches: the same result. More recently, Sandi Kerr, a member of Christ the Redeemer, was experiencing stabbing headaches for three weeks after she fell and hit her head hard. The pain was so severe that several times she was near-suicidal. Leslie and I visited her in May 2015. Again, the same result—for eight months now, she has had no headaches, not even the minor ones she had before her fall.

Additional healings since 2005 involved retired attorney Harry Lyles and former law enforcement officer, Ed Litaker, whose advanced cancers went into sudden remission after I prayed with them, significantly extending their leases on life. Also there was my cousin, Michael Smith of West Virginia, who had severe gout up until a time when I visited him in 2007 and prayed for him. Mike swears that this prayer with him was instrumental in the gout disappearing for many years after that date. I am deeply humbled, of course, and consider this a "praise report" solely for the One God who did the healing.

There have been many telephone prayers with great results. Former paralegal Lynelle Howard insists that one such prayer in 2013 greatly relieved her of the acute pain in her back.

And there is a Kenyan immigrant, Peter Owuor, who has been plagued by pancreatitis and says my prayers helped ease and relieve his pain. Of course, Peter had medical treatment, too, but to God be all the glory. All I or anyone else can do is serve a conduit for God's healing power.

My son David and I have long had a "father-son" relationship such that we can pray for each other and see great healings. One memorable time, about 2011, occurred when both injured ourselves at our Lake Martin retreat.

David had sprained his ribs water skiing, and I had badly sprained my ankle coming down some broken stairs from our porch. As David prayed for me that night, back home in Montgomery, I could feel the pain and pressure subsiding. Before I went to bed, I was feeling no pain. And all praise be to God, because the next morning David felt no strain or pain in his ribs.

Additionally, my office manager, Amy Strickland, has unfortunately suffered her share of injuries related to three car accidents. Over the last 19 years, Amy has undergone five back surgeries, two neck surgeries, and five knee surgeries. Further, she has been diagnosed and treated for cancer three times. Two different times Mahesh prayed for her over the telephone. Each time, through the grace of God, prayers, and modern medicine, Amy has made a full recovery.

Some of Amy's recovery time has taken longer than anticipated, but she has been able to bounce back and not miss a step in her work with the firm. Further, since Amy has endured so many medical procedures, she can share her story with personal injury clients suffering catastrophic injuries. Amy, a person of genuine faith, has also shared the power of prayer. I have prayed with Amy too many times to count.

I've never claimed to be 100 percent effective in healing, and I'm not. Nor is Mahesh Chavda nor anyone else. Nonetheless, there have been so many times when good results occur after prayer that it is certainly worth trying. There is nothing to lose and much to gain.

I have learned some principles along the way. First, as Mahesh says, there are obstacles to the healing ministry. The biggest by far is what he calls "doubt" or "unbelief" that God can heal you. The second he calls "unforgiveness." If there is anyone you haven't forgiven, you must do so, and do so completely. That includes forgiving one's own self. Unforgiveness of oneself, also known as "guilt," can "gum up the works." After all, I explain to friends who consider themselves too sinful, that is why Christ died on the cross for us, to forgive us for our sins. We need to sincerely repent and let God open up the channels for healing.

Another principle is to envision that you've allowed your body, hands, and spirit to be appropriated by our Lord Jesus, such that *our* hands become transformed into *his* hands. After all, we are God's creation, and our hands truly belong to God anyway.

It is also important, as much as possible, to let go of one's own self-consciousness and try to tap into, or become a part of, the Lord's great compassionate love.

It is also helpful in praying for someone to help "prep" them—prepare them, by getting them to release their unforgiveness, or let go of their doubt. Jesus himself, the Gospel says, encountered no great results in his ministry in his hometown, namely Nazareth, where people doubted who he was. Therefore, if the person on the receiving end is not receptive, it can be a huge foil to the move of God's holy spirit, and the healing that comes with it.

St. Paul, who had a profoundly effective healing ministry, said, "We live by faith, not by sight" (2 Corinthians 5:7; see also Acts 19:11).

In my preparation, I often use metaphors, such as a sponge soaking up water, or the pulling force of a magnet. The idea is that someone praying for others is only a conduit for God's spirit. We are not the source of the power, not for a moment. But it is also very helpful to "spark" the faith of the person on the receiving end of the prayer. That is, spark them, so that like the sponge, he or she can soak up "rivers of living water" flowing from Christ, and flowing from the Holy Spirit, both a part of the same Godhead.

It is these principles and these practices which those of us who restarted Christ the Redeemer try to practice in the healing ministry. As recently as Sunday, October 11, 2015, we prayed at Christ the Redeemer for Lothar Donde, a former client of mine, about 75 years old. He has been suffering from painful rheumatoid arthritis. That Sunday, when Lothar came, he said he really needed to be carried in on a cot, he was in such pain. At the end of the service, about five or six of us gathered around Lothar, laid hands on him, and prayed. While we were doing so, Lothar let loose with a "wow," as he felt all his pain go away. When we were finished, Lothar stood up, and started jumping up and down, completely pain-free. This is just one of the many such healings that continue to amaze us at Christ the Redeemer.

Janie Wall, a long-time member and one-time assistant lay minister of Christ the Redeemer, is a huge believer in the Holy Spirit's power to touch and heal people today. So also is Peggy Gelpi. So also are Steve and Marie Hixon, and Michael and Sandi Kerr. So also is my dear better half, Leslie McPhillips.

Leslie also received a wonderful prayer over the telephone from Mahesh Chavda at Baptist Hospital in 2003 when her blood count got dangerously high due to a burst appendix. It could have killed her, but thank you, Lord, for being there with her.

Of course, opportunities to pray for people do not require a church or a hospital. One can do it anywhere: at work, at play, while traveling, or by chance.

Ironically, on my 69th birthday on November 13, 2015, I was the beneficiary of someone else's healing prayers. While I was sitting in my aisle seat on an airplane in Charlotte, North Carolina, before take-off, suddenly I was struck on the head by a hard metallic suitcase falling from the bin above. The blow stung me, and it cut my bald head and left ear, with both left bleeding. After the stewardess wiped away the blood and applied a Band-Aid, I noticed a young, thin college-age Korean girl. It was her lack of strength in pushing the suitcase up that caused it to fall in the first place. She was mortified, embarrassed, and in tears, as she apologized and tried to hand me a card. After I returned from the bathroom, I noticed her in the middle seat of our aisle. Her head was bowed, and her hands were cupped as in prayer. Suddenly I felt the pain in my head go away. I told her not to worry. I was okay.

As described earlier concerning my episode with depression, one can pray for one's own healing and see results. Again, earnest faith on the part of the recipient is key, but it is God and his compassionate love that does the work. A letter to God may bring surprising results.

THE HEALING MINISTRY IS also for relationships. On Sunday, November 15, 2015, at Christ the Redeemer, responding to tensions and strains in the Jumbo marriage, eight of us laid hands on Chichi and Success Jumbo, and their one-year-old son, earnestly praying. Both husband and wife were touched and subsequently reported an amazing improvement in their marriage.

Certainly, the resurrection of Christ the Redeemer Church has emboldened our ministry. However, many of my most encouraging fellow prayer warriors in the healing ministry come from other denominations and from many walks of life. Locally, that includes the Reverend Tom Bridges, chaplain at the Montgomery city and county jails, and the Reverend Carmen Falcione of the Gathering. Both are brethren in the Lord with Holy Spirit- empowered gifts in the healing ministry. And there are others.

Part of "staying healed" is avoiding the anxiety that often underlies, or abets, an illness in the first place. Of course, I distinguish between a lesser degree of anxiety, known as "healthy concern," which can motivate one to avoid dangers and resolve problems.

For several years now, I habitually begin every morning, just before perusing the newspaper, with carefully reading Sara Young's daily devotional book, *Jesus Calling: Enjoying Peace in His Presence.* A portion of one annual daily reading, hitting at the book's theme, attributes to God the following advice:

> Anxiety is a result of envisioning the future without Me. So the best

defense against worry is staying in communication with Me. When you
turn your thoughts towards Me, you can think more positively. Remember
to listen, as well as to speak, making your thoughts a dialogue with Me.
Luke 12:22–26; Ephesians 3:20–21

While this life is the beginning of a greater life beyond the grave, this life
is very important. God sent us Jesus to show us the way, the truth and the
life (John 14:6). Praise God that he taught us, through Jesus, that his healing power is still alive and well in this 21st century! Praise God that Jesus
has also opened the door to Eternal Life (John 6:40), which is the biggest
healing of all.

Part IV

Summing Up

39

Alabama Can Rise, Montgomery Must Lead

Alabama is a great state in many ways, with great people, virgin forests, navigable pristine rivers and gorgeous great lakes for recreation. We also have many cultural opportunities, historical places worth preserving, some nationally ranked education programs, dynamic churches and synagogues, successful football teams, and many charitable organizations and civic clubs.

Sadly, Alabama also leads the nation in many negative ways, with a regressive tax system, poorly funded public schools, grossly overcrowded prisons, disappearing mental health services, recently enacted needlessly inconvenient barriers to registering and/or exercising the right to vote, and inadequately funded health services for the aged, children, infirm, and poor. Not surprisingly to me and many in the civil rights community, the Alabamians most hurting from these negatives, percentage-wise, are members of minority groups.

Why this paradox? Why this seeming inconsistency? What can be done about it? This book would be incomplete without considering this fundamental contradiction at the heart of living, learning, earning a living, and exercising public leadership in Alabama. No one has a magic wand, but what reasonable solutions exist? And do we have the public will to try them?

My perspective on such matters has been gained from growing up in Cullman, Guntersville, and Birmingham in the '40s, '50s and '60s, with roots deep in Mobile, Baldwin, Perry and Greene counties. Add to that a Tennessee military education in high school (59–64), an Ivy League college and law school education (64–71), and four years on Wall Street as an attorney and you get a guy with a varied background, enabling him to see more than the surface of things.

One thing I can see is that Alabama's problems are not exclusive to Alabama. Nationally, electing Barack Obama as president was an accomplishment, due in part to his unique set of skills but also to an increasingly non-white electorate and many white voters of conscience. Given, however, the high disparity in income between whites and blacks, vestiges of injustice still impact many African Americans across the nation, not just in Alabama. With entrenched white prejudice going back to the nation's founding, we still have a long way to go.

Many Americans, black and white, sung and unsung, are fighting daily battles against racial injustice. That includes employment discrimination, racial profiling, and police brutality. It also includes the battle to lessen economic injustice, which disproportionately adversely affects the poor and therefore the black and brown.

On Sunday, October 25, 2015, the *New York Times'* lead article was entitled, "The Disproportionate Risk of Driving While Black." The coverage included a detailed study of fourteen police agencies in Connecticut, North Carolina, Illinois, and Rhode Island. The results unsurprisingly reflected a nationwide phenomenon of racial profiling. National uproar erupts periodically, as it did in New Jersey in the 1990s when state troopers admitted focusing on minority drivers for traffic stops in hopes of catching drug carriers.

So, as I said, Alabama's problems are not necessarily unique, but they are our problems, and because of our demographics and our tragic racial history, compounded by our lamentable legacy of demagogic, race-baiting politics, our problems may be more severe than those in other states.

It has now been more than 40 years since my wife Leslie and I returned to Montgomery, where I became engaged in Alabama's legal and political worlds, including two statewide political campaigns lasting a year each.

As a result I have been in every county of Alabama, every city, and almost every municipality. Yet living outside the state and traveling worldwide have broadened my perspective. Based on that, I have developed some ideas about the two key questions: what needs to be done to improve Alabama, and who should take the lead in doing it.

The brief answer to the first question is a new state constitution, a more progressive tax system, home rule for towns and counties, and a combination of faith, prayer and action. The brief answer to the latter question is Montgomery.

Yes, Montgomery is the state capital, the seat of state government, Montgomery is a city, and Montgomery is a people, nearly 300,000 strong, if you count the closely adjacent suburban communities. All three identities are why Montgomery should take the lead in making Alabama better.

MONTGOMERY, THE CAPITAL

Let me address the first issue first, namely of what Montgomery, the state capital needs to do.

Recently, Dr. Jim Vickrey, a retired educator from Troy University and former president of the University of Montevallo, laid it on us thick at the Montgomery Lions Club at its meeting of September 11, 2015. Vickrey prophetically challenged the listening audience about the future viability of K-12 public education in Montgomery and in Alabama. Vickrey quoted Franklin D. Roosevelt to the dual effect that the quality of democratic choice-making at the ballot box and the quality and quantity of future workforces in the area is dependent upon the state of public education. He said:

> In Alabama and in its capital city, the two greatest barriers to progress in education are the 1901 Constitution—the ultimate source of every single major problem Alabama faces—and white flight from public education. As long as the white economic base of Montgomery continues to flee from public schools because of their racial composition, our city will suffer. If we leave it mainly to black students from families with fewer resources to pay more in taxes, our public schools will continue to erode.

Professor Vickrey boldly added:

> To the extent that that is true, the economy of the Montgomery area will continue to be adversely affected, if not stunted. Everyone living and working here, without regard to race, will be negatively impacted.

So Vickrey challenged our Lions to confront and reverse inept local and state leadership, pass a new constitution, and fund public education. Cheers! I couldn't agree with him more.

Let's face up to the truth. The 1901 Constitution is an anachronistic relic of bygone days. It contains Jim Crow laws prohibiting interracial marriage and infringing upon other basic civil rights for minorities. Its bitter legacy contributes to ongoing deep evils such as racial profiling, not only in traffic stops, but also in "red-lining" of bank loans. It is also far more likely that victims of police brutality are black.

A badly needed initiative is to end judicial policies such as bail bonds that fall heaviest on the poor. Blacks are disproportionately poor, but so are many whites.

In January 2015, a poor woman in Clanton, Alabama, suffering serious mental and physical health problems, was arrested and taken to jail for shoplifting and three other misdemeanors. She was told that if she had $2,000 she could post bail and leave. If not, she could wait a week to see a judge. Her only income was her monthly food stamp allotment.

To his great credit, civil rights lawyer Alec Karakatsanis sued the City of Clanton, saying its policies discriminated against the poor by imprisoning them, while allowing those with money to go free. The response was immediate. Clanton agreed to release most of its misdemeanor defendants quickly, without posting bond. Now all defendants get to see a judge within 48 hours. We need more civil rights initiatives like this, hopefully creating a rippling effect on bail, seizure, fines and other practices.

Dr. Vickrey points out that although it has been diminished by federal court rulings, our outdated constitution contains more than 892 amendments, prohibits home rule, blunts local initiative, promotes regressive taxation, and plainly embarrasses our state.

Indeed, Dr. Vickrey says the prohibition of home rule was the primary mechanism by which the framers of the 1901 Constitution disenfranchised poor white and black Alabamians.

If you don't believe Jim Vickrey or me, then ask the preeminent authority on Alabama history, Dr. Wayne Flynt, emeritus professor of history at Auburn University. He has written brilliantly about how the Alabama Constitution of 1901 was fraudulently ratified by Bourbon aristocrats to disenfranchise black voters (and had the same effect, to a lesser degree, on poor whites). For 115 years now, state, county, and local government leaders have been saddled with the most inefficient and ineffective state constitution in America, and their constituents have paid a heavy price.

A new constitution has been ballyhooed ever since Leslie and I returned to Alabama in 1975. I remember that gubernatorial candidate George McMillan, in 1982, made it the central plank of his platform. Yet here we are, three decades later, with less being said and nothing done.

I call upon politicians of all stripes to join together for the common good of Alabama and demand that a constitutional convention take place in Montgomery at the earliest date possible.

Making a difference is the Alabama Appleseed Center for Law and Justice and its dedicated leaders John Pickens, Shay Farley, and Craig Baab. They are dealing with pressing public policy issues facing Alabama—from prison reform, to payday/title loan reform, to consumer protection, to constitutional reform, access to justice in civil legal matters, and children's hunger in Alabama's public schools.

I'd be remiss not to mention Alabama Arise, the "Citizen's Policy Project" that I have supported for many years. Not associated with any church, this organization is inspired by dedicated individuals who run it. They have long supported a new constitution. Arise's top policy priorities for 2016 are (a) adequate state budgets, (b) tax reform, (c) death penalty reform, (d) payday and title lending reform, and (e) voting rights legislation. These reforms would help Alabama as a whole, and Montgomery would benefit too. I support them all.

It is reprehensible that the poverty rate among Alabama's children, already bad, is worsening. The 2015 *Alabama Kids Count* data book shows nearly 27 percent, roughly 300,000 children, live in impoverished households that make $25,000 or less a year for a family of four. That statistic is up from 21.5 percent in 2000, reported by the *Montgomery Advertiser* in December 2015.

"Almost half of those 300,000 children live in extreme poverty, defined as an annual income of less than $12,000, and their numbers have rapidly increased," the *Advertiser* editorialist bemoaned. And disproportionately these children are African American or Hispanic.

A more progressive, reform-minded government, unafraid-to-tax where it won't hurt that much, will contribute to a better economy, better public schools, and less poverty. A new constitution will help accomplish that.

Objective observers of all political stripes agree that Alabama's prisons and mental health system are in a disgraceful condition. The inhumane prisons house much more than double their design capacity, and any inmate has a substantial chance of being molested, beaten up, knifed, or killed. I am especially critical of the Alabama Board of Pardons and Paroles, for that entity's hard-hearted, unmerciful position of keeping incarcerated inmates who've already served ample time but may have committed minor disciplinary offenses, such as wrongfully using a cell phone.

Mental health facilities have also been wrongfully cut back, due to the so-called budget crunch. Many legislators worship a false idol called "No New Taxes." Alabama's citizenry would easily absorb some modest new taxes that few would feel. After all, we have the lowest property taxes of any state in the country.

The Alabama Department of Public Health, while it has many dedicated employees, could also be much sharper in certain areas. I have represented a number of its employees over the years who have been mistreated.

What it comes down to, basically, is that the poor and the mentally disabled have little if any political power. Therefore, the Alabama legislators ignore them. This often results in tragedies that conscientious Alabamians should be ashamed of.

The state capital, via its legislature, must call a convention to draft and ratify a new, efficient 21st-century constitution.

MONTGOMERY, THE CITY

Montgomery, as a city, must continue to shape itself up as the beautiful city that it is—historic, entertaining, and a future national magnet for industry, tourists, education, and the military. What more can our city do? Montgomery's energetic mayor, Todd Strange, the Montgomery City Council, and the Montgomery County Commission are to be commended for many progressive initiatives in recent years, especially in the downtown area. Making Montgomery more user-friendly and attractive to out-of-towners is paramount. Already basking in its recognition by *USA Today* as "America's best historic city," there is no good reason why Montgomery shouldn't start attracting national conventions for doctors, lawyers, engineers, teachers, and other professionals. It may need some more hotel rooms, but it is obvious that Montgomery has much to offer, more than most places.

Certainly "the Alley" in downtown Montgomery, looking like the French Quarter of New Orleans, has been a great move. Likewise, the Montgomery Biscuits professional baseball team, the Riverwalk Stadium, and a growing number of quality restaurants have spruced up and brightened the downtown area.

Fortunately, General Sherman pursued his incendiary march from Atlanta to Savannah and left intact Montgomery's many antebellum cottages and mansions. Our city's Confederate history is second only to that of Richmond, Virginia.

On the other hand, Montgomery's civil rights history is second to none. We have the Rosa Parks Museum, the Civil Rights Memorial, the Freedom Rides Museum, ASU's National Center for the Study of Civil Rights and African-American Culture, the federal courthouse, and all the historic markers reminding us of Montgomery's leading role in moving past slavery and segregation. We also have the Dexter Avenue King Memorial Church, the First Baptist Church Ripley, and numerous other civil rights landmarks and churches. That includes the former homes of Martin Luther King Jr., Rosa Parks, E. D. Nixon, Ralph Abernathy, and Rufus Lewis, as well as the childhood home of Nat King Cole. Tourism potential is unlimited, and it is not restricted to African American tourists; all races enjoy these civil right tours.

Add to that a world-class Shakespeare Theater, the world's only Scott and Zelda Fitzgerald Museum, the Hank Williams Museum, and the several large theaters and engaging performance venues, and you can see why *USA Today* got so carried away.

Montgomery and Alabama are fortunate to have several top-notch historians who have recorded and celebrated our colorful history. That includes Mary Ann Neeley, a prolific author and famous for giving walking tours of downtown Montgomery. Retired University of Michigan historian Mills Thornton has published the definitive history of the civil rights movement in Alabama. Jeff Benton, retired Air Force officer and former Montgomery Academy teacher, is a leading authority on 18th- and 19th-century Alabama history. Ed Bridges, former Archives director, is a fascinating writer and speaker. Historian Richard Bailey has chronicled the lives of influential African Americans, especially in Reconstruction-era Alabama. Randall Williams of NewSouth Books has edited the writings of all the afore-named historians and has artfully written a number of history pieces himself. Dorothy Autry, former ASU history chair, has made great contributions.

The Montgomery County Historical Commission and its long-time leaders James Fuller and Rusty Gregory deserve the community's appreciation for their tireless efforts in preserving Montgomery's history.

I modestly add that this book, the 2005 edition of *The People's Lawyer*, and my *History of Christ the Redeemer Episcopal Church* throw me into the dubious category of the "frustrated historian." If so, my interest began in the 1950s with collecting stamps and coins from which I gleaned so much history and geography. I was a third-generation stamp collector, following my father and grandfather, the two elder Julian McPhillipses. Mom and Dad added to the fever with their lives and stories.

Finally, I majored in history at Princeton, and had fun writing a 90-page thesis on French communists in the resistance against the Nazis, 1939–44. That work, drawn upon research in France the summers of 1965 and 1967, also bolstered my French language skills and deepened my appreciation of history's international scope.

We have some great high schools in Montgomery. On the private school side that includes St. James School, Montgomery Academy, Trinity, Catholic, and Alabama Christian. St. James is fortunate to have the dynamic, young Larry McLemore as its new headmaster. He replaced another great headmaster, Melba Richardson, who pioneered many great initiatives at St. James. Except for LAMP, St. James had the most National Merit semifinalists of any school in Montgomery for the school year 2015–16. Ann Caesar of Catholic, its president, has also helped elevate that school.

On the public school side are Robert E. Lee, Sidney Lanier, Jeff Davis, George Washington Carver, and Park Crossing, plus the three top-notch magnet high schools: LAMP (academic), Brewbaker (technology), and Booker T. Washington (arts).

However, the LAMP magnet high school is in a class by itself—public or private—consistently ranking in recent years among the nation's top 25 high schools. In 2013, it was ranked the No. 1 magnet high school in America; 17 seniors in its 2016 class were named National Merit semifinalists.

Good college educations can be had locally at Auburn University Montgomery, Alabama State University, Huntingdon College, Faulkner University, and Troy University Montgomery. None are perfect and some are dealing with great challenges, but overall the educational quality offered is something to celebrate.

Montgomery has been extraordinarily fortunate for many years to have both Maxwell Air Force Base and Gunter Air Force Station. The leaders they constantly attract enrich and broaden Montgomery. Many retire here, to Montgomery's benefit.

Montgomery's economy is stable but could be better. Industrial giant Hyundai, the Korean car manufacturer, leads the way. In 2014 Hyundai's total sales in Alabama were $7 billion. Hyundai accounted for twenty percent, or $2.4 billion, of Montgomery's entire economy. Add all the nearby supplier plants, and the auto industry is a juggernaut that feeds a ton of people. Statewide, the auto industry helps preserve for millions the civil right to eat.

Other industries, like Rheem Manufacturing, plus state and federal government, employ many. The big hospitals also supply an enormous number of jobs. However, Montgomery's hospitals are not even ranked in the top ten of the state, and too many people catch staph infections at Baptist hospitals in the Montgomery area. I know this because of all the complaining parties who call me. As WSFA says about low-grading restaurants, "Hospitals, shape up."

Still it is Montgomery's high number of small businesses, including suppliers of goods and services, that keep this city spinning and puts food on the most tables. That includes our McPhillips Shinbaum law firm. With our current 15 employees, and as many as 25 in the late '90s, our firm not only feeds our staff, but like many other law firms, we help our clients put food on the table. As one can imagine, there are many economic aspects of injustice issues.

Inasmuch as my firm has represented many employees over the years in wrongful dismissal or workman's compensation suits, I have never been a favorite of the business community. Yet in 1995, due to my Princeton wrestling connections, I was largely responsible for enticing Feldmere, Inc., of Syracuse, New York, to expand its canister plant operations, with 200 employees, to Montgomery. For a very short while, I was the darling of the Chamber of Commerce. My brother Frank McPhillips of Birmingham, whom I believe to be the top bond attorney in Alabama, whipped through about 95 agreements as he helped Feldmere get financing for its new Montgomery plant under the Wallace-Cater Act.

Montgomery, as a city, is full of wonderful neighborhoods. When my father first moved our family here in 1962, we lived in the beautiful, stately Garden District. Our house was a modest two-story bungalow at 1329 S. McDonough Street, adjacent to the Church of the Ascension, where Dad ministered. I could roll out of bed at the last moment for church services.

When Leslie and I moved back to Montgomery in 1975, we rented a house for one year in Gay Meadows. The next five years we lived in a ranch-style brick home in Normandale. Many good people lived in both neighborhoods. We had great neighbors.

After searching the city intently in 1979–80, we finally found, bought, and restored the historic home at 831 Felder Avenue in Old Cloverdale. We have now been there for 35 years and have thoroughly enjoyed both our home and our beautiful historic neighborhood.

My point is that Montgomery contains many wonderful neighborhoods, which collectively make for a great city. We just need to practice the "good neighbor" policy all over the city, from east to west, from north to south, and in the central part, including downtown.

Some would say this ambition is Pollyannaish. Yet, it is doable, even if it requires hard work. We should all be good neighbors, one to another, no matter what section of town we live in.

Montgomery must learn to celebrate these assets better, and promote them to the world. In return, this gem of a Southern city we live in will develop into a national and potentially cosmopolitan city.

Montgomery mayors Bobby Bright and Todd Strange and numerous civic and business leaders have all done their parts in the 21st century, as has both mayors' top executive assistant, Michael Briddell. I also applaud Public Safety Director Chris Murphy for his efforts to make law enforcement more "user-friendly."

Likewise, *Montgomery Advertiser* publisher Bob Granfeldt, executive editor Tom Clifford, and former editorial page editor Jim Earnhardt have taken the daily newspaper, a venerable institution since 1829, to new heights. The paper manages to stir up local interest with penetrating reporter-columnist Josh Moon and engaging features writer Kym Klass. Semi-retired columnist Al Benn, a good friend of 40 years, also does an engaging "good news column" about Montgomery-Selma area personalities and events. Al originally made his name as a civil rights reporter.

In this age of online media, the *Advertiser* is the only daily newspaper left among the four major cities of Alabama, including Birmingham, Mobile, and Huntsville. That is a big plus for Montgomery. The *Advertiser* does much more than report the news. It also is stirring up the "social conscience" of its readership.

The *Advertiser* practices what it preaches, as reflected by its own employees helping with community needs on the annual Make a Difference Day. Bravo for editors Clifford and Rick Harmon, reporters Rebecca Burylo and Andrew Yawn for their carpentry work in October 2015, restoring local dwellings in the House-to-House program in Montgomery.

Likewise, Bob Martin, owner and editor of the *Montgomery Independent*, has long run a good weekly newspaper, challenging local officials with courageous editorials. Jamal Thomas of *Gumptown* has created a new magazine widely circulated in Montgomery's black community. Virginia Saunders of *The Pride of Montgomery* and the editors of *River Region Living* keep Montgomery supplied with two lively, monthly magazines. Former public television producers Sandra Polizos and Bob Corley successfully switched to print media with their magazine for seniors, *Prime*.

MONTGOMERY, THE PEOPLE

Finally, as to the third issue, what can the people of the City of Montgomery do as individuals?

I've always thought many people from Montgomery, though by no means all, have a sense that there is something special about Montgomery. I thought so years ago in the early 1960s, when my family moved to Montgomery for several years. There is a spirit here not seen elsewhere in Alabama.

I noticed in the early 1960s, at the Episcopals' Camp McDowell in north Alabama, that young girls my age from Montgomery seemed more spirited, more lively, than young girls from elsewhere. I ended up in 1962–64 dating Betty Scott, a Garden District neighbor, met though the Church of the Ascension, where Dad ministered. I also went out with Melville Douglass, daughter of St. John's Episcopal rector, the Reverend Charlie Douglass. I also enjoyed taking Priscilla Crommelin, daughter of Navy Captain Quentin Crommelin, to two balls. Coming from a military background, Priscilla must have liked the SMA uniform I wore as a boarding student at Sewanee.

The point I am making is that all three young ladies had a lively spirit and spunk. Maybe they were shades of the colorful Zelda Sayre.

Zelda Sayre Fitzgerald herself, and young Willie Thompson, our new Fitzgerald Museum executive director who has deep roots in Montgomery, also represent the spark that characterizes Montgomery at its best. There are many engaging personalities in the capital city. If you don't believe it, just meet Tommy Gallion, and listen to his melodious voice for a while—just don't ever get on his bad side. Charlie Price, the retired Montgomery Chief Circuit Judge, despite all his dignity, is also quite the personality, sometimes quite humorously so.

Montgomery is full of interesting, eclectic personalities. There are many lively people in churches, civic clubs, literary clubs, and other charitable organizations. They exist in most every neighborhood. Some are more liberal, others more conservative, and many are varying degrees in between. We can all learn to better respect one another, uphold mutual dignity, and enjoy the humanity we have in common. We are all God's children.

We would be remiss not to acknowledge the many hard problems still facing Montgomery. That is why Montgomery genuinely needs a police force, a fire department, a district attorney's office, and other law enforcement and support personnel in all neighborhoods of Montgomery. People are still killing and robbing each other, or stealing from neighbors. Others are battling each other, husbands and wives abusing each other, married couples running around on each other, and kids shooting each other. Identity theft, cybercrime, and cyberbullying are much too prevalent and need to be stopped.

Likewise, terrorism, whether international, domestic, or local, at whatever level must be fought as effectively as possible, with law enforcement and the civilian population cooperating as fully as possible.

I applaud U.S. Attorney George Beck for successfully pursuing pockets of prostitution and/or human trafficking that have occasionally waved their ugly heads, especially on West South Boulevard. George is also due much credit, as is Montgomery County District Attorney Daryl Bailey, for successfully pursuing the organized trade of illegal drugs. Illegal narcotics, especially heroin and other hard drugs, have taken or ruined many lives.

Is this human nature? Yes, but such things can be dealt with and improved, especially if we learn how to work together. Tough love and law enforcement are necessary, but I call on churches, schools, neighborhoods, and people of good will, regardless of race, gender, religion, or socioeconomic class, to come together, even pray together, in common purpose for these problems, and reduce them.

Forgiveness and reconciliation are the highest arts of both the Christian and Jewish faiths. We as a people, in Montgomery and everywhere, must learn to practice these basic spiritual principles more. In doing so, a spirit, really the Holy Spirit, is loosened and becomes contagious. Joy and peace are its fruits.

More is already being done in Montgomery's black community. The efforts of Lee High School wrestling coach Phillip Brooks, described in chapter 31, in teaching young kids how to wrestle, how to keep off the streets, and how not to shoot each other, is an exciting example! I helped draft the bylaws for Phillip's Peace on the Streets Training and Tutoring Center, Inc. I also plan to show the young wrestlers a few special moves and techniques, although, at 69, I better avoid wrestling too hard.

Reaching the young black male portion of our population is essential. I have two relatively young such men working with my law firm, namely Kaylon Jenkins and Carlton Avery. They are both big "family men." For 18 years, Kaylon has served process for us and is our firm chaplain. Carlton is my right-hand paralegal. Both are committed Christians, well-disciplined personally, and are great examples. I know both inspire many other young African Americans. They also inspire many older white folk, like me.

Pastor Edward J. Nettles has famously said "enough is enough" when it comes to guns. Nettles must also be encouraged and assisted. The pastor has much support in the Montgomery area already, but he needs more. I do all I can to discourage young people from carrying guns, whenever I get a chance, which oftentimes is in my office.

It is past time for reasonable gun control measures to be asserted, and enforced, in Montgomery, before we have an outbreak that kills and maims many innocent people. Law enforcement has a justifiable need for guns, and let hunters keep their rifles. But pistols and automatic guns should be banned for youthful citizens under a certain age, like 35 or 40.

I am excited about the "Youth City" development in Montgomery's old Montgomery Mall. It was originally inspired by the visionary pastor Kyle Searcy of Fresh Anointing Church. The Montgomery County Commission recently gave it a huge financial boost with a $100,000 check. Youth City will take up 80,000 square feet inside the Mall and will sponsor fun, leadership, and learning programs after school and during the summer. The goal is to create healthier choices among youths, and to encourage a drug-free and nonviolent lifestyle. Thank you, Lord. Other cities, take note.

I am also excited about what County Commissioner Dan Harris has done in spearheading a summer jobs program for unemployed teens. He also helped restore voting places in a run-down area of South Boulevard. Dan has a law office in my Perry High Office Building, so I see him frequently, and stay up to date on his efforts.

The Reverend Jay Wolf, pastor of First Baptist Church, Perry Street, has been a leader in expressing concerns about young black males caught up in a violent environment. These crimes continue to claim lives each year, and they make "double victims," as the perpetrators get sent away for life sentences or worse.

An especially exciting ministry is Common Ground, which fights violence and provides mentors and after-school activities for young people in Washington Park, Gibbs Village, and low-income neighborhoods. Bravo, and thanks to its leaders and supporters, including the Central Alabama Community Foundation, which recently gave Common Ground $100,000 for an anti-violence grant. I also know that my friends at the Beasley Allen law firm have been quite helpful to Common Ground. My own son David McPhillips has also helped Common Ground and attended some of their Sunday worship services.

Leslie and I enjoy supporting Reality and Truth Ministries, founded in 2008 by our down-the-street neighbor, LaDonna Brendle. She has focused its mission on downtown Montgomery and Tel Aviv, Israel. In Montgomery, they minister to the homeless and poor by providing daily meals and a day shelter with the amenities of home, including showers, haircuts, clothing, furnishings, and financial and legal assistance. Bible studies are also provided.

Another potent Montgomery-area ministry to the homeless is known as Hope Inspired Ministries. Featured by the *Montgomery Advertiser* in October 2015, in recognition of World Homeless Day, this ministry serves the chronically unemployed by preparing and equipping them through a 13-week job training course. This program seeks to transform by providing relationship training, life skills, employment skills, GED preparation, and internships with local businesses. Bravo again!

Yet another ministry for the homeless, featured in an Al Benn story in the *Montgomery Advertiser,* was the Mid-Alabama Coalition for the Homeless. The more people help to address this real problem, the kinder and gentler city we become.

A long-time ministry/service to the community has been Montgomery's Habitat for Humanity. In 1984, Leslie and I gave this organization two lots with old houses on them on Cramer Avenue, near Decatur Street. Attorney

Mark Chambless, a young 31 years old at the time, received the gift for the organization. Instead of being rehabbed, the old houses were torn down and new homes built on their lots. More of this type of rehabilitation is needed in Montgomery and is actually being done in the House-to-House home restoration efforts, a volunteer agency.

The Pure in Heart Outreach Ministry, organized in 1996 by Josie Marie Knott, on Edgar D. Nixon Avenue on the west side of Montgomery, is another good example of a neighborhood ministry that helps to feed and clothe the poor. Bravo.

Another exciting work is that of the Reverend Carmen Falcione in his ecumenical, nondenominational ministry, The Gathering. Likewise, the Reverend Tom Bridges of Let God Arise Ministries goes into the Montgomery city and county jails to minister to inmates.

Some of Montgomery's biggest churches, namely Frazer Methodist, Fresh Anointing, First Methodist, First Baptist, Trinity Presbyterian, Dexter Avenue King Memorial Baptist, and the Episcopal Church of the Ascension also have great outreach ministries, as do hundreds of other churches in the greater Montgomery area. Save-A-Life and Cope are both doing great work to save unborn children.

I am especially grateful to First Methodist, a stone's throw from where I live, for its Respite Ministries. That group provides rest or respite for people, in their church and well outside, who are taking care of family and friends with dementia and Alzheimer's. Since both my mother and maternal grandmother suffered in the end with extended dementia or Alzheimer's illnesses, I am especially supportive of this work.

Obviously, all these churches and ministries are doing much, but can do more, if their congregations will commit their resources, financial and voluntary, to do more. Professional groups (lawyers, doctors, teachers, accountants, etc.) and churches must also do more to identify and assist those struggling with depression or other mental health burdens.

Suicide prevention is possible, but greater efforts must be made to detect the suffering and bring transformational help. Such help exists, especially in the spiritual realm. I know what it's like to be a family survivor victim, having lost my brother David that way almost 40 years ago. I hear about way too many suicides around town and elsewhere. Whatever our religious or occupational background, we must be more vigilant, and sensitive.

Montgomery must continue to encourage such citywide traditional youth programs as Cub Scouts, Boy Scouts, Girl Scouts, and YMCA. Likewise, such charitable efforts as giving blood to the Red Cross and other such life-support entities must always be active. I include groups supporting suicide prevention and helping suicide victims.

United Way, the grandfather of all charity fund-raising groups, must continue to be supported strongly by as many local citizens as possible, whether with a widow's mite or a large corporation's big donation. So many charitable service agencies rely on this help.

Two exciting recent developments have sprung from local churches getting into the educational arena to help underprivileged kids. One is Trinity Presbyterian's development of the Montgomery Christian School in the Garden District. My wife Leslie has been a substantial contributor since it opened its doors five years ago.

The other is the Valiant Cross Academy, a new faith-based, all-boys school that just opened its doors on August 17, 2015. Two brothers of African American descent, Anthony and Fredrick Brock are using River City Church's property in downtown Montgomery to teach discipline, self-worth, prosperity, and the Christian faith to at-risk youth.

Bravo for these initiatives. They are exactly what I'm talking about. The *Montgomery Advertiser* had a great feature story on Valiant Cross Academy in October 2015. Thanks again to the *Advertiser* for encouraging local charities, volunteer efforts, and good causes.

Other great ministries include New Birth Ministries, helping people maintain freedom from substance abuse, and Renascence Ministries, helping ex-inmates adjust. They and many other ministries are making a positive difference in Montgomery. They are living the "Word of God."

My sometimes paralegal, Vicki Morrison, now an English professor at Troy University Montgomery, told me to include the dynamic ministry of Pastor Vincent Rosato and his wife, Mary, and their Friendship Mission for Men and Friendship Mission for Women, which serves homeless and displaced men, women, and children. Rev. Cliff Terrell and his Gospel Tabernacle Church of God in Christ are also impacting many, or so he tells me, on Fridays at the Montgomery Lions Club.

The Montgomery Lions Club itself contributes to many charitable causes in Montgomery, as do the many other civic clubs, Kiwanis, Rotary, Civitan, and other Lions Clubs. All these help make Montgomery a better place to live in.

Speaking of the Montgomery Lions Club, I will have been a member of that venerable institution for 40 years, as of January 2016. Historically rowdy and fun-loving, our club has become increasingly diverse, with more women and African Americans. (McPhillips Shinbaum, LLP now has four members, including officer manager Amy Strickland, partner Joe Guillot, paralegal Carlton Avery, and me). Member Alva Lambert often leaves us in stitches laughing at his impersonations of famous voices.

The Montgomery Kiwanis Club also deserves great appreciation for its annual running of the Alabama National State Fair in and around the Garrett Coliseum. The fair is a lot of fun, especially for kids, and raises much money for worthy local causes.

The name of organizations fighting cancer in Montgomery are amazing, including the pink-colored Joy of Life Foundation that sponsors annual fund-raising marches, to fight breast cancer.

MACOA, the Montgomery Area Community Organization on Aging, wonderfully delivers "Meals on Wheels" to many needy seniors who might not eat otherwise. It also delivers other indispensable services. Three cheers for these guys. My law partner Joe Guillot is on its board of directors.

Also impacting others is the television show "Conversations with Carol and Julian" originated by Carol Jones, but continued with my help. That ministry, through cable television, reaches many in Montgomery, with a religious and counseling message, spiced with humor. Carol's husband, Mike, helps keeping this ministry moving.

In September 2015, Montgomery participated in the International Day of Peace. The website *Peace within Montgomery* reads "we can spark the creation of peace with justice (aka peace plus teeth) which should ripple out globally. That's the kind of vision we need. As Isaiah the prophet poetically stated, "Without a vision, a people perishes."

In October 2015, hundreds of religious activists walked through downtown Montgomery praying for the victims of the massacre that claimed the lives of nine college students in Oregon and many other similar victims of school shootings. This annual River Region Prayer Walk is a good thing. They just need to get the word out better publicly, through the churches and media, so that more people will know in advance, and can join them.

Another great organization in Montgomery is the Alabama World Affairs Council. I have been on its board of directors since 1980, when it began. It has brought in many great speakers over the years, many of national reputation. This not only keeps our local citizens better informed, but enhances Montgomery's visibility as a player in national affairs. We cannot become too narrow-minded or parochial about local issues. We, as a city populace, must be vigilant to stay informed about national and international issues.

This includes staying informed about environmental issues and the growing ecological crisis brought about by global warming. The evidence of pollutants, waste, and swelling oceans is indisputable. The damage is undeniable. Montgomery can help lead the way here also.

Towards that end, I commend Susan Carmichael, head of the Montgomery Clean City Commission and Jon Broadway of the Montgomery Transportation Coalition for raising local consciousness about how, and where, we can make Montgomery a cleaner city for all of us to live in.

The Fellowship of Christian Athletes (FCA) has enormously inspired its membership over the years, resulting in better family values, good sportsmanship, and a great love of God. Although evangelistic, its broad outreach extends to Jews, Hindus, Muslims, agnostics and atheists. *Woodlawn* is a must-see movie, reflecting how the FCA in the early 1970s sparked Birmingham-area schools to peacefully transform to integrated teams. I helped co-found the FCA at Princeton University in 1965 along with Bill Bradley (whose presidential campaign I chaired in Alabama in 2000). The FCA does much good in Alabama, and Montgomerians should support it strongly.

It helps a city's citizens to be athletic. Increasing numbers of our citizens are running in races that raise monies for charities, but it also helps to lower blood pressures for bodies.

Likewise, I was thrilled to see Montgomery named as a "bike friendly" city by the League of American Bicyclists. This has delighted my 88-year-old second cousin once removed, David Sanderson, who moved to Montgomery to live in the John Knox Manor independent living home. My elderly cousin is still riding a bike, which says something about why he is still alive and healthy at his age.

We are many ministers, accountants, engineers, doctors, nurses, teachers, lawyers, mechanics, plumbers, carpenters, restaurateurs, and average ordinary people who make up Montgomery. Together we can make Montgomery and the world, a better place to live in, with a humble degree of community pride. We must work together more, however, with this mutual goal and vision in mind.

I speak to all demographic sectors of our population: young, old, black, white, and brown, male and female, and all socio-economic groups, when I say that, even though many good things are already being done, we can all do better. We must have a heart for our fellow citizens, and love one another more. Pope Francis' visit to the USA stressed all of this. He couldn't have been more correct. He spoke to all religious groups, those more secularly-minded, and the non-religious when the Pope stressed civility, mutual respect, and compassion. I couldn't agree with him more. Pope Francis is my hero.

As can be seen by the preceding review of local organizations, providing needed local services, Montgomery is already doing much of what needs to be done.

Just before this book went to press, I had the good fortune of having my dear friend, Michael Briddell, speak to the Montgomery Lions Club in December 2015. Michael, top executive assistant to Mayor Strange, said the mayor's vision for the City of Montgomery was to have a city that is "safe, vibrant, and growing." Mike reeled off award-winning statistics for the fire department and said the new police chief, Ernest Finley, was making the police more "user-friendly" with a new "park, walk, and talk" campaign.

Michael, in his prior career as a professional journalist, lived in metropolitan areas all over the U.S. He believes Montgomery already compares quite favorably with the others. Michael's goal, and that of the mayor's office, was to make Montgomery "the Garden Spot of North America." Sounds good, and I agree that it is possible.

Montgomery, as a people, must develop a collective sense of living the Great Commandment. That is, we must first learn to love God with all our heart, all our soul, all our mind, and all our body. Yet, the second part is of this commandment is like unto the first, namely that we should really love our neighbors as ourselves. Montgomery can lead this movement.

That is why Montgomery needs to be re-inspired and re-motivated by the Great Commandment given us 2,000 years ago. If that happens, what a city we could become. Cynics and skeptics are correct that it will not be easy, but they are incorrect if they think it is impossible. With God's help, and the City's proper self-organization, together with public and private resources, Montgomery could help lead Alabama into a "new era of greatness." The City of Montgomery must make it a goal. That is the first step.

If that happens, and if the spirit reflected in Second Chronicles 7:14 catches fire, God would not only heal Montgomery, but transform Montgomery from that "Shining City on the Hill" to a "Shining Metropolis on Many Hills." In the process, Montgomery would become a leader and example for others in Alabama and in the world. It would not be just for Montgomery's glory, but it would be, and must be, for God's greater glory.

40

Closing Comments

Life is a journey. Learning its true meaning and purpose is every person's challenge. The greatest truth to learn, in my opinion, is that God is absolutely awesome, amazing, and ultimately in charge. Knowledge and power revolve around him, not us. It often takes a lifetime to realize this, or to fully realize that he is the "ground of our being." That is, were it not for God's creating us in the first place, we would not exist, or would not be, at least on planet Earth.

None of us had any choice in what gender, race, nationality, or socio-economic group we were born into or with what genes or which parents. A humble awareness of this truth tends to temper one's feeling of pride in one's own accomplishments. Yet, our innate humanity will not allow us to escape some measure of satisfaction in living life well.

A deep sense of gratitude to God, hungering and thirsting for expression, is in all our souls, whether we realize it or not. To the extent we repress it, a latent dissatisfaction begins to well up, no matter how much we may satisfy other fleeting desires for such as wealth, power, security, sex, or other temporal things.

We also learn that the obstacles, pitfalls, and potholes common to all humanity are part of God's plan for us all. Indeed these foibles ultimately can be a cause for rejoicing, because God uses them to bring us closer to him. To quote scripture, "it is in our weakness that God's strength is made perfect" (2 Corinthians 12:9). God's strength then becomes our rod and staff (Psalm 23:4) in fighting injustice and helping neighbors and strangers in need.

Yes, we live in a world of mystery and wonder. Yet that is part of the excitement or adventure of life. It should not be a stumbling block. As a teenager, I wanted answers to these profound, ultimate life-purpose questions. As I grew older, I learned that many of these answers will not come until we enter the greater life beyond the grave.

I do believe that God laid the foundation with his prophets and leaders of the Old Testament world, but he then intervened even more directly when he sent us Jesus, as part of himself, to give us a road map for life. That map is laid out in the New Testament, especially in the Gospels and Epistles. The disciples and apostles spread his Word, as God breathed his spirit on all of them and the scriptures as well (2 Timothy 3:16).

After getting past a childhood ambition to become a professional athlete, or to continue in my family's canning food business, my earliest career leaning was to follow in Dad's footsteps and become a priest of the Episcopal Church. That lasted through my high school years at Sewanee Military Academy and the first half of the Princeton years. Dad wisely encouraged me to get the law degree, due to its great potential usage.

I realize now, as I approach my 70s, the wisdom of Dad's encouragement, and the opportunities it has given me. Yet, ringing clearly underneath was my mother's repeated reminder of the Lord's words that "to those to whom much is given, much is required" (Luke 12:48). The parable of the talents (Matthew 25:14-30), and the ringing words of the Sermon on the Mount (Matthew 5:3-16) have also been influential in my life.

I also believe that every day is important and a "gift" (quoting the Reverend John Claypool). "This is the day that the Lord has made; let us rejoice and be glad in it" (Psalms 118:24; see also Philippians 4:19).

I am also fully cognizant, as I get closer to this life's end, that we cannot take anything material to heaven with us. I therefore take seriously the words of our Lord, who said poetically, "Gather not up for yourselves treasures on earth, where thieves break in and steal, and rust and moth doth corrupt, but treasures in heaven . . . " (Matthew 6:19-20).

I have been raised in the orthodox Christian doctrine that salvation is by God's grace, love, and mercy, and that there is nothing we can do to earn our way into it (Romans 9:15-16; Matthew 19:25-26). Nonetheless, it is also orthodox to believe there will be a degree of accountability, and that our actions in this life matter, not only for this world, but in the world to come (Matthew 12:36; Romans 14:12).

If that is so, then what is the yardstick? Jesus told us quite plainly. It is the two-part "Great Commandment": (1) Love God with all of our heart, soul, and mind. (2) The second part, he said, was "like unto the first," namely to love our neighbor as ourselves (Matthew 22:37–39).

I also believe the Ten Commandments are a wonderful guide (Exodus 20:2-17). When their public display was attacked some years ago, I had Muslim and Hindu friends tell me they believed in the Ten Commandments. Of course, our Jewish and Christian brethren should also, although it is obvious that not everyone does. Particularly troubling to some is the seventh commandment about not committing adultery.

The first two commandments are exceedingly important. Both deal with prohibitions against idolatry: (1) Thou shalt have no other gods before me; and (2) Thou shalt not worship any graven image. It's not by coincidence that these two commandments are the top two. They are that important. They are part of the spiritual DNA God has placed deeply in our psyche.

Idolatry is a subtle thing. It sneaks up on people. By definition, idolatry involves allowing yourself to love anything more than you love God. All humans fall into this practice at some time in their life. The more it happens, and the deeper it goes, the more one pays a negative price. The less one does it, and the more one loves God the most, the more a spirit of peace and joy falls upon you worth more than gold and silver.

Where have I learned the above? The answer is "life experience over 69 years." Scripture reinforces these lessons, and the Holy Spirit confirms the truth.

Of course, as human beings we all fall short. I was raised at a high school that was not just military, but religious, namely Sewanee Military Academy, in the church town of Sewanee, Tennessee. That was where my Dad had studied in seminary to be a priest from 1959–62. In Sewanee, I learned the classic definition of sin, namely that it was "separation from God." I believe there are many general subclasses of sin, including sins of commission, sins of omission, sins of disposition, sins of misplaced priorities, and sins of not loving God with our whole heart. In our twice-daily prayers, Leslie and I try to make confession and repentance a regular part of our communication with God.

I admit that I have my faults. One is the need for more patience, although I tend to think that impatience with injustice may be more of a virtue. Still I need to work on "more patience" generally. One of my greatest faults, I readily recognize, is the need to be more humble. Sometimes I am closer to being there, at other times far away. There are other faults.

I thank God that he is the one to whom I can genuinely turn to and repent for my sins. There is nothing like the cathartic, or cleansing, flow of the Holy Spirit, whether in private prayers of confession, or at Holy Communion.

Montgomery has been a great city to live in for over 40 years. I enjoy the diversity of its people, many of whom come to see me in my law practice. We've also enjoyed a great diversity of people in the latter years at Christ the Redeemer Episcopal Church. The praise and worship music, its healing ministry, and other spiritual components strengthen my walk.

The quest for justice, and standing up to bullies causing injustice, has been my life's purpose and motivation. It has been daunting at times, but, for the most part, it has been exciting, even exhilarating. While tough-mindedness is often necessary, I believe that kindness, gentleness, and sensitivity are also important. Likewise, broad-mindedness is more effective than narrow-mindedness.

I am against proselytizing, which is always counterproductive. Low-key evangelism, reflected more in one's deeds than words, can be very effective for spreading the Gospel. It is important, however, to accord others a mutual, reciprocal respect, regardless of how different that other person's faith, or lack of faith, may be.

My wonderful life partner and wife of 42 years is the former J. Leslie Burton. I am speechless in looking for adequate words to describe her and thank her. Leslie has given me the firm foundation to pursue my life's journey and, most importantly, she has made the voyage with me. Leslie has also taken the leadership in raising three fine children, who are producing a growing brood of lovable grandchildren.

I am deeply humbled, and I say again, thank you, Lord, for Leslie and all the blessings of life. But I thank God most especially for sending us Jesus as Lord, to open the door to Life Eternal. I don't know how many years I have left. Few of us do. We could be called home tomorrow. Yet even at my age 69, I could live 20–30 more years. I hope and pray it is a good while longer, and that I maintain decent health, so I can continue to serve others in need. Another reason is that I am curious and interested in seeing how things shape up in the years ahead. And I want to do my part to help them shape up in a positive way.

I recognize that this life, however long it may be, is an instant in eternity. I further realize that this life is a preparatory stage for that greater life beyond the grave. I look forward someday to seeing Jesus face to face. Although not in a hurry, I also look forward to another stimulating stage of existence that reflects the incredible love of God. I also look forward to seeing family members and friends who have predeceased me.

The great truth is that "only God is God," and to him be all honor, glory, and praise!

Appendices

NEAR-DEATH EXPERIENCES
IN UNDERGROUND GARAGES

Did I ever tell you about the two times I was almost killed? They were both in underground parking garages." This parenthetical remark by Julian is an illustration that casual conversations with him rarely proceed in a straight line.

While high-profile cases such as Julian handles can earn attorneys a growing conglomerate of enemies over the years of their careers, it's ironic that Julian's two close brushes with death both came accidentally.

In 1986, Julian and fellow attorney Gary Atchison were defending a Montgomery fireman in a termination review, in the mayor's office. When McPhillips arrived at City Hall, he found all the parking places on the street taken and, running tight for time, parked in the underground garage at the nearby Madison Hotel.

It had rained heavily the night before and Julian noticed that the underground lot was mostly flooded. Giving up on trying to keep his feet dry, he settled for walking in the spots where the water level appeared lowest. But a few yards later, stepping into an apparent shallow spot, his footing disappeared completely and he sank precipitously into what turned out to be an open manhole, whose cover a worker had apparently removed to help speed drainage but had neglected to mark with a barrier.

By instinct, Julian's arms shot outward and he found himself barely suspended at the manhole's rim, as the force of the water's suction exerted powerful pressure to pull him under from the neck down.

After he caught his breath and regained his bearings, he was able to gradually hoist himself from the maelstrom and to get one foot, then finally the other, on solid ground.

"It was absolutely terrifying," he recalls. "I have no doubt that if I had been much smaller physically, or maybe older and somewhat frail, it would have drowned me. I'd have ended up somewhere in the Alabama River."

Julian drove home and — before changing into dry clothes — called Atchison, told him what had happened, swore him to secrecy, and asked him to carry on the hearing until Julian could drive back downtown.

A short time later, he strolled into the hearing room as casually as he could manage, and was met by laughter from all sides. Atchison had caved in and explained Julian's delay. Which may have been, Julian reflects, sound legal strategy on Atchison's part. In any event, the review board was in a sufficiently good mood to quickly rule in favor of his and Atchison's client.

A medical checkup found that, except for some painfully bruised ribs, Julian was okay. The hotel offered him an official apology which, seeing as it was attached to a $1,000 check, he "graciously accepted."

That night, at a lawyers' party, the word of Julian's mishap had quickly spread before he arrived. Present at the party was Alabama Bar Association president Walter Byars, who chuckled, "McPhillips, I heard what happened. You're invincible, man!"

As it turned out, Byars's compliment was also prophetic. In 1993, Julian and Leslie were in Atlanta, where Julian was preparing for a Eleventh Circuit Court of Appeals argument on behalf of his client Marcia Edwards. The McPhillipses spent the night at the Peachtree Hotel, and once again parked in an underground garage. The next morning, Julian went down to get a book he had left in his car. As he was walking back up the ramp, out of nowhere came a red, ten-feet-long metal guard arm, which apparently had gotten stuck in the "up" position after the last car went through, and chose the exact moment of Julian's passage to come back down. Miraculously, the heavy pole just missed the top of Julian's head, instead scraping down the front of his face: knocking his glasses off, bloodying his nose, and toppling him onto his back, dazed, on the concrete.

After Julian recovered his composure, he realized how close he had come to death. If he had passed under the arm a split second later, the barrier could have cracked his skull like a hammer splitting a pecan.

At that moment, Julian recalls "thanking God the Father, Son, and Holy Spirit," and rushing back to the room to get at least partially cleaned up before the court session began.

On the way to the courtroom, he remembers debating with himself about whether to preface his remarks to the judges with a description of the accident. He finally decided against telling, not only because the story sounded so incredible, but because it also would have taken away valuable time from his client's argument.

"As it was," he says, "I guess the judges thought I had been in a fist fight."

Subsequently, the Peachtree Hotel also gave Julian a $1,000 apology.

"I wouldn't recommend it as a way to earn money," he says.

APPENDIX 2

BRIEF HISTORY OF KING PHARR

In 1946, the McPhillips family brought King Pharr Canning Company, a major vegetable canning operation, to Cullman. Led by chairman Julian B. McPhillips of Mobile and his two sons Julian L. McPhillips and W. Warren McPhillips (returning from Navy service in the Pacific), the local plant became Cullman's biggest employer, ultimately employing up to 400 people locally, many hundreds more indirectly in harvesting crops, and over 1000 employees in all its plants.

King Pharr Canning Company was headquartered in Cullman. It canned and shipped 33 vegetables nationally, including peas, green beans, Irish potatoes, okra, tomatoes, pimentos, sweet potatoes, and blackberries. At its peak in 1959, King Pharr had over 2,000 individual growers

on contract, and produced 30,000,000 cans annually. King Pharr's impact on the local economy was enormous. It also had plants in Selma, Uniontown, Georgia, and Louisiana. The business closed in 1976.

(1950's) Warren McPhillips, Lilybel & Julian B. McPhillips, and Julian L. McPhillips

A Dedication of the King Pharr Canning Company Historic Marker

Friday, December 19, 2014
9:00 a.m.
Site of former King Pharr Canning Co. Plant
Cullman, Alabama

APPENDIX 3

CHRIST THE REDEEMER
EPISCOPAL CHURCH
RESURRECTED
(All Saints Sunday)
November 1, 2015

Let the Glory of the LORD fill this House — Mahesh Chavel

Sunday Services – 6:00 p.m.

I can do all things through Christ who strengthens me. – Philippians 4:13

APPENDIX 4

ALABAMA JOURNAL

(Established 1888)
Published Every Week Day by
THE ADVERTISER CO.
Second class postage paid at Montgomery, Alabama

CARMAGE WALLS _____ President and Publisher
HAROLD MARTIN _____ Associate Publisher
WILLIAM H. McDONALD ____ Editorial Page Editor
RAY JENKINS _____ Managing Editor
GUYTON PARKS _____ General Manager

C. M. STANLEY, Editor Emeritus

Full Report of THE ASSOCIATED PRESS (AP)
THE UNITED PRESS INTERNATIONAL (UPI)

PAGE 4   MONTGOMERY, ALA., FRIDAY, NOVEMBER 29, 1963

LETTERS to the Editor

Your name and address must be given on letter ★ But upon request name will sometimes be withheld at the Editor's discretion ★ We reserve the right to shorten letters ★ No poetry please ★ Repeat: No letter will be printed unless Editor knows who wrote it.

A Letter From A Teen-Ager Who Didn't Cheer

Editor, Alabama Journal:

My teen-age son is a high school student away at school in Sewanee, Tenn., and I could not help but wonder about his reactions to the tragic events of this past weekend. Today I received this letter from him written on Friday a few hours after the announcement was made that President Kennedy died.

It seemed to me that the hope and inspiration expressed in his letter might be helpful to other teen-agers if shared with them.

REV. JULIAN L. McPHILLIPS
Montgomery.

_____

Nov. 22

Dear Mom and Dad:

What a dreadful tragedy has occurred. The assassination of President Kennedy would seem like an impossibility in our day and time. Yet, it has happened and the whole world is mourning.

The sorrow and grief of his death, to me, is inexpressible. We have truly lost one of our greatest presidents, a man who was responsible for so much improvement and progress in our land and throughout the world.

The whole corps of cadets was informed at lunchtime today that President Kennedy had been shot, along with the Governor of Texas. The silence and gloom that fell on the corps was halting.

After lunch, everyone went to the Study Hall and from 1:00 to 2:30 we watched the reports on President Kennedy come in until it was finally announced that he had died.

I was so moved emotionally that I found it hard to keep back the tears. After gaining my composure some time later, I have had time to let something be absorbed which seemed like a fantastic unreality at first.

The meaning and significance of his death will be felt not only in our country but throughout the world. Rather than letting this even put the country in confusion and turmoil, I hope it so motivates conscientious citizens and lovers of peace, freedom, and justice that they will be determined enough to do something to help get our country and the people of the world back on the right road.

I don't think I can ever remember being so sorrowful, yet I honestly say that I am filled with a strong inspiration and incentive to give myself for a cause for the betterment of mankind, as this great man who died in Dallas did.

When such events as this can happen, it can not help but open my mind to the great need for reform, but also the great need for people who will strive for reform. About the only thing right now a person can do is pray, pray for God to be with Mrs. Kennedy and her family, our new President, Lyndon Johnson, and our nation and the whole world in this time of great crisis.

I hope that this event will really tie our people together in a bond of unity, peace, and mutual respect as citizens and human beings. This could serve to do our country some good, to make us strive for the high ideals for which President Kennedy stood. I think, hope and believe God will make something good come out of what, at the present, seems so terrible.

I don't know how to end or really adequately begin to express myself at a time like this. How have you, Mom and Dad, taken this tragedy? I'd like to hear your views concerning the national, political, and world effects of today's disaster. Give my best to the rest.

Love,
JUTSY

Sewanee, Tenn.

KNOW YOUR SCRIPTURE:

Whatsoever a man soweth that shall he also reap.—Galatians 6:7.

APPENDIX 5

OPINION

First Amendment to the
of religion or prohibiting the
or the right of the people pea

FRIDAY, DECEMBER 5, 2014

MONTGOMERYADVERTISER.COM

ALABAMA VOICES » Julian McPhillips

Alabama case recalls Ferguson

I must respectfully disagree with the USA TODAY editorial in the Advertiser that the grand jury's no indictment in Ferguson, Mo., deserves deference. The reason it does not is because of the prosecutor's extremely close ties to the police and the one-sided nature of a grand jury presentation.

It's the fox guarding the henhouse. No one represented the slain victim inside the grand jury room.

America is in dire trouble if a fairer method of determining criminal liability of a police officer shooting and killing an innocent and unarmed civilian is not reached. As national columnist Dana Milbank has proclaimed, "The Missouri prosecutor is the face of injustice."

Worse than Trayvon Martin's death in Florida and Michael Brown's killing in Missouri is what happened recently in Alexander City, Ala., when a 21-year-old African-American male was killed by local police.

Emerson Crayton Jr. was the victim. After getting off from work, Crayton stopped at the Huddle House, the only restaurant open after midnight in Alex City. Father of a 2-year-old girl, young Crayton had no gun or weapon on him. He was simply hungry and wanted something to eat. A white waitress, unhappy with Emerson's voice, hurled the F-word at him. Crayton returned the description and left

Huddle House, telling it to keep its food and money.

According to multiple eyewitnesses and earwitnesses, not once did young Emerson speak any threatening words towards anyone at Huddle House. Yet, as Mr. Crayton was leaving, a Huddle House employee followed him, screaming at him while calling for a police officer next door.

In response, a young white Alex City police officer came running over. Never identifying himself as an officer, he shot Mr. Crayton five times, killing him. An investigation by the Alexander City police confirmed that Mr. Crayton had no weapon.

Eyewitnesses say Mr. Crayton was not aware of the policeman's presence in the dark of the night. The victim had committed no crime. He was not a fleeing felon. He was not speeding away down a highway, nor was he threatening the safety of others. Mr. Crayton's windows were up, and his car doors shut, with music impairing his hearing.

Alexander City and neighboring Dadeville, where Mr. Crayton lived, are in an uproar over the innocent killing of this young African American male, with nothing being done about it.

Over 1,000 blue t-shirts were sold the first week afterwards, with the words "No Justice; No Peace." Almost a thousand attend-

ed his funeral. Hundreds have marched on the Alex City police station to demand justice.

The community has absolutely no faith in law enforcement or in the Tallapoosa County district attorney's office. To the credit of civil rights leaders, no violence has occurred, as compared to Ferguson.

Unlike George Zimmerman in Trayvon Martin's case, this was not a "stand your ground" defense. The policeman was not attacked by Mr. Crayton, and multiple witnesses say the officer was never endangered by Mr. Crayton's car.

Yet the local district attorney quickly closed ranks behind the policeman, with whom his office works regularly. Like Ferguson, like Alex City. A grand jury returned no indictment. Family and friends and many others, especially in the African-American community, but many Caucasians as well, are incensed at what they perceive as a cover-up.

Lawyers say a prosecutor can indict a ham sandwich if he wants to. Conversely, great crime can be whitewashed. I except Montgomery County's outstanding district attorney from this rule, but do not except the DAs of Ferguson, Mo., and of Alexander City, Ala.

Montgomery lawyer Julian McPhillips represents the administration of Emerson Crayton Jr.'s estate.

APPENDIX 6

Montgomery Advertiser

OPINION

Jim Earnhardt | jearnhardt@gannett.com | 261-1524 | montgomeryadvertiser.com/opinion

PAGE 5A

MONDAY, JUNE 11, 2012

Congress shall make no law respecting an establishment of religion or prohibiting the free exercise thereof, or abridging the freedom of speech, or of the press, or the right of the people peaceably to assemble, and to petition the Government for a redress of grievances. — *First Amendment to the Constitution*

ALABAMA VOICES: » JULIAN MCPHILLIPS

Compensation for family due

My dear friend Vanzetta McPherson is an articulate columnist, attorney and former judge. I appreciate her saying an apology is due the Whitehurst family by the city of Montgomery and its police department, but I must respectfully and strongly disagree with her view that no compensation is due.

Vanzetta's premise is that a case once was pursued unsuccessfully, which constitutes binding precedent. She suggests that accommodating the White-hursts opens the city up to "subsequent requests." I readily concede the city has no legal obligation per se, but insist that it has a strong moral obligation.

Further, an apology without compensation has a hollow ring to it, suggesting that money is more important than life. Further, as I contended before the

City Council last Tuesday, the White-hurst case is so unprecedented, and so undisputed, as to its egregious wrong-doing. There is no other comparable case.

Even the police now admit they were wrong in shooting an unarmed White-hurst, not a fleeing felon, in the back, and then planting a gun beside his hand to make it look like Whitehurst had shot at then first. The Whitehurst case is now taught at the Montgomery Police Academy as an example of what police officers should not do. The shooter, Donny Foster, died last year.

The famous Todd Road case, of which Ms. McPherson was an attorney for African Americans in conflict with local police, was quite different. No life was lost, and there was fault on both

sides. Surely the city of Montgomery's legal office, gifted at denying claims, can quickly pour cold water on attempts by any other plaintiffs to piggyback on a Whitehurst family payment.

The mother of Bernard Whitehurst Jr. pursued a civil suit in 1976-77, represented by Donald Watkins. Their case was gutted by a judge who made openly and harshly prejudicial comments but refused to recuse himself. The Fifth Circuit affirmed. The Whitehursts, including the widow and infant children, never got their day in court. The statute of limitations has long ago run out.

Obviously, no amount of money will ever adequately compensate the White-hurst family for all the years of pain and injury they have suffered. The city's

police depriving the innocent Mr. White-hurst of his life meant that three toddlers and one baby were raised without a father, and Florence Whitehurst has been denied her husband all these years.

A first-class book will someday share "the truth is stranger than fiction" story that gripped Montgomery for several years, leading to the resignations of the city's mayor, chief of police and other top officials. Wouldn't it be great if the final chapter reported that the City Council and mayor of Montgomery did the morally correct thing in 2012 by not only apologizing, but also by courageously compensating the victims?

Julian McPhillips practices law in Montgomery. He is representing the Whitehurst family without compensation.

APPENDIX 7

Eastern Bloc Countries Seek Peaceful Revolution

By JULIAN McPHILLIPS

Breathtaking! Historic! Sweeping!

The Citizen Ambassador delegation of 20 U.S. lawyers and spouses searched for appropriate words to describe the peaceful revolutionary changes taking place in Czechoslovakia, Hungary, and Poland.

People to People, an organization founded by Dwight Eisenhower in 1956, sponsored our group as its first set of lawyers ever to visit these Eastern Bloc countries.

Following an orientation session at Kennedy Airport on May 24 in New York, we arrived in Prague, Czechoslovakia, the next morning. Greeted by a cheerful young tour guide who once ranked nationally in tennis (and played with Martina Navratilova), we skipped from one interesting meeting to another, with intermittent sightseeing. Prague remains a beautiful city.

Our first session began with two gentlemen from the Czechoslovak Society of Foreign Relations. Discussions centered on such topics of Czechoslovakian law as dispute resolution and civil conflicts involving trade matters. The next day we were briefed at the U.S. Embassy by Ambassador Julian Niemczyk and several attaches. Another day's highlight involved a spirited give-and-take session at the Prague University Law School with Professor Kopal and the faculty of law.

Czechoslovakia is the most conservative and unchanged of the three countries visited. Reflecting its more cautious approach, Czech officials described 1968 reformer Alexander Dubcek as weak and bankrupt, while

the law school professors avoided questions on the topic.

A number of Czech officials and professors attended our farewell dinner. The mood was relaxed and convivial. Earlier in the day, President Bush announced a 20 percent troop reduction in Europe, while Gorbachev countered with word that 385,000 Soviet troops were being removed from Eastern Europe.

The middle leg of our journey brought us to Hungary, economically the most advanced of the three countries. Budapest is a beehive of activity. American tourists and Western capitalists come and go.

The day we arrived in Hungary — May 30 — historic legislation was passed by the Parliament privatizing the economy. The next day, Dr. Gabor Komaromi, head of the Ministry of Justice, explained how formerly state-owned industries would be sold to private investors, including foreign nationals. Important guarantees allow foreigners to take profits out of Hungary in hard currency. Hungarian corporations may be 100 percent owned by foreign nationals, and these corporations can own Hungarian land.

That communism has not worked, that Hungarians aspire to the good life of the capitalist world, and that they are no longer afraid of being crushed by the Soviets, as they were in 1956, is manifest. A new, hopeful spirit resonates. One Hungarian official gave us a piece of metal framed with the message:

"This is the last part of the iron curtain! All other parts have been used for the building of the bridge of friendship between East and West."

McPhillips

Alabama Voices

McDonald's does a booming hamburger business in Budapest. Citibank is entrenched; incredibly, its English manager stated that it had not suffered one bad loan in the past three years. McCann-Erickson has already expanded its American-based advertising empire into Budapest.

Another good example is one-year-old Levi Strauss Budapest Company. It has carved out an operation free of union and party interference and enjoys a five-year tax holiday due to the special status accorded foreign ventures. Its workers make twice the average salary of Hungarian garment workers, and its work force has achieved production levels considered remarkable by Hungarian experts and Western observers.

We arrived in Warsaw, Poland, the day after the country's first open election since the Soviets established hegemony after World War II. Solidarity posters were everywhere, and excitement was in the air. The votes were still being counted when we arrived on Tuesday, June 6. By Thursday, it was clear that Solidarity, the independent trade union party, had gained an overwhelming victory.

Solidarity virtually swept the new 100-seat senate and stood one seat away from capturing the entire 35 percent of the seats permitted to be contested in the 460-seat sejm, or lower house. What was even more amazing is that only two of the 35 high Communist party officials and their allies who ran unopposed got the 50 percent of the total vote cast which was necessary for re-election.

According to one high Warsaw University official, Solidarity leader Lech Walesa is accorded an heroic status in most Polish homes. "One Polish national is more popular, however, namely Pope John Paul II. Most Polish families have at least two or three of his pictures in their home.

America is popular in Poland. Many Poles have U.S. relatives, and large avenues are named after presidents Wilson and Roosevelt. The former's initiative restored previously divided Poland following World War I. Incredibly, our tour guide's 6-year-old son was a walking encyclopedia of biographical information on American presidents. Indeed, he was far more knowledgeable on the subject than any of us lawyers.

The broad public support of Solidarity and its clear agenda for economic reform should ultimately attract the same kind of foreign capital to Poland now going to Hungary. Warsaw, almost completely destroyed by the Nazis but largely rebuilt, is eager to lead the way. Anxiety remains, however. Given the historic domination of Poland by Prussians, Germans, and Russians, many Poles can hardly believe the relative freedom they are now enjoying.

It was truly exhilarating to witness these historic changes. It is endemic to

the human spirit to be free, and where there is a will, sooner or later, there appears to be a way. The Poles, the Hungarians, and the Czechs see on television and in their travels the prosperity enjoyed by the West Germans, the Austrians, the French, and the Americans. Pragmatically, they seem more interested now in the end result than in the means to achieve it. If that means throwing out old tools and using a common approach, they are eager to do so.

Many would contend that the changes taking place would not be possible in the absence of "perestroika" and "glasnost" instigated by Gorbachev and spilling over into the Eastern Bloc. This may be so, but the countries visited appear eager to take advantage of the opportunity.

What does all of this say to America, to Alabama, and their people. First, we should re-examine our stereotypes and recognize changing realities. People are people everywhere. Secondly, there are new markets for aspiring entrepreneurs, and money to be made.

Surely, there are risks — one big problem is the wide disparity between official and unofficial exchange rates in both Czechoslovakia and Poland.

Finally, we should always remember that we share a common bond with all humanity — whatever our differences may be — and there is much more to be gained by peace and mutual understanding than by the real wars of the cold wars of yesteryear.

Montgomery attorney Julian McPhillips was a member of the Citizen Ambassador legal delegation to Eastern Europe from May 24 until June 10.

APPENDIX 8

OTHER VIEWS

Montgomery, Alabama • Thursday, October 1, 1987   PAGE 13A

Kayaking Trip A Reminder Of Need To Protect Rivers

By JULIAN McPHILLIPS

The glistening white of the rapids is signal to the adrenalin. The rumble building to a roar quickens the senses. Ahead is a five-foot wave leaping out of a narrow space between the canyon wall and water-whipped rocks.

All at once the kayak soars upward, then bellies forward into the next surge of water. A quick, strong turn of the paddle avoids collision with a boulder half-buried in the waves.

On the banks of the Salmon River, a visual feast tempers the soul and relaxes the mind. On one side a granite cliff rises a thousand feet skyward; on the other, big-horn sheep stoically eye the intruder.

Such was part of the wilderness adventure enjoyed by my wife Leslie, 6 year-old daughter Grace, and me in Idaho during the third week in August.

A party of 15 launched forward on three rubber rafts and two kayaks on Monday morning. Left behind were watches, telephones, television, plumbing, and any other sign of civilization. Nights were spent in tents. Five children softened the pace and gladdened the hearts. Led by my cousins Joe and Fran Tonsmeire of Salmon, who moved from Mobile to Idaho 16 years ago, the group became as one large family, camping out at night under the stars.

Wildlife was everywhere. On two different occasions, black bear were spotted. Once, after lunch on a sandy beach, we watched a bear swim from the opposite side of the river, and approach our site. Excitement quickened. Our boats shoved off. A highlight, no doubt, but no need to test her further.

Moose, coyote, deer, eagle, grouse, and rattlesnake also greeted our number. However, only the yellowjackets dared pester our party. I became a champion swatter.

Bang, splash, twist, and turn. Waves drenching the river raft cooled off the sun, a welcome refresher. By the end of the trip, man-made waves leaped out of buckets as water-fights ensued. Laughter spiced the melee.

My daughter joined her cousin Amy in digging holes on sandy river beaches. Their laughter was music to the ear. Grace and her daddy strengthened an already-strong father-daughter bond, bouncing over the waves, going on hikes, and telling and listening to ghost stories at night.

And at night everyone pitched in. With dried river wood as fuel, gour-

Alabama Voices

met meals were cooked and served. Hope of shedding those extra pounds evaporated with the morning dew. But he fellowship of the campsite was a greater reward.

Never have the stars been clearer and more playful at night. Contemplating the handiwork of our Creator in the heavens and on earth was indeed spiritually uplifting.

Other diversion enlightened the voyage. At one point, thermal springs provided a natural hot-tub amid the trees and the rocks. At other locations, the painting of ancient Indians graced the cavern walls. A pioneer gold mine was inspected, as were the abandoned cabins of early trappers and explorers. Children fished for salmon. And our guides shared stories, at once romantic and tragic, of the early travelers of the Salmon.

Nature hikes up sparkling creek beds and trails leading to mile-high vistas were healthy exercise for mind, body, and spirit, integrating all three.

A mass of twisting foam. Elephant-size boulders. A bucking raft with bow pitching upward. The rafters screaming. The boat swerving the rocks, hanging for a moment in mid-air, then retreating down the back of the wave. These were the most indelible impressions of our bobbing journey down the famed Salmon River.

Given the challenging rapids, swift-running current, and constant slope of the Salmon, the early pioneers called it the "River of No Return." Today those who journey down this magical river cannot help but feel a magnetic attraction to return.

A return-to-nature experience is something which Americans and Alabamians are doing in increasing numbers. The fun my family and I enjoyed on the Salmon River in Idaho can be experienced on a lesser scale in Central Alabama. Bull Dog

Bend on the Cahaba River in Bibb County is a throwback to another era. Just hop into a canoe and bounce down some intermediate level rapids. Exciting rivers in Florida, Georgia, and North Carolina also becken, some with rapids more daring than the Salmon.

There is a formidable challenge to all Alabamians in maintaining our precious natural resources, particularly our rivers, mountains, lakes and forests. As we finish the last years of the 20th Century, the danger to these jewels of nature becomes ever greater, the battle increasingly severe.

In Montgomery alone, a real threat to the purity of our drinking water exists. National and international companies want to take advantage of our ignorance and desire for industry at any cost and build hazardous-waste sites nearby.

Only a few years ago, a band of determined local citizens, known as the Safe Energy Alliance of Central Alabama, barely prevented a nuclear fuel plant from being built six miles from our Capital City. Most Alabamians do not realize how lucky they are in being saved the cancerous consequences of this plant.

We cannot take the great outdoors for granted. We cannot let down our guard. We in Alabama, as the people of Idaho, have much of which to be proud. We also have much to protect. There is a big fight ahead, but the fight is worth fighting.

But in dodging the rapids, or stopping the polluters, the stake is high. Our children and grandchildren, years from now, will look back on our efforts or lack thereof. Let's give them the opportunity to enjoy the same good life our forefathers have passed down to us.

The writer is a Montgomery attorney who has been active in environmental matters.

APPENDIX 9

Montgomery, Alabama ● Thursday, August 9, 1990   PAGE 9A

OTHER VIEWS

Pilgrimage Renews Religion

By JULIAN McPHILLIPS

"Al..le..lu..jah. Al..le..lu..jah! Give thanks to our Risen Lord! Al..le..jah!"

Spontaneously echoed this hymn of praise sung by an Australian priest and his wife upon entering the little cave containing Lazarus' tomb. Instantly, my wife Leslie and I joined in the melody, as did a young Irish priest from Egypt.

Words cannot describe the feeling. All sensed strongly the Holy Spirit was with us. Joy and peace overcame us. It was one of many touching moments during our recent 2½-week spiritual pilgrimage around Israel, ending on June 22.

Fellow Montgomerians Mark and Vicki Tusken of Christ the Redeemer Episcopal Church joined Leslie and me as part of a 36-member group based at St. George's College in Jerusalem. Approximately 40 percent Australian, and 40 percent American, with the remaining 20 percent a mixture of English, Irish, and New Zealander, we were a diverse group, sharing the English language and our Christian faith.

Among the highlights were: The Church of the Nativity in Bethlehem, containing a grotto inside, marking the birthplace of Jesus. The archeological discovery under a Catholic convent in Nazareth of what many scholars believe was Christ's boyhood home. The blue Sea of Galilee, including Peter's home in Capernaum near a first century synagogue where Jesus taught. Cana, where Jesus turned water into wine. Mount Tabor, site of the Transfiguration. The Church of the Anunciation, where Mary was visited by the angel Gabriel. The mount of the Beatitudes, where Jesus preached his famous "Sermon on the Mount." The Judean Desert, where our Lord defeated temptation over 40 days and 40 nights. The Garden of Gethsemane and the Mount of Olives. The ancient stone-cobbled road where Christ carried the cross and endured the crown of thorns. The Church of the Resurrection, preserving the rock of Golgatha, and adjacent to it, the tomb where Jesus rose from the dead.

All of these were precious, precious moments. By the end of the journey, everyone agreed that his (or her) Christian faith had been greatly nourished and strengthened.

Also visited were many famous Old Testament sites, including the City of David, Hezekiah's

Alabama Voices

Tunnel, the Canaanite tells of Antipater and Megiddo, and the valley of the Armageddon. The famous Temple steps and the Wailing Wall in Jerusalem are "must" stops for Jews entering Israel, as well as for many Gentiles. Qumran, home of the Dead Sea Scrolls, which authenticated much of the Old Testament, was most interesting. Masada and Gaamla, mountain fortresses where first century Jews heroically resisted the Romans, were other exciting stops. No wonder Jews of every nationality claim Israel as their historic home.

Also included was the leading Moslem shrine, the Dome of the Rock, constructed on the site of the ancient Jewish temples. That location is a source of continuing friction between certain Jews and Moslems. After Mecca and Medina, Jerusalem is the holiest Islamic site in the Middle East.

And so it is that Israel continues as a wonderful blessing for Christians, Jews and Muslims alike. We have all sprung from these same Abrahamic roots. Yet sadly and ironically, a centuries-old bitterness and hatred continue to divide Arabs and Jews in Israel.

Many Americans stay away from Israel due to the TV image of Palestinian commandos and Israeli soldiers shooting it out. Yet, even though St. George's College is in a Palestinian neighborhood of Jerusalem, we all felt safe. Turmoil is typically overplayed by the media, but machine guns and jeeps abound, especially in the Palestinian sectors of Jerusalem and the West Bank.

Unfortunately, much-needed moderation and reason are in retreat. Extremism in the defense of passionately held principles is a great virtue on both sides. But a terrible price is being exacted.

Since the Intifadeh (or Palestinian uprising) began two-and-one-half years ago in Israel, 947 Palestinians have been killed. Of that number, 230 have lost their lives at the hands of fellow Palestinians. Suspected trouble-makers are often detained or imprisoned without charges. Refugee camps are in poor condition. The

frustration level is high. Once we witnessed a hand-to-hand slugfest between Palestinians in the narrow market streets of Jerusalem. Other Palestinians quickly broke it up. Nonetheless, tension remains, and most Arab stores close at 1 p.m. in support of the Intifadeh. Unfortunately, those hurt most by this partial strike are the Arab store-owners.

Given the polarization, very few people in Israel see shades of gray. It's all black and white. Even Americans too quickly take sides. One mild-mannered Midwesterner traveling with our group become suddenly agitated, comparing Israeli treatment of the Palestinians to Nazi brutalization of the Jews.

Another group member politely responded that such a comparison was grossly inaccurate, insulting to the Jews, and a disservice to the cause of peace. He added that the recent history of the Jews (the holocaust in Europe) and their present geography (surrounded by hostile Arab states) made American standards of civil liberties impractical.

And so the debate, and the fight, intensifies, and then deescalates, in the regular rhythmic phases.

We in Alabama need to learn more about this vitally important part of the world. Our roots are in Jerusalem. What we are today, religiously, is because of what happened in this land. What we are today, in terms of world politics, is closely related to the current events of this ancient country.

Given the strategic significance of contemporary Israel, its vast impact on our Judeo-Christian heritage, and its potential for enriching the faiths of Christians, Jews and Moslems alike, Alabamians would do well to experience first-hand this fascinating place. Surely, our citizenship ends not at the borders of Alabama, or of America, but rather extends to the four corners of the world through a common bond with all humanity. This is really what Israel is all about.

Many inexpensive opportunities for travel and study in Israel exist, particularly through religious organizations. Whether it be responding to a desire for spiritual growth, or whether it be a desire to better understand the Byzantine politics of the Middle East, go ye to Israel and discover for yourself.

McPhillips is a Montgomery attorney.

APPENDIX 10

THE MONTGOMERY
Independent
Alabama's State Capital News Source

FEBRUARY 27, 2014 - VOL. 51, No. 8   40 PAGES - THREE SECTIONS   75 CENTS

Local attorney and wife visit Antarctic, 'the last frontier'

By JULIAN MCPHILLIPS

IN HIGH SPIRITS ABOARD THE FRENCH SHIP, L'Austral, our Antarctic Expedition tackled the world's last frontier this past February 3 - 12, 2014. Organized by Gohagen Co. of Chicago, the 200 Americans and Europeans, ranging in age from 17 to 88, were on more of a scientific exploration than a vacation. Prepped en route by experts on Antarctica's topography, geography, astronomy, wild life, history and politics, the voyage from Tierra del Fuego, Argentina to Antarctica and back was a grand combination of discovery and adventure.

Spectacular, breath-taking, majestic...such adjectives spontaneously ascend in describing Antarctica's melange of snow-covered mountains, icebergs, black volcanic sand beaches, and pristine bays, seen on water or enjoyed on land. Several strenuous hikes, including a 5 kilometer trek up and down icy mountain passes at Deception Island were challenging but exhilarating.

Penguins were legion, seals abundant, and whales frequently sighted. Exotic birds, including the broad-winged albatross, were also seen. All was captured by my wife's camera, often on zodiac excursions, sometimes on land.

Julian McPhillips (4th from right) and wife Leslie (3rd from right) say hello from *way down under* along with friends they met on journey.

Early explorers from Britain, Norway, and France braved harsh conditions, as did whalers whose remnant outposts remain to be seen. Although discovered by some in the 1800s, it was not until the early 1900s that Antarctica started seeping into the world's consciousness.

Many nations have claims on Antarctic land

Harvard astronomy professor **David Aquilar** captivated his fellow travelers, describing Antarctica's vantage point on outer space, and the substantial likelihood of intelligent life on earth-like planets in other solar systems.

Brown geology professor **Peter Gromet** explained plate tectonics and how Antarctica was once a part of Gondwana, the southern continental land mass now represented by present day South America, Africa, Australia, and India. 250 million years ago, he added, there was one contiguous land mass called Pangea.

Duke professor **Andy Read** educated us about whales worldwide, and especially those in the Antarctic seas. Penn professor **Irina Marinov**, of Romanian origin, provided insight into climate changes in the Southern Ocean and the developing ozone hole over Antarctica. **Carla**

Thorson of the World Affairs Council of San Francisco discussed the historic development of national claims, and related international politics.

The original eight nations making sovereign claims, some overlapping, over the huge land mass of Antarctica were Argentina, Australia, Britain, Chile, France, New Zealand, Norway and the United States.

Norway, said Ms. Thorson, had by right the greatest claim, since its explorer **Amundsen** was the first to make it to the South Pole. English explorer **Ernest Shakleton's** heroic 1915 journey to the frozen continent has been memorialized in books and a gripping movie.

In 1952, disputes over rival Antarctic claims made war seem inevitable. However, in 1957-58, international scientists working together gave momentum towards an International Treaty signed in Washington,

D.C. on December 1, 1959.

The above-named countries, plus Belgium, Sweden, Japan, and the Soviet Union were all signatories. Today peaceful settlement procedures exist, military action is prohibited, and no new claims can be made. Rich in mineral deposits, including oil and g··· the continent is currently   -limits for such exploitation.

Antarctica remains a forbidden, mysterious continent to many. Increasingly, it is piquing the imagination of world travelers. To me, it was a breath-catching epiphany, as my wife **Leslie** and I celebrated our 40th anniversary. As we continue our journey in life, we rejoice in the magnificent diversity of God's creation.

Julian McPhillips is a local attorney.

APPENDIX II

IN YOUR WORDS

MONTGOMERY ADVERTISER » SUNDAY, MARCH 15, 2015 » 5E

ALABAMA VOICES » Julian McPhillips

Seeing Cuba in transition

Want to go to Cuba? It's still not as easy as other Caribbean Islands, but it's opening up. My wife, Leslie, and I traveled recently via an educational tour, since ordinary tourism from America is not yet here.

Our hearty band of 12 kicked off from Miami. With a short hop over, we arrived in Havana. A billboard at the airport heralded "The Socialist Revolution." Automobiles from the 1940s and '50s whizzed by.

Our first stop was at Revolution Square. A monument to 19th century hero Jose St. Marti soars upwards over 300 feet. An image of national hero Che Guevara adorned an adjacent building. The Fidel Castro-led revolution of 1959 continues today, but now with a softer tone.

Today, Havana contains more than 2 million people. When Castro took over, the government nationalized private industry and tightly controlled the economy. In 1993, self-employment was authorized, and recently it has surged.

Given Cuba's 11 million citizens, a vast consumer market exists. Economic liberalization is already attracting foreign capital.

crime is minimal, and the murder rate is exceedingly low.

Cuba is proud of its distinctive cigars and great sugar production, but tobacco, coffee, citrus fruit, nickel, cobalt and rum are all exported national products.

Cuba leads in biomedical research, especially in the fight against diabetes. Cuba has helped develop PPG to lower cholesterol and as a pain killer for cancer treatments. These advances are exported to many countries.

Religion in Cuba, despite governmental discouragement after the revolution, is still vibrant among the older set, but less so among the younger.

For many of African or mixed heritage, Catholicism has merged with a Santeria religion, giving rise to many saints and superstitions. American missionaries are already making inroads.

We enjoyed upbeat Cuban music on multiple occasions, especially when enhanced by lovely Latin maidens dancing. A variety of drums, thumped to an African-flamenco beat, and accompanied by a shaking chequere', elevated the senses.

Increased Cuban-American commerce will surely benefit both countries. Cuba's brand of socialism is always adjusting, having surely noticed China's success with capitalism.

One area of the economy never "socialized" was the restaurant business. Fine dining is run out of people's homes called "paladors." Guests are served on porches and roof-top patios. Havana now boasts over 2,000 private restaurants, offering tasty cuisine from traditional Cuban to gourmet dishes of other nationalities.

We enjoyed dinner at the Palador Mercaderes in renovated Old Havana, as musicians crooned Cuban ballads, and breezes circulated through high-ceilinged rooms.

Since the revolution began, Cuba has emphasized education, medicine and sports. However, infrastructure needs have suffered, as can be seen by crumbling buildings and pot-holed sidewalks. Guns are outlawed. Accordingly,

Cuban artists also produce many dazzling oil paintings, at prices invitingly low. The museums need work, but neo-classical Spanish architecture of the 1800s and early 1900s is extraordinary. The historic National Hotel, visited twice by our group, has been declared a UNESCO World Heritage Site.

My wife and I enjoyed an early morning stroll along Havana's "Malecon," the concrete boardwalk, crumbling due to frequent waves splashing over the walls.

Our motley dozen, mostly from the southeastern U.S., enjoyed contact with local Cubans not only in Havana, but also in Veradero, Cinnfuegos, Sancti Spiritus, Santa Clara and Trinidad. Cuba is a big country geographically, about as wide as California is long.

We also met many tourist groups from all over the world, including Iceland, Belgium, Sweden, Canada, and Slovakia, plus Asian and Latin

See CUBA » 6E

Cuba

Continued » 5E

American countries. Cuban tourism is only now opening to its big USA neighbor above. Come before the flood tide explodes.

Yes, in reaction to foreign exploitation, the Cuban revolution nationalized industries, confiscated private property and threatened U.S. security. Yet Castro cleared out Mafia strongholds and other corrupt interests, including the drug trade. Many Cuban locals consider Fidel and his brother Raul as heroes, yet millions of Cuban-Americans will always view the brothers as villains.

Elections exist in 365 municipalities and 16 provinces for legislative and executive officials, suggesting democracy at those levels. On the other hand, free speech criticizing the national government can be a ticket to jail.

Parts of Cuba, with horse-drawn carts, are very Third World-like, and rough edges remain. Only 5 percent of Cubans have access to the Internet.

This was a fascinating time to witness Cuba in transition. Come see for yourself, and surely you will be intrigued.

Julian McPhillips
practices law in Montgomery.

APPENDIX 12

OPINION

First Amendment to
of religion or prohibiting
or the right of the people

MONDAY, FEBRUARY 2, 2015

MONTGOMERYADVERTISER.COM

ALABAMA VOICES » Julian McPhillips

Petition President Obama to pardon Don Siegelman

I grieve not only for Don Siegelman and his family but for Alabama over how badly our former governor, lieutenant governor, attorney general and secretary of state has been treated in his 49-day round trip journey from Oakdale Prison in Louisiana to Montgomery.

Mr. Siegelman was shackled, handcuffed, chained, "box"-ed and locked before each trip of this seven-week journey, which consisted of five buses, five vans and three airplanes. He was contained by over 70 U.S. marshals and countless jail and prison officers.

He was taken to Oklahoma twice, to Jacksonville, Fla., to Harrisburg, Pa., and to Altanta twice. He was also in the Montgomery County jail three times.

Don was always kept in solitary confinement. The Montgomery jail cell was all steel, except for the cement floor, and the lights were never off.

If one treated an animal that badly and inhumanely, there would be a cruelty to animals criminal charge against the perpetrator. A normal drive by car would have taken seven hours from Oakdale to Montgomery.

How much more did it cost the federal government in seven weeks with 70 marshals?

It's also been six months now since I complained to the Federal Bureau of Prisons about how a $250 check I sent Don at its Iowa headquarters was embezzled by the Prison Bureau itself. The Montgomery bank from whom I obtained the cashier's check has proof the check was deposited into a Cleveland account -- someone else's account. Siegelman never got it.

I've complained repeatedly to the U.S. Justice Department, to the FBP itself and to other law enforcement sources, but never got a response. Welcome to the federal prison system, a law unto itself.

I don't agree with Don Siegelman on everything, but this hardworking man gave his blood, sweat, tears, life and energy for over 30 years to make Alabama a better place for its citizens. This is no way to treat the worst of our criminals, much less someone who did much good for our state.

Don't forget that Don Siegelman was convicted of bribery because of two large contributions

Richard Scrushy helped obtain, not from Scrushy's own pocket but from two corporations.

The money didn't go to Siegelman personally, nor to his election campaign, but to retire the debt of a statewide lottery campaign. That lottery, by the way, had it been successful, would have contributed millions to public schools in Alabama. What a terrible crime Don committed.

All Richard Scrushy allegedly received was reappointment to a state board on which he had served on for many years under three previous governors. Scrushy didn't even want the appointment, he insisted to me, because he was tired of serving on the board.

I urge Americans everywhere, and especially Alabamians, to write President Obama and urge him to commute Siegelman's sentence, and halt this grave injustice and inhumane treatment to which Don has been so painfully subjected. Rise up, write and be heard.

Julian McPhillips practices law in Montgomery. He once represented Richard Scrushy in civil matters unrelated to the Siegelman case.

APPENDIX 13

Montgomery Advertiser

OPINION

Jim Earnhardt | jearnhardt@gannett.com | 261-1524 | montgomeryadvertiser.com/opinion

PAGE 9A

TUESDAY, MAY 22, 2012

> Congress shall make no law respecting an establishment of religion or prohibiting the free exercise thereof; or abridging the freedom of speech, or of the press, or the right of the people peaceably to assemble, and to petition the Government for a redress of grievances. — *First Amendment to the Constitution*

ALABAMA VOICES: JULIAN MCPHILLIPS

Millions denied pain relief

One of the biggest scandals in health care in America today is the failure of insurance companies to cover prolotherapy.

What is prolotherapy, why is it so helpful, and what can it do for millions of Americans?

Prolotherapy provides amazing relief — non-surgically, and fairly quickly — for people with joint problems in their backs, knees, shoulders, elbows or hips. It has helped my back and knees.

Prolotherapy is a series of injections of a substance called "dextrose 50 percent," which basically is highly concentrated sugar water. It is not a steroid or cortisone, but once injected, it "proliferates" into the tissue around a joint. Hence, the name "prolotherapy."

The proliferation process causes the body's own natural healing mechanisms to fight back, which in turn strengthens a person's tendons and ligaments. That in turn strengthens the joint area, allowing the joint to breathe better and begin to heal.

Back in 1999, I was in my early 50s, and I injured my back while wrestling with high-school wrestlers. I had herniated discs. It was painful to sit down. The next eight to nine months were an odyssey of exploring healing options, including seeing three different chiropractors and two orthopedic doctors. The relief from the former was only temporary, and the advice of the latter was not to do surgery, except as a last option, due to the risks.

In the early fall that year, I discovered from a local osteopath the amazing healing power of prolotherapy. Even after the first treatment, I was feeling much better. After three or four applications, I was back to 100 percent. In 2007-2008, at the age of 61, I was back to wrestling with high-schoolers with no back problems whatsoever.

A former United States Surgeon General, Dr. C. Everett Koop, wrote a preface to the book "Prolo Your Pain Away," by Ross Hauser M.D., in which he described the enormous pain he had with his back until age 40, when he discovered prolotherapy, and what a huge relief and major long-term healing he received from it.

Unfortunately, the reason why prolotherapy is used so little is that all major health insurance companies, including the monopolistic Blue Cross/Blue Shield, refuse to pay the low cost (about $200 per set of injections) for the treatment. Instead, the insurers end up paying for much more expensive surgery. This keeps many surgeons busy and more profitable, but the insurance industry pays from $5,000 to $20,000 or more per surgery.

This scandal is largely unknown and certainly unsung. Prolotherapy would not only save billions in health care costs were it more widely used, but numerous people needlessly suffering excruciating pain would be healed.

Since health insurance companies do not cover it, the only people who get prolotherapy are those who pay for it out of their own pockets. Obviously, others could afford it but don't know about it due to self-serving silence or lack of awareness about the treatment in the medical and insurance fields.

Julian McPhillips practices law in Montgomery.

INDEX